PROUD SERVANT

PROUD SERVANT

The Memoirs of a Career Ambassador

ELLIS O. BRIGGS

THE KENT STATE UNIVERSITY PRESS

Kent, Ohio, & London, England

Library of Congress Catalog Card Number 97-36506

ISBN 0-87338-588-8

Manufactured in the United States of America

04 03 02 01 00 99 98   5 4 3 2 1

Library of Congress Cataloging-in-Publication Data

Briggs, Ellis, 1899–

   Proud servant : the memoirs of a career ambassador / by Ellis
Ormsbee Briggs.

    p.   cm.

   Includes bibliographical references and index.

   ISBN 0-87338-588-8 (cloth : alk. paper) ∞

   1. Briggs, Ellis, 1899–   . 2. Ambassadors—United States—
Biography.   3. United States—Foreign relations—20th century.
I. Title.

IN PROCESS

327.73′092—DC21   97-36506

British Library Cataloging-in-Publication data are available.

DEDICATED TO MY GRANDCHILDREN

Everett, Catherine, Allen, Lucy, and Church

Every very great house is full of proud servants.

— J U V E N A L , *Satire* 5,66

CONTENTS

by Monteagle Stearns

Ellis O. Briggs entered the Foreign Service of the United States in 1925, one year after Congress had enacted legislation creating a professional diplomatic service to replace the discredited system of spoils and patronage that had governed the selection of American diplomats in the nineteenth and early twentieth centuries. The Rogers Act of 1924 combined the theretofore separate American diplomatic and consular services and established for both uniform rules of appointment and promotion based for the first time on principles of merit and competition. Ambassador Briggs retired in 1962, having presented his credentials as chief of mission in seven foreign capitals, ranging geographically (and politically) from Rio de Janeiro to Prague, Athens, and Seoul. Health problems prevented him from serving as ambassador in an eighth capital, Madrid, where the Kennedy administration proposed to send him at the time of his retirement.

Therefore, in a literal sense, the personal history of Ellis Briggs is also a history of modern American diplomacy. Or, as he might have said as he watched with mounting exasperation the resurgence of patronage and the erosion of professional standards in the years after his retirement, a history of the rise and fall of modern American diplomacy. The man himself embodied most of the virtues, and a few of the faults, of the first crop of diplomats produced by the Rogers Act. A down-to-earth New Englander with a degree from Dartmouth and an abiding love of the outdoors, Briggs provided an instant corrective to the popular image of American diplomats as cookie-pushers whose vision is permanently impaired by the strain of trying to see two sides to every question.

I first met Ambassador Briggs in Belgrade in 1959. He and his wife, Lucy, were on their way to their new post in Athens in a Mercedes purchased the week before in Germany. I was a young second secretary at the embassy in Athens and had been dispatched to Belgrade to assist the ambassador-designate with driving chores on the last leg of his journey and to provide any Greek language help he might require in crossing the border from Yugoslavia into Greece. Mindful that I would be spending two days or more with the ambassador before he arrived at his new post, the embassy had laden me with briefing books covering every possible subject into which he might care to inquire, from personnel problems to the latest figures on Greece's balance of payments. Ambassador Briggs was already a Foreign Service legend, and his reputation as a warm-hearted but formidably demanding curmudgeon had preceded him. The journey, however, passed agreeably and uneventfully. The talk was mainly of Latin America and the recent Castro takeover in Cuba. My briefing books remained unopened. At last, as we drove through the fertile plain of Thessaly, the ambassador had a question about Greece. Unfortunately, the answer was neither in my briefing books nor my head. "This looks like good shooting country," he said. "Do you have any ringnecked pheasants around here?" (He forgave me my ignorance about Greek game birds. And when, soon after his arrival, I was fortunate enough to marry the daughter of his predecessor in Athens, and her father was unable to be present to give away the bride, Ambassador Briggs volunteered to do the honors — although he much preferred hunting clothes to striped pants and Tennessee sour mash to champagne.)

Having a great aversion to salon diplomacy and the theorizing of pundits, Ambassador Briggs was not especially reflective or intellectual in his approach to foreign affairs. In reaching decisions he tended to rely on his intuition, which was good, and his judgment of people, which was even better. Well before the "management" specialists arrived on the scene, Briggs had the ability to take charge of a large diplomatic mission and make it work. But his greatest virtue, I think, was his possession of what Harold Nicolson called "moral precision," which is to say total honesty, a passion to report things as he saw them and to make policy recommendations he thought were right, regardless of conventional wisdom in Washington.

Needless to say, his recommendations were not always right and not always followed when they were right. In Greece he was quickly labeled a reactionary by the ever-sensitive Greek Left, primarily because he did not agree with them that an election victory of Greek conservatives had been invalidated by fraud at the polls. At the same time, by keeping a tight rein on the size and scope of American military and intelligence activities in Greece, Ambassador Briggs was making a more significant contribution to the health of Greek democracy than his critics realized. This concern to play by the rules and to keep the conduct of American foreign policy true to American values, as he understood them, permeates his memoirs. It is a virtue even rarer today than it was then.

I once heard a glib foreign policy expert refer disparagingly to an American ambassador whom he deemed too deferential to a foreign despot, adding that it confirmed his belief that Foreign Service officers were too polite to stand up to tyrants. The career of Ellis Briggs, a diplomat of the old school, effectively refutes that canard. He was expelled from his first ambassadorial post in the Dominican Republic because Nelson Rockefeller, the newly appointed coordinator of Inter-American affairs, thought he was being too hard on the Dominican dictator, Rafael Trujillo. He earned the undying enmity of Juan Perón in Argentina, and he despised the anti-Communist demagogue Joseph McCarthy as much as he did the Czech commissar Kliment Gottwald. In fact, the record of American foreign policy shows that palship with dictators usually comes easier to career politicians than to career diplomats, whether it be Nelson Rockefeller and Trujillo, Franklin Roosevelt and "Uncle Joe" Stalin, or Richard Nixon and Leonid Brezhnev.

For anyone who knew him, the voice that speaks from these pages is unmistakably that of Ellis Briggs. For those who did not, his patriotism, his blunt honesty, and his keen eye for people and places will reveal a dimension of professional diplomacy too little recognized by public opinion and too seldom appreciated by political policymakers. That same honesty and eye for detail, coupled with the extraordinary range of his career, make his memoirs a remarkable document. Even his blind spots — his antipathy for the Peace Corps, for example, and for do-good diplomacy in general — are representative attitudes of his generation of diplomats. You find the same themes in the memoirs of George Kennan, a very different kind of person who nevertheless operated from many of the same premises.

What the reader has in hand is virtually a first-person account of American diplomacy between the end of the Great War to the height of the Cold War. The problems in the management of American foreign policy that Ambassador Briggs describes so passionately — the effort required to get Washington to see events abroad clearly, to act on them decisively, and to contain the vast, self-serving bureaucratic apparatus that impedes effective action — all continue to clog the wheels of American diplomacy. Most of these problems are worse than they were when Ellis Briggs left the Foreign Service. The pity is that there are fewer voices inside and outside government to say so and fewer experienced hands to begin the task of rebuilding a strong, "morally precise" American diplomacy — a diplomacy cleansed once more of the corrosive effects of the spoils system and again worthy of America's place in the world.

PREFACE

In 1975, during his last summer, Ellis Ormsbee Briggs finished his personal reminiscences of the American Foreign Service. He took his title, *Proud Servant*, from Juvenal: "Every very great house is full of proud servants."[1]

This autobiography has been described by one critic as a history of the beginnings of the professional Foreign Service. It is that, and more. Ambassador Briggs's life (1899–1976) was one of devotion: to his wife, Lucy, and to his family; to Dartmouth College; to the woods and fields of Maine; and to his country. This devotion is reflected in the pages that follow.

Ellis Briggs was born December 1, 1899, in Watertown, Massachusetts. At age fourteen he became partially blind in one eye and for three years was tutored at home in Riverdale, New York, and at the family farm in Topsfield, Washington County, Maine. His tutor was a Dartmouth graduate, and this led him to matriculate at Dartmouth in 1917. Such was his attachment to the college that when he retired, in 1962, he made his home in Hanover, New Hampshire.

After graduating from Dartmouth in 1921, he taught secondary school at Robert College in Istanbul and was a freelance short story writer for *Collier's* and *The Smart Set* before entering the Foreign Service in 1925. For the next thirty-seven years he served in Peru, Cuba, and Chile; with brief tours in Liberia (1932) and China (1945); intermittently at the Department of State in Washington, D.C.; and as ambassador to seven countries: the Dominican Republic, Uruguay, Czechoslovakia, Korea, Peru, Brazil, and Greece. Confirmed as ambassador to Spain in 1962, he was unable to take up his duties because of illness and he retired.

Ellis Briggs reached the highest rank attainable in the Foreign Service, career ambassador, held the record number of U.S. ambassadorships, and received the Medal of Freedom from President Eisenhower for his service in Korea.

---

1. *Maxima quaeque domus servis est plena superbus.* Juvenal, *Satire* 5, 66. In *Putnam's Complete Book of Quotations, Proverbs, and Household Words* (G. P. Putnam's Sons, 1926, p. 574a.

He was also the author of three books, each related to some aspect of his career: *Shots Heard Round the World* (1957), *Farewell to Foggy Bottom* (1964), and *Anatomy of Diplomacy* (1968).

Lucy Barnard Briggs
Lucy Therina Briggs
Everett Ellis Briggs

Angus and the Acolytes

Although many decades have passed since that spring term in Washington when I burned incense at the shrine of Angus Macdonald Crawford, the image of that remarkable man remains: an articulate, intolerant, and sedentary Buddha, with a lame foot in a built-up boot, and the rasping cough of an overweight smoker. During the 1920s, Angus prepared almost half of all the candidates who succeeded in passing the State Department's Foreign Service examinations. Since only a small proportion of those who took the tests attended Angus's classes, his was no small achievement.

His attitude was mercenary. He taught to make money, and he was good at it. As a dispenser of organized information in the fields of government, history, and foreign affairs, in bouillon-cube concentration and with a lasting flavor, he had no peer. He understood the sweep of events and the impact of decisive personalities upon them. He had an encyclopedic knowledge and a sense of proportion that led him to reject inessential details; his sardonic humor garnished an account with an incident, often frivolous or discreditable, that brought the scene alive and made it memorable.

In the international arena he admired winners: Bismarck over Napoleon III, Cavour over the Hapsburgs, Lenin over Tsar Nicholas, Senator Lodge over Woodrow Wilson. He had few tears for the vanquished. The crusading spirit that had already begun to tarnish American foreign policy possessed no charms for Angus Crawford.

There was nothing in the rumor, fostered by envious competitors, that Angus had a special pipeline into the Department of State, much less that he had advance access to the examinations. What he did have was a collection of past examination papers that he studied with care and astuteness, seeking a pattern that, in conjunction with his comprehension of current events, might furnish clues to impending questions. He became so successful that eventually the State Department selected an erudite ex-Princeton professor with a mandate to devise an Angus-proof set of examinations. This bureaucratic harassment, along with tobacco, lack of exercise, and other in-dulgences, possibly shortened Angus's career, but they did not detract from his reputation.[1]

I called on Angus Crawford one spring morning in 1925, with the sun warm on the Potomac and the privet buds already turning the hedges bright green around Georgetown gardens. Angus, in his lair on New Hampshire Avenue, was snorting over his double chins and tapping one cigarette after another on the arm of an overstuffed chair that resembled, when he sat in it, the throne of an irascible monarch. He told me, civilly enough, that it was his custom to reject for his courses those who after an interview seemed to be unpromising material for diplomacy.

Those whom he accepted were therefore pleased by his recognition of their superior potential, but I cannot remember many petitioners whom he turned down, and I do recall several durable candidates who attended his classes several years running and never did manage to enter the Foreign Ser-vice. Such persistent clients were uncommon, however, for he was unsympa-thetic toward failure even though the tuition dollars of one candidate were as negotiable as those of another.

Angus began by asking me questions. I replied that after getting a bache-lor's degree, majoring in English and history, I had spent two years as an in-structor at Robert College in Constantinople. There followed two years of freelancing while I awaited the enactment of legislation that would, I hoped, render State Department service a slightly less precarious livelihood. After the passage in 1924 of the Rogers Act, establishing the American Foreign Service, I recognized the need for more systematic preparation than I could generate alone, several years away from undergraduate textbooks. Hence my visit.

Angus grunted, and his questions became more specific. Why had the British in 1920 been so stupid as to back the Greeks in their disastrous Ana-tolian adventure against a Turkey rejuvenated by Mustafa Kemal Pasha? What was my impression of the Allied control of Constantinople as a form of international administration? How about the missionaries and their irra-tional belief that the Armenians — Michael Arlen excepted — were worth

1. The former Princetonian was Joseph Coy Green, then serving in the Western Euro-pean Division, who later had a distinguished career, until he retired in 1953, as ambas-sador to Jordan. Among those he supervised over the years were Charles Yost, a career ambassador chosen by President Nixon in 1969 to head the UN mission, and John Sloan Dickey, later president of Dartmouth College. At Princeton, before joining the State De-partment, Green had as students no fewer than twelve men who subsequently became ambassadors, including George Kennan, Walton Butterworth, and Livingston Merchant.

{ P R O U D   S E R V A N T }

saving? And did I take seriously a Near East petroleum thing called the Chester Concession?

At the time I assumed Angus had some special interest in the Levant, a personal familiarity with events in that area. Later I realized that he could have duplicated the performance with a candidate from Yale-in-China, or a young man who had prospected for gold in Ecuador, or raised sheep in New Zealand. His outlook straddled the continents, and his curiosity, seasoned with the belief that most politicians were knaves, was as omnivorous as the appetite of a raccoon.

I replied as best I could. I said that in the Near East the British were still infected, a century after his exploits, by the romanticism of Lord Byron: maybe, I ventured, the star of empire had started to decline. I declared more confidently that if there was a worse form of administration than multilateral control of a conquered capital by the victors, it had yet to be devised; inter-ally rivalries were reducing Constantinople to a shambles and the Turks, emboldened by the fall of Lloyd George and the discomfiture of Lord Curzon at Lausanne, were already talking about moving their capital to Ankara, in the middle of nowhere in Anatolia. As for the missionaries, they were becoming an anachronism. They would soon bend to the rising winds of nationalism or be swept away by them. The Chester Concession, I hazarded, was a manifestation of the eagerness of the West for oil. If the oil was there, in the barren and quarrelsome Near East, capital would be forthcoming one way or another. (This was some years before solid gold Cadillacs began replacing stallions in Arabian stables.)

Angus grunted again and asked, more amiably, why, if I nourished those heretical views, I wanted to enter the diplomatic service. He held up a pudgy paw. "Don't tell me. That is one of the key questions on the oral examination. They never miss it. The successful reply should be brief, diffident, and under no circumstances should you fail to include a reference to your dedication to the responsibilities of public service. So between now and July dream up a good answer."

He collected $100 in advance, remarking that an additional $100 would be due on the first days of May and June. (One hundred dollars was not confetti in 1925; the yearly tuition of Ivy League colleges came to less than the cost of Angus's three-month cram course.) Here, he said, was a schedule of reading. I could buy the books at Brentano's on F Street. His lectures would start the following Monday morning, 10 to 12:30, five days a week. When I inquired whether his lectures covered all of the subjects required by the State Department, his snort was disparaging.

"Except arithmetic. If you haven't learned to add and subtract, that's too bad. And I don't teach languages. Here's a list of language teachers. They send me their names. I don't recommend them. I suppose you picked up Levantine French in Constantinople. Don't admit it. If you studied Turkish, don't admit that either. Get yourself sent to Samsun, or Aleppo. . . ."

He wrote down my name and asked where I lived — a question that presently left me further beholden to him. I said I was looking for something quiet and reasonably priced, preferably within walking distance of his establishment. Did he have any suggestions?

"Washington," he observed, "has all kinds of places. Overbuilt during the war and hasn't caught up with itself yet." He gave the problem his attention. "Get you a card to the University Club if you want. Small rooms, good swimming pool. Noisy." He named a bachelor apartment on I Street. Then there were, he said, some new apartments, very elegant, near DuPont Circle, "Good but expensive."

When I repeated that something quiet and economical was what I had in mind, Angus heaved himself up and hobbled to an untidy desk where he churned up the papers. He unearthed a slip, which he gave me.

And that was how I came to live, until my first assignment abroad fifteen months later, in a third floor room at 1775 Church Street, in the house of a Mrs. Fenton, whose contribution to my entry into the Foreign Service was second only to that of Angus Crawford. Angus described Church Street as "a lane sandwiched between P and Q Streets, with an Episcopal church at the 18th Street end of it. Tell Mrs. Fenton I sent you. Don't try to smuggle a girl in."

Thither I repaired and was aware of my good fortune, for in addition to my room, Mrs. Fenton provided breakfast and supper for ten or a dozen other Foreign Service aspirants, young men camped in the neighborhood, and her dining room became a haven for nourishment as well as a platform where diplomacy has rarely been more ardently debated.

Her cook went marketing with Mrs. Fenton after breakfast. The meals they provided were magnificent, and how Mrs. Fenton managed to make any money out of us remains to this day inexplicable. These remarkable viands were consumed amid noisy and protracted arguments about barratry and hot pursuit, about Caprivi's Finger and the Drago Doctrine, about the fate of the Romanovs and the grim boasts of the Bolsheviki, about the Fourteen Points, and about the notion, the validity of which Angus questioned, that Latin America was really important to the United States.

Thus the cherry blossoms were succeeded by the dogwood, and the dogwood in turn by the honeysuckle. By the end of May, the hot weather had descended on Washington, without the benison of air conditioning and with a smallpox scare that had the whole town revaccinated and itching. Angus reminded us that until the turn of the century — only twenty-five years before — the American capital was classified an "unhealthy post" by several countries, including Great Britain.

The written examinations were torture, not because they were so difficult in themselves — on the contrary, diligent application to Angus's lectures paid off handsomely — but because of the Washington weather. The papers stuck to my forearm, and drops of perspiration blurred my answers. At the desk in front was a young woman named Polly, another of Angus's clients, and I can still see her cotton dress sticking to her shoulders.

The oral part of the exam in my day was given at once, starting the day after the writtens ended, and it was open to any candidate who believed he had done sufficiently well on the written tests to warrant the effort. In 1925 the oral ordeal was compounded by the custom of taking five applicants at a time for their interview. While one was examined, the other four sat side by side on a bench, tense and fidgeting, each praying that the panelists — who included the undersecretary of state and two of the four assistant secretaries — would not run out of easy questions before it was his turn to be interviewed.

Six weeks later I had my first official message from the Department of State. Signed "Your obedient servant, for the Secretary of State, J. Butler Wright, Assistant Secretary," it informed me that I had passed with a rating of 84.69 (80 was passing). It was shortly followed by another communication informing me that I had been appointed a Foreign Service officer, unclassified, "with compensation at the rate of $2,500 per annum." In short, I was in.[2]

In 1938, shortly after Angus's death, I wrote the following words about his impact on the acolytes of the 1920s:

It used to be the boast of the late Angus Crawford . . . that he covered in a single lecture "all the history of Latin America since 1800" — that everything the examinations had asked in upwards of twenty years was contained in that single lecture. . . .

---

2. My first commission, dated September 22, 1925, was signed by President Coolidge and countersigned by Frank B. Kellogg as secretary of state; my last one was signed by President Kennedy and Secretary of State Dean Rusk, thirty-seven years later.

And as Angus Crawford boasted, so it was; for that lecture was Angus at his best, and his best was a memorable adventure. For two hours and a half, history marched before you like veteran soldiers on parade; you had the precise sequence of battalions, the movement and the color, the sense of direction and control. You forgot the man, heaving with emphatic gesture; you forgot springtime Washington and even the impending examinations — but you knew Miranda and Bolívar. You felt the wind that moves the reeds along the marshy shores of Lake Junín, and you rode beside San Martín at Ayacucho. You saw the dust splash of bullets on adobe when Maximilian fell at Querétaro, and you were there on the Malecón in 1898 when the *Maine* steamed past Morro Castle toward manifest destiny. You saw the first steam shovel tear the red earth when men severed the continents of Culebra. All these you saw and you sensed the drama. . . . You felt the pulse of nations stirring on a great continent.

Angus Crawford touched a map, and twenty countries were alive; it was an unforgettable adventure.[3]

Angus would probably have snorted, but I still say he was a magnificent teacher.

---

3. From the *Foreign Service Journal*, September 1938. Reprinted by permission.

The Foreign Service School

The Rogers Act, intended to establish the American Foreign Service as a competitive, nonpolitical, professional career, was enacted in 1924, replacing the separate diplomatic and consular branches. Simultaneously there came into existence in the Department of State, in Room 100 on the ground floor of the old State War Navy Building, a modest enterprise called the Foreign Service School.

The idea behind the school was that it was wasteful to launch candidates who had just succeeded in passing the examinations straight into service abroad without prior home office indoctrination. Moreover, the effect of a first chief is always important to a beginner, and both the quality and the interest of American officials serving around the world varied from post to post and country to country. Accordingly, there was organized a course of several months in the State Department before a new officer was sent to his first foreign assignment. Until after World War II, the Foreign Service School remained an unpretentious institution, concentrating on unraveling consular regulations and on language instruction.

It was likewise decided that all new officers should go abroad as vice consuls. There were a number of reasons: consular work was more tangible than diplomatic endeavor, and it was also more measurable, in that a record was kept of the number of visas and passports issued, the number of ships arriving and departing, and the number of invoices certified, together with a description of the merchandise and the value of each shipment.

Consular work also brought those performing it into contact with people: foreigners seeking immigration visas as well as American citizens seeking passports, and foreign officials. Since success in diplomacy depends to an important degree on the ability to inspire confidence, the decision to start junior officers in consulates was sensible and designed to assess their future usefulness in diplomacy.

The first head of the Foreign Service School was a debonair bachelor named William Dawson, who wore a bow tie of the kind later popularized by President Truman. A Midwesterner, he entered the Foreign Service via the Ecole Libre des Sciences Politiques; in 1908 his first post was St. Petersburg, the capital of tsarist Russia, as vice and deputy consul general (an imposing title since abandoned). Seven posts and eighteen years later, now a full-fledged consul general, he was summoned to Washington. Intelligent, sympathetic, and interested in young people, Bill Dawson was in the best sense a professional diplomatist, dedicated to his career and to those who shared it with him.

Consul General Dawson decided that it would be desirable for us to become familiar with the principal foreign affairs matters confronting our government. He invited the chiefs of the six geographic divisions of the State Department to lecture to us: Western Europe, Eastern Europe, the Near East, the Far East, Latin America, and Mexico.

The division chiefs were well informed. We learned the status, and some of the details, of all manner of projects and problems. Those chiefly concerning the United States in the mid-1920s had to do, as they do today, with national security. The disarmament conference of 1922 had settled the naval ratios of the Great Powers, but other disarmament aspects remained major issues. Avoiding an arms race was a widespread preoccupation. So was the rehabilitation of ravaged Europe, especially Germany, ruined by inflation and by a vengeful treaty.

The State Department tiptoed warily around the League of Nations, with an eye on the isolationists in the Senate.

Russia and the United States had no relations. Stalin was watched by a small band of Kremlinologists in the State Department, many of whom were regarded as eccentric.

In Nicaragua the Marines were chasing Augusto Sandino on the forested heights above Jinotega. Other Marines were restoring order in Haiti. Elsewhere in Latin America, orators denounced intervention, which shortly was forsworn by a repentant Washington.

In the Far East the United States was prodding European powers to relinquish special rights in China, precisely as the United States later hectored its allies after World War II to get on with the business of relinquishing colonies. Japan, frustrated by the Washington Naval Treaty and humiliated by the Immigration Act, was beginning to dream of a Co-Prosperity Sphere that would exclude non-Asians from the region.

This was American diplomacy in 1926. One was impressed then, as on many occasions thereafter, by the essential decency of United States objectives.

There was little in the world that the United States coveted — no alien territory, no domination of others, no spheres of special influence, no exclusive privileges. When we intervened in the Caribbean, it was to clean up something beyond the local ability to handle, and we departed as soon as we could. During an intervention the people of the country often had better food, more freedom, better health, and more money than they enjoyed before the Marines came, or after the Marines departed.

If a peak of naiveté was reached two years later in the Kellogg-Briand Pact, the purposes motivating the renunciation of war as an instrument of national policy nevertheless were those of men striving to create a better world and to live at peace with their neighbors.

For the United States it was, until the disastrous collapse of the stock market in 1929, a prosperous decade. The national mood, after Harding, was well attuned to the spirit of cautious, unaggressive President Coolidge, whose idea of what was good for the country was to support business. If Coolidge discouraged flamboyant adventures in foreign affairs, he likewise managed to keep the ship of state out of hot water.

All this was perceived, more or less, by William Dawson's protégés. After we had exhausted the wares of those handling policy matters for the State Department, Mr. Dawson decided that we should learn something about other agencies whose responsibilities in the foreign field brought them into contact with the Foreign Service. The Commerce Department, under the energetic Mr. Hoover, was putting commercial attachés in embassies and trade commissioners in consulates. Treasury was responsible not only for duties and customs but also for the control of narcotics. Justice, through the Immigration and Naturalization Service, would soon handle the visas that we, as vice consuls, would issue to foreign travelers. Agriculture was responsible for keeping the United States free of hoof-and-mouth disease and for promoting the sale of American farm products in overseas markets.

Mr. Dawson was a first-class linguist, fluent in French, German, and Spanish. It was at the Foreign Service School that he inaugurated his famous "language lunches," held in one of the downtown restaurants. Three times a week he would preside over a meal during which the participants were permitted to speak only that day's chosen language. I then knew no German or Spanish; my attendance at the French luncheons possibly accounted for the fact that I never was sent to a post in a French-speaking country.

There was a baker's dozen of junior officers in the class of 1926, more than half of us Angus Crawford alumni. We were sworn in as Foreign Service officers, unclassified (C), by the chief clerk of the State Department, an imposing functionary who was the keeper of the Great Seal and sundry other oddments having to do with certifications required of the Secretary of State.

Under the Rogers Act there were eight Foreign Service grades, classes 8 to 1, in ascending order of rank, plus an unclassified grade for probationers; the latter was in turn divided into three steps, A, B, C. We all began at unclassified (C), the lowest level, and our salary was $2,500 per year, minus 5 percent for retirement. That brought my first monthly paycheck, for November 1925, to just under $200. The top salary of a Class 1 officer in 1925 was $10,000, which was also the stipend of a minister plenipotentiary. (A Cabinet officer received $12,000.)

As soon as we had been sworn in, Consul General Dawson had asked for an appointment to present us to the secretary of state. We trooped solemnly upstairs to the second floor, where, after being taken in hand by Eddie Savoy, the black factotum who served every secretary of state from John Hay to Dean Acheson, we were duly introduced to Frank B. Kellogg, a lawyer from Minnesota, who after duty as ambassador at the Court of St. James's was named by President Coolidge to fill the shoes of Charles Evans Hughes — a large order that Mr. Kellogg was probably the first to recognize. He greeted us affably, recalling the significant role played by his predecessor in establishing the Foreign Service, and he wished us well in our period of training for diplomacy.

The Washington of 1926 was a far cry from the strangulated horror that it became after World War II. The small town atmosphere that prevailed during the nineteenth century, and until World War I, was still in evidence in the era of Coolidge. Washington was a town of wide, tree-shaded streets and low buildings. It was a town of trolley cars and easy distances, gracious parks and readily accessible countryside, with little mechanized traffic and no thruways defacing the landscape. It was a town not deafened every few seconds, day and night, by airplanes roaring up the Potomac Valley. It was, however, a town with a robust social life befitting the capital of a strong and growing nation.

The young men of the Foreign Service School found themselves in considerable demand. Diplomats, in theory at any rate, are people who take regular exercise, bathe frequently, and can cope with the social amenities. Washington has always been a place with more young women than men, many of the former brought there by solvent parents with social or political ambitions. Helping the debutantes were eagle-eyed matrons, of impeccably correct if sometimes slightly desiccated social stock.

Government officialdom was also generous in extending us hospitality. Cabinet wives had at-homes on Sunday afternoons during the winter. So did the wives of assistant secretaries of state. We were encouraged to attend these affairs and to pass cakes and teacups in circumstances of the utmost gentility. That may not have been the origin of the expression "cookie-pusher," but admittedly it did little to dispel it.

Fledgling diplomats likewise paid their respects at the White House. At the front door we left our official cards, the right-hand corner turned down; Miss Cornelia Bassel, Dawson's assistant, had seen to it that each card had the proper engraving and dimensions. We were told that in due course we would receive invitations to attend a presidential diplomatic reception.

"Prohibition" in 1926 was a word that took up a disproportionate amount of the country's attention; it cast a blight across the land for more than a decade. Yet it afflicted the young men of the Foreign Service School relatively lightly. Bootlegging was an established enterprise, and many bootleggers were reliable. There were also the foreign embassies and legations. The Volstead Act, named for an otherwise unmemorable congressman whose legislation purported to implement the Eighteenth Amendment, did not apply to foreign diplomats. They had extraterritorial rights. They were not subject to the laws of the country. They imported their liquor and they served it to literally everybody who was anybody in the capital, including members of Congress who voted dry but drank wet.

Diplomatic immunity was of special interest to young men studying the practical aspects of their profession. Not only were the foreign missions entitled to import their supplies, but the State Department was obligated to establish a procedure whereby diplomatic liquors, eyed by hijackers and other predatory elements, could safely reach their destinations on Massachusetts Avenue and on 16th Street. These pampered cargoes were imported through Baltimore and transported, like currency and securities between banks, from the Patuxent to the District of Columbia.

In the mid-1920s the entire American foreign affairs establishment was housed in the old State War Navy Building. The Navy Department had already moved down 17th Street toward salt water. The secretary of war still had his office in the building, on the third floor on the west side; and on the fourth floor, overlooking the White House, was the ornate suite held available for General John J. Pershing, commander of United States forces in World War I.

With its high ceilings, massive walls, and long tessellated corridors, the State War Navy Building was one of the coolest and most comfortable edifices in Washington. It was undoubtedly one of the ugliest on the outside, being all gimcracks and Victorian curlicues, but with great mahogany doors that were dignified and handsome on the inside. The swinging shutters shielding each door were likewise impressive (until Secretary of State Stettinius had them painted, in honor of his "team," a ghastly blend of artichoke and pistachio).

State Department personnel, including the corps of messengers presided over by Eddie Savoy, numbered approximately seven hundred people. Every spring it was the custom to have a photograph taken in front of the steps, on the south side of the building. The secretary of state stood in the middle of the front row, flanked by the undersecretary and the four assistant secretaries. Around and behind them were the chiefs of the geographic divisions, each with a cluster of officers, each officer responsible for relations with one or more countries. Behind them in turn were all the rank and file of American diplomacy: code clerks, researchers, messengers, historians, file clerks, translators, and stenographers — the last group shepherded by a severe individual named Mr. Russ, who was suspicious of young men, including Foreign Service officers, unclassified (C), who roamed about the department; he believed these young men had designs on his youthful and innocent charges.

Mr. Dawson decided it was time to concentrate on our foreign assignments. To this end we were each provided with a form on which to specify post preferences and to state our reasons. The State Department was under no compulsion to honor these choices. Service was at the discretion of the secretary of state, which meant the Office of Personnel and the geographic divisions, which made known to Personnel their requirements. Nevertheless, within the limitations of what are still termed "the exigencies of the Service," a genuine effort was made to match posts with preferences.

Between the submission of our post preferences and the announcement of our destinations, Consul General Dawson did a moderate amount of proselytizing. It was thus no surprise to me when I drew Callao, Peru, although my first choice had been Harbin, Manchuria.

The ten Foreign Service officers comprising the class of 1926 were proud of the venerable establishment they had joined. We worked hard to prepare ourselves for our foreign assignments. Mornings we studied the consular regulations, a forbidding compilation with heavy green covers and a contraption that allowed the book to be taken apart so a revised sheet could be substituted for an obsolete one. The prose was technical and uninspired, except for one splendid chapter heading: "Marriages," it read, "Consuls not to celebrate."

This arresting directive called attention to the fact that with the termination of certain extraterritorial rights that American citizens had enjoyed during the nineteenth century in China, Persia, Egypt, and elsewhere, the performance of weddings by consuls would no longer be permitted. The phrase "not to celebrate," we were instructed, meant not to administer the nuptial vows, which henceforth would be the task of a padre. A Consul was, however, authorized to be present at the request of an American participant, and to issue under his hand and the consular seal a certificate declaring that the wedding had taken place in accordance with the laws of the country. Thereafter, consuls were indeed known to celebrate.

We were frequently given examinations by Mr. Dawson, tests covering various phases of consular activity. Those having to do with the new immigration law were the most complex; the regulations governing the Immigration Act of 1924 covered several hundred pages.

We then had individual photographs taken for our diplomatic passports; Miss Bassel insisted that this be done downtown, instead of at one of the four-for-a-dollar Pennsylvania Avenue studios that catered to the public. She reminded us that the secretary of state personally signed diplomatic passports. She told us that Secretary Hughes made a practice of looking at each picture before he signed the passport and of insisting upon a respectable likeness. Diplomatic passports were issued to members of a profession. They testified to a special position, and they called upon foreign governments to recognize that position. Whereas passports issued to the general public had to be renewed at regular intervals, diplomatic passports were of unlimited validity, subject only to State Department endorsement as the bearer moved from one country to another.

As a parting gesture, the Foreign Service School gave a dinner in honor of Consul General Dawson. We toasted him and each other, and we drank to the health of such brethren in absentia as Secretary Kellogg, Ambassador Grew, Angus Crawford, Eddie Savoy, and Mr. Russ, the guardian of the State Department secretarial contingent. We also raised our glasses to Mrs. Coolidge and Cornelia Bassel. The details of the affair were not altogether clear the following morning.

Then, clutching our steamship tickets and our diplomatic passports, we of the Class of 1926 went our separate ways.[1] On July 8, 1926, just one year from the date of my oral examination, I sailed for Peru on the SS *Santa Luisa* of the Grace Line.

1. Six members of the class were to serve thirty or more years in the Foreign Service. The last to retire was David Bruce; he was the only American diplomat who served as ambassador to Germany, France, and Great Britain.

Young Mr. United States in the Port of Callao

In Peru my first ambassador was Miles Poindexter, a Republican from the state of Washington. My second was Alexander P. Moore of Pittsburgh. "Uncle Alec" came to Peru two years after my arrival, when I was promoted from vice consul in Callao to third secretary in Lima, the City of Kings, seven miles inland from the port.

Strictly speaking, I was not a member of Ambassador Poindexter's staff; consulates were not absorbed into embassies until fifteen years later, in one of the streamlining operations from which American diplomacy has periodically suffered. The embassy, a combined office and residence with a total staff of fewer than ten people, was on the other side of town from the consulate general, beyond the Plaza San Martín. It was a sprawling, one-story colonial building that stretched back and back in a series of patios. The cobbled entrance had once admitted carriages. Iron grilles protected the windows. The rooms on either side of the first patio were the chancery, with living quarters behind them. The kitchen and servants' rooms were farther back still. The whole building covered several acres.

My first view of my first ambassador was of a tall, bald gentleman, formally dressed, stretched at full length across the top of his desk. In one hand he held a large magnifying glass with an oblong lens. With the other hand, he was slowly moving a lighted lamp, trying to focus on a spot under the magnifying glass.

"They're boring right through the mahogany!" I heard him exclaim. He observed a hesitant figure in the doorway. "Come in," he invited. "There, see his head? That brownish dot? By Gad, you can almost hear him chewing!" He put down the lamp. "You the new vice consul?"

Diplomatic offices in the 1920s were equipped with elephantine wooden desks purchased in Grand Rapids. Under the mahogany veneer was a layer of American softwood. This filling was an irresistible target for termites, the Peruvian *comejenes*. Ambassador Poindexter had such a desk, and at the time of my arrival it had been thoroughly riddled by the wood-chewing larvae.

One always cherishes a special interest in and affection for his first post. Sentiment apart, Peru is the most fascinating country in South America. It has a history that goes back to the edges of time, culminating in the civilization of the Incas, which Pizarro destroyed with one, still incredible blow. Peru became a viceroyalty of Spain, and for three hundred years the wealth of the Indies poured into Europe. Then came Bolívar, the antithesis of Pizarro, to found a republic that celebrated its centenary in 1924, two years before I reached Lima.

Geographically, the variety of Peru is endless. I first saw the long, arid coastline from the ship at Talara — a desert cut through now and then by the greenest of valleys, where irrigation canals that predated the Incas were still spreading the precious moisture of thin rivers. Behind, to the east, towers the sierra, and hidden from the coast lie glaciers at twenty thousand feet. So abruptly do the Andes rise from the sea that the continental divide of South America is scarcely one hundred miles from the Pacific, with the Atlantic three thousand miles to the east.

On the inland side the land falls away almost as sharply into the rain forests of the great tributaries — the Ucayali, the Marañón, the Huallaga, the Apurímac; these and other mighty streams come together to form the Amazon River. Locked in the sierra are deposits of silver and vanadium and copper, and of the gold that first beckoned the conquistadors. It is a vast empire, still a land of adventure.

Something of this Ambassador Poindexter conveyed that afternoon while the mist of winter moistened the patio tiles and termites bored through his desktop. No armchair representative, Mr. Poindexter had visited the cotton and sugar haciendas of the coast, and the mines fifteen thousand feet above sea level. He had slid down the eastern side of San Ramón, where there was talk of building an airstrip for planes that would then switch to floats for the six-hundred-mile flight downriver to Iquitos, Peru's Atlantic port on the Amazon, twenty-five hundred miles from the mouth of the river.

"The overriding problem in Peru," the ambassador told me, "is the Indian problem." Not the primitive tribesmen of the Amazon jungle; those Indians, he said, were comparatively few in number. He meant the Indians of the sierra, the indigenous people who made up the bulk of the population of the Republic. Although they were enfranchised and no longer tied to the soil, their way of life nevertheless differed little from the serfdom of the colonial era. Now, as transportation developed, they were beginning to drift to the coast towns and to Lima — dissatisfied, unintegrated, with little prospect of employment.

I was to see a good deal of my first American ambassador. Later he helped me find the biggest frog in the world.[1] He encouraged other activities that enriched the life of a junior vice consul. He represented the United States with dignity, if not brilliance, and was reportedly the first man to call attention to the enormous and then unexplored fishing resources of Peru. I owe him a debt for his interest in a very junior officer.

The American consulate general in Lima was a mile from the embassy, in a downtown office building one block from W. R. Grace and Company, the leading American firm in Peru; two blocks from the Lima branch of the National City Bank of New York; and three blocks from the Plaza de Armas, where in the ancient cathedral the bones of Pizarro were displayed in a glass case. The twin towers of the cathedral looked across the square to the Presidential Palace, where in the garden was a fig tree that the tough Spanish captain was supposed to have planted in 1535.

My immediate chief in the consulate general, George Makinson, was a mild, gray man, with occasional flashes of temper. He lived in constant dread lest the Department of State should, as he put it, "come back at him." Never having served in Washington, he saw the State Department as a figure of menace. He was convinced that when a telegram arrived over the signature "Kellogg," the message had been personally signed, if not personally dictated, by the secretary of state himself. He was a considerate chief, naively impressed by having a graduate of the new Foreign Service School on his staff. The consul general was assisted by an imperturbable consul, Nelson Park, whose Spanish was fluent. The consul dictated letters in Spanish, handled all callers who did not speak English, and in point of fact was the wheelhorse of the office, a very competent public servant.

My own bailiwick, which I viewed with great pride, was the two-room branch office in the port of Callao, operated for the benefit of American shipping. It was on a side street close to the waterfront and the part where the *capitanía* — the office of the captain of the port — was located. My outer office had a stout railing designed to deter belligerent seamen. It separated the public from the official sector, which was occupied by Carlos, my Peruvian clerk, whose joy was the telephone. When it rang, I would hear him

1. As described in *Shots Heard Around the World* (Viking Press, 1957): a story of the earnest attempt of a vice consul to fill the request of a frog grower (for the frogs' legs market) in Louisiana for the legendary Peruvian "biggest frog in the world."

say "Consulado general de los Estados Unidos de América, oficina de Callao. Habla Carlos," and I would know that we were in business. Later, when my own Spanish became serviceable, I had an extension telephone put on my desk, but when it rang, I always waited for Carlos to answer; otherwise his pride in his official status would have been diminished.

I occupied the inner office, where I reviewed regulations and read documents, including the maritime notices in the local newspaper. I had a small desk (not from Grand Rapids) and a safe. The safe contained the heavy impression seal reading "Consulate General of the United States of America, Callao–Lima, Peru" and some consular fee stamps, mostly in $5 denominations, for the bills of health I issued to northbound foreign vessels. In the main drawer we kept the ship's papers while an American vessel was in port, together with blank marine notes of protest and other documentary forms. There were wafer seals, some blue and some red, and a cash drawer with a small amount of Peruvian and American currency. We did not issue visas in Callao, except on crew lists for American vessels, which were certified gratis; most fee-producing services were handled in Lima.

Not all my consular business was with the captains of American vessels. The consulate was equally responsible for the welfare of American seamen. One difficulty in discharging that responsibility was that not all the young men who went down to the sea in ships were deserving of the solicitude lavished on them by Congress. A life at sea, forecastle to command, was no longer the ambition of many American youngsters. American seamen were well paid by international standards; some of them were not worth one-tenth of what they were getting. Others, worth even less in terms of the American merchant marine, were as tough as the copper bars they watched the stevedores load at Callao, where waterfront establishments were geared to their off-duty diversions.

An American seaman could not be discharged from his vessel except with the assent of the consul and in the consul's presence. This was intended to protect a seaman from the exploitation that might follow discharge on a foreign strand. The provision did not, however, cover deserters or seamen left behind through carelessness when their vessel weighed anchor. The law provided that such seamen, if they were destitute, were entitled to board and lodging at the expense of the American government until they could be shipped out on another vessel. In order to discourage desertion, a seaman reshipped abroad could not automatically claim regular wages; he often returned to the United States as a "workaway," at twenty-five cents a month, for which he was supposed to perform regular duties.

　　　　{ P R O U D   S E R V A N T }

In practice the consul had a good deal of leeway because he was the one who determined when a sailor was destitute; the finding on that score was not subject to reversal, although it was not infrequently subject to debate.

The reputation of a consul in this particular often governed the density of traffic into his office. Ports where the consul was reported to be a "tough son-of-a-bitch" with little regard for the amenities were ports where the police seldom had to be summoned to deal with unruly clients pounding on the railing and demanding their rights or the scalp of the consul. Ports where a hard-luck story was good for ten days of idleness at government expense soon were congested. The reason why a seaman missed his ship varied with the ingenuity of the sailor. Some were left behind because "that bastard the bosun" lied about sailing time. Others claimed a Mickey Finn in "the one bottle of beer I had all evening." Still others declared they had forgotten to read the sailing notice at the head of the accommodation ladder.

Sometimes a seaman, his ship gone, was escorted to the consulate by a local gendarme with a bill from one of the neighborhood bars or bordellos. Such accounts were usually suspect; those who extended credit to seamen did not long stay in business. On the other hand, failure to pay could land a seaman in jail — not the most luxurious establishment between Panama and Cape Horn — pending developments. The consulate had no funds for that kind of indebtedness. Those cases, however, provided opportunities for the practice of diplomacy. The general idea was that if the creditor would not press charges, the consul would "see what could be done" — no guarantee of performance.

In the course of these activities the consul got to know not only assorted local authorities but also ship chandlers, customs brokers and agents, and the principal entrepreneurs of the city. Practical solutions with a mixture of toughness and compassion straightened out more types of cases than were defined in the shipping statutes and the Consular Regulations.

Callao might not be the finest city in South America, but it had movement and variety; a port is always a place where things happen. It was the terminus of the great Central Railroad; it was the gateway to Lima. The harbor was protected by San Lorenzo Island, a barren shoulder rising a thousand feet straight out of the ocean, whitened on the seaward side by deposits of guano. When the wind flowed, citizens did not have to be reminded of their industrious feathered neighbors — out of sight was no longer out of mind.

Callao harbor was often invaded by jellyfish, some of which were nearly as large across as umbrellas, with long, poisonous streamers. They were occasionally so thick that ships had to stop pumping in salt water. Since there were no docks, vessels anchored half a mile offshore, loading and discharging with lighters. Launches plied back and forth between ships, and there was an inadequate pier called the Muelle y Dársena, where customs and baggage handling took place amid scenes of riotous confusion. The construction of proper port works — breakwater, piers, docks, and cargo facilities — was one of the ambitions of President Leguía. The work was finally completed in the 1930s.

Callao at this time was a town with virtually no residential area. Few people other than those whose trades or professions demanded it had their homes there. The office workers, those employed by ship chandlers and their agents, as well as government officials, either lived in Lima, which was connected to the port by tram and bus service as well as a railroad, or in one of the Lima suburbs. Callao was not a "bedroom town" except in a somewhat restricted sense of the term, catering to very transient transients. On the other hand, it boasted several excellent restaurants, notably Salón Blanco, where the vice consul was diverted to find that if he paid in cash for a meal, he paid the full amount, but if he ran a monthly bill, 10 percent was deducted from the total. Salón Blanco specialized in prawns, in tiny scallops called *señoritas,* in thin-shelled clams, and in other delicacies from the cold Humboldt Current. In return for meals aboard ship, I used to invite skippers and pursers to lunch at the Salón Blanco, washing down seafood with the excellent local beer poured from large, dark brown bottles.

I had little to do with our embassy in Lima during this period except for my services on pouch days. That was a task I enjoyed the first few times, but thereafter viewed with decreasing enthusiasm because of what I regarded as the inefficiency of the ambassador's underlings. They rarely produced the diplomatic pouches in time for me to convey them with dignity to the custody of the northbound ship.

Except for cables, communication with Washington was by "despatch," and the despatches were sent by diplomatic pouches carried by mail ships, twelve days from Callao to New York. Diplomatic pouches, constructed of heavy and presumably tamperproof material, were inventoried and sealed in the chancery. There were no couriers, so an American clerk brought them to my Callao office. I was unable to prove that he dawdled en route, or stopped for a drink on the way, but he was almost always so late that it was a close thing to get the pouches to the vessel, ten or fifteen minutes by launch across choppy waters. That was a trip that had to be performed by the vice consul, who rated no consular launch but had to hire one of the *fleteros.* Once aboard, he obtained a receipt from the second mate, in charge of the mails, which receipt was duly delivered to the embassy the following morning.

Ships usually sailed at 6 P.M. If the pouch arrived late in Callao, this could cause the vice consul endless trouble. The skippers of Grace ships were encouraged by the company to make a fetish of punctuality. Punctuality in arrival. Punctuality in departure. When the blue peter was lowered, 6 P.M. meant 6 P.M., and not 6:15 or 6:30. Not a few friends of departing West Coasters, celebrating on the veranda overlooking the swimming pool, were carried to the next port — Salaverry or Chimbote or Talara — and were teased about it for the rest of their Peruvian service. The American vice consul had no desire to join that fraternity. Several times, however, I climbed aboard ship while the anchor was coming up, feeling the vibration as the dripping links clanked on the main deck forward. Once the vessel was actually under way, anchor up and the propeller turning, when I reached the top of the accommodation ladder. That time the captain rang down his engines, but what he said through his megaphone when I departed did not make good hearing.

The consulate general had to get its official mail to the embassy by noon on pouch days. I never could understand why it took so many hours to close the pouches and get them to Callao. I suspected, intolerantly, that the chancery staff slept late and did not start typing their reports until midday. Later, when I myself was dictating those reports, I was amazed to discover how many things happened on pouch days.

Meanwhile, my Spanish, under these varied auspices, was making strides that Consul General Dawson would have approved. Taking the advice of the ambassador, I became a boarder in Miraflores. As Mr. Poindexter had surmised, it took a great deal of doing. The food at the first place was so ferociously seasoned that only a man weaned on Tabasco sauce could long have survived it. At another, a predatory mother turned out to have two even more predatory daughters. At the third, where I stayed several months, there was hot water only on Saturdays. Lima is in the tropics, twelve degrees from the equator, but from May through October — the months of winter mist and fog along the coast — the dampness in unheated houses is pervasive and chilly. Lowering myself into a tub of icy water every morning was the roughest experience since I had earned my commission.

Thus 1926 merged into 1927. One of the principal events in 1927 was the flight across the Atlantic of Charles Lindbergh, which triggered the development of commercial aviation on the west coast of South America. The thrill over this achievement was a universal phenomenon. Peru was ripe for the age of aviation. It took ten days for a ship to travel, with intermediate calls, from one end of the Peruvian coast to the other, from Tumbes to Ilo. The two railroads, the Central from Callao, and the Southern from Mollendo to Lake Titicaca and Cuzco, although marvels of engineering, did not connect with one another or knit the country together. Outside Lima the seven-mile highway from Callao was the only hard-surface road in the Republic. Finally, except for fog in the winter, which rarely reached the ground and invariably thinned out by two thousand feet above sea level, the weather was almost perfect for flying — an important consideration before radar and instrument landings.

The first crossing of the Andes had already been made, by a pilot-mechanic named Slim Faucett, but it was more of a stunt than a promise, and he crash-landed on a strip of sand beside an Amazon tributary. A projected Iquitos air service was later surveyed, and the first plane was flown in by Commander Jasper Grow of the United States Naval Mission to Peru and operated initially by the Peruvian Navy. Jasper Grow's planes took one day to go from San Ramón to Iquitos, and for the first time Peru's *oriente* became part of the Republic.

Before that, the overland trip from Lima to Iquitos had taken from three to five weeks, depending on the weather: up the Andes by railroad to Oroya, crossing the divide at Ticlio, at sixteen thousand feet — the highest standard-gauge line in the world — from Oroya by truck to San Ramón on the eastern slope of the cordillera, then across the Pichis Trail by muleback and canoe to Pucallpa on the Yurimaguas River, and finally to Iquitos by launch.

So arduous was this travel that Peruvian officials appointed in Lima to serve in Iquitos went from Callao by ship through the Panama Canal and across the Atlantic to Liverpool. There they boarded a vessel of the Booth Line that took them back across the Atlantic to Belem, Brazil, at the mouth of the Amazon, and then slowly by river up to Iquitos. That voyage took from three to four months but was preferable, in the eyes of the *limeño* officials, to the Pichis Trail crossing.

Two other aviation pioneers in Peru were Collett E. Woolman and Harold Harris, who at the time of the Lindbergh flight in 1927 were busy dusting the cotton belonging to Pedro Beltrán, a young Peruvian graduate of Oxford who was later Peruvian ambassador to Washington and prime minister of his country. Pedro's hacienda was in the Cañete Valley, south of Lima, and he was the first cotton grower in South America to tackle army worms from the air by crop dusting. Woolman and Harris's modest enterprise, Huff Daland Dusters, was based in Monroe, Louisiana. These two young men later founded Peruvian Airways Limited, the first link in the chain that soon became Pan American Grace Airways, called Panagra, owned half by Grace and Company and half by Pan American Airways.[2]

Woolman and Harris were frequent callers at the consulate general. Harris had been an army test pilot with records to his name, and claimed to be the first member of the Caterpillar Club.[3] He gave me my first flight in Peru — in the empty dust hopper of his plane, which afforded a poor view of the country and brought on an attack of sneezing. I was relieved when we set down on Pedro's hacienda, on a field not much larger than a poncho.

The American embassy in Peru was involved in these flight developments. Woolman and Harris were duly presented to President Leguía, whose interest was immediate and potent. Exciting things began to happen. At first there were little single-engine planes holding five passengers. No flight crew. If mother became ill, she handed the baby to the pilot, who held the baby until mother felt better.

It was an important event, in May 1929, when the first air mail from Peru reached the United States in six and a half days, half the time it took by steamship. Even more important to Peru, later in the same year, was the arrival of the first of the new trimotor Fords, which more than doubled the passenger-carrying capacity of the single-motor Fairchilds.

This took place during the tour of duty of my next ambassador, Alexander P. Moore, and while it may not have been Ambassador Moore's most important diplomatic achievement, it may have been his most spectacular one.

2. At the beginning the Grace connection was enormously the more important, for Grace had offices all the way from the Canal Zone to Santiago and Valparaiso, plus nearly a century of experience in dealing with west coast problems. Pan American Airways, before the word "world" was added, in 1928 had a single ninety-mile service, one round-trip flight a day between Key West and Havana. Shortly thereafter Lindbergh, as a consultant, mapped routes for Panair around the Caribbean.

When Woolman left Peru, he founded Delta Airlines, of which for years he was president. Harold Harris remained as operating head of Panagra until World War II. He then operated MTC, the worldwide Military Transport Command, retiring with the rank of brigadier general. After that Harris was president of Northwest Orient Airlines, during which service he rescued me, when I was American ambassador to Korea, from President Rhee's two bears. (See *Shots Heard Around the World,* chap. 10, in which President Rhee sends a present of two bears to President Eisenhower.) In the 1960s Panagra was absorbed by Braniff International.

3. The Caterpillar Club was founded in the days when parachutes were made of silk. If the pilot bailed out of a crippled plane and survived, he was automatically a member.

After the Peruvian link was started, with single-engine planes that skipped up and down the coast of Peru, the energetic Harold Harris obtained rights in Ecuador and on the Island of Tumaco, off the coast of Colombia. Panama was now within range of Lima, and the first service to the north of Peru used amphibians from Talara to Guayaquil and thence north to the Canal Zone. The single-engine planes were cramped and inadequate, and from day to day, passenger demand was increasing. It was with pride, therefore, that we learned in 1929 that Peru would soon receive the first of the new Ford trimotor aircraft — the last word in safety, comfort, and convenience. Moreover, the first one would be named *Santa Rosa* for the patron saint of Peru, and would be christened by the archbishop of Lima, assisted by the daughter of President Leguía. The plane was shipped from New York, and unloaded and reassembled at Durán, the landing strip across the river from Guayaquil, Ecuador.

The first flight would be to the City of Kings, and the American ambassador, with an eye to showmanship, arranged to have the ceremony take place not at the airport, which was then some distance south of Lima, but at the race track on the edge of the city. It would be on Sunday afternoon, in the middle of the races, in the presence of President Leguía, members of the Peruvian government (including the foreign minister in his gray top hat), the diplomatic corps, and Lima society. Harris was at first dubious about landing on the oval or, once there, taking off again with a full load of honored guests for an inaugural ride over the city. To save weight, he would have to land and take off with as little fuel aboard as possible.

Tape measure in hand, I paced off the race track while Harris, who had not yet piloted a Ford trimotor, made notes and calculations. By taking down the fence at either end of the oval, some extra yardage was obtained. It remained for Harris to get the plane and to make a few practice landings within the oval, but by that time Ambassador Moore was far ahead of him with plans for the ceremony. Fortunately, Harris received the plane a week in advance and did practice landings on measured terrain at Las Palmas, beyond the city, until he was sure he had a safe leeway for the race track landing.[4]

4. The trimotor Ford, with no retractable landing gear and no cowling around the three motors, and with a thick single wing, had so much drag it could almost be landed on a pasture. The last time I flew in one was with Ernest Hemingway and Winston Guest, plus shotguns and ammunition and much equipment, for a duck hunt at the mouth of the Agabama River in Cuba. The pilot got us down by scraping the top frond of a royal palm at the near edge of the field with his tail wheel; he explained that if he did not feel

The christening of the *Santa Rosa* was a great success. Harold Harris made an impressive landing and then deployed the plane to the race track itself, directly in front of the presidential box. Everything went according to schedule until it came to the takeoff with the twelve guests of honor — seventeen were found to have crowded aboard. It took an extra half-hour to sort out that one, during which the president impatiently waited for the next race, and Harris and the third secretary of embassy (which I had become in 1928) aged visibly.

---

the slight jar of the wheel scraping the *yagua,* he circled and tried again, because otherwise he would overshoot the field and nose into the river. When he came back for us two days later, we watched, and sure enough, that was the way he landed. Cuba was the last place to use the trimotor Ford commercially — in 1941, after Pearl Harbor.

In the Footsteps of Pizarro

The Foreign Service in 1928 had seven hundred officers, of whom less than a quarter had been members of the old Diplomatic Service before it was merged with the Consular Branch in 1924. These diplomatic officers had several things in common. By and large, they had not been enthusiastic about the merger of the two corps, on the ground that it might dilute the prestige of their profession, which some of them regarded as a cut above the tasks performed by consuls. This was not altogether a matter of snobbery. As one of them expressed it; "You don't have to have been a coal miner to run a coal business."

These diplomats were of necessity men of wealth. The old Diplomatic Service was so poorly paid that no one who could not contribute upward of $15,000 or $20,000 a year to the expenses of his post could accept a commission in it. A number of officers commanded large fortunes. The roster had names like Armour (meat), Bliss (of Dumbarton Oaks), Kirk (soap), Wilson (shirts), Grew and Phillips (Beacon Hill), Pabst (beer), Harriman (banking), Laughlin (steel), and Schoellkopf (electric power).

Prior to 1924, the highest diplomatic salary below that of ambassador was paid to the counselor of the American embassy in London — the officer then second to the ambassador — who received $3,750 per annum. The expenses of that office — house, servants, horses, automobile, clubs, official entertaining, travel, shooting in Scotland, and fishing in Ireland and Norway — came to at least ten times that amount. There were no allowances. London, to be sure, was expensive, but so were Paris, Rome, Vienna, Berlin, St. Petersburg, Tokyo, Rio de Janeiro, and Buenos Aires. One could get by for less in Asunción, Oslo, or Sofia.

The remarkable thing about the old Diplomatic Service was that there were so few dilettantes and so large a proportion of dedicated and competent officers. There were some drones, of course. One was serving with Ambassador Poindexter when I reached Lima; he was amiable, stuffy, and harmless. Notified of his transfer to Turkey and looking forward to Constantinople, he wailed loudly when an office was established in the new capital of Ankara, in the wastelands of Anatolia. Last we heard of him, the only outdoor exercise he was getting — there being no golf or polo in Ankara — was a twice-a-week walk to the railway station, where, by arrangement with a porter of the Ankara car of the Simplon-Orient Express, he received a box of gardenias from Paris. These he presented to a lady from Budapest with whom he was sharing his exile.

It should not be supposed that those diplomatic officers lacked esprit de corps or refused to serve in dangerous places. Most of them went without argument from the fleshpots of western Europe to remote jurisdictions in Central America, the Far East, or the Balkans. What they did have in common, however, was an aversion to serving with an ambassador of whom they did not approve. Moreover, with a service so small, they all knew each other on a first-name basis, so that when a difficult or objectionable chieftain was identified, the word got around and plans were laid to avoid, if possible, going to that capital.

Having no background of that sort and a warm pride in being a Foreign Service officer, I found this attitude distasteful. It seems fair to observe, however, that if I had been paying $2,000 or $3,000 a month of my own money for the privilege of working for the United States abroad, my attitude might have been different.

Ambassador Poindexter resigned, and Alexander P. Moore was appointed in his place. There was no rush of diplomats toward Lima, which perhaps explains why I was switched from the consulate general in Peru to our embassy in Peru with the rank of third secretary. I applied for home leave so I could begin my diplomatic career with a bride to share it with me.[1]

The ambassador had not arrived in Lima when I left, so when I reached New York, I called on him in his suite at the Plaza. He was sailing in a few days for Callao, and in the meantime was receiving visits from executives and businessmen with interests in Peru.

1. I was the only third secretary in the Lima diplomatic corps. Inflation of titles had already set in, and even the smallest countries like Costa Rica and Haiti had begun to recognize no rank below first or second secretary. As a result, I was always at the foot of the table, down by the toothpicks and the spare finger bowls. The only man I ranked was the assistant military attaché of the Chinese legation, a first lieutenant in the Chinese army. Since we were usually too far away to be able to hear speeches — a not unmixed blessing — we used to play tic-tac-toe on the tablecloth, marking the squares with the tines of a fork. I cannot remember ever winning a game from him.

Mr. Moore has been variously described, but no one ever said he was not a colorful character or accused him of being the soft-boiled egg in an Easter basket. At the age of twelve he started peddling newspapers, and before long he was publishing the paper. He dabbled in the stock market and made a great deal of money. He contributed generously to the Republican Party. In 1912 he married Lillian Russell, the actress who in the early 1900s used to stop traffic along Broadway. Mr. Moore survived her.

Ambassador Moore had served in Spain for two years by appointment of President Harding. The rumor had it that Mrs. Moore wanted to go to China, but that Secretary Hughes intervened, pointing out that Peking was a legation, not an embassy. "Raise it to an embassy," Uncle Alec demanded. When the secretary of state declined to cooperate, Madrid resulted. While there, Mr. Moore learned little Spanish, but he developed an affection for the royal family of Spain that was equaled only by the offhand way he treated its members.

At the Plaza the ambassador received me in the purple satin dressing gown that was his official uniform for the daytime transaction of business. Evenings he wore a dinner jacket, with a high Alfred de Musset bow tie, but between 11 A.M., when he started most days, and dinnertime, the purple dressing gown saw almost uninterrupted service. This afternoon he was smoking a cigar, scattering ashes. His hands, heavily veined, looked older than his face.

We talked of Peru. I did not much care for his attitude toward his predecessor; I had not yet learned that almost every ambassador is critical of whatever went on in his country before he got there. Ambassador Moore had already decided that there were two things of interest to him in the land of the Incas: finding American enterprises to develop the country, including bankers to provide the capital, and settling the long-standing dispute between Peru and Chile over the territories of Tacna and Arica.

"They better settle it," said the ambassador. "Bankers don't buy lawsuits." Was it true, he asked me, that the entire piece of disputed real estate was worthless?

"Except maybe to Bolivia," I agreed. I explained that the railroad went from Arica up through the mountains to La Paz, and since Bolivia had lost her Pacific territory to Chile in 1884, she had always wanted it back. Bolivia was not, however, a party to the current negotiations.

"Which are getting nowhere fast," said Mr. Moore. He added, apparently with relish, that those same negotiations had given General Pershing so painful a toothache that he had resigned, but Secretary Kellogg was all for getting on with a settlement. "Nervous Nellie chasing a peace prize," he observed disrespectfully. "See you in July," he said, waving his cigar.

The return voyage south involved me for the first time with the General Accounting Office in Washington. The subject was reimbursement for my wife's steamship ticket. In those days an officer's transportation and that of his family was paid by the government *only* if the State Department transferred him. No matter how long you had been abroad, you paid your own way when you came back to the United States on vacation. So when I filed my account, submitting the ticket for one bride, New York to Callao, the bill was thrown back in my face, with the kind of prose the General Accounting Office saves to spit in the eye of a government traveler. Research disclosed that if my wife had accompanied me to Peru in 1926, when I first went there, instead of when I returned from leave in 1928, her fare would indeed have been chargeable to the government, but as it was, she was just a bride on vacation; no tinkle from Uncle Sam's cash register. It did no good to point out that I was, in fact, being transferred, from vice consul in Callao to third secretary in Lima. The corresponding trolley fare came to the equivalent of thirteen cents — no stopover in New York included.

Those voyages by ship before World War II were splendid experiences. Modern travelers by jet plane — across an ocean by daylight, or overnight to Buenos Aires — have no idea what they are missing. You sailed from New York at noon on Thursday, and on Sunday the ship passed Watling's Island (Columbus's San Salvador, his first landfall); not many hours later you saw lights on the eastern tip of Cuba; then Panama, six days from New York, the transit of the Canal, with a buffet on deck and a breeze off Gatun Lake, the white cranes on Barro Colorado Island so close you could almost touch them, and the Continental Divide at Culebra. The ruins of old Panama were much the same as when the pirate Henry Morgan left them. And there was time that evening for a drink at Kelly's Ritz or the Hotel Tivoli. Next day the motion of the vessel, cradled at last by the Pacific, had a rhythm different from that of the choppy Caribbean. In the South American winter the officers put on blue uniforms for Talara, three degrees south of the equator; it was the first port washed by the cold Humboldt Current. Two days later, there was San Lorenzo Island off the starboard bow as the ship nosed in among the jellyfish in Callao harbor.

There were few tourist travelers in those days; shore facilities and accommodations were still too primitive to lure many away from the attractions of Europe. The men and women traveling to the Rainless Coast were the hewers of wood and the drawers of water — the doers, not the time wasters.

They were mining and construction engineers, geologists, mechanics, archaeologists, employees of banks and companies with export interest, searchers for petroleum, a bride now and then, heading apprehensively for Chuquicamata or Cerro de Pasco, a sprinkling of government officials. The other half of the passengers were Chilean and Peruvian, who mixed well enough with each other so long as the subject was not Tacna or Arica. They were businessmen, doctors, schoolchildren and college students, the latter loudly bilingual, with now and then a *Latino* diplomat or a wealthy *hacendado* returning via New York from Madrid or Paris. The ship's menus were in English and Spanish, and both languages were spoken in the purser's office. The barmen were Chinese, unintelligible in either language but good at arithmetic.

Our arrival in Callao was memorable. We were met and informed that as a welcome to the bride and groom, Ambassador Moore had sent his Rolls Royce to the landing to bring us to Lima.

The ambassadorial automobile was the only Rolls Royce in Peru, but it would have been a conspicuous vehicle even in a covey of Rolls Royces. The radiator and hood were gunmetal, polished and shining like a silver mirror. The body of the car was painted a purply sort of dark red — a very special paint job — and on the center panel of each rear door was painted the shield of the United States. It was not quite so large as the official shield over the embassy doorway, but it was visible for some distance in clear weather. The chauffeur, whose Indian face I remembered from the Poindexter menage, wore a uniform the same shade of red as the coachwork, with silver braid matching the gunmetal. Over the visor his cap had an American Army officer's insignia, silverplated. This unorthodox use of the cap ornament caused pain to the military attaché, which the ambassador ignored. Altogether the effect was as edifying to the arriving travelers as it must have been electrifying to the citizens of Peru who first saw it.[2]

At the special diplomatic landing where the Rolls was parked, there were always a policeman and a customs official on duty — to make sure that the *estado* was not defrauded of revenue by unauthorized passengers trying to make a taxfree landing. As a vice consul I had been allowed to land there as a

2. It was not until the late 1930s that the American government began supplying official transportation for its chiefs of mission. Before that the only officers with official cars were the attachés of the two armed services. Ambassadors bought their own cars, hired their own chauffeurs, and bought their uniforms. Even transportation of the automobile between posts was paid for by the ambassador.

courtesy, and often I was accompanied ashore by a captain or a purser en route to a meal at the Salón Blanco. On such occasions I would indicate my guest, saying to the guards, "El señor capitán del vapor Santa Luisa" (or "El señor contador" if he was the purser). The two Peruvians would salute me and say politely, "Que pasen, señores," which raised my stock with the American merchant marine. Now, as a real diplomat at last, I could use this special landing in my own right; it was a pleasant sensation.

Our arrival at the landing, while elegant, was to have repercussions. They had nothing to do with the ambassador's Rolls Royce, but they did have to do with my diplomatic immunity.

Peru had granted a match monopoly to the Kruger interests in Sweden for a substantial sum. Kruger had received exclusive rights to manufacture and sell matches in Peru, and was eager to recoup the investment, including matchmaking machinery imported from Stockholm that produced much better matches than those previously available. The matches were called *La Llama,* which in Spanish means both "the flame" and the Andean beast of burden. Each box had a bright yellow label with a likeness of the animal upon it. And each box cost at retail the equivalent of four American cents for half the number of matches contained in a one-cent box of American matches.

Not only were the monopoly aspects irritating to many Americans, but the enforcement provisions were so harsh as to become a source of repeated friction between the Peruvian government and the American consulate general. There was a fine for using foreign matches — £10 or $40 — and notices to that effect were posted around the ship before the first Peruvian port was reached. Lighters were forbidden, and anyone using one was subject both to a fine and to confiscation of the lighter. But travelers from the north, including American transients, were careless or forgetful. Moreover, agents provocateurs, called *pesquisadores,* frequented bars and hotel lobbies in Lima. Producing a cigarette, they would ask for a light and then pounce on the offender.

American visitors were constantly being arrested, whereat loud and bitter complaint would be registered with the consulate general. The penalty was a heavy one for possession of something that in the United States was taken for granted, even given away at cigar counters. Equally outraging to the unfortunate culprit was the problem, once apprehended, of getting unmeshed from the Peruvian bureaucracy in time to get back aboard ship. Vessels had been missed while cases were being disposed of. In Callao, as vice consul I had been able to persuade the Grace office to supply Peruvian matches to members of the ship's crew going ashore, thus saving many headaches, but somehow that never worked with the passengers. Thus the consulate general in Lima had a case or two every time a ship arrived, and the ill will thus generated was out of proportion, it seemed to me, to whatever benefits accrued to Peru from the monopoly.

During the call of the *Santa Teresa* at Balboa, my wife and I visited the Canal Zone commissary and purchased, along with other supplies for housekeeping in Lima, $10 worth of Canal Zone matches. They came neatly packed in sealed containers, each container conspicuously labeled with a blown-up replica of the label on the individual box. We had not realized that $10 bought so many matches. These and the rest of our Canal Zone purchases were stowed in our stateroom, and hence went ashore with us as luggage.

The customs guard at the diplomatic landing could not possibly fail to identify this abundant supply of contraband matches. On a penalty basis, they represented a fortune almost as large as the amount raised to ransom Atahualpa. The guard, however, made no objection, for ours was clearly diplomatic luggage. There was the truck marked Embajada Americana; there was the Rolls Royce with the American emblem on the door. The *aduanero* courteously said nothing, but he made a note on his pad, according to his instructions.

On my first day in my new office in the chancery, my first caller was the honorary Swedish consul general, who was simultaneously the head of the Compañía Fosforera del Perú, the national match monopoly. He was very correct, and very reproving. Sven Karrel was a tall man who reminded me of Axel Heyst in Conrad's *Victory,* except that he had no guardsman's mustache to enhance the dignity of his bearing. I liked Sven. It was evident, however, that Swedish-American friendship was about to be severely tested.

Sven Karrel conceded that I was within my rights in importing the matches. Diplomats had special privileges. As consul general of Sweden, he understood my situation. But he could not forbear to add that the amount spent by even the most profligate match-consuming diplomat could not possibly come to more than a few *soles* a month, a nothing in the budget of an American household. He likewise conceded, politely, that my Canal Zone matches were intended for my personal use. His concern should not be misinterpreted as implying that an American official would countenance selling them in the black market. Certainly not. But the effect on Peruvian guests in my house would not be good — they would put a box or two in their pockets and use them elsewhere. Probably not very important, but not good for the *monopolio.* Not good, but supportable.

What really disturbed him, Sven declared, was the problem of my servants — and he obviously envisaged a retinue of them — to whom these foreign matches would be an irresistible temptation. The servants would steal them — a few boxes at a time — and the illegal matches would get into circulation, and that would be bad — very bad — for the Compañía Fosforera del Perú, of which he had the honor to be president.

I protested. I said the matches were already in the stockroom at my house, locked with a padlock. I said I was sure there would be no black market leakage attributable to my household. I could give him my most solemn assurance.

Sven bowed in acknowledgment of the assurance, but he was plainly unappeased. He had, however, one more thing to say. "I haf," he said, "one suggestion, but it will depend upon your cooperation. I cannot insist upon it." This was the formal Swede — the consul general addressing a colleague. "I haf," he repeated, "one suggestion. It will be expensive for me, but not for you. But it depends upon your cooperation."

And that was how, on my first Sunday as a married diplomat in Peru, there was produced the damnedest bonfire since the last auto-da-fé of the Spanish Inquisition. Ours was not in the Plaza de Armas, but three thousand feet up, on the flank of one of the coastal mountains. It was a diplomatic triumph for Sweden, although the United States emerged with honor.

We had a picnic luncheon, high enough on the road so we were above the winter fog, and appeared to perch on an island surrounded by a sea of cotton with the bare ridges of the Andes for an eastern boundary. We were above the mist in clear, warm sunshine; the only vegetation consisted of cactuses of varying sizes and descriptions, some with bright flowers, and all with sharp spines. We had dry martinis and aquavit, and tart Peruvian wine from the Ica Valley. We had cold fried chicken, and *escabeche*. There were avocados with dark brown skins and green-yellow meat, smooth as butter.

There were various toasts, and various responses. Punctiliously we toasted Peru and Sweden and the success of the match monopoly, and at the end of the meal we made a bonfire of $10 worth of Canal Zone safety matches.

Back in Lima that afternoon, the president of the Compañía Fosforera del Perú solemnly delivered to Lucy an equivalent number of boxes of national monopoly Peruvian matches. They went into the locked storeroom, to be doled out a few boxes at a time. When Lucy and I were transferred from Peru, the remaining matches were with equal formality returned to the donor. Ambassador Moore approved of the bonfire. He said it was smart public relations.

Working for Ambassador Moore was not, however, all picnics and match burning. In the 1920s the normal complement of embassy Lima was four officers, including the ambassador. That made it a middle-sized mission as things went at the time, but we had only three — the counselor and myself in addition to Mr. Moore — which testified to the agility of successive first secretaries in wiggling out of the assignment. At the time I resented this, chiefly because it doubled the work reaching the desk of the third secretary, but looking back, I realize what an unusual opportunity it gave me to participate in operations that normally would have been undertaken by a more experienced officer.

I found the work endlessly absorbing. As a vice consul I had dealt with crises such as lost travelers' checks, missed steamship connections, an arrest for using a cigarette lighter in the lobby of the Gran Hotel Bolívar, the demand of an important *político* for an emergency visa. Solutions of these problems were important to the clients concerned, but they were hardly of moment — except perhaps in an ill-defined aggregate — in the relations between the two countries.

Diplomacy, at least Uncle Alec's brand, dealt strictly with bilateral relations and with the power that influenced them. He sensed at once where the power lay in Peru: with President Leguía, and not in the hands of his ministers. On embassy business I went to the beautiful old Torre Tagle Palace, the Peruvian Foreign Office, far more often than did the ambassador. Except when he presented his credentials, the autographed letter from President Coolidge countersigned by Secretary of State Kellogg, Ambassador Moore paid almost no attention to the foreign minister, a comic little man with a bald head who dutifully went to the race track each Sunday because President Leguía owned race horses. The foreign minister wore a gray top hat that was too large for him, reminding those admitted to the presidential box not of Ascot but of the Mad Hatter at Alice's tea party. The ambassador cultivated the president, and they got on well together; he also went to the races, the Rolls Royce in attendance, but he complained to the president that betting there was no fun. When a presidential horse paid off, all you got back was your money; when you bet on anybody else's horse, you lost the price of the ticket.

For Peruvian society as such the ambassador had little use, except that he was soon playing poker with those sufficiently solvent (and optimistic) to take him on. He told the counselor of embassy to "dispose of the social nonsense" and not to bother him with it.

In official entertaining, however, Uncle Alec was not remiss. Being essentially a nocturnal animal, he enjoyed the glitter, the movement, and the late hours. He himself never drank anything alcoholic, but he knew the prestige value of serving superior wines, even if half his guests could not tell the difference.

Uncle Alec was not philosophical, nor was he concerned with someone else's social problems. About the plight of the Indians of the Peruvian sierra, Ambassador Moore, unlike Ambassador Poindexter, knew little and cared less. To him the future of the Indians was the business of Peru, not of the United States government. Travel in Peru? Why travel, when Lima was the only comfortable place in the country?

5

Uncle Alec Settles Tacna-Arica

It should not be supposed that Mr. Moore was not a working ambassador. He was physically sedentary, but his mind was rarely idle. The accuracy of his observation that "bankers don't buy lawsuits" was demonstrated when loan negotiations initiated by President Leguía faltered and the lenders began talking, privately, about the strained relations between Peru and Chile. After an exchange of cables with Washington, the ambassador decided that a further and active effort ought to be made to get the problem of Tacna-Arica off the agenda.

The dispute over these two barren provinces had been playing for so many years that no one could remember when Peru and Chile had not been denouncing one another. The denunciations were coupled with recriminations and dark threats of unilateral action. Nearly two generations of Peruvian children had been taught to regard Chile as their natural enemy.

Angus Crawford, in his famous summary of Latin America in one lecture, used to cite an incident to illustrate how difficult it is, after an event, to get at the facts of history. Angus described two versions of the battle of Arica, fought in 1880. According to one, the brave Peruvian commander, defeated but defiant, spurred his charger and leaped off the top of the Morro, plunging to his death several hundred feet below. Death before defeat — and Lima schoolchildren for half a century were taught to cheer when this brave exploit was described by the teacher.

The Chilean version of the same event was that the defeated Peruvians were fleeing in disorder, every man for himself, and that Colonel Bolognesi, the Peruvian commander, outdistancing all the others, was galloping so fast that he was unable to pull up. Horse and man fell off the edge of the cliff, screaming with terror.

Not in dispute was who won the war. The descendants of the tough Araucanian Indians decisively defeated both Peru and Bolivia, acquiring a strip of the Rainless Coast and rendering Bolivia a landlocked country. Chile also occupied the two southern Peruvian provinces of Tacna and Arica, with a provision in the Treaty of Ancón for a plebiscite ten years later (in 1894) to determine whether they would remain Chilean or revert to Peru. Bolivia was not consulted. At the time nobody paid much attention to Bolivia.

The plebiscite had not been held, and during all the intervening years Peru regularly complained, and the two countries continued to argue about it and to denounce one another. When Chile, on the eve of World War I, ordered from Great Britain the battleship *Almirante Latorre,* nearly thirty thousand tons, Peru could hardly wait to order four submarines from the Electric Boat Company. Peru ordered the U-boats although it was well known that Chile could not afford to operate a piece of armor as a battleship; in fact, a saying was current up and down the coast that every time the *Almirante Latorre* blew its whistle, the Chilean peso dropped ten points. Peru likewise could ill afford the submarines.

Peru refused to buy Chilean fruit and boycotted the excellent light wines of the Central Valley, the best wines produced in the Western Hemisphere. Peru also deprived herself of the succulent *langostas,* the best clawless lobsters in the world, because they came from Robinson Crusoe's Juan Fernández Island, a Chilean possession.

Peru also hectored Chilean shipping. As a vice consul I had observed that in *noticias marítimas* — the official shipping notices that listed vessels arriving, loading, and departing — there was a notation, every time a Chilean vessel reached Callao, that the master had been fined five Peruvian pounds for "carelessly blowing his whistle and disturbing the guano birds." No captain except a Chilean captain incurred that penalty, which was strictly a one-way weapon, for half a dozen Chilean ships, including two in the New York service, called regularly at Peruvian ports. No Peruvian vessel went to Chile.

Various efforts to mediate the dispute were made by the inter-American family, but one after another the peacemakers burned their fingers or, in the case of General Pershing, infected a tooth, and gave it up. The Tacna-Arica dispute proved to be the most durable menace to peace in the Western Hemisphere.

When the United States was asked to extend its good offices, the postponed plebiscite was declared to be on. That was the origin of the Pershing presence on an American warship rolling in the Pacific swell off Arica. He was supposed to make sure that the plebiscite was fair and aboveboard.

That was well intentioned but unrealistic. It is impossible to conduct a fair plebiscite when the area in dispute is occupied by one of the parties to the dispute. That should be an axiom of international relations. With the best of goodwill (which here was lacking) the occupying power will, one way or another, stack the cards in its own favor.

The Peruvians alleged that Peruvian residents of the provinces were being disqualified; the eligibility of even lifetime residents was being questioned. They claimed intimidation and duress. They charged that Peruvians were being brutalized by the Chilean police. Finally, they alleged that Chile was importing voters from down the coast and lodging them in military barracks pending plebiscite day. The Peruvians said that every time a Peruvian was finally qualified, two Chileans were accepted.

Perched on his battleship, like a pelican on a buoy, General Pershing had no way of investigating these allegations.

The plebiscite might perhaps have worked if the United States, as the power invited to extend its good offices, had taken over the administration of the provinces for the period of registration and balloting. The area was, after all, not very large and, except for the towns of Tacna and Arica, was thinly populated. A few hundred American troops could doubtless have exercised police power and maintained order; a few score could have operated the polls. But the American government was not invited to do this.

The plebiscite was called off. Relations between Peru and Chile were more strained than ever.

That was the situation on Ambassador Moore's arrival in 1928. Peru was convinced, with some reason, that if a fair plebiscite could be held, Peru would win; therefore Peru was prepared to continue to agitate against perfidious Chile, vandal of the Pacific. Peruvian politicians made loud noises. The editorial pages of *El Comercio* and *La Prensa* came smoking from the Lima presses. The four Peruvian submarines sailed up and down the Peruvian coast, waiting for the *Almirante Latorre* to appear in their periscopes.

The fine levied by Peru against Chilean captains who disturbed the guano birds was doubled.

To the practical brain of the American ambassador, there was nothing insoluble about the problem. To him, the proposition ran something like this: (1) Settlement of the dispute would benefit both countries, each of which was pleading for capital development. (In the late 1920s, the United States was full of bankers looking for profitable investment, and of American citizens ready to buy foreign bonds.) (2) Treaty or no treaty, the plebiscite had been a silly idea in the first place. (3) The alternative was a negotiated settlement, and the time for its was now. (4) The only negotiated settlement that made sense was to divide the area, giving Chile the southern province, Arica, and giving Tacna to Peru.

Moore calculated that Chile, with the poorer claim, would be more amenable than Peru, which had been preaching *revindicación* for decades, demanding the return of both provinces. Besides, Chile would be getting Arica with its harbor and railroad, the more valuable of the two areas.

The task, therefore, was to win over Peru, which meant winning over President Leguía — a dictator, but a patriotic Peruvian dictator with a grasp of statesmanship.

To that task Ambassador Moore dedicated himself with vigor, astuteness, and tenacity. He admired the diminutive president of Peru. They were both politicians; the character of each contained hard metal. As individuals they liked each other. Moreover, the president spoke English, so their conversations were conducted without an interpreter who might have been too terrified to render some of the ambassador's observations.

The first thing Ambassador Moore was able to do, with an assist from Ambassador Culbertson, his opposite number in Santiago, was to promote an exchange of ambassadors between Peru and Chile. Diplomatic relations had been maintained, tenuously at times, but for years the respective embassies had been manned by chargés d'affaires. A chargé, no matter how competent, lacks the prestige and the influence that go with ambassadorial status. Moore had few illusions about their accomplishing much with respect to the substance of the dispute, which in any case was being handled by the United States as mediator, but he believed that if a Chilean of stature could come to Lima, his mere presence might improve the atmosphere. Firebrand speeches and editorials might be cooled. The voice of reason might now and then be raised. It seemed worth trying, and after considerable discussion, President Leguía agreed. This initiative was fruitful largely because Chile sent to Peru an ex-president of the Republic, a gentleman of commanding presence, who proved to be a synonym for the word *simpático*. Don Emiliano Figueroa Larrain was a man of good family; he had a patriarchal beard below a twinkling eye. Chilean wine began flowing in Peru for the first time since the War of the Pacific. Peruvian society, standoffish at first, began flocking to Don Emiliano's parties.

These activities were reflected in greatly augmented cable traffic among Washington, Lima, and Santiago. I soon found myself swamped by my regular chores plus nighttime coding and decoding. There were no coding machines and, except for a few of the largest posts in Europe, there were no code clerks. Messages were enciphered and decoded by junior officers, whether or not they had a talent for that specialized operation. As the only junior office in embassy Lima, I soon discovered that a six-hour night over code books decreased my efficiency during the following ten-hour day. Uncle Alec thereupon recruited a couple of new vice consuls to be my assistants. More, he furnished unlimited amounts of coffee. Lucy used to drive in from the suburbs and scramble eggs at 2 A.M. Sometimes she was joined by the ambassador, wearing a dinner jacket and his Alfred de Musset tie, upon his return from poker or from roulette at the country club.

In the midst of these activities there occurred the American election of 1928, closely followed by the announcement that President-elect Hoover would make a tour of South America — the first such voyage to be made by so exalted an American official. He would sail down the West Coast on a warship, cross the Andes by train, and sail north aboard another navy vessel via Buenos Aires and Rio de Janeiro. As a mining engineer, Herbert Hoover's name was already known in Peru, where he would spend two days in the American embassy after his visit to Quito. The Peruvians were thrilled. For the moment, Tacna and Arica were in abeyance.

When I recall subsequent visits of high-ranking officials, especially after the airplane cast its blight upon rational diplomacy, the Hoover visit to Peru seems a model of simplicity and lack of ostentation. Accompanying the president-elect were Mrs. Hoover, a lady of quiet charm; Herbert Hoover, Jr. (who was to be undersecretary of state twenty-five years later); and, as adviser, ambassador Henry Fletcher, a competent and experienced senior diplomat. There must have been a security agent or two and clerical personnel; they were so unobtrusive that they left no impression.

There was a banquet in the Presidential Palace, which I recall because it was the first time I had seen the gold viceregal dinner service. As usual I was at the foot of the table. There were meetings: the mine owners urged a higher price for copper; the sugar and cotton growers, a better market for cotton and sugar. During his private talk with President Leguía, Mr. Hoover, coached by Ambassador Fletcher and Uncle Alec, made a pitch for an early settlement of the dispute with Chile.

The visit catered to the self-importance of Latin American countries; then, as now, they complained about being taken for granted. But diplomatically, little new ground was broken. On the contrary, hopes were raised that could not possibly be fulfilled except with congressional action, which was not forthcoming. Mr. Hoover learned little about the continent that he had not known before. Those countries he did not visit experienced hurt feelings. And such goodwill as was generated in Peru was compromised by the sack of Callao by the exuberant sailors from the USS *Maryland*, Mr. Hoover's transporting vessel.

The year 1929 dawned with hopes ascendant. The break in the Tacna-Arica deadlock came when President Leguía finally agreed "in principle" that a division of the territory would be acceptable, provided a Peruvian port could be found for the inland town of Tacna, which had hitherto shipped its oranges and vegetables through Arica.

"In principle," remarked Uncle Alec as we drove back to the embassy, "means in diplomacy that you plan to run out on it first chance you get. But it is the first time the president has agreed to drop the claim to both provinces. We're in business!"

On his next visit to the president, the ambassador took Commander Jasper Grow with him. Grow belonged to the Naval Mission, in which capacity he had been instrumental in establishing the air service to the Amazon port of Iquitos. For this exploit, and also because he had a blonde and vivacious wife, Jasper Grow stood well with the president. Uncle Alec had a map session with Grow before their appointment with the president. On large-scale maps the southern coast of Peru looked encouragingly indented. After the meeting the ambassador emphasized that Jasper had better find a port site for Tacna, or else. He pointed out that with modern equipment a road could easily be built to connect Tacna with the seacoast across a strip of intervening desert. Commander Grow got the idea. He departed to crank up his airplane and that, in essence, is the way the problem was finally settled.

Shortly after the Tacna port site was decided upon, the ambassador made a quick trip to the United States, leaving his butler in charge of the residence. Soon the idle chef had a fight with the butler and resigned his job, whereupon the counselor of embassy hired him.

The counselor had been in the service thirty years, against my four. I nevertheless told him that, no matter what were the facts of the case, Mr. Moore would be convinced that as soon as he had left, the counselor had stolen his chef. The counselor maintained that the chef had declared he would not again work for Ambassador Moore.

The ambassador's rage was immediate, loud, articulate, and punitive. Thenceforth, gatherings at the embassy did not include the counselor or his wife, a German baroness who had not been restrained in expressing her contempt for her husband's boss. The counselor was informed that he could still use his office in the embassy, but beginning now, all documents — telegrams, dispatches, accounts, whatnot — would bypass his desk. As far as the ambassador was concerned, the counselor had ceased to be a member of his staff.

Soon Lima society had another reason to enjoy the goings-on at the American embassy: the arrival of Uncle Alec's friend Mrs. Smith for an extended visit. She engaged a suite at the Hotel Bolívar, one hundred yards down the street from the embassy.

Just where Mrs. Smith fit in was never altogether clear. Reportedly, Uncle Alec and her late husband had once been business associates, and after his death Uncle Alec had helped her with her investments. She was twenty years younger than Mr. Moore; her clothes were expensive and theatrical; and she was filled with extrovert good humor. She used to reach the embassy about 10:30 in the morning, and when I was summoned half an hour later to bring in the telegrams, Mrs. Smith would be sitting on the foot of the ambassador's bed, which had a pale purple coverlet, several shades lighter than Uncle Alec's dressing gown, which he wore over pale purple silk pajamas. A breakfast tray would be before him, Mrs. Smith would be balancing a coffee cup, and the American ambassador would be about to light his first cigar of the day.

All of which bears on events because of the warming effect Mrs. Smith had on the ambassadorial disposition. What with long days, personality clashes, efforts to keep out of the line of fire in a battle in which I believed my professional colleague was grievously at fault, and the pressure of official business as the Tacna-Arica negotiations entered their final phase, the contribution of Mrs. Smith toward keeping Uncle Alec in good spirits was one for which my wife and I remained everlastingly grateful. She soothed him and cheered him up, and the life of his youthful subordinate was correspondingly brightened.

Commander Grow brought back encouraging reports about a Tacna port site. A hassle began about what contribution Chile should make to the construction of facilities for Peru. This did not seem insoluble because, once the hatchet had been buried, either country would be in a position to borrow from American investors.

In the course of this debate, which involved many telegrams and more joint coding operations with my vice consul pals, Uncle Alec became incensed with his opposite number, the American Ambassador to Chile, and sent him a message of blistering, gratuitous rudeness. Ambassador Culbertson, a lawyer and an economist, was occasionally extremely long-winded. Their falling out proved to be a break for the coding contingent, because Ambassador Culbertson was so enraged that, in addition to telegraphing Moore's message to Secretary Kellogg in the hopes that Kellogg might remonstrate, he stopped repeating *his* Tacna-Arica telegrams to Lima, thus considerably lightening the workload of the three amateur code clerks.

The incident is also noted because of the light it sheds on Mr. Moore's character. He had guessed that Secretary Kellogg, who was soon to be replaced by Henry Stimson and was ardently desirous of winding up the Tacna-Arica dispute during his own stewardship, would in effect disavow a quarrel between two American ambassadors. On the chance that Secretary Kellogg might not, Mr. Moore — like a general who has occupied an exposed salient — had a retreat in readiness. He had abstracted from context a sentence by Ambassador Culbertson, which if interpreted in a certain way, seemed somewhat discreditable. In context, it seemed to me that the meaning was clear and the sentence unexceptionable, but on the receipt of a more-in-sorrow-than-in-anger squeak from Nervous Nellie, Ambassador Moore promptly telegraphed in reply, "If Culbertson meant what I thought he did, then obviously I wanted no part of it" — carefully avoiding saying what the interpretation was that he was finding objectionable.

I also recall the incident because it was about 1 A.M. when I took the text of the Kellogg wrist-slapping telegram to the Lima Country Club for the ambassador. I had by that time seen enough of my chief to decide that this particular message should be taken to him without delay: he would be interested to know that he had guessed right about the secretary of state. So I put away the code books, burned our work sheets, stamped on the ashes, locked the safe and the doors to the code room, buttoned up the chancery and headed for the country club. The American ambassador, in his dinner jacket, was playing roulette and his luck was evidently in. Mrs. Smith, who did not gamble, was kibitzing beside him. The casino was crowded. The give-and-take was unmistakable: a young diplomat of the American embassy passing an important message to the American ambassador.

Uncle Alec took the message and read it through his cigar smoke. The croupier obligingly withheld the spin while the ambassador read and everyone stopped talking.

The American ambassador smiled broadly. His voice was heard from one end of the room to the other. Addressing me, he proclaimed, "Tell your wife to buy a new dress and send me the bill, and get yourself a new suit, those pants are worn through."

For days our contemporaries kept asking my wife if she had her new dress yet, and asking me if I had been to the tailor. To Uncle Alec, his had been a rational offer. He was indebted to us for overtime work. One paid his debt, and that was that; then it was over and done with. He was genuinely puzzled and slightly resentful that we did not take him up. He thought our inertia was silly. Why an impecunious third secretary would not jump at the chance to improve his wife's wardrobe was beyond him.

The final obstacle of the Tacna-Arica settlement was Bolivia, and it was raised from an unlikely quarter: Secretary Kellogg. The press sensed that an agreement was imminent. Word reached La Paz and went from there to Washington. Fernando Diez de Medina, the Bolivian foreign minister, obtained an appointment with the secretary of state and had hysterics all over the second floor of the State Department. His case was deserving of sympathy. By force, Bolivia had been deprived of her Pacific coastline. The value of the two territories to Peru and Chile was insignificant compared with their value to Bolivia, which was blocked from access to the sea. The port facilities offered Bolivia at Arica could be a fraud; Bolivian commerce would be at the mercy of Chile.

Kellogg, despite his eagerness for a settlement, was impressed. He agreed to relay the Bolivian plea to the disputants. Uncle Alec had no bias against Bolivia, but he was sure that injecting a third party at this late date would mean no settlement in any predictable future. Bolivia's cue, in his opinion, was to await the settlement between Peru and Chile and then to present her case, perhaps with the support of the United States as the recent mediator. He said so, in unambiguous terms, and the code books once again experienced heat treatment. Peru and Chile, consulted, turned their backs on Bolivia.[1]

The Tacna-Arica settlement was a personal triumph for Ambassador Moore, but it was also a triumph of statesmanship over narrow nationalism, with credit to President Leguía. Although the bitterness against Chile has been dissipated by time, it was not a solution universally popular in Peru, and it was a factor in Leguía's overthrow in 1930. Yet at the time, Leguía

---

1. The Tacna-Arica settlement led directly to the Chaco War of 1932–1936, a conflict so overshadowed by World War II that it has been almost forgotten. Yet one hundred thousand men died in it, mostly Bolivian soldiers — peasants from the altiplano who, used to the thin air of the sierra, could scarcely move, much less fight, in the "green hell" of the tropical Chaco. What impelled Bolivia was the search for an outlet to the sea. Frustrated on the Pacific, Bolivia dreamed of reaching the River Plate and thence the Atlantic. The warlike Paraguayans, the same Indians who for three years in the nineteenth century held off the combined forces of Brazil, Uruguay, and Argentina, mowed down the Bolivians in every engagement. The Chaco War, finally settled in 1938 largely through the efforts of the American negotiator Spruille Braden, cost more lives than the struggle for independence of the colonies from Spain in the preceding century.

weathered the criticism with relative ease, and the photograph of him, flanked by the ambassadors of the United States and Chile, is a lasting reminder of the fact that the path of the peacemaker is across terrain that is as unstable as quicksand. The photograph shows President Leguía and Ambassadors Moore and Figueroa, with the fig tree supposed to have been planted in 1535 by Pizarro in the background. Remembering the group photographs that used to be taken by the State Department, I was sorry that others concerned in the settlement could not have been grouped around their principals. On the American side they would have included, in addition to me and my two fellow amateur code clerks, Bill Folger and Joe Jones of United Press (whose probity as correspondents and whose good advice as friends smoothed many rough edges), and, by no means last or least, Mrs. Smith, whose contribution has too long been unrecorded.

Looking back, the rest of our stay in Peru was a pleasant anticlimax. Ambassador Moore departed, and the counselor with the ex-baroness was replaced by a bright and intelligent senior officer with a gay and attractive wife — Freddy and Katie Mayer. Relations within the chancery were for the first time without tensions. Ambassador Moore was expected to return, but months went by and he did not. He failed to write. Then we finally heard that President Hoover had named him ambassador to Poland. And one day I received a telegram instructing me to report to the Department of State for duty. I was transferred to Washington.

Lucy and I sailed north on a ship that called at Guayaquil, and there, going ashore in a launch, I read in an Ecuadoran newspaper that Ambassador Alexander P. Moore, 1867–1930, was dead. We had not known that he was ill. To us he had always seemed indestructible.

Mr. Hoover's State Department

"The Western European Division," said Freddy Hibbard with relish, quoting a Georgetown dowager whose credentials permitted her to regard most secretaries of state since John Hay as upstarts, "is the only one that is socially possible." This was irritating to colleagues toiling over the problems of other areas of the world, like the Islamic scholars striving in the Near East Division under Allen Dulles, or the old China hands bewailing the loss of special privileges in Peking and Shanghai, or those who were trying to untangle the Platt Amendment in Latin America.

Socially possible or not, the matters dealt with by the Western European Division were often more important in 1930 than happenings in other parts of the world. Recognition of this gave its officers a sense of prestige and of participating in the march of events. Furthermore, WE — as the division was known within the State Department — was realistic in its approach to foreign relations, believing that facile solutions and predictable changes are rarer than politicians, on either side of the Atlantic, were wont to proclaim.

The division had a strong tradition of professional competence, and it also had the readiest access to the secretary of state, whose office was one floor down, thirty seconds from the desk of the chief of the Western European Division. Finally, although creative work was held in esteem in WE — both the Marshall Plan and NATO were born in the division after World War II — there was skepticism about the usefulness of evangelism as an instrument of diplomacy.

Freddy Hibbard's comment notwithstanding, my first emotion on learning that I had been assigned to the Western European Division was not one of elation. Although neither then nor later did I aspire to become a specialist in any one part of the world, I had nevertheless hoped that my rigorous four-year tour of duty in Peru might be followed in Washington by something relevant to that experience.

Instead, my first WE assignment had to do with the nonself-governing parts of the British Empire, about which at the time I knew practically nothing. Moreover, except for rubber in Southeast Asia, already preempted by an economist colleague, there was little in the area that was then of more than marginal interest to the United States.

My bailiwick included India, plus Burma, Malaya, the Straits Settlements, and Singapore. It included all of the crown colonies, from Sierra Leone and the Gold Coast to Trinidad, British Honduras, and the Bahamas, and across the Pacific to the Fiji Islands and Hong Kong. The principal cities in this far-flung jurisdiction were manned by American consuls general, officials of uninhibited verbosity. Their despatches came by mail, as they were not encouraged by the State Department to transmit their revelations by costly cable, and reached Washington from two to three months after signature. These worthy gentlemen may have lived like characters from Joseph Conrad or Somerset Maugham, but their prose was the prose of bureaucracy. Ninety percent of the contents of my "in" basket was shortly marked "File," and that was generally the end of it.

In short, I had all of the British Empire except the parts that counted. The affairs of the United Kingdom, Canada, Australia and New Zealand, and the Union of South Africa were being dealt with by officers senior to me who knew something about the areas they served.

Great Britain, for instance, was the domain of Freddy Hibbard, who in the 1920s had been in Embassy London with the Kelloggs. In WE much of Freddy's time seemed to be spent in the leisurely reading of the *London Times,* which reached Washington by steamship a week or ten days late, and in lengthy telephone conversations with members of the British embassy whom he addressed variously as Pinkie, or Bubbles, or Nigel, with a good deal of ribald chitchat thrown in. But when Bill Castle, an ex-chief of WE who was now assistant secretary of state, wanted a quick interpretation of an item of parliamentary debate in London, Freddy could produce one in a matter of seconds. He was faster still with the latest scandal in Soho, but only to those whom he described as qualified inquirers.[1]

---

1. Freddy was from Texas, a state for which his admiration was restrained. He spoke Spanish with an El Paso accent, French with a Parisian accent, and English with a Texan accent. My first experience with him, when I reported to Room 300, was overhearing a telephone conversation with, as it later turned out, Mrs. Alice Roosevelt Longworth, who was inviting Freddy to dinner. He was relating, as a sociological note, the reply of his maid when he had warned her that morning to knock before entering his room, lest she find him unclothed. She had briskly replied, "That wouldn't be no treat to me, Mr. Hibbard!"

My initial office arrangements were not conducive to contemplative effort, far less to concentration. I was one of four occupants of Room 300 (two floors above Room 100, which housed the Foreign Service School). Room 300 was on the southeast corner of the building, and so far as location went, it was one of the best in the department, the windows on one side overlooking the executive offices and the White House garden, and on the other side, the park stretching toward the Washington Monument and the Tidal Basin.

Just outside Room 300 was the narrow entrance to the office of the chief of the Western European Division. This was occupied by his two personable assistants, Mrs. Wilcox and Mrs. Palcho, by chairs for use by those waiting to see the chief, and by an oil painting of Lord Ashburton, who with Daniel Webster drew the northeastern boundary of the state of Maine. Those finding the chief busy often declined the offered chairs and instead stuck their heads into Room 300, exchanging gossip with Freddy Hibbard or asking Noel Field how the League Covenant was getting on, or importuning Paul Culbertson about the latest from the Quai d'Orsay. Paul, the younger brother of our ambassador to Chile, wore two hats: that of economist, which he wore soberly, and that of Mr. France, which he wore jauntily. As economist, Paul had the only lively issue in my entire jurisdiction, the rubber of Southeast Asia.

There were also transients. Officers back from the field left their dispatch cases on our windowsills, sometimes cadging extra tables and transacting their local business over whichever one of our four telephones happened not to be in use. Room 300, in sum, could hardly have been a less auspicious place to work in if we had sold railroad and theater tickets as well as the bright and shining tokens of diplomacy. And yet work in it we did, answering one another's phones in whatever language we could manage, taking messages, receiving callers, and drafting notes for signature by the secretary of state, addressed to the ambassadors and ministers whose countries were within the WE area. I soon discovered that if I had a task of substance before me, the time to do it was Saturday morning or Sunday, when Room 300 was comparatively peaceful.

These were the dark Depression days of 1930, yet the bureaucrats in the capital probably suffered less from hard times than most segments of the population. We took a salary cut but prices were low, the currency was stable, and our reduced income was at least assured. Few other earners could say as much during the early 1930s, and certainly not President Hoover, who had been elected in 1928 on a platform of two chickens in every pot, two cars in every garage. The pots and the garages now were empty, but the nearest the Depression came to many of us in Washington was the invasion of the bonus marchers, who camped messily on the Anacostia flats until evicted on White House orders.

In the beginning of my tour of duty as the State Department recipient of rubber reports from the Far East, I carried them across the room to Paul Culbertson, who, after absorbing their contents, got them with all speed to Commerce and Agriculture. I soon found it tedious to be merely a transmitting agent, because rubber, unlike Gandhi and Nehru and the other disturbers of colonial peace whose undertakings left the Potomac pulse unruffled, was capable of raising Washington blood pressure. The rubber boom in Brazil had ended, and synthetic rubber was still a decade ahead. The plantation rubber from Southeast Asia was the principal source of supply of a commodity of which the United States was already the world's greatest consumer. It was President Hoover himself who, while secretary of Commerce in the Coolidge administration, denounced a project whereby the British, later in collaboration with the Dutch, sought to control the market and dictate the price that the American motorist would have to pay to put tires on his automobile.

Henry Ford and Harvey Firestone, friends of the president, were accordingly encouraged to establish their own plantations in Brazil and Liberia, respectively, and meanwhile the American government shook an indignant finger under noses in London and The Hague, seeking thereby to influence Singapore and Rangoon and Batavia. As Mr. Outlying-Chunks-of-the-British-Empire, I was aware that this was going on, but irked because I had no part in it beyond handing papers to Paul Culbertson.

Something of this I conveyed to J. Theodore Marriner, the chief of the Western European Division, the first time he summoned me to his office. Beneath his disdainful manner was a real competence, as successive secretaries of state discovered. Although he looked and sometimes acted like a dilettante, he was in fact hardworking and conscientious and an astute and skillful negotiator. His specialties were the political problems stemming from World War I, particularly as they involved France, Great Britain, and Germany, but he had a finger in disarmament and in other European pies that threatened to overheat in our diplomatic oven.

Privately, he was interested in royalty and was impressed by dynastic rank and ramifications; his knowledge of the *Almanach de Gotha* and Burke's

Peerage would have impressed a chamberlain. The lower classes did not interest him, and he was dubious about the ability of colonial peoples to master the tools of self-government. He would have deplored the post–World War II eagerness to establish irresponsible, unviable new countries as contrary to common sense, statesmanship, and the best interests of the inhabitants.[2]

Ted agreed that my shreds and shards of empire hardly constituted a life-work, but he pointed out that they made few demands during a period when I was getting settled in Washington. With a four-year rule in the assignment of Foreign Service officers to the department, there was a constant turnover during which new duties and opportunities became available. He would keep my situation in mind.

A few weeks later, after the desk officer for Spain having completed his Washington service, I was given that country, to my great satisfaction. Further reshuffles dealt me the three Scandinavian countries and Holland. It was explained that all four of them were so civilized that nothing unseemly was expected to occur. As for the Dutch East Indies, they were next door to the British colonial territories I was already monitoring. So now I had Spain, ripe for turmoil, together with Norway, Sweden, Denmark, and the Netherlands, which were not — five more countries to look after in addition to my original pile of British colonial chips. Business was looking up.

Peering down the tunnel of years, I cannot remember a single thing that happened in Sweden during my stewardship except that the Swedish legation in Washington added my name to their invitation list, hospitably bidding me to superlative food amid unmemorable participants. Madame Briggs did not share in these adventures because she was temporarily out of circulation pending the arrival of our daughter, born during our first Washington winter.

Norway, Denmark, and Holland did provide items of business while their affairs came under my microscope. The Department of the Interior, with jurisdiction over Alaska, became seized with the notion that the economy of the territory would benefit from the introduction of musk oxen then resident in Greenland. These docile and heavily upholstered animals would provide hair that could be woven into garments, plus steaks for deserving Eski-

---

2. An ironic as well as tragic event cost Marriner his life four years later. After service in Paris, he was appointed consul general in Beirut as a cover for diplomatic duties in the Near East. He was murdered in the doorway of his office by an embittered Lebanese visa applicant, of whose existence Marriner was not even aware.

mos and milk for deserving Eskimo children. Today the project would have attracted at least a dozen different Washington agencies. Then it involved only Interior, the Maritime Commission, the Coast Guard, the Smithsonian Institution (which hitherto I had assumed, incorrectly, dealt only with stuffed animals and taxidermists) and the State Department — meaning me, the recently appointed Mr. Denmark.

Denmark was the key to the arrangement, since Denmark owned Greenland, where the unsuspecting musk oxen gamboled on the glaciers. Denmark agreed to sell twenty-four beasts to the United States and to help round them up. The State Department, meaning me, gave the project its blessing. The musk oxen were collected, Denmark was paid, and the animals were embarked on their long voyage to Alaska via the Panama Canal. Up to that point everything had gone smoothly and there had been no publicity.

Panama is warmer than Greenland. The musk oxen, unable to shed their winter overcoats, would likely melt en route. At the instance of their worried seagoing keepers from the Smithsonian, a special refrigeration vessel was mobilized to provide a flow of ice cakes in which the perspiring musk oxen could be packed while in transit to the Panama Canal and until the Pacific breeze carried the first promise of Alaskan winter.

The episode did not escape the vigilant eye of the newspaper *Estrella de Panamá,* which decided that the story possessed a timely how-to-keep-cool-in-the-tropics interest and published it. The press associations picked it up, and soon someone at the National Geographic Society telephoned Room 300, wanting to know, in a reproachful voice, why the society had not been informed in advance. The Department of the Interior, also queried, predicted that herds of musk oxen would shortly be grazing from Sitka to Point Barrow, to the profit of the citizens of the territory and the credit of the enterprising Department of the Interior.

Whereupon the methodical Norwegians, first checking with the newly assigned Mr. Norway in the State Department — again, meaning me — sent an official note of complaint conceived in indignation and hurt feelings. Norway declared to the secretary of state that northeast Greenland was territory belonging to the Norwegian government. The legation accordingly wished to protest this unauthorized trespass as well as the theft of assets, the rightful property of the Crown of Norway, which demanded compensation. In WE we were astonished. I had never heard of a Norwegian claim to Greenland, and no one else in the division had either. The research staff upstairs speedily vouched for the existence of the Norwegian claim; they prepared an erudite and lengthy memorandum addressed to the secretary of state, and they sent it via Room 300, where it languished.

The Norwegian note was written in English. Most diplomatic missions in Washington, then as now, wrote their notes either in French or in the language of the sending country, accompanied by an English translation marked "Unofficial Text." Norway was one of the few countries that conducted its business in English, having discovered that this accelerated the handling by the Potomac bureaucracy of matters of interest to them; usually the English was faultless. In the musk oxen case, however, some indignant Viking had stumbled over his dictionary. The note read: "The Royal Norwegian Legation accordingly wishes to protest, in a most emphatic manner, against this arbitrary and illegal seizure of mush oxes on the Norwegian territory of Greenland."

Eventually, Secretary Stimson signed a soothing message confected by Mr. Norway (me) with the assistance of François Colt DeWolf, a deft and knowledgeable lawyer attached to the division. Our reply was to the effect that the American government was sorry that Norway felt that way, but that a careful and sympathetic review of the facts (here François and I drew upon the memorandum from the research sleuths upstairs) supported the conclusion that Denmark, not Norway, was the recognized and rightful possessor of the island of Greenland. The American government in those circumstances was, regretfully, unable to entertain the Norwegian protest and considered the matter closed. Last I heard, years after Alaska had become a state, the Danish Norwegian mush oxes were living on moss, lichen, and muskeg, and thriving on them.

My next brush with international fauna involved mice — Dutch mice with voracious appetites and untidy habits, who were not themselves edible but who modified my eating habits thereafter. Along with tulip bulbs, wooden shoes, duck feathers, and lace bonnets, the thrifty Dutch exported caraway seeds sought by American bakers. Control over the entry of caraway seeds was the responsibility of the Treasury Department through the Customs Service, and of the Department of Agriculture.

It appeared, further, that caraway seeds in bulk, as for international shipment, are attractive to mice, especially Dutch mice, something apparently well, if not favorably, known to the trade, including wholesale caraway seed importers.

Word of the enthusiasm of Dutch mice for caraway seeds reached the State Department via the Netherlands legation, which sent a commercial secretary to inquire — informally, as a prelude to possible diplomatic representation — why a certain action had been taken by the United States authorities. This action was delicately described as "lowering the mouse tolerance" below the previously existing "reasonable level."

It took me longer to find out what the specialists considered a "reasonable level" of mouse in caraway seed might be, and why it was proposed to modify that level, than it did to get the musk oxen from Greenland to Alaska. I did succeed, however, in persuading the Dutch chargé d'affaires not to write an official note on the subject but to pursue the matter in direct consultation with the constituted authorities.

We obligingly put the Dutch in touch with the bureaucrats in question. The result of their negotiations was the substitution of metal for cardboard and wooden caraway seed containers, to the frustration of the caraway seed-eating Dutch mice.

My other Dutch adventure was the result of carelessness, and hence in diplomacy reprehensible. What was worse, it brought me to the unfavorable attention of the secretary of state. It would not have happened had I not been the only officer in WE one Sunday. I would have done better, as my wife observed, had I been helping her push the baby carriage across the Taft Bridge in Rock Creek Park instead of trying to write President Hoover's reply to the presentation of credentials speech of Salvador de Madariaga, the first ambassador of the Spanish Republic after the overthrow of King Alfonso XIII. The ambassador, a literary figure, was to be received in the White House on Tuesday, which was only forty-eight hours from the Sunday in question.

My own literary efforts on behalf of President Hoover were being defeated by a series of interruptions and harassments. Finding me present, the departmental telephone operator concluded I was on duty and kept referring incoming calls to my vulnerable extension. Finally, and in irritation, I told the operator to stop ringing me, and in consequence one of the newspaper correspondents, balked at getting through, prowled up from the press room to ask whether anything special was stirring.

Nothing was. I told him about the Spanish ambassador, but the correspondent already knew about Salvador de Madariaga; he had called at the Spanish embassy in the hopes of getting something on the attitude of the Republican regime toward the existing American telephone concession. What else was cooking? Surely there must be some news out of Europe, what with defaulting debtors and the economy of the succession states sliding into the Danube in the wake of the Kreditanstalt failure. How about it?

Eager to get on with the Hoover speech, I finally threw the correspondent the smallest bone I could find, a telegram I remembered from having gone through the divisional folder on my arrival to see whether there was anything of interest to the areas I dealt with. This was a domestic message, included because it related to Holland. It was a telegram, filed in New York, from the Association of Duck Feather Producers of Long Island. In several hundred abrasive words the association took the secretary of state to task for allegedly favoring a reduction in the tariff on imported duck feathers.

The association implied that behind every house from Flatbush Avenue to Montauk Point, white American ducks were raised for the market, and that these ducks would be discriminated against in favor of cheap foreign competition. The secretary was reminded that breeders of Long Island ducks were voters who would not condone a betrayal of their interests. It was a truculent message, and the title of the sender, executive director of the Association of Duck Feather Producers of Long Island, suggested embattled farmers, muskets in hand, rallying to the flag sacred to Betsy Ross and Barbara Fritchie.

I did not give the correspondent a copy of this minatory effort, the original of which was, after all, addressed to the secretary of state, but I permitted him to read it in hopes of getting rid of him. The result was on page 1 of Monday morning's *New York Times.* In a box often reserved for the periodic wisdom of Will Rogers was an item the gist of which was conveyed by the headline: "Duck Feather Diplomacy: Long Island breeders chide Secretary Stimson, threaten to bolt Republican Party." Secretary Stimson lived on Long Island. He was not amused by the item.

These seashells dredged up by the tides of time are not presented because of their intrinsic value or historical consequence, but because they are in their way representative of the kinds of questions that, added all together, still make up the dunes and promontories, if not the coral reefs, of foreign affairs. There are more important questions, of course. The North Atlantic Treaty Organization today binds two of the three Scandinavian countries more closely to the United States than was the case before the shared hazards of World War II. Sweden, by offering safe haven to American deserters during the 1960s, for a while attracted considerable American attention. The new Republic of Indonesia, arising from the ashes of the Netherlands East Indies, often is more important to the United States than is Holland.

That those four countries which used to have the attention of one officer in the State Department for perhaps two hours per day now require for the maintenance of relations the activities of scores of busy workers goes some way toward explaining why the State Department is the size it is.

Having survived the ire of Secretary Stimson — he was placated by Ted Marriner, who gave him my text of the proposed presidential reply to the Spanish ambassador, which text the secretary endorsed and left at the White House that morning — I found increasing satisfaction in the work of the division in the pleasantly informal personal relationships. My colleagues rarely took themselves seriously but invariably took their work to heart as well as to mind, with a pride in performance that reflected credit on professional diplomacy. Our foreign opposite numbers in Washington proved equally stimulating. The associations thus formed were renewed across the years by chance encounters in Havana and Montevideo and Prague, in Rio de Janeiro and Seoul and Athens, and invariably with the pleasure that accompanies shared experiences and remembered endeavor.

I soon found myself spending less time on fragments of empire and more on Spain, which, when I reached the desk, was already ripe for revolution. Our ambassador in Madrid was Irwin Laughlin, experienced, conscientious, but not bright. He was assisted by Counselor John Wiley, tough and articulate, who remained as chargé d'affaires when the ambassador departed in the wake of the deposed king. The Madrid roster also contained a name synonymous with power from Niagara Falls — little of which, however, had reached the diplomatic member of the family. It was John Carter, another of the Room 300 operators, who coined the jingle

> So here's to Walter Schoellkopf,
> Alumnus of Cascadilla,
> The only living diplomat
> Who's dumber than Padilla.

(Padilla was the last Bourbon-appointed ambassador to serve in Washington. He used to assure Ted Marriner several times a week that Primo de Rivera had matters in hand, and that the popularity of the monarchy had never been higher.)

Ambassador Laughlin was so staunchly loyal to the monarchy that he refused, almost until the day of the king's departure, to believe that the Republicans had any appreciable backing. Wiley knew better, and said so when he could, so that the Spanish Revolution was not a surprise to WE, but it did produce a problem requiring immediate high-level Washington consideration.

This had to do with asylum and what the ambassador should do about the cardinal archbishop if the latter should seek American embassy protection. The church in Spain, reactionary and entrenched, had long been a principal supporter of the monarchy. It was hence suspect among Spanish Republicans and labor leaders, many of whom viewed the archbishop with animosity. Liberals in the United States welcomed the revolution and remained pro-Republican throughout the bloody civil war that erupted in 1936. On the other hand, the humanitarian interests of the United States would have been outraged if the archbishop were thrown to the mob because of American embassy indifference.

The record of the United States with regard to diplomatic asylum has been uncertain except in the New World, where we view the granting of asylum with disfavor. Washington had recently declined to sign the inter-American convention on asylum. Under this the republics of Latin America were destined to be hosts, every time a revolution occurred, to scores and at times to hundreds of vanquished Outs fleeing the vengeance of the victorious Ins. Those refugees camped for weeks and sometimes months at a time in the legations and embassies in Latin American capitals whenever a violent change of government occurred. A check with the Latin American Division confirmed the fact that American representatives in that area were being instructed to grant diplomatic asylum in no circumstances. Consistency, then, cast a vote against the Spanish archbishop.

Ambassador Laughlin had reported the receipt of a plea — one of those "If I should try to come, would you let me in?" approaches — and the urgency of a reply was emphasized by reports of deteriorating conditions in Madrid, where crowds were surging about looking for likely targets, including ecclesiastical ones.

Marriner was out of town and the acting chief of WE was Pierre Boal,[3] with whom I had served briefly in Lima. Pierre was nothing if not resourceful. In five minutes we mapped out the kind of message we thought Secretary Stimson should send, and in less than an hour we had it on paper. I still think it was a sound decision and a good piece of drafting.

---

3. Pierre de Lagarde Boal (1895–1966), a landed gentleman from Boalsberg, Pennsylvania, entered diplomacy after piloting Spads in the Lafayette Escadrille in World War I. He was a descendant of Christopher Columbus, so it was perhaps appropriate that he should interest himself in the fate of a Spanish archbishop.

The proposed telegram instructed Ambassador Laughlin to get word to the archbishop, not in writing, to the effect that although the ambassador deeply sympathized and earnestly desired to be of any possible assistance to His Eminence, the declared policy of the American government, as set forth on numerous occasions, was to discourage the use of diplomatic missions as havens during political upheavals. Therefore the archbishop would understand that the ambassador could give no assurances in response to His Eminence's inquiry.

Having launched that bureaucratic prose, our message continued in a confidential aside to the ambassador that if, notwithstanding the foregoing negative answer, the archbishop should suddenly come pounding up the Avenida, pursued by a mob clearly bent on his destruction, the archbishop should not be refused admission to the embassy premises. (Those premises were not far from the archbishop's palace, so the possibility was by no means remote.)

On his return, Marriner promptly dubbed our effort the "hang your clothes on a hickory limb but don't go near the water" telegram, but he nevertheless took our draft to Secretary Stimson and succeeded in selling it to him. He reported that before signing, the secretary phoned the gist of it to President Hoover.

The incident illustrates how foreign policy is often made in response to a situation demanding action rather than evolving from theory or being spun from gossamer webbing in the ivory tower of bureaucratic or academic planning. Once something has been done, it becomes the raw material of precedent; three or four precedents tied up in a paper bag equal a policy neatly packaged. Planning can be useful, too, especially in establishing priorities and identifying objectives, but planning fails when it seeks to become too specific. The number of variants to which foreign affairs are subject makes it impossible to describe in advance a proposed action that will take cognizance of all of them. If you do, as Dean Acheson once observed, at some point Liechtenstein exclaims, "The hell with it!"—and the whole planned edifice collapses.

In the case of the threatened archbishop, Pierre and I checked with the Latin American Division, but we consulted no planners and we looked up no precedents. There is rarely time to do so when the pin is pulled from the diplomatic grenade or the diplomatic barn starts burning. Some background we possessed — academic, plus on-the-job training — but mostly we concentrated on doing what we thought was practical and feasible within the terms of reference suddenly presented. That, I repeat, is how foreign policy is not infrequently confected.

In those early days following the departure of King Alfonso, we in the State Department were faced with another, if less urgent, decision: when to recognize the revolutionary Republican regime, which, notwithstanding the existence of chaotic conditions here and there, seemed to be doing a creditable job in taking over the administration of the country amid a good deal of popular rejoicing. American conservative opinion was generally silent if unenthusiastic. Liberal opinion, supported by much of the American press, welcomed Spanish events, seeing them as another milestone in the evolution of Europe away from monarchical institutions and toward democracy.

In terms of United States interest, it did not seem to make much difference, one way or the other, whether we recognized at once or waited for others to do so.

The most important United States investment at the time of the revolution was the telephone monopoly, established in the previous decade by I.T.&T. with an assist from Alexander P. Moore, then American ambassador in Madrid. Transatlantic phone service had been established in the 1920s, but it was uncertain at the outset and expensive, and the State Department, as usual, had few funds to devote to it. IT&T itself was importuned by Sosthenes Behn, grand vizier of IT&T, to get on the phone with John Wiley in Embassy Madrid, at the expense of IT&T, and ascertain what was happening. The fact that the call would go through company headquarters in New York, where it would be no trick to monitor it, was not mentioned; it was not mentioned because in WE we concluded that it did not really matter. What was important was firsthand, up-to-the-minute news, beating the fastest cable service by several hours.

WE was the first office in the State Department to use the telephone for on-the-spot reporting of developments by one of our embassies. We were correspondingly elated, little realizing how great a nuisance to diplomacy the abuse of the phone would become even before improved techniques rendered the service itself faster and more efficient than it was following the Spanish Revolution.

The existence of the large American communications investment in Spain was not the controlling factor in the decision to recognize the new Spanish regime, but it was nevertheless not a factor that was ignored. Wiley was soon instructed to seek from the newly established authorities an explicit assurance that the contract entered into by the predecessor government would be honored by the new.

The course recommended by WE, which then and in retrospect seemed a sensible one, was to decide on recognition, the standard criteria having been met, but to defer the act itself (the formal notification) until after recognition had been extended by neighboring European countries with more at stake in Spain than the United States. The most important of these was Great Britain, which in addition to investments and political considerations, was dynastically connected, Alfonso's queen being a granddaughter of Queen Victoria.

While our recommendation on recognition awaited approval downstairs, there came another of those unexpected but inevitable complications, the occurrence of which is so beguiling to those who follow the day-to-day practice of diplomacy. The Navy Department suddenly telephoned and an admiral demanded, "What do we do about the *Juan Sebastián de Elcano?*"

I told the admiral he had me there, and who was *Juan Sebastián de Elcano?* It turned out it was a vessel — the training ship of the Spanish Navy, scheduled to make a courtesy visit to the port of New York in accordance with arrangements approved several months before.

"It is customary," explained the admiral, "for a foreign naval vessel to salute the Battery at the entrance of the New York harbor. In New York they want to know whether to return the salute because we haven't yet recognized the new Spanish government. The *Juan Sebastián de Elcano* will be off Sandy Hook at daybreak tomorrow. So what do I tell New York?"

The admiral's phone call came at 4:15 that afternoon. Recognition would not be extended for two or three days, at the earliest. The Spanish school ship, its midshipmen looking forward to fun and games along Riverside Drive, would be sighting the towers of Manhattan (and the naval saluting station in the lower bay) in approximately fifteen hours. I told the admiral I would call him back.

The State Department instructions to the navy, conveyed by telephone with an offer to confirm by letter the next day, were that the admiral should forthwith find himself a Spanish-speaking junior naval officer and send him down the bay by launch to intercept the arriving *Juan Sebastián de Elcano* before that vessel reached the saluting point. There the junior officer should board the training ship and explain to the Spanish admiral that since there had not yet been sufficient time for the government of the United States to extend recognition to the new regime in Spain, the American authorities would not be in a position to return the salute fired by the *Juan Sebastián de Elcano*. In those circumstances the Spanish ship would doubtless decide not to salute. I added that it would be appropriate to assure the Spanish admiral that the unusual saluting situation implied no lack of consideration for Spain nor any lessening of the hospitality that the United States Navy hoped to have the privilege of extending to the officers, midshipmen, and crew of the arriving vessel.

"In explaining all that," I told the admiral, "the point to get across is that since we haven't recognized, we cannot return their salute — and to have the message sink in before the Spanish admiral has a chance to light his firecrackers."

The American admiral may not have thought much of my naval idiom, but he rang off with a cheerful "Aye, Aye, Sir," which was memorable because it was the first time a flag officer had said that to me.

The next day the admiral was back on the phone in high nautical good humor. He said the *Juan Sebastián de Elcano* was a sailing ship with auxiliary power and had made a slow Atlantic crossing. He had just talked to New York, where the previous evening they had found themselves an officer fresh out of Annapolis who was bilingual in Spanish. "Made him an aide, and put so much gold braid on his shoulder he was top-heavy with it." Everything went fine — the briefing of the officer, the launch trip before sunrise, the meeting off Sandy Hook, and the boarding of the *Juan Sebastián de Elcano*.

"Everything went smoothly," repeated the admiral, "until our man reached that part of his story about not enough time since the Spanish Revolution for the American government to recognize. At that point, the Spanish admiral suddenly blew up and shouted "What revolution? A revolution in Spain? My God . . . ."

The radio on the *Elcano* had gone dead five days out of Las Palmas, and they had sailed all the way across the Atlantic without communications. So when the American boarded their ship, that was the first they had heard of the overthrow of their king and of the establishment of the Spanish Republic. We recognized the new Spanish government two days later, and when the *Juan Sebastián de Elcano* departed New York at the end of the visit, saluting courtesies were meticulously observed.

In the second year of my Washington assignment, I was able to shuck off the British Empire fragments. This enabled me to devote more time to Spain, where I hoped to be posted at the end of my service in WE.[4]

4. It was almost thirty years later that President Kennedy nominated me to be ambassador to Spain — a post that ill health forced me to decline.

Meanwhile, officers, junior and not so junior, came and went through Room 300. Prentiss Gilbert, our expert on Central Europe, was assigned to Geneva. Ted Marriner, chief of the division, went to Paris as number two to ex-Senator Walter Edge, who like most political appointees, did not speak the language of his post. Ted in effect would run the brand new embassy office beside the Hotel Crillon.

Marriner's successor proved to be an equally competent and considerate chief, although two men could scarcely have differed more widely in character and work habits. Ted was amusing, cynical, intellectually and socially a snob; he was a bachelor without independent means, a man from Maine who entered diplomacy via Dartmouth College. His successor, Jay Pierrepont Moffat, was steady, intelligent, and literal-minded, with no great sense of humor. A wealthy New Yorker who graduated from Harvard, he married the eldest of Ambassador Joseph Grew's three daughters. Pierrepont was dependable — a rare and priceless virtue in a chief. You could set your watch when Moffat emerged from his doorway on 19th Street, furled umbrella in hand, or by the time, just before nine, when he paused at the Metropolitan Club to scan the *Wall Street Journal,* or by the moment, just after ten, when from his office he spoke to his broker in New York, on which occasions he was not to be interrupted by anything short of a summons from the secretary of state himself. You always knew where Pierrepont Moffat could be found — he was meticulous about leaving word of engagements — and, wherever he was, he was accessible to his colleagues and ready to transact business, which was the diplomacy of the United States. He also was a first-rate officer.[5]

Foreign Service officers in the 1930s made up a substantial proportion of those performing substantive work in the Department of State. There were other officers with permanent tenure in Washington whose training, specialized knowledge, and experience in finding paths through the increasingly dense jungle of bureaucracy were indispensable to the solution of our problems. The teamwork between the permanent staff and the Foreign Service was by no means perfect, but with an organization so small that it did not take a newcomer long to find out who did what, the arrangement functioned with surprising efficiency. It broke down after the war, with the inva-

5. Jay Pierrepont Moffat (1896–1943), like Marriner before him, had his career tragically and unexpectedly cut short as he was reaching the peak of his performance. Appointed minister to Canada just before the mission was to be raised to embassy status, he died of a blood clot after the briefest of illnesses.

sion of hundreds of enthusiastic amateurs — too many to assimilate, and too many of them suffering from an illusion of mission and a palpitating eagerness to remake foreign societies.

The Love of Liberty Brought Us Here

The year 1931 brought another change in my responsibilities in WE, my acquisition of Liberia. I was to learn that the size of a country does not necessarily govern the amount of time required to handle its affairs; in fact Secretary Stimson was to remark that if he had to spend as much time per acre on the British Empire as he did on Liberia, ten secretaries of state would be needed for Scotland alone, with an additional man for the Channel Islands.

The Western European Division occupied itself with Liberia for the reason that the rest of Africa, barring only Ethiopia and Egypt, which belonged to the Near East Division, was either a colonial dependency of a European power or else it was the Union of South Africa, whose foreign affairs were being handled by London. Since nine-tenths of the African continent belonged to W.E., and since Liberia was bounded on the north by the British colony of Sierra Leone, the natural thing was to put Liberia into the Western European Division.

I got myself into Liberia incautiously, as a volunteer. A crisis had developed when the American chargé d'affaires in Monrovia seized the occasion of a reception at the British legation in honor of the king's birthday as a chance to mix so much scotch with so much champagne that he not only entered into a loud altercation with the president of the Republic, but he also conveyed to that beleaguered guest various home truths concerning the administration of the country and the character of its administrators, including the chief executive. The American chargé further declared that if Liberia did not mend its ways, a United States warship would teach the Americo-Liberians a lesson.

Among those present was the manager of the Firestone rubber plantation, which enterprise included a radio company established for communication between Akron, Ohio, and Monrovia. Shaken, the manager sent a long message to his principals, in which he predicted that the removal of the American chargé would immediately be demanded by the outraged Liberian president. He requested that his communication be brought urgently to the attention of the State Department.

No country likes to have its representative kicked out. However, because of the Firestone warning, an annoyed Mr. Stimson was able to greet the Liberian representative with false heartiness and to say, before his startled caller could present his note requesting the recall of the American chargé, that his visit gave the secretary the opportunity to inform him of the appointment of a new American representative to Monrovia who would arrive there at the earliest possible date.

That was the point at which the reckless individual who authors this chronicle, scenting excitement, volunteered to act as Mr. Liberia for the duration of the mission of Sam Reber, who had been a fellow vice consul in Peru.

The West African Republic of Liberia, whose national motto is "The Love of Liberty Brought Us Here," is the size of Ohio. That may have commended Liberia to the Firestone Rubber Company after several years of exploration that carried their botanists to Mexico and Central America, Brazil, the Philippines, and even to Sarawak on the island of Borneo. The fact that Liberia is nearer to Akron, Ohio, than is the Far East, and also that Liberia's climate approximates that of the upper Amazon Valley, where natural rubber originated, no doubt influenced the decision.

Of equal validity, at least to Harvey Firestone, Sr., was the notion that Liberia, having been founded by Americans, remained a "moral protectorate" of the United States, the original American Colonization Society having received a grant from Congress in 1817 and the American government having been instrumental in helping the society to establish the Republic of Liberia as a haven for freed slaves thirty years later. Firestone reasoned that if rubber could not be grown under the American flag, Liberia, with its special ties to the United States, might prove the next best place to grow it. Harvey Firestone, Jr., signed the plantation agreement with Liberia in 1926, some four years before I joined the Western European Division.

I was to spend much time trying to define "moral protectorate" as used by the Firestones, and to track down its implications. The phrase was also used by American missionaries, by Negro organizations in the United States, and by an occasional angry European statesman. In every case some sort of action by the United States was being demanded.

I discovered that the history of Liberia is a long string of difficulties spaced close together. Some resulted from adverse natural conditions: the Grain Coast, five degrees from the equator and with two hundred inches of rainfall annually, might not, by United States standards, be regarded as a garden spot in which to found a republic. Some Liberian difficulties resulted from inexperience, some from hostile neighbors and unsympathetic colonial powers, and many — especially since the turn of the century – from the convoluted chicaneries of the Americo-Liberians themselves, the descendants of the colonizing freedmen who constituted themselves the governing class just as the whites of South Africa monopolized power in that area.

Repeatedly when facing bankruptcy, threatened revolution or epidemic, or exasperated European powers, Liberia appealed to the United States, which often came to the rescue with a proviso attached that was supposed to guarantee reforms on the part of the Liberian government. Performance rarely followed, the Liberian leaders having developed a specialized technique compounded of demagogic patriotism, racist emotional appeal, and misrepresentation that defeated the most talented efforts of foreign advisers while preserving the fruits of power for the elite minority.

The Firestone rubber enterprise, by bringing substantial amounts of money into Liberia, increased the take of the politicians by raising the revenues they could divert to themselves. From such sources, taken in conjunction with Harvey Firestone's "moral protectorate," flowed the "Liberian problem" with which I was destined to wrestle in the 1930s.

At the end of World War I, three-fourths of all the rubber produced in the world was consumed in the United States, which did not grow one pound of it. The Firestone plantation was an American reply, warmly endorsed in Washington, to the Stevenson Rubber Restriction Act of 1922, whereby the British sought to control — and raise — the price of rubber. In 1922 the price was 14 cents a pound, and long before it reached $1.23 (some three years later) the United States was proclaiming its pain and its indignation.

Every time rubber went up 1 cent, it cost the American consumer another $8 million. While it lasted, the Stevenson plan cost the United States economy more than one billion gold dollars, not an insignificant sum in the 1920s. Cheerfully examining the other side of the coin, Winston Churchill, colonial minister at the time of the Stevenson plan, observed that "one of our principal means of paying . . . our [World War I] debt to the United States is in the provision of rubber."

The tribulations of the corporation from Akron, Ohio, doing business eight thousand miles from home began almost at once. They form so integral a part of the Liberian story of that period that it is appropriate to record that the Firestones generally behaved with patience, fortitude, and forbearance, and that the company showed greater concern for the welfare of the Liberian natives than did the Americo-Liberians who governed them.

To the Firestone desire to break the British-Dutch rubber monopoly was joined a recognition of the responsibility to society of a powerful company establishing itself in a primitive environment, among tribesmen whose paramount chiefs may have worn battered top hats as badges of office but whose responses to jungle life were geared to witch doctors and voodoo.

Mindful of the exploitation of African natives that remains so dark a page in history, and also of the importance of establishing a dependable and contented labor supply, Firestone specified to the Liberian government before its operations began that native labor must have the right to bargain for its employment without government intervention and be free to work or depart, as each man saw fit. Firestone thereby hoped to forestall efforts by the Liberian government to require work permits or otherwise to intervene in the process of recruiting, to the detriment of the laborers.

When the company saw the plantation payrolls disappearing into the pockets of Levantine traders, Firestone organized the United States Trading Company to operate stores on the edge of the jungle and a bank in Monrovia to service those operations. Thus Firestone incurred the hostility of the traders and at the same time aroused suspicion on the part of the Liberian government.

Nevertheless, plantation roads were pushed through the forest, hospitals were built, towns and villages were established. For the first time ideas of sanitation and public health were promoted. The transformation was not unlike what took place in Panama during the first decade of the twentieth century, except that whereas the Panama Canal was a government enterprise, the Firestones developed their Liberian plantation with their own money.

By the early 1930s, from a standing start in 1927, nearly sixty thousand jungle acres had been cleared and planted, and over ten million bud-grafted, high-yielding rubber trees were approaching production.

The judgment of the Firestones in dealing with the Liberian government was less successful than their plantation operation, even if their intentions were good. Here the company was often out of its depth. Firestone representatives were unprepared for the local compound of agreement and promises — the latter often delivered with a startling command of ornate, polysyllabic prose — that led either to no performance or to the frustration of the objective through inertia or fraud.

The highway to the plantation was a case in point. At the outset the plantation area was accessible only by the Du River, which Firestone dredged for transportation of latex in barges. A road soon proved essential, however, but the one existing highway leading from the capital toward the interior was in deplorable condition and ended short of the plantation. Firestone offered to rebuild and extend the road, including bridges and culverts, provided the government would admit the materials and equipment duty free. The Liberian government declared this was a splendid idea and supplied the corresponding authorization.

When cement and steel began to arrive, only a trickle reached the road. There were delays in the customhouse. Invoices were mislaid, then disappeared altogether. Barges overturned in the surf between freighter and shore. A warehouse fire of undetermined origin damaged cement bags. Presently the mansions of Liberian officials started to undergo renovation and repairs; some houses that had been unfinished for years were completed, including an extra story and a cement wall around the garden.

A telephone line to connect Monrovia with the plantation fared no better. Wire was purchased and the line was strung under Firestone supervision. Communication was established, and the president of the Republic held an inaugural conversation with the Firestone manager at the plantation. A few days later communication ceased. Telephone wire has a multitude of uses in the tropics. Miles of wire simply disappeared, along with the glass insulators, which were popular neck ornaments for jungle virgins. "Elephants," said the Liberian government. Worse was to come.

The Firestones unwisely raised a loan for the Liberian government. First they sought to persuade the American government to furnish the credit. That was in accord with the "moral protectorate" ideas espoused by Harvey Firestone, Sr. When the secretary of state demurred, the company turned to New York bankers, representing to them that in the face of the British investment of hundreds of millions of dollars in rubber production in the Far East, the relatively insignificant amount asked by Liberia ($5 million) ought readily to be forthcoming. Finally the Firestones themselves organized the Finance Corporation of America to handle the issue, with the National City Bank of New York as fiscal agent. The State Department, gratified by this display of private initiative, agreed to assume certain functions under the loan agreement with respect to arbitration and the appointment of a financial adviser should Liberia so request — which Liberia did.

The loan, however, netted the Liberian government not the anticipated $5 million but approximately $2 million, most of which went to retire prior obligations. Disagreements arose and grew increasingly bitter, certering on Liberian violations of the loan agreement and on the extent of the financial adviser's authority over Liberian finances. The Firestones in turn refused to underwrite further bonds until the financial adviser was satisfied. The State Department, as a party to the loan agreement, was immediately involved. Matters reached an explosive stage during the incumbency of Minister Charles E. Mitchell, and in December 1932 Liberia repudiated the loan altogether, denouncing the adviser, the Firestones, and the departing American representative.[1]

While these things were enlivening Monrovia, Akron, and Washington, still darker clouds were gathering. The cry of "slavery" was raised against the land of freed slaves.

In 1929, two years after the rubber plantation began, an American missionary on the West African coast reported a traffic in Liberian "boys" – that is, tribal Liberians. They were being rounded up and shipped from Liberia, charged the missionary, to the Spanish island of Fernando Po in the Gulf of Guinea. Liberian officials were reportedly engaged in this traffic, utilizing the Liberian Army to gather the "boys" for shipment.

Washington was shocked. A sizzling message was dispatched to Monrovia for delivery to the Liberian government. The first sentence went as follows:

I am directed by the Secretary of State to advise your Excellency that there have come to the attention of the government of the United States reports bearing reliable evidence of authenticity which will definitely indicate that existing conditions incident to the so-called export of labor from Liberia to Fernando Po have resulted in the development of a system which seems hardly distinguishable from organized slave trade, and that in the enforcement of this system the Liberian Frontier Force and the service and influences of certain high government officials are constantly and systematically used . . . .

"Hardly distinguishable from organized slave trade" was an abrasive indictment of the descendants of freed slaves. That marathon sentence conveyed an accusation that could not be ignored. The Liberian government nevertheless decided to brazen it out, to admit nothing. Proof might be

1. Minister Mitchell, a black banker from West Virginia who was selected for his post by the Republican National Committee, was a veteran of the Spanish-American War who had lost a leg in combat. When I first met him in Washington, he used a thumb tack instead of a garter. He told me that when he was younger, one morning after a party, he had pushed a thumb tack into his good leg my mistake, a most awakening experience. As a defensive measure against Liberian termites, at my suggestion, he exchanged his wooden leg for a British contraption made of aluminum.

harder to come by than allegation. By the time an investigation could be organized, trails could be smudged and tracks obliterated. Liberia accordingly rejected the charges with an indignant "categorial denial" to which was added the statement that Liberia would have no objection "to this question being investigated by a competent, impartial, and unprejudiced commission." This invitation was followed by an equally reckless statement to the League of Nations denouncing the charges as propaganda, and inviting appointment of a commission.

Appoint a commission the League of Nations eagerly did, and the group proceeded at once to Liberia. The Christy Report was submitted in September 1930, fifteen months after the dispatch of the American note.[2]

The League commissioners minced few words in denouncing the leaders of the black republic. They declared that although slave markets and slave trading "in the classic sense" (whatever that means) did not exist in Liberia, nevertheless the Liberian natives shipped abroad as contract laborers had been recruited "under conditions of criminal compulsion scarcely distinguishable from slave raiding and slave trading."

The commission also dealt with the Americo-Liberian custom of taking native servants as "pawns." In theory it was possible for a pawn to redeem himself, but when that did not occur, the pawn was in fact a slave. The commission noted that the prevailing price for a pawn was £6 for a woman and £4 for a man; children brought less.

Here it is useful to recognize two factors that are sometimes overlooked. The first is that the Liberian ruling caste (the Americo-Liberians descended from the freed slaves) numbered about 15,000 in a population of approximately 1,500,000 natives. The elite 1 percent who monopolized government had little affinity with tribal Liberia. Few of the forebears of the blacks who colonized Liberia came originally from the Grain Coast, which was selected by the American Colonization Society because it was the only part of West Africa not already preempted by European powers. The Americo-Liberians were as alien to the tribes inhabiting the interior as Europeans or Orientals would have been. Intermarriage had occurred, but control of affairs by the Americo-Liberian minority was never challenged.

---

2. The commission was headed by Dr. Cuthbert Christy, an Englishman. The American government named Dr. Charles S. Johnson, a black educator. Their report was published by the State Department as *Report of the International Commission of Inquiry into the Existence of Slavery and Forced Labor in the Republic of Liberia,* Publication No. 147 (1931).

Furthermore, tribal Liberia spoke over two dozen dialects, many unintelligible to others, a circumstance that facilitated control over the natives, who found it difficult to combine to resist exploitation.

The second factor is that slavery has deep roots on the Dark Continent, existing long before slaves were brought to the New World. Those roots remained in the twentieth century to be tapped by the Americo-Liberians. The original colonists may have remembered their motto "The Love of Liberty Brought Us Here," and may even have cherished that uplifting sentiment, but the ambition of their descendants was not to carry the torch of freedom into dark corners but to live the kind of life they imagined was enjoyed by the governing caste in the American South in the decades before the Civil War. Hence those mansions in and around Monrovia, occupied by Americo-Liberians and staffed by natives held as "pawns" in indefinite servitude.

In the United States an outcry followed by publication of the Christy Report. Essays bemoaning the "tragic irony" of Liberia blossomed on editorial pages. There were denunciations and demands to the president and the secretary of state that something be done. Missionary, educational, and philanthropic organizations held meetings, some of which I attended as Mr. Liberia of the State Department. They passed pained and eloquent resolutions. The Firestones beat a path from Akron to the White House and to the Western European Division of the State Department.

At the League of Nations there was keening and wailing, and soon after the Christy Report the British government (the United States not being a League of Nations member) placed the Liberian matter on the agenda of the next council meeting at Geneva.

In Monrovia these manifestations blew a scorching breath down the collective government neck, and it was recognized that gestures would have to be made. President King obligingly resigned. So did Vice President Yancey. The surviving Fernando Po laborers were brought to Liberia. There was much to-do about atonement and house cleaning, proclaimed by the Liberian secretary of state, Mr. Grimes, and reported upon by my friend Sam Reber. Liberia then declared to the League of Nations that the government desired to do the right thing, but that it lacked the resources necessary to carry out the sweeping reforms that were projected. That declaration led the League to appoint a special committee, and when Mr. Mitchell became American minister to Liberia, Reber was detailed to Europe as the American member. The committee in turn appointed a group of administrative experts who were directed to formulate specific recommendations to be adopted by the Liberian government.

That was the quiver of porcupine quills inherited first by Sam Reber, then by the frustrated Mr. Mitchell, and now by me.

It was fashionable in 1933 for disappointed educators, missionaries, philanthropists, and internationally minded public servants who had devoted much thought and attention to the welfare of Liberia to declare that the country, after behaving badly, had been "saved by the bell" from the retribution it so richly deserved. By the time the League of Nations got around to admonishing Liberia, crises of greater importance elsewhere in the world had allowed a respite to the West African transgressor.

Such a conclusion seems an oversimplification. It is true that it was the luck of an unrepentant Liberia to be brought to book at a time when the pages of the League Covenant were so tattered that condemnation by Geneva meant little. The League of Nations had been endowed with none of the attributes of power or sovereignty. It could be competent in a political matter only to the extent that its principal members were prepared to act together. That was not the case when the League confronted Liberia, which itself was a sovereign state, if one of the most unprepossessing.

The League of Nations' experience with Liberia had, on the other hand, features relevant to the illusion widely cherished in the United States in the post–World War II period that it is possible to modify the behavior (and even the culture) of another country, and that it is a worthy thing to do, particularly if the target country is what is euphemistically termed "less developed" or "emerging." The objective is more admirable still if the torch of democracy is brandished.

My skepticism about the value of that sort of activist diplomacy traces back to our Liberian mission in 1933, even granting that Liberia probably represented a special case and that the Americo-Liberians showed unusual dexterity in seducing their constitution, prostituting their nationalism, and betraying their freed-slave heritage while they utilized all three as instruments for political survival.

In 1933 the idea of sending a special United States mission to Liberia to try to accomplish what previous emissaries had failed to do arose in the Western European Division; Secretary Stimson adopted it and made the project a reality. The secretary had devoted much interest and a disproportionate amount of his time to Liberia, getting nowhere. He felt both challenged and baffled. An aroused secretary of state not only found the candidate but he sponsored the mission to the incoming Washington administration. A personal friend of the president-elect (who was later to make Stimson the secretary of war), Stimson was able to kindle Mr. Roosevelt's interest in Liberia at a time when most overtures of the Hoover administration, seeking to bridge the gap between the elections in 1932 and the inauguration in 1933, were being rejected. Stimson's executive assistant, Harry McBride, who years before had himself served in Liberia, was able to fortify the efforts of the Western European Division and was invaluable to those of us who worked on day-to-day matters affecting West Africa.

Secretary Stimson's candidate for the Liberian mission was Major General Blanton Winship, retiring judge advocate general of the army, a gentleman from Macon, Georgia. A century before, Winship's family had freed some of those who had gone to Liberia. When Stimson was governor-general of the Philippines, Winship was on his staff, and their association was renewed when Stimson came to Washington as Hoover's secretary of state.

Winship at sixty was a splendid figure of a soldier: erect, precise, disciplined, and in top physical condition. He had an abundance of dark hair (which I suspected he tinted to suppress the gray), and a carefully groomed white mustache. His eyes flashed when he talked and when he spied a pretty girl. The general, a bachelor, was much in demand among upper-echelon Washington hostesses. He was a member of "The Family at 1718 H Street," along with Joe Grew, Billy Phillips, Archie Butt, Henry Fletcher, and other leaders of the cotillion era in Washington.

General Winship read the Liberian file, and I answered his questions. Not a man to shirk a duty, the general held an attitude toward the proposal that was not unlike that of General Marshall a dozen years later when he was asked by President Truman if he would take on China. General Winship said he would go, provided the State Department would assign him an officer familiar with the background to serve as his assistant, and to conduct the routine work of the legation in Monrovia.

I had seen the Liberian writing on the State Department wall soon after Sam Reber left Washington in 1930; I even admitted to General Winship, an avid sportsman, that I enjoyed bird shooting. I was appointed. The next thing I did, however, was to take a leaf from the general's book: I told Pierrepont Moffat that to be of maximum value to the special representative, our mission ought to include a clerk to handle accounts, to help with the coding, and to do the administrative chores.

Our clerk proved difficult to find. The State Department, mindful of health hazards in Liberia, decreed that only volunteers should go to Monrovia. (The department also vetoed the presence of wives and families.) Our volunteer was Alure Gallant, a cricketlike Rhode Islander of French Canadian extraction, found in one of the administrative cubbyholes in the State

Department. Gallant was scared almost every minute he was in Liberia, yet he worked for us faithfully and well, and we were deeply indebted to him.

Thus I abandoned my wife and daughter in Washington on the eve of the 1933 presidential inauguration. With General Winship I sailed for England on March 1, wafted onward by a press release issued by the State Department the previous day:

> Believing that the acceptance by Liberia of international assistance looking toward the reorganization of Liberian administration offered the best guarantee of Liberian reforms, the American government has participated in the work of the Liberian Committee of the League of Nations at Geneva. The American government last October [1932] endorsed the program elaborated by the Liberian Committee, and forwarded it to the Firestone interests as a basis for certain modifications in the contract between them in Liberia.
>
> The progress toward the rehabilitation of Liberian finances and a sounder general understanding between this country and Liberia has been blocked by a series of recent occurrences and it is clear that a reexamination by a special American representative on the ground is necessary. . . . A special representative is being sent to Monrovia in an effort to provide a solution safeguarding American rights in Liberia and restoring at the same time a situation which will permit our further efforts to assist Liberia.

The press release announced that General Blanton Winship had been designated "Representative of the President of the United States on Special Mission to Liberia, with the Personal Rank of Ambassador." The general was the first to receive that resounding Rooseveltian title, which the president was shortly to debase by according it to scores of White House travelers, no matter how frivolous or superfluous their mission. In fact, there were times during World War II when in the principal bar of any Allied capital a salted peanut could not be thrown without bouncing it off a stranger "with the Personal Rank of Ambassador," not infrequently traveling without the knowledge of the American ambassador accredited to the country. As the first holder of the title, however, the general was gratified, the press took notice, and the Liberians were impressed.

In London we were received by Viscount Cecil, who expressed various opinions about various Liberian officials. Toward the Liberian secretary of state his attitude was one of refined but virulent distaste. "Mr. Grimes possesses," declared his Lordship, "only the most elementary knowledge of the meaning of veracity." If we could nevertheless get Liberia back in line, Lord Cecil said he would reconvene the League committee in Geneva.

We waited until the last day before having our yellow fever inoculations. These had only recently been perfected, and in 1933 London was one of the few places in the world where they were given — ours were numbers 49, 50, and 51 at the Institute of Tropical Medicine. Instead of the prick in the arm and the mild reaction of later inoculations, we received a vigorous dosage from a wide and menacing needle, and we were upended by it. Miserably we crawled aboard SS *Wahehe* at Southampton, and we sailed south with raging fevers. The general and I were up in three days — he spotted me thirty years — and playing deck tennis, but the *Wahehe* was almost to the Canary Islands before our bedraggled clerk ventured out of his cabin. The poor man was tempted, I suspect, to desert us at Tenerife, and might have, except that he could not speak Spanish. At sea the next day we donned white suits, and the captain warned us that henceforth we should not cross so little as an unshaded deck space without wearing our sun helmets.

Thus we came thirteen days from Southampton to anchor, one scorching noon, off a town on a ridge at right angles to the muddy discharge of the Mesurado River, a town of low buildings and galvanized iron roofs streaked with rust. The encroaching forest shimmered in the haze. A launch appeared to be flying the American flag, but as the craft approached, we could see that although the red and white stripes were familiar, the blue field bore a single star.

We came ashore in a surf boat, our cased shotguns wrapped in our raincoats and ourselves drenched in warm salt spray. This was Monrovia, named in honor of the fifth president of the United States.

The business of our mission was to produce an acceptable reform plan ("plan of assistance," as the League committee called it) and to take the plan to Geneva for adoption as the League of Nations' response to the request received from an ostensibly repentant Liberia following the slavery disclosures. The original League project was too expensive for a country whose budget was less than $1 million per annum. The ensuing discussion about what Liberia could afford had been obscured by the dispute with the financial adviser, and when Liberia repudiated the Firestone loan, the prospects for reform were jeopardized still further. Those were the "recent occurrences" referred to in the State Department press release describing General Winship's mission.

The problem was thus simple as to objectives but complicated by the multiplicity of elements involved, including, in addition to Liberia, the State Department, the League committee (on which half a dozen nationalities were represented), and the Firestones as creditors under the defaulted loan agreement.

At the time of our mission, diplomatic relations between Liberia and the United States had been suspended. There is no such thing in diplomacy as "unrecognizing" a country; Washington had not broken relations over Liberian behavior that the United States had publicly denounced. No new American minister or chargé d'affaires had been appointed after Mr. Mitchell's departure, and Liberia had merely been "notified" of the Winship mission. That somewhat anomalous situation was not without its advantages, in that we wasted no time on digressions of protocol and social activities were kept to a minimum. Racial feeling had no part in this. On the contrary, General Winship later told his Georgia friends he felt very much at home in Monrovia society, since the guests usually included one or two who bore names identified with the early years of Macon, Atlanta, and the surrounding counties.

There were discomforts enough in Monrovia without plunging into local society. Our legation, a two-story combined office and residence, was the most thoroughly screened building in Africa — and the stuffiest. The house had screened porches around all four sides, and it had screen doors instead of solid wooden doors except to the bedrooms, which had both screen doors and wooden doors. Each bed was equipped with cotton netting suspended in damp folds from the ceiling. The netting was carefully tucked in, last thing at night. These precautions meant that between the sleeper and the mosquito-infested outside world there were four or five separate layers of screening, so that it took an enterprising puff of wind to penetrate to the bedside. To the equatorial heat was added humidity that approached 100 percent, so that feathers in our pillows turned rancid and had to be changed every few days. Mildew formed on almost everything. The lock of my steamer trunk turned green; my silk hat in its box became the shade of the bark on the north side of a New England pine tree.

Our bathing took place on the rear veranda of the legation, in the presence of a houseboy who replaced the five-gallon tin of warm water with a second one midway through the shower, when the bather was covered with soapsuds. Since we used rainwater, the suds were abundant, and it took the last drop from the second five-gallon can to rinse away the bubbles.

There were insects of all sizes, upholstery, and colors, from termites to infinitesimal things that got through the screens and clustered around our gasoline pressure lamps, making typing a torture. There were flying beetles that, colliding with a wall, shook the building, and cockroaches with three-inch antennae that scurried out from under things, disappearing into crevices that looked too small to accommodate a gnat.

We had two unfriendly house cats Sam Reber had christened Aegypti and Anopheles after the mosquitoes, and a gaunt, untidy monkey. The monkey stayed in the garden, wearing a belt attached to a length of light chain; she provided additional income for our cook by periodically slipping her belt and trespassing on neighboring property, where she pulled up vegetables and rattled tin cans. She was returned by an irate "property owner," who demanded one shilling for damages sustained. We paid the shilling the first week but then informed the cook that future indemnities would be deducted from his wages, whereupon the monkey stayed at home. She was fascinated by our shower bath, which she admired from the branch of a tree, shaking her chain and making faces. She was a cheerful, harmless little beast, but Gallant, our clerk, lived in dread lest she slip her belt during his ablutions and bite him.

We were received by the president of Liberia, Mr. Barclay, and we met several times a week with Secretary of State Grimes. It was uphill work. We soon decided that Viscount Cecil's observation about Grimes's imperfect acquaintance with veracity was the understatement of the century. A large man with protruding, poached-egg eyes, Grimes looked like a prototypical golliwog. He had some forensic ability, and a bullfrog voice lent a kind of raffish aplomb to his undertakings. In conversation Secretary Grimes used long words in preference to short ones, with a smattering of foreign phrases. I once heard him tell the general, after an ornate polysyllabic expression of regret: "Although I myself am not au courant with the intricacies of that matter, I shall inquire of my locum tenens." General Winship blinked.

Grimes's circumlocutions almost invariably added up to misrepresentation. He lied so habitually that sometimes he did so when no discernible purpose was served. I experimented with a formula based on the proposition that by taking the opposite of any statement attributed to the secretary of state of Liberia, an approximation of the truth was obtained. This proved a sterile exercise, but dealing with Grimes nevertheless fit into the through-the-looking-glass circumstances of local political life. Things that were irrational — at times almost lunatic — were constantly happening in Monrovia in a logical, even inevitable, manner.

For instance, the Liberian budget was prepared each year by the executive, debated by the legislature, and solemnly enacted in Liberian dollars. But there were no Liberian dollars. The only money in Liberia was the palm tree shilling of British West Africa, the currency of Sierra Leone, the Gold Coast, and Nigeria, a silver coin at par with the British shilling. The Firestone payroll distributed palm tree shillings; so did General Winship and I when we hired beaters to flush the fast-flying African guinea fowl on afternoons when we hunted the savanna lands and cassava patches inland from Monrovia.

Taxes, duties, levies, and fees of every description were expressed in nonexistent Liberian dollars, which were then laboriously converted into palm tree shillings.

Again, the Americo-Liberian elite had recently been stung by foreign criticism: a European magazine had noted disparagingly that not only did many of the legislators go barefoot in Congress, a sign of unsophisticated behavior, but that grass and even weeds grew in the main street of the capital. With nerves still sensitive following the slavery charges, Liberia reacted with unaccustomed vigor. The legislature passed a resolution with a preamble acknowledging the relevance of suitable attire to the dignity of lawmaking; it directed the sergeant at arms of Congress henceforth not to admit any member who was not wearing shoes.

The emporium on Broadway of Isaac Alkmin, dealer in shoes, did a brief thriving business, only to have the legislators discover that for men accustomed to going barefoot, new shoes can be excruciatingly uncomfortable. Thereafter one saw the unshod members of Congress sauntering toward the capitol, each legislator followed by a houseboy with a shoe box balanced on his head. Upon arrival, the barefoot congressman would seat himself on the portico of Congress, don his new shoes, and hobble into the building.

The tidying up of Broadway was still in progress when General Winship and I arrived. The city jail was near the legation, and we used to see batches of prisoners let out from time to time, under guard, to weed Broadway. It would have been more efficient to issue a small scythe to each prisoner, but perhaps more difficult in that case to shepherd them back to jail. The weeding was accordingly done by hand, and by the time one block was cleared, last week's stretch of Broadway again demanded attention.

Our mission was to draft, in conjunction with the Liberian secretary of state, a practical plan of assistance for adoption by the League of Nations. We persisted and persevered, and after a good deal of stalling by Liberia, we got a revised and simplified project on paper, "approved in principle" by the Liberian president, which the general believed ought in practice to be workable.

We thereupon called in a passing northbound ship to take us and Mr. Grimes to Europe to attend the League of Nations session in Geneva. The vessel turned out to be the old *Canada* of the Fabre, once of the Boston Mediterranean service, and now of the Monrovia waterfront. "Two pipes," they marveled, and no one could remember when a ship of that size had last graced the roadstead. Our prestige was enhanced by the dimensions of the vessel, and we departed in style.

In Geneva, Secretary of State Grimes at once set out to obstruct consideration of our project. The general and I then encountered trouble with Harvey Firestone, Jr., who was willing to make generous concessions on the loan contract (thus in effect supplying the funds to underwrite the League program of assistance), but on the understanding that the chief adviser would be an American citizen.

Both General Winship and Secretary Grimes opposed this, for different reasons. The general was against writing into the League of Nations contract that the chief adviser, a League appointee, should be of any specific nationality; Winship regarded that as incompatible with the international sponsorship of the program. Privately, he apprehended that an American chief adviser, in addition to the American financial adviser already stipulated on the loan contract, would saddle the United States indefinitely with the Liberian problem, an outcome we did not consider to be in the national interest. In any case, the important thing was the authority of the chief adviser, not the color of his passport.

Grimes opposed an American because he knew the Firestones wanted one. In order to complicate the issue further, Grimes made a speech declaring that Liberia would view with equal disfavor either a British or a French chief adviser, "since both Great Britain and France have colonial dependencies contiguous to Liberia's frontiers."

"No contiguous adviser," proclaimed Grimes, savoring the adjective. "And," he continued piously, "no American, because an American might be embarrassed by having to make a decision adverse to bondholders of his own nationality."

Finally the general persuaded Harvey to withdraw his insistence that the chief adviser be an American, and this troublesome matter was settled.

Grimes next produced a series of distortions, irrelevancies, and misstatements so preposterous that General Winship ordered me to prepare a written rebuttal. The rebuttal turned out to be a lengthy document, carefully blue-penciled by the general to delete anything that might savor of heat, rancor, or derision.

"The American representative has examined in detail the statement made by Mr. Grimes," declared the general, "and in many instances he has been able to check the allegations with the original record. The American representative finds Mr. Grimes' statement inaccurate and misleading, and his conclusions without foundation . . . ."

Appended was a catalog of prevarications on the part of our Liberian colleague, each followed by the corresponding correction: "The Liberian Secretary of State says . . ." followed by the facts. Insofar as Viscount Cecil and the League committee were concerned, our statement was conclusive. Secretary Grimes glowered as the committee proceeded, paragraph by paragraph, to adopt the project in substantially the form in which we had drafted it in Monrovia.

At the final Geneva session Lord Cecil reminded the Liberian representative that the action of the committee was being taken in response to a request by Liberia for assistance, following disclosure of conditions that shocked the civilized world. The plan now formulated was the result of intensive and disinterested effort over a protracted period. The plan had been framed to help Liberia, and the only way that could be done was by giving the chief adviser sufficient authority to accomplish the reforms Liberia said it wanted. In effect, declared Lord Cecil, Liberia could now take it or leave it — the plan of assistance was not subject to further whittling down by the beneficiary.

We adjourned. Secretary Hull cabled General Winship his congratulations, and the State Department issued a public statement that the American government expected Liberia to accept the plan and would be pleased to cooperate in its successful execution. On the other hand, should Liberia reject it, "such action could only be construed as opposition to reform; . . . and indifference to the welfare of the native peoples of Liberia."

The final outcome surprised few students of Liberian behavior. Ironically, the opposition of the Americo-Liberian ruling caste was strengthened by the very constitution that the American Colonization Society had so proudly given to Liberia in 1847. That constitution, patterned on ours, envisaged a degree of political sophistication that turned out to be lacking in those who found themselves deposited on the margin of the steaming West African jungle, charter in hand, among indigenous peoples ripe for exploitation.

Dictatorship by the descendants of the freed slaves was the result, but an unusual aspect of it was the retention of the original constitution, which the

Americo-Liberian leaders shrewdly concluded would be useful as a facade behind which to retire when danger threatened. This the Liberian government proceeded to do when faced with the League of Nations plan of assistance, adoption of which might have jeopardized the preservation of their monopoly of power.

Secretary Grimes returned to Monrovia with the League plan in his pocket. In January 1934, after debate during which the Constitution of 1847 figured largely, the legislature authorized "acceptance" of the plan, but with reservations — constitutional reservations — undermining the authority of the proposed chief adviser. These reservations, in the opinion of the League Council, were in fact the equivalent of rejection. Washington agreed. The League of Nations washed its hands of Liberia.

In World War II, Liberia declared for the Allies and the country prospered. Monrovia's airport was built to accommodate war planes being flown from the shoulder of Brazil. Deposits of iron ore were discovered up-country from Monrovia. Latex flowed from the Firestone plantation. By then, General Winship had been appointed governor of Puerto Rico, and I was serving in our embassy in Cuba for the second time.

Cuba with Jefferson Caffery

I was in Geneva, still wrestling with Liberia, when I received a letter from the chief of the Western European Division that was to enrich my life and advance my career by exposing me to one of diplomacy's most astute practitioners. Pierrepont Moffat's letter, dated September 28, 1933, read:

> You are in the position, happy or unhappy, where two groups in the Department are fighting for your services. Caffery is particularly anxious to have you go down to Cuba with him and in view of the really critical situation there, the Personnel Board felt that the Western European Division must forego [*sic*] its claim on you for the last three or four months of your service in the Department. . . . I do think this change offers a great professional opportunity and no Chief of Division has a right to withhold such a chance from one of his officers . . . .

Like many juniors in the Foreign Service, I had heard about Jefferson Caffery, but I had never met him, and I was curious to know why he was "particularly anxious" to have me join his staff. The answer throws light on the Caffery economy of effort as well as on the confidence Caffery had in the accuracy of his own assessment of competence, in this case the competence of H. Freeman Matthews,[1] a contemporary of mine whose previous service with Caffery had convinced him that Matthews was one of the ablest men in the service. Having overcome the view of the Personnel Board that Matthews was too junior for the number-two job in Havana, Caffery assigned to him the task of selecting the rest of the staff. It followed that all of us had to be junior to Matthews, which resulted in a youthful, and hence

---

1. H. Freeman "Doc" Matthews (1899–1986) graduated from Princeton in 1921, the year I graduated from Dartmouth. He had preceded me by two years into the Foreign Service.

presumably durable, aggregation eagerly facing the rigors of Havana exposure. We did not know how rigorous until we got there.

When I returned to Washington a few weeks later, I called on Mr. Caffery, who was then still serving as assistant secretary of state. The interview was not an unqualified success. Caffery expressed little interest in West Africa, with whose problems I had struggled night and day for over two years. He wanted to know how soon I could get to Havana, whether Matthews had already gone to take over from the departing Ambassador Welles. Mrs. Matthews was still in the United States; my wife was to get in touch with her about joining us later, depending on developments. He himself hoped to arrive in December. When could I start for Havana?

My impression after that Potomac interview was that my new boss was abrupt, sharp, and somewhat inarticulate. The abruptness I soon discovered was a part of his economy of effort. During business hours Caffery went to the heart of the problem without wasting time on small talk or digressions. His inarticulateness, on the other hand, denoted no imprecision in marshaling his ideas; on the contrary, his ideas raced ahead of his vocal cords. Consequently he sometimes mumbled or left sentences unfinished. What was equally disconcerting, he sometimes skipped the verb or even the object of the verb, leaving the listener to puzzle out what he wanted to have done. This propensity complicated operations for those who made the mistake of trying to guess what the ambassador meant, as I found out the hard way in Cuba a few weeks later when the ambassador sent me to ascertain from Carlos Hevia, minister of agriculture in the unrecognized provisional government, whether the Cuban authorities were taking seriously the capers of the Uruguayan minister, who was rushing about volunteering good offices to quarreling political factions.

At the time I thought Ambassador Caffery wanted me to find out about "Uruguay and *tasajo*" — dried beef, an important export item from the River Plate to the Caribbean, whereas what interested the ambassador was "Uruguay good offices." My report did not enhance my prestige as the newly arrived second secretary of embassy. When presently I carried my frustration to Doc Matthews, he gave me good advice and I took it. Next time I was given an assignment, I said to my ambassador, diffidently but with insistence, "I'm sorry, Sir, but I didn't understand a damn word you said." Mr. Caffery scowled, then smiled, and thereafter I obtained both verb and object before leaving the ambassadorial presence.

In the early 1930s the plight of many Cubans had little to do with their government, good or bad. It lay in the worldwide depression. The price of sugar, a world commodity, had dropped to half a cent a pound — 50 cents the hundredweight — and the economy of Cuba wilted like a decapitated flower. Around the silent and deserted mills, worn sugar bags did duty as jackets. Cubans, like their northern neighbors who had been assured in 1928 of two cars in every garage and who thereafter blamed the makers of those promises when their stomachs as well as their garages were empty, blamed their troubles on their president, Gerardo Machado. But unlike the Americans, who waited for the 1932 elections to vent their disenchantment, the Cubans started plotting the overthrow of their government.

President Machado retaliated. Reports of rough treatment of political opponents and of the suppression of civil liberties soon began circulating in the United States. Then the vice president of Cuba was brutally assassinated. Reprisals by Machado followed. Concern in the United States, fanned by the press, flamed into indignation. There were demands, echoing those heard in 1898, that Washington take action.

There was an excuse for American intervention, because in 1933 the Platt Amendment was still on the books, servitude written into the Cuban Constitution at the instance of the United States. The Platt Amendment authorized the American government to intervene, in specified circumstances, for the good of Cuba. Under it, the United States had intervened several times, with varying results, including a growing belief among the Cuban people that the way to embarrass their own government was to provoke an intervention, and among critics of the United States throughout Latin America that the way to embarrass Washington was to wave the Platt Amendment in Washington's face.

Earlier political upheavals in Cuba were conducted with some restraint and, once the tyrant of the moment had prudently fled to Miami, with considerable regard for the amenities. Enough of the tyrant's associates were rounded up and lodged in Cabanas Fortress or Príncipe Prison to satisfy the patriotic fervor of the new redeemers of the Republic, whose promises of reform lasted about as long as it took the prisoners to buy their way out of jail. And throughout whatever confusion punctuated the affair there was always the prospect, comforting to many citizens of Cuba, that if things became too complicated, the United States, by reason of the Platt Amendment, could be counted upon to send a gunboat. Bluejackets would land, troublemakers would be admonished, new credits would be extended, and pretty soon business in the rich and fertile Pearl of the Antilles would again be conducted with decorum.

The Hoover administration, concluding that the Platt Amendment had outlived such usefulness as it may have possessed in the early years following the Spanish-American War, was planning to abrogate it when Hoover was voted out of office.

The incoming Roosevelt administration nailed its flag to the Good Neighbor Policy enunciated in the inaugural address on March 4, 1933. While publicly denouncing intervention, Roosevelt nevertheless schemed to oust the president of Cuba, whose behavior had alienated large segments of American as well as Cuban opinion. Roosevelt instructed Sumner Welles, his first ambassador in Havana, to get rid of President Machado. A few months later Machado was overthrown.[2]

Three weeks after Machado's overthrow, the provisional president, Carlos Manuel de Céspedes, Ambassador Welles's handpicked successor to Machado, was himself ejected from office by an improbable combination of left-wing university professors, incendiary students, and the noncommissioned officers of the Cuban Army led by Sergeant Fulgencio Batista, who was destined to dominate the political life of Cuba for most of the next quarter-century.

Washington worried and fretted. Ambassador Welles, an able public servant but not the best judge of character, was unlucky. When Machado fled, Welles was a hero and the new provisional president, the son of a nineteenth-century Cuban patriot, was greeted with enthusiasm. Had Welles left then, his reputation might have remained intact, but he elected to stay in Cuba, hoping to see his handiwork approved. Instead, Welles saw it violently dismembered.

Céspedes could not control the forces, generated during the repressions of Machado, that were explosively liberated by Machado's downfall. Moreover, for the first time since independence, more than the politicians were involved in a revolution. Labor found itself incited by student radicals and by Communist agitators who demanded the nationalization of the sugar industry, seizure of the railroads, and the expropriation of public utilities. Revolutionaries punctuated their demands by throwing bombs, and soon Havana was in an uproar.

The ousted Céspedes was replaced by a panel of professors, and then by one of their own number, Dr. Ramón Grau San Martín, a charismatic med-

2. Cuban plotting against Machado redoubled when Washington's attitude became known in Havana upon Welles's arrival. Machado was toppled on August 12, 1933. Secretary of State Hull in his *Memoirs* (chapter 22) describes Ambassador Welles as Roosevelt's "mediator among the various factions in Cuba," evidently seeking to play down the American role in expelling a president.

ical doctor who was afflicted with oratory. Dr. Grau made little sense but charmed many listeners, who began calling themselves *los revolucionarios auténticos* — the authentic revolutionaries, Auténticos for short.[3]

Meanwhile, Batista set about consolidating control over the Cuban Army. Those resenting this initiative presently congregated in the Hotel Nacional, a luxurious headquarters in which to plot but not tactically defensible. Batista, now a colonel, surrounded the grounds with soldiers while the gunboat *Patria* rocked on the edge of the gulf stream, lobbing four-inch shells at Havana's newest hotel, an inviting target. Casualties were light because the building was soundly constructed and the aim of the *Patria* gunners was uncertain. The ex-officers held out as long as their ammunition lasted (which was several hours), but after that Batista was the undisputed head of the armed forces. It was on that foundation that he was soon to erect his political career.

In the capital, however, bombs continued to explode, killing innocent people. Business was at a standstill. Two of the largest sugar mills on the island, American owned, were seized by their workers. Grau applauded. Washington withheld recognition.

Ambassador Wells, alarmed by these doings, momentarily forgot the Good Neighbor Policy. He cabled Washington, urging armed intervention. Instead, President Roosevelt sent the light cruiser *Richmond* to Havana with orders not to land forces "unless necessary to evacuate American citizens." Secretary of State Hull sought to pacify critics by characterizing the action as a "precautionary measure" without the "slightest intention of intervening or interfering in Cuba's domestic affairs."

Welles, one of the architects of the Good Neighbor Policy, decided it was high time for him to leave Cuba and to exchange places with Assistant Secretary of State Jefferson Caffery, under an arrangement approved by President Roosevelt early in the administration: Welles to Havana to get rid of President Machado, then Welles to Washington to take charge of Latin American affairs, and Caffery to Cuba as ambassador.

A few days after my initial conversation with Mr. Caffery in Washington, I abandoned my wife and daughter for the second time in 1933. I drove our automobile the fifteen hundred miles between the District of Columbia and Key West, where I embarked on the ferry for Havana. Five hours later the gray fortress of Morro Castle was visible. Doc Matthews welcomed me to Cuba.

---

3. The Auténticos were to elect Dr. Grau San Martín president eleven years later. His reform administration attracted a record proportion of crackpots and scoundrels.

The embassy chancery was at Avenida Misiones, on the square backed by the Presidential Palace, facing the narrow entrance to the harbor with Morro Castle on the opposite side of the channel. Two blocks away was the Prado, and the Malecón extended from the lower end of the park along the coast toward Vedado. Ours was a splendid address in terms of central location and access to government offices, but by the same token we were often in line of fire either from guards stationed on the roof of the Presidential Palace, shooting at real or imaginary snipers, or from the not-so-imaginary snipers themselves. When Machado fled, arms depots and arsenals were raided by jubilant mobs including the most unruly elements from the university. Those guns were now being fired from doorways and rooftops, sometimes in anger, sometimes to test the weapons, and other times just to make noise, which has always been a popular diversion in Cuba. Shooting a machine gun from the roof became the equivalent of lighting firecrackers on the Fourth of July in the United States.

The chancery was a three-story, triangular structure with a walled roof where, following the arrival of the USS *Richmond,* Ambassador Welles established a radio shack for communication with the admiral. Three bluejackets camped in the building beside the code room, working eight-hour shifts. Sandbags piled on the coping were often punctured during the night by stray bullets fired from neighboring buildings. The three sailors were nevertheless the envy of their mates aboard ship because off duty they had access to the fleshpots of Havana — a privilege denied the other enlisted men for many weeks, until a provisional government was recognized by Washington.

When I arrived, Ambassador Caffery was still in the United States, but the new staff had already begun replacing those who had served with Ambassador Welles and his Republican predecessor, Ambassador Harry S. Guggenheim. One of the things that differentiated the old hands from the newcomers was that when gunfire was heard, the newcomers rushed to embassy windows to see what was happening, whereas the old hands, invariably led by Jim Flexer, bumped into one another getting to the stairwell, a haven protected by several thicknesses of wall from bullets striking the building.

When Ambassador Caffery arrived in December 1933, the same month my wife and daughter arrived on the SS *Morro Castle,* the tasks facing the embassy were both urgent and complex: how to find someone in Cuba capable of damping down the violence and curbing the disorders; how to encourage the more responsible elements to support those objectives; how to safeguard the large and important American community as well as its large investments without landing bluejackets or marines.

Also, how to get business moving; how to revive the lagging sugar industry; how to write a new commercial treaty; how to abrogate the Platt Amendment; and then how to convince Cuba that it should henceforth stand on its own feet.

In short — how to mobilize men, money, and ideas, and do so without creating the impression that the American government was manipulating the actors, or the embassy was pulling the strings.

Relations with the State Department required careful handling. Assistant Secretary Welles was an expert on Cuba in his own right; he had ideas about personalities as well as about policy. There was also young Larry Duggan, who had been given special responsibility for the work of our mission. And there was the secretary of state himself, whose interest dated back to 1898, when, as a lanky youth from Tennessee, Sergeant Hull came sweating ashore to fight in the Spanish-American War. Cordell Hull and Sumner Welles did not always see eye to eye, another factor affecting the work of embassy Havana.

Among the talents that Caffery brought to revolution-torn Cuba was a rare ability to size up men and their motives, and to gauge the strengths and weaknesses of those occupying public office. Although in his spare time, relaxing, he had a catholic taste in companions and was kept abreast by them of all sorts of trivial gossip and chitchat, in his official capacity he did not suffer drones gladly. In fact, the new ambassador was so brusque with a procession of early Cuban callers that few of them returned to bother him a second time. The word got around that the new envoy was tough and apparently not interested in "exchanging impressions" — a favorite way to spend time in the Cuban political arena. Mr. Caffery could not have cared less. Popularity he regarded as an overrated tool in diplomacy.

On the other hand, the ambassador accepted the visits of a thoroughly raffish Havana character, who was dubbed by Matthews and me "the Bailarina." But by no stretch of the imagination did he resemble a ballet dancer, being both overweight and deeply impregnated with Chanel No. 5. Puffing up the single flight of stairs to the ambassador's office used to make the Bailarina heave like a winded porpoise, whereupon out would come his silk handkerchief and the air would tingle with expensive perfume.

The easy access of this disreputable individual to the ambassadorial lair used to puzzle members of the community, but the explanation was simple: the Bailarina was useful to Caffery as a channel of communication between the chancery and some of those who were beginning to wield political power in Cuba. Caffery exploited this without permitting his pudgy messenger to take advantage of the relationship.

In addition, the Bailarina amused the ambassador, whose private life was somewhat austere. No plump beagle following a rabbit was more diligent than the Bailarina in pursuit of the extracurricular activities of certain politicians, and he relished recounting pieces of succulent intelligence to an understanding audience who, although immune to those temptations himself, was nevertheless entertained by the escapades and pretensions of others.

Ambassador Caffery never ate lunch. A glass of milk sometimes, with a sandwich consumed rather messily among the papers on his desk, but no proper meal between breakfast and dinner. That practice had something to do with weight control and with his early morning exercise. It was also connected with self-discipline, with which Mr. Caffery was abundantly supplied. He was not, however, one to urge his private arrangements on others. Having attended early Mass with Walter Donnelly, he used to reach the chancery about 10:30, receiving elaborate salutes from González and Iglesias, the two uniformed Cuban policemen at the entrance, and a hearty "Good morning, Mr. Ambassador" from Amalia, our robust and cheerful telephone operator. In strict interpretation of international usage the Cuban policemen should have remained outside the building, but years before, someone had installed them inside the doorway, where they took messages, helped Amalia with the switchboard, and made themselves generally useful. They were amiable and kindly, and we held them in affection.

Ambassador Caffery was not an effusive chief. He rarely expressed either praise or censure. It was enough if a man did his work according to the standards Caffery set, in which case what was done with the rest of one's time was primarily one's own business — always provided that it did not diminish the prestige of the mission. Prestige he rightly held to be a powerful ingredient in successful diplomacy.

As the embassy surveyed the new prospects, clearly the first priority was getting rid of Provisional President Grau, provided it could be accomplished without provoking a reign of terror on the part of his bomb-throwing constituents. Since Ambassador Caffery has published no memoirs, one can only conjecture about the moments it took during their first interview for the ambassador to conclude that the doctor-president was addled.

There was simultaneously the problem of who should succeed Grau. Batista, whom Caffery at once identified as a leader, lacked experience. He was still feeling his way into the intricacies of his Cuban undertakings. Controlling the armed forces, Batista could be the equilibrium, the steadying influence behind a regime, but he was not yet ready for the driver's seat.

Moreover, Batista, who had helped overthrow Welles's personally selected provisional president, was hardly popular with the former envoy, who now occupied high position in Washington. To the patrician Welles (Groton and Harvard), there was little to arouse his enthusiasm when he contemplated this swarthy ex-enlisted man, of mixed blood and unimpressive antecedents, who not only had evicted President Céspedes from office but also had single-handed cashiered the officer corps of the Cuban Army. Selling Batista to Welles was not an overnight proposition.

Nevertheless, five weeks from Caffery's arrival, Grau was out of office. The intolerance of the provisional president, coupled with his ineptness, helped topple his edifice of its own weight, the doctor angrily resigning as various political associates withdrew their support. He declared himself a martyr sacrificed on a reactionary altar.

After Dr. Grau resigned, an acquaintance of mine, Carlos Hevia, the minister of agriculture in the previous administration and a 1920 graduate of Annapolis, became provisional president. In his ministerial capacity Hevia had given me assurances that he would do what he could to restore to their American owners two sugar mills whose seizure Grau had approved. Ambassador Caffery sent me to the Presidential Palace to cash in on Hevia's promise.

The Palacio Presidencial was one hundred yards from the chancery. To say that on the day after Grau's resignation the premises were in a state of confusion gives scant idea of the ability of the Cuban political animal to churn up the pasture. Armed soldiers dashed in and out of the entrance, showing bits of paper to each other. Conspirational civilians, revolvers bulging in their pockets, swarmed about inner doors, coming and going. Groups stood about, engaging in loud altercations punctuated by gestures. With the windows closed against the January wind off the Bahama Channel, the air was blue with smoke. Cigarette stubs littered the marble floor and cigar butts overflowed the ashtrays.

As the only foreigner in evidence, I was immediately conspicuous. A submachine gun barred my way and a lieutenant, in need of a shave, demanded my identity and business. Those stated, I was given polite attention and presently was conducted upstairs, my escort apologizing that the elevator was no longer working. "Nuevo presidente, ascensor malogrado," said my guide cheerfully. "New president, busted elevator."

The deposed Machado, who had governed Cuba for eight years with an envious eye on the arrangements for visitors adopted in Fascist Italy by Mussolini, had done himself in comparable style in Havana. His Hall of Mirrors was a vast office across which the caller had to walk, conspicuously alone, in order to approach the executive desk, an elephantine piece of furniture sustained by thick gilt legs. Behind this fortress, dwarfed by it, was Carlos Hevia. He came forward to greet me in English.

When I referred to his new status and congratulated him on it, Hevia shrugged and remarked he did not know how long it would last, but in any case, before we discussed business, there was something he wanted to show me. Inviting me to his side of the desk, he opened the wide center drawer. The first thing I identified was an automatic pistol beside an open box of .45 caliber cartridges, but what President Hevia was pointing at was a pile of telegraph and cable forms that he handed to me.

The messages were in English. "Hold 'em, pal." "Attaboy, Carlos." "President Hevia forever." "Sink the Army. Up with the Navy" — all testifying to the popularity of former Midshipman Hevia.

Provisional President Hevia remembered his promise. He had a draft decree already prepared and signed it in my presence. Summoning a secretary, he dictated a telegram to the military commander in Santiago de Cuba in Oriente Province, quoting the decree and directing that it be put into effect forthwith: the two sugar mills, Central Chaparra and Central Delicias, were to be restored to the Cuban American Sugar Company. Although Hevia occupied the presidential office for only two days before retiring in favor of the venerable Colonel Mendieta, the Hevia decree was honored by the succeeding administration. The company had its two properties returned in time for grinding of the 1934 *zafra*.[4]

Recognition by the United States of the new provisional government of Cuba was shortly facilitated by Secretary Hull himself, who was on his way home from the Montevideo Conference. His ship put in at Key West so he could confer with Ambassador Caffery and then shorten the trip by making the last leg by train from Florida. A four-stack destroyer of World War I vintage was mobilized to make the rough crossing of the Strait of Florida so the ambassador could keep the appointment. After talking with Caffrey, the secretary agreed, subject to President Roosevelt's concurrence, that on Mr. Hull's return to Washington, formal recognition would be extended to the provisional government of Carlos Mendieta.

4. Carlos Hevia, an honest and honorable man, ran for president almost twenty years later. He was the leading candidate when by a coup d'état former President Batista once again installed himself in the Presidential Palace. Hevia, who deserved well of his country, died in Miami while Batista was still president.

Now, after nearly six months, we faced a regime with which the embassy could deal on an official and, we hoped, cordial basis. The first round was over. From that point on, things slowly began to get better.

President Carlos Mendieta (always known as Colonel Mendieta) was honest and a good presence. He was not bright, but he was a veteran of the Cuban War of Independence and was regarded as a reliable elder statesman. With his military background Mendieta believed that the duties of the armed forces included restoration of public order and security. He got on well with Batista, whose power and ambitions were growing.

Urgency courts were established to deal with terrorism and violence. Antonio Guiteras, Dr. Grau's minister of the interior, was finally exterminated in a clash with troops near Matanzas. The National University was at long last raided, amid imprecations and threats from the Auténticos, abetted by many of the students and professors. Their indignation over this violation of academic freedom was by no means diminished by the discovery on university premises of a huge cache of explosives and an arsenal of rifles and machine guns. Stored with the explosives were fuses and sections of iron pipe, threaded at each end, bored to encase dynamite sticks.[5] These confiscated adjuncts to higher education were removed from the university to Camp Columbia, where Batista showed them to Ambassador Caffery. Sensible Cubans applauded, and Mendieta's stock rose.

The Platt Amendment was next on the agenda. If the part played by President Roosevelt in getting rid of Machado was of debatable statesmanship, there was no denying the sincerity of Washington's efforts to assist Cuba once recognition had been extended to an acceptable successor government. The actual drafting of the new treaty was done in Washington, with embassy participation focused on facilitating the dispatch of helpful instructions from the Cuban Ministry of State to the Cuban ambassador in Washington. That involved liaison by Doc Matthews with the Foreign Ministry, which was headed by a self-important individual who greatly admired his own talents as an international lawyer. In essence the matter was simple: a renunciation by the United States of certain conditions imposed with the best of intentions thirty years before.

Through the Bailarina, Mr. Caffery sent certain observations to President Mendieta. In conveying the president's reply the Bailarina delighted us by remarking that if Cuba really wanted to regain its prosperity, "It ought to buy

5. On the day in April 1934 when our son was born, over twenty of these homemade bombs exploded within earshot of my wife's Vedado hospital.

the foreign minister for what he is worth, and then sell him for what he thinks he's worth." This cheered Matthews in his subsequent dealings with the minister, whose pride was piqued at having to negotiate below the ambassadorial level. In any event, President Mendieta told his foreign minister to behave, and the treaty work went forward.

In an agreement approved by the U.S. Senate in the record time of two days, the United States formally renounced the right to intervene in Cuba as established in 1920 by the Platt Amendment, and gave up all special rights with the exception of the Guantánamo Naval Station, deemed essential to the defense of the Panama Canal.

In Cuba, on ratification, there was feasting and jollity. The Cuban government declared a three-day holiday. *La Enmienda Platt* was burned in effigy in a great bonfire in the park in front of the embassy chancery amid cheers and expressions of goodwill. That night, the festival spirit continuing, three persons were killed and fifteen wounded by stray bullets fired by those celebrating what Pepín Rivero, in his influential newspaper *Diario de la Marina*, described as "the coming of age of the Republic."

The business community, encouraged by the good feeling engendered by the treaty, as well as by the eclipse of Dr. Grau and the success of the efforts to contain the depredations of his vindictive supporters, took heart. They were further stimulated by a 25 percent reduction in the American tariff on sugar and by the prospects for an early trade agreement.

The Trade Agreement Act, passed in July 1934, was the special concern of Cordell Hull, whose primary interest during his long years as secretary of state lay in the liberalization of international trade, which he regarded as the key to Free World prosperity. His theory was that in a series of bilateral negotiations, the products of greatest concern to each pair of countries would, after bargaining, receive lower tariff treatment, which would then, through the operation of the most-favored-nation principle, be extended to other countries. The result would be that tariffs worldwide would gradually be pushed down, and international trade would benefit. It was a sound idea.[6] Another important aspect was that the agreement negotiated under the Trade Agreement Act did not have to be submitted to the Senate for

---

6. The Trade Agreement Act with Cuba was to be unique, however, in that it granted "exclusive and preferential reductions in duties" that were not extended to third countries. This served to perpetuate the special relationship established by the Convention of 1902, with its 20 percent differential in favor of Cuban products entering the United States.

approval, thus removing it from the political pressures and logrolling that had so often characterized tariff measures in the past.

The agreement with Cuba was the first to be reached under Secretary Hull's program. Most of the negotiations took place in Havana, beginning almost as soon as the Mendieta government had been recognized, and before the act itself had become law. A young tariff expert named Harry Turkel was dispatched by the State Department to assist us, and the daily hassles with our Cuban opposite numbers were conducted by our very able commercial attaché, Walter Donnelly. The ambassador gave general guidance to the negotiations and followed daily reports from Donnelly, but he attended few of the negotiation sessions. He was available to unblock a logjam, should one occur, but he did not occupy his time arguing about pineapple shoots or the periods during which Cuba would be permitted to ship alligator pears to the American market. In short, Caffery conserved his ammunition for important targets, and especially for sugar.

The commercial attaché in his then separate office in Havana had responsibility for other commodities, but sugar, accounting for upward of 75 percent of Cuban exports, was the lifeblood of the economy. Sugar was the very fabric of Cuban society. Sugar was politics. Therefore sugar was moved from the attaché's office to the embassy chancery, where it received special attention. It became the province of Doc Matthews, and with the ambassador's approval, I became Doc's understudy on sugar. I set myself to learn something about it.

The problem was straightforward, but in practice it was hemmed in by political considerations and irrational restrictions, one effect of which was to lower the return received by the Cuban producer. Another was to raise the price paid by the American consumer.

Sugarcane grows in warm countries. Cane is planted, and months later it is hacked down with a machete — unskilled but very arduous labor. Crushing the cane between steel rollers extracts the juice, which after various treatments produces raw sugar or refined sugar. Along the way, molasses is inescapably produced, which has a variety of uses, including cattle feed, fertilizer, and rum. (It is also possible to make rum direct from the cane juice.) What is left of the stalks when the juice has been squeezed out is bagasse, a cellulose product that can be compressed for fuel.

Those are all relatively intelligible operations involving a variety of skills, from agriculture and industrial engineering to chemistry, railroading, town management, and labor relations. They are all comprehensible even to a layman. The process, from dumping the cane into the hopper in front of the first rollers to the emergence of sticky raw sugar poured from a chute into heavy jute bags that, when filled, weigh 325 pounds each, is impressive but not bewildering.

Not so the marketing, the complexity of which derives from the fact that sugarcane grows in so many places that production tends to outstrip consumption, and that many of the noncane countries elect, for nationalistic reasons, to produce beet sugar at a higher cost than cane. Cane sugar is then further penalized by tariffs or quotas or both.

In the United States, for example, sixteen states produce beet sugar and three (Louisiana, Florida, and Hawaii) produce cane. At times their representatives, the thirty-two sugar senators, have formed the most cohesive, powerful, and disciplined block of legislators in Congress. Their word is literally law insofar as sugar entering the United States from abroad is concerned. Moreover, although under a different system the aggregate savings would be immense, the American consumer is apparently unmoved that a product which at the supermarket might cost five cents a pound instead costs twenty, because sugar is a comparatively minor item in the total spent to fill that day's market basket.

Since 1934 the American market has been divided among domestic and offshore producers, through legislation establishing a series of escalating and contracting formulas that require an army of bureaucrats in the Department of Agriculture to administer. The first objective is to support American producers, who, even with the artificial advantage of tariff and quota, are unable to supply United States requirements, and without formidable protection would not be able to compete at all with foreign lower-cost production. The second objective is to benefit "friendly" producing countries, such as Cuba (until Castro), various other New World suppliers, and the Philippines, while at the same time assuring that American needs will be met. That is done by awarding to foreign producers portions of the so-called American deficit, and since the American price is far above the world price, foreign producers scramble to obtain these quotas and to share in the business. The size of each quota sometimes spells the difference between profit and loss on that country's sugar crop as a whole.

For nearly thirty years, until Castro's behavior left Washington no choice but to close the door, Cuba's United States quota did in fact often represent the difference between poverty and prosperity for that country.

This system resulted, however, in frantic and undignified efforts by Cuba every time quotas came up for revision in the American Congress. In practice it fell to the State Department to advocate the Cuban case, with the Cubans

understandably resenting both their economic dependence and their suppli-
cant relationship. About the best that can be said for the American tariff/
quota system, which added hundreds of millions of dollars to the annual
sugar bill paid by its citizens, is that it corresponded to the political realities
within the United States (including the sugar senators) and that, if humanely
administered in Washington, it would allow Cuba, the lowest-cost producer,
a sufficient share of the American market to sustain the economy of the island, if not to permit it to expand at the rate desired by the Cuban people.

In the last analysis, however, this system could not fail to affect Cuba's
pride, morale, and outlook as a sovereign state. In fact, many Cubans were
later to complain that although the abrogation of the Platt Amendment
freed Cuba from a political servitude, United States sugar legislation perpet-
uated an economic servitude that was equally humiliating and pernicious.

These views, however, were for the future. In the fall of 1934, as the next
grinding season approached, our Cuban friends were much more impressed
by the further drop of 40 percent in the American sugar tariff obtained
through the Trade Agreement Act than they were by the ethics of their long-
time bilateral relationship with the United States.

With its American market controlled by the quota system, Cuba also participated in international agreements seeking to render the world market
less disorderly. The result was the establishment within Cuba of a complex
pattern of regulations that often defied rational analysis. Each of approximately 160 sugar mills received its individual quota based largely on past
performance. Beyond that figure the mill could not grind, regardless of the
amount of cane still standing in the fields. Each quota was then subdivided
into segments representing administration (mill-owned) cane and *colono*
cane, which was grown by adjacent farmers and committed to that mill for
grinding. Since the *colono* farms varied in size from a few acres to thousands
of acres each, the bookkeeping problem alone, in days before computers,
was formidable.

It was arbitrarily established by the Sugar Coordination Law, enacted
while we were in Cuba, that mill-owned cane could not exceed 12 percent of
the total. This was aimed at *latifundismo* (absentee ownership), a favorite
target of the post-Machado liberals (as it was of Ché Guevara and his merry
men, who nearly wrecked production a generation later). On leased land
5 percent of the value of the cane was ruled to be rent. The balance was divided 48 percent to the mill and 47 percent to the grower. The formula for
determining value on which cane-cutting and sugar mill wages were based
was still more convoluted; called the *promedio*, or average, it utilized the

American price, the world market price, and the domestic price, in the proportion that each bore to the total estimated crop.

These and related matters were administered, with remarkable efficiency, by the Cuban Sugar Stabilization Institute, a government agency. Its operations were vigilantly monitored by two other official organizations, the Mill Owners (or Hacendados) Association and the Association of Colonos.[7]

Not all these mysteries were immediately revealed to the fledgling sugar expert of the Havana embassy. There was no lack of willing instructors from our widening circle of Cuban friends, including both *hacendados* and *colonos,* as well as from the American mill owners and managers who during the eight or nine months of the dead season, when their mills were idle, often congregated at the American Club on the Prado with articulate notions about the role of Washington in Cuban-American relations. Their consensus was that until the advent of Dr. Grau and his Auténticos, along with Communist and other agitators bent on poisoning the minds of cane cutters and mill workers against "foreign exploitation," relations between Americans and Cubans on matters pertaining to sugar had remained excellent for years.

The mill owners, whatever their nationality, proved almost homicidally hospitable, so that even before I had learned the sucrose content of blackstrap molasses or the difference between administration and *colono* cane, I found myself invited to visit mills on the island. My indoctrination was facilitated in extraordinarily congenial circumstances. Those invitations not only got me into the glorious Cuban countryside but also encouraged me to carry a shotgun in a land teeming with pigeons, quail, wild guinea fowl, and, from November through February, migratory ducks whose nesting grounds lay icebound. In fact, it was not until my first duck shoot in Cuba that I realized ducks did not have to be pursued in conditions of extreme physical exposure and discomfort.

My affection for the island and for the Cuban people grew with these rural visits. Life on the haciendas had for me all the charm that life on the pampas had a century ago for W. H. Hudson. I awoke each morning with more things to do than one day could possibly encompass, and all of them

---

7. See Dr. Ramiro Guerra's influential and erudite treatise *Azúcar y Población en las Antillas* (Havana, 1927). (An English translation of a later edition was published in 1964 by Yale University Press, under the title *Sugar and Society in the Caribbean.*) The late Dr. Guerra was a personal friend, but I never went along with his proposition that American influence was mainly responsible for converting independent Cuban farmers into a "peasant proletariat." That metamorphosis was achieved by Moscow, not Washington, in the 1960s.

{ P R O U D   S E R V A N T }

delightful. Left to my own devices, I would probably have tried to visit each of the 160 mills scattered from Pinar del Río to Oriente — a project that would have kept me outside the office for most of my tour of duty. As it was, I had to settle for weekends, and splendid weekends they were.

There is something about the Cuban dawn that enriches all subsequent recollection. As the night retreats, gorgeous colors parade across the eastern sky. The dew is heavy, and when the light comes, it clothes each palm frond with diamonds. Out of the earth still warm from yesterday's sun there comes a freshness compounded of moist roots under leaf mold, of opening flowers, and of ripening vegetation. A violent land by day, Cuba wakens gently, but by the time the first golden ray sets the dew ablaze, country people are astir. Wood smoke films the thatched *bohíos*, where coffee from the hills around the Agabama River is mixed with twice its weight of sugar, quick combustion with which the *campesino* greets the daylight.

Those sunrises often found me halfway to Matanzas, eastbound on the Carretera Central, ticking off the kilometer posts on my way to dove shooting in a rice field with a sugar mill close by. That meant I was up by 3 A.M., having declined that Saturday night's frolic, and it often meant a pause, before taking the Central Highway, for scrambled eggs at the Culebrina on the edge of the Vedado, a breakfast consumed while greeting homeward-bound fiesta survivors. When you yourself have a night's rest behind you, there is something eupeptic about encountering friends in crumpled evening clothes, frayed by their indulgences, still trying to prolong yesterday.

Thus fortified, I would remember that my rice field was eighty miles away. Abandoning the Culebrina, I would see that all across the night sky the stars were beginning to flicker. There was a dawn breeze off the Gulf Stream, with the scent of sea grapes in it. The Cuban winter day promised to be fine.

So passed the weeks and months of my Havana assignment. Having watched the economy of the country come back to life, the embassy found itself involved in political developments. Washington prodded us to urge the provisional government to get on with the business of holding democratic elections. That was meddlesome of Washington, but perhaps not so much so as it might have been in other jurisdictions. Many Cubans had become so accustomed to presenting their problems to Tío Sam that they continued to do so, calling upon the United States for assistance in the solution of the recurring dilemmas. That meant that embassy Havana at that time was more concerned than most missions in the domestic affairs of the country. They may have been good or bad, but it was a fact in the political life of Cuba during the 1930s.

Colonel Batista, having acted upon sound advice solicited from Ambassador Caffery, by the middle of 1935 had managed to put down most of the terrorism that had plagued the island ever since Machado fell. There was no longer organized resistance to the provisional government, and the job of pacification had been accomplished with a minimum of repression and bloodshed even though in the process the center of political gravity had shifted from the Presidential Palace toward military headquarters at Camp Columbia.

A main reason for the delay in elections was that the political parties could not agree on an electoral statute setting forth the ground rules. Each group sought to have included provisions that would benefit its own adherents at the expense of other candidates. In that sort of maneuvering the politicians proved as slippery as eels, and as inventive as small boys dreaming up reasons to skip Sunday school. General principles were readily agreed to, often expressed in eloquent phrases that echoed with patriotic fervor, but someone invariably added a gimmick that, when discovered by the opposition, evoked outcries and recriminations in the course of which entire paragraphs and articles previously agreed upon were angrily rejected. Cuban parliamentary lawyers had a genius for that sort of composition. In record time they could produce a statute that appeared to be of general applicability, dedicated to the public good, that, when unraveled, turned out to exempt from taxation a citizen born on February 15, 1912, whose mother's name was Giocochea, and who now lived in Varadero.

Washington became more and more impatient. Nor was Sumner Welles soothed when the politicians took time out to debate, and eventually to enact, a new divorce law the purpose of which, not mentioned, was to divert some of the lucrative matrimonial traffic away from Reno and into the coffers of Havana. While this was cooking, the electoral statute was left in the icebox.[8]

Finally the provisional government appealed to the United States for electoral law assistance, and at that point Doc Matthews, a loyal son of Princeton, had the excellent idea of nominating the president of his university, Dr. Harold Dodds, who, Matthews remembered, had in an earlier incarnation drafted an electoral law for Nicaragua. Apprised of his availability, the provisional government duly extended an invitation.

8. The Cuban divorce law never proved the tourist attraction its proponents anticipated. It remained on the books long enough, however, to be taken advantage of by an appreciable portion of the Havana Social Regis-

Dr. Dodds was a fortunate choice. Not only did he know his electoral onions but he was sagacious and cooperative, and he recognized good diplomatic advice when he heard it.

Reporters present and magnesium flares blazing, Dr. Dodds interviewed officials of the provisional government. He next met separately but openly with leaders of the various political parties except the Auténticos, who, glowering, refused to participate. He then met, in protracted unpublicized sessions, with Dr. Arturo Manas. Manas was not a politician. He was one of the most capable lawyers in Cuba. Matthews, who was not a lawyer, had one of the most practical of minds. He recognized what was needed — a simple and workable statute with no collapsible ballot boxes and no booby traps concealed in the verbiage. Among Manas, Matthews, and Dr. Dodds, with Ambassador Caffery in the background, such a statute was speedily confected within the embassy.

The provisional government bought that text intact, heaving a great sigh of relief. It pinned a decoration upon the departing president of Princeton.

Elections duly took place, and by Caribbean criteria they were fairly held; most of the ballots were counted. On January 10, 1936, Dr. Miguel Mariano Gómez, a veteran *político* of more than average repute, was declared the winner. Washington burst out in a rash of delight, and Miguel Mariano was invited, as president-elect, to visit the United States. His triumphal tour testified to the goodwill of the American people toward Cuba. President Gómez was inaugurated on May 20, 1936, the national holiday of the Republic.

For Sumner Welles it was a day of special satisfaction; for almost the first time since he left Cuba, with the cruiser *Richmond* standing by to evacuate endangered Americans, Mr. Welles believed he could see the light of tranquil progress at the end of a long, corkscrew tunnel.

In Havana, we at the embassy were not so sure. Dr. Gómez had returned from his American trip so filled with the sound of welcoming speeches and of his own patriotic replies that even before Inauguration Day there were signs that he was overestimating his political strength, that he was ignoring the erosion of political power by the military. His American trip may have been fine publicity for the Good Neighbor Policy, but it had dangerously inflated his own self-confidence. We apprehended that should President Gómez attempt prematurely to restore to the presidency the power it had wielded before the fall of Machado, that effort could set him on a collision course with Colonel Batista, who had long since ceased to be the bewildered victor of the Hotel Nacional battle. Batista had grown into a tough and seasoned *político,* accustomed to command.

Unfortunately for himself, President Gómez chose to challenge the chief of staff not only too soon but on the worst terrain Gómez could have chosen, the area of rural education.

Fulgencio Batista was born in poverty in a small town near the northeast coast of Cuba. He grew up beside one of the United Fruit Company estates, empty land that was rapidly being transformed, with a huge investment of American capital, energy, and foresight, into one of the great sugar plantations of the Caribbean, giving employment to hundreds of Cubans at wage levels never approached during the preceding four centuries. Batista's childhood was nevertheless impoverished. Apologists were later to declare that his attitude toward "big business" derived from this early experience, viewing the gap between the lush living of the "exploiters" and the condition of the peasant farmers of eastern Cuba. The accuracy of this estimate is debatable; the fact is that Batista rose through his own qualities of determination and leadership, first to staff sergeant at army headquarters and then to *jefe político.* This was in itself a refutation of the notion that Cuba was a land where opportunities were limited by wealth, favoritism, or family.

Batista was sincere in his desire to improve the conditions of life in rural Cuba, which was most of the island. Having worked hard to acquire a limited education, he was especially determined that every youngster should have access to at least the rudiments of knowledge. In furtherance of this ambition the project closest to Batista's heart was the *escuela rural,* the Cuban equivalent of the little red schoolhouse of nineteenth-century New England. Utilizing the Cuban Army, Batista was establishing such schools as fast as they could be built.

In my travels outside Havana I had stumbled upon a number of these small enterprises, and I had seen what they were doing. By 1936 my sugar mill/hunting trips had taken me all the way from Cape Maisí, beside the Windward Passage, almost within sight of the blue hills of Haiti, to Cape San Antonio, which juts into the Yucatán Channel facing Mexico. Each school was taught by a noncommissioned soldier, often recruited by taking a country schoolteacher and putting him in uniform, a step that improved the economic status of the teacher while giving him increased prestige in the community.

Each little school was built of palm, with thatched roof and open windows, and a small playground around it. Tall trees often shaded the area. The advent of a foreigner carrying a shotgun occasioned immediate interest. The teacher assenting, I used to recruit a couple of boys to shinny up a palm trunk and knock down a coconut, the green end of which was then sliced off with a machete so that the parched visitor could clap his lips to the cool *agua de coco*, the most refreshing drink a tired hunter can find in the tropics.

Education followed a leisurely pace in an *escuela rural*. My thirst for coconut water quenched, I would be invited to rest beside the teacher's *bohío* with a cup of sizzling, overpoweringly sweet black coffee, while we gossiped about education and the probable whereabouts of wild guinea fowl, which the teacher remembered having heard along the edge of a canebrake a few hundred meters down the road. Yes, he could spare the two tree-climbing boys; the place was beyond that patch of *manigua* brush where the land sloped toward the river. The boys could show me the way. Along the bank there was also a *dormitorio* of pigeons. Later in the day, if luck had smiled upon our efforts, I would leave a wild guinea or perhaps a pair of slate blue *torcaza* doves at the teacher's *bohío*.

Back in Havana, Ambassador Caffery encouraged me to report some of these encounters to Colonel Batista, whose interest was affable and intelligent. Batista knew his countryside. The questions he asked showed a grasp that would have done credit to the minister of education. There was no doubt but that the *escuela rural* was the apple of the eye of the chief of staff of the army.

Colonel Batista now proposed to establish, in order to accelerate his school-building program, a small per bag tax on sugar that would be easy to collect because the production statistics were already on record. The tax would require legislation, but a new Congress had been elected along with the new chief executive and, following the inauguration of President Gómez, the legislature was in session.

This, then, was the proposal that President Gómez decided to oppose in order, as he saw it, to reestablish the supremacy of civilian administration and at the same time put the military in general, and Colonel Batista in particular, back in its place.

The president announced that he opposed the tax bill. The tax bill was passed. President Gómez vetoed it, and the pig was in the fire.

We warned Washington, but such was the euphoria produced by the Gómez visit to the United States, where he had been entertained by both President Roosevelt and Secretary Hull, and by the peaceful inauguration in Havana (the end, Washington hoped, of the long revolutionary period), that the warning predictions of the embassy did not really sink in. At least they did not sink in until we cabled, shortly before Christmas 1936, that President Gómez was being impeached by Congress and that his prospects for survival did not look good.

Washington's yelp was pure anguish, and it was simultaneously implied that if Miguel Mariano were thrown to the dogs, Embassy Havana might find itself in the doghouse. He was, and we were.

The impeachment proceedings were based, with an irony typical of Cuban politics, not on the president's having vetoed a piece of tax legislation; President Gómez was so clearly within his constitutional rights as to be impregnable on that score. He was instead impeached for allegedly having used improper tactics, before the bill was passed, in an attempt to block passage of the measure. Various legislators deposed to that effect, declaring that they had been the objects of a gross abuse of executive power disrespectful of the Congress and demeaning to the dignity of its members. This was declared in the indictment to demonstrate President Gómez's unfitness to discharge the duties of the high office to which he had mistakenly been elected. The facts of the situation were precisely the reverse: Batista had used the kinds of pressure of which Miguel Mariano was accused in order to obtain congressional approval of the measure that the president then vetoed. But Batista controlled the legislators. The adherents of the president were shouted down.

The final proceedings took place at night — our Latin cousins seem to have an incurable preference for nocturnal adventures — and Ambassador Caffery arranged, via the Bailarina, to have a play-by-play rendering of the drama telephoned from the Capitolio to Doc Matthews at the chancery. The ambassador, having accurately gauged the situation, went home to bed.

In Congress, 'twas the night before Christmas, and all through the house every creature was stirring — and the mouse was the unfortunate Miguel Mariano Gómez.

I remember dozing while Doc and I waited for the final word, my chin on the blotter on the top of my desk. Our code clerk waited upstairs. We had a message ready to encipher except for the voting score on the impeachment charges. It was a carefully drafted cable already approved by the ambassador, and we were aware that it would not cause joy beside the Potomac. In substance, the embassy declared that we shared Washington's disappointment at this distressing turn of events. Many honest Cubans could not but decry this harsh resort to dictatorial methods, this prostitution of the democratic process (which we put in because it was true and also because it looked good on the record).

The message went on to point out, however, that Dr. Gómez had been extraordinarily reckless in challenging Batista almost at the outset of his administration, before his own political strength had been tested, and on an issue where popular sentiment could not be mobilized to support his position. The message observed that much as we might deplore the situation created by the Gómez-Batista clash, the steps.taken by Congress were in accord (we did not say "strict accord") with the constitution, and that immediately following the vote of impeachment the vice president, Dr. Federico Laredo Bru, had been sworn in as chief of state. He was even now the president of Cuba.

Since the constitution had been complied with, the embassy remarked (rather meanly) that no question arose over extending recognition; President Laredo Bru represented a legal continuation of the previous administration.

Washington gagged, but Batista had won his ball game and Washington knew it. The matter of recognition was not raised by the State Department, and the embassy continued to do business with the constituted authorities. Moreover, Laredo Bru made a surprisingly successful president. A veteran, as was Mendieta, of the Cuban War of Independence, Laredo Bru was a rather colorless replica of his more hearty predecessor. But Laredo Bru was enough of a political realist to comprehend where the power lay; he acted with circumspection. The angry waters quickly subsided.

The embassy was accused in various quarters of having engineered the Gómez impeachment. That was nonsense. We knew Miguel Mariano personally and liked him. We knew that he was genuinely friendly to the United States. Laredo Bru was an unknown quality. There was no conceivable profit in seeking the downfall of the first elected president of Cuba in a decade. Had Dr. Gómez discussed his proposed veto in advance, Ambassador Caffery would doubtless have indicated the political folly of his course. The ambassador could be sharp and direct in a private conversation. But Gómez returned to Havana from the American visit with his self-esteem so inflated that no such talk took place. Had Batista, on the other hand, raised with Caffery the subject of possible impeachment, the ambassador would almost certainly have sought to discourage him, if only on the grounds of complicating Batista's relations with Washington — which was exactly what happened.[9]

Ambassador Caffery had now been dealing with Cuba for approaching four years, and he watched with satisfaction as the Laredo Bru administration settled into the groove of government in frictionless collaboration with Camp Columbia. It was, his colleagues in the embassy agreed, as good a government as Cuba was likely to get in the immediate future, and it was

9. By 1938, two years after the impeachment of Gómez, Batista was so forgiven in Washington that the State Department did not object to an invitation extended to the chief of staff of the army to visit military installations in the United States.

certainly an improvement over the last elected administration, which ended with the revolution against Machado. Reaching Havana in a period of chaos, with an unfriendly eccentric unrecognized by the United States in the saddle, Mr. Caffery had witnessed immense changes along the Malecón. By the quiet and effective use of his office, combined with uncommon professional skill, the ambassador had influenced those changes to a marked degree and in directions favorable to the relations between Cuba and the United States.

No self-advertising ambassador, Caffery had made few public speeches. His lack of soaring oratory disappointed listeners accustomed to forensic acrobatics (as many Cubans were), but that was not Mr. Caffery's way. Adulation was not his goal. Respect, yes, but not applause from the bleachers. Moreover, much of his day-to-day work was done behind the scenes without attracting public attention, or else conducted through trusted members of his staff whose devotion to "the Chief" testified to the quality of his leadership. Caffery got results with a minimum of commotion.

Notwithstanding the disappointment that prevailed in Washington over the Gómez impeachment, Ambassador Caffery's achievements were recognized in our own capital when, in 1937, Secretary Hull proposed that he be transferred to Rio de Janeiro, then the most important capital in Latin America. President Roosevelt endorsed the move, and Sumner Welles, albeit still shaking his head over Colonel Batista's abrupt disposal of Dr. Gómez, agreed.

The group of officers whom Doc Matthews had assembled in 1933 for Ambassador Caffery was disbanded. Doc was assigned to embassy Paris, and although he still had twenty-five years of service ahead of him — when he retired in 1962, he was the ranking officer in the entire Foreign Service — he never returned to Latin America, for whose apparently incurable problems he expressed increasing distaste. Walter Donnelly, our able and civilized commercial attaché, accompanied Ambassador Caffery to Rio. He was to conclude his career, after several ambassadorships, as high commissioner to Germany. Nonie Griggs, the ambassador's private secretary, who used to grumble whenever the Bailarina came in because the Bailarina used the same expensive perfume as Nonie's wife, also headed for Brazil with the ambassador.[10]

10. Many years later, at a State Department ceremony in November 1971 honoring Jefferson Caffery on the approach of his eighty-fifth birthday, the citation noted that during his forty-five years in diplomacy, two-thirds of them as chief of mission accredited to six different countries, more than two dozen of Caffery's "trainees" later became ambassadors. That record, which has never been approached in the American diplomatic service, included seven men who had served with him in Havana.

One of Nonie's early tasks in Brazil was to make the arrangements for an ambassadorial wedding, celebrated in the Cathedral of Rio de Janeiro. There Jefferson Caffery, to the chagrin of the society scribes in Havana, who had repeatedly sought to connect his name with one or another lovely and eligible Cuban candidate, married Miss Gertrude McCarthy of Chicago.

After Cuba, I found myself returning to Washington as assistant chief of the Latin American Division under Larry Duggan. My wife and I were pleased. Lucy said it was high time that our Auténtico son started learning American English to go with his Cuban Spanish.

President Roosevelt Conducts Foreign Policy

The position of chief of a State Department geographic division in the 1930s was not an exalted one, but neither was it insignificant. The chief and his assistant were close enough to the focus of decision making to watch power as a functioning phenomenon. Just as the State Department itself was physically next door to the White House in that enlightened era, so the papers we drafted were frequently carried to President Roosevelt by the secretary of state. When one of our documents was approved, sensations of accomplishment gladdened the author.

Proximity to wielders of political power also allowed the observer to witness their weaknesses. In the decades since Franklin Roosevelt's death, his stature as a world statesman has been exhaustively debated. By contrast, the impact of Roosevelt on the *conduct* of foreign affairs has received less attention. Winston Churchill is reported to have said, "War is too important to be left to the generals." President Roosevelt paraphrased that by denigrating his appointed diplomatic officials, repeatedly going over their heads or gleefully organizing end runs around them. Sometimes ignoring his ambassadors, at other times Roosevelt injected himself into operational details. Disciplined evaluation of foreign situations was not the rule in the White House; the professional who dealt in facts was often replaced by the necromancer who dealt in bubbles.

By belittling diplomats Roosevelt impaired the prestige of their office, thus lowering the ability of diplomats to serve him. In this the president acted within his constitutional prerogatives, but on the corps of commissioned officers known as the Foreign Service the effect was often adverse and at times almost lethal.

Professional diplomats would agree that there exists a "feel" for diplomacy, and for what at a given moment may be feasible or possible in the relations of one country with another. They are also inclined to give weight to the lessons of history, and to draw upon their own accumulated experience.

They have learned that few situations in foreign affairs can be solved by an inspired equation, or even by a stroke of genius. Most international problems yield, when they do yield, to the mounting pressure of events rather than to a magic formula. Thus diplomats generally mistrust adventurism, not because they themselves are not adventurous but because it has produced so few successes.

In his relations with a superior the Foreign Service officer is sometimes cast in the unhappy role of a Cassandra. That role is seldom applauded by those on whose behalf it is exercised, and in the case of President Roosevelt it also ran counter to his penchant for playing hunches. This included an early one that soon developed into the conviction that he himself possessed a unique flair for diplomatic operations.

Most presidents absorbed in policy decisions direct, but they do not implement. Not so the thirty-second president of the United States, who was rarely happier than when he was tinkering with a piece of government machinery. He derived a perverse pleasure from taking a complicated gadget apart blindfolded, to show he was good at it, and then trying to reassemble the pieces. When he found a pocketful of wheels and springs left over, the presidential solution was to appoint a commission or to pound the machine with a hammer.

In the realm of Foreign Service management the first such exercise that I witnessed had to do with the kinds of women that President Roosevelt thought his diplomats should marry; the second involved the eligibility of diplomats for military service.

As to the first, the American ambassador to the Soviet Union had complained that there were not enough American women in his mission. William Bullitt had gone to Moscow following a decade of compaigning in favor of resuming diplomatic relations with Russia. As a friend of Roosevelt he had played a part in the Roosevelt-Litvinov agreement in 1933 whereby relations were restored. When shortly thereafter Bullitt presented his credentials in the Kremlin as American ambassador, he was still convinced that cordial relations with the Soviet government might follow. Able, but quarrelsome and opinionated, Bullitt at that time had direct access to the White House; in communicating with the president he did not always bother to go through the State Department.

The State Department, desiring to give Ambassador Bullitt the strongest possible backing, picked officers of superior ability to serve with him in Moscow. The ranking officer was John Wiley, whose performance as counselor in Madrid I had admired in the Western European Division. A junior was George Kennan, who a decade later was to galvanize the Truman administration with his memorandum on the sources of Soviet conduct, which message led to the doctrine of containment.

Ambassador Bullitt, a Main Line Philadelphia product, had not remarried after his divorce, and therefore the wife of the counselor was his ranking lady, the ambassador's official hostess. What the State Department had failed to note or, perhaps noting, had dismissed as of secondary importance, was that neither Wiley nor Kennan had a native-born American wife. Mrs. Wiley was Polish; Mrs. Kennan, Norwegian. Both were naturalized American citizens, and each was a talented lady. (Charles Thayer was then a bachelor.)

With his cosmopolitan background it is doubtful whether the ambassador was trying to establish a Little America in the heart of Red Russia. Nevertheless, what Bullitt wanted, clearly, was "American, not foreign, women." He demanded that something be done about it.

The first intimation of trouble to reach the State Department was a presidential request for information about "foreign wives married to Foreign Service officers." In the Division of Personnel noses were quickly counted. Upward of 20 percent of the wives of Foreign Service officers had been born outside the United States. That, commented the Division of Personnel, was an understandable proportion in an organization whose entering candidates were in their twenties — many of them going abroad as bachelors — eligible, personable, and not unattractive to indigenous maidens. Almost without exception the foreign-born wives had become naturalized American citizens. Almost without exception they were loyal to their adopted country and dedicated to the advancement of the careers of their husbands.

When informed of "upward of 20 percent," President Roosevelt, incited by Bullitt, caught fire. He decreed that henceforth Foreign Service officers must obtain in advance the secretary of state's permission to marry a foreigner. To underline his view of such nefarious mating, the president added that together with a request for permission to marry, each officer must tender his resignation. Investigating the character and antecedents of the bride thus became a preliminary to granting permission or to accepting the resignation — whichever happened first.

With my American wife I was not vulnerable to this ukase, but I was incensed by it. The regulation itself was offensive, and the insult to foreign-born wives seemed both unwarranted and gratuitous. In the decade since I went forth as a vice consul, I had come to know a good many foreign-born wives; all except one had been assets to their husbands. Some of them had proved more cosmopolitan than their American-born sisters. Some had fit more smoothly into the Foreign Service. Their culture shock was less, possibly because they generally spoke more languages than American brides did. In sum, the foreign-born wives, now naturalized American citizens, were assets to their husbands and to the Foreign Service alike.

The humane way to handle a situation such as the one complained of by Ambassador Bullitt would have been through a confidential circular. (Such documents, in the days before copies, did not find their way almost automatically to the press.) A circular could have acknowledged the contribution of wives — all wives — to the success of a diplomatic career. It could then have pointed out that as a practical matter, at a time of mounting international tensions the country of origin of the spouse was one of the factors that had to be taken into account in personnel placement. Thus an officer married to the daughter of a French official might not be assigned to Berlin, nor one married to the niece of a Loyalist leader, to Franco Spain. Such an admonition, plus alertness on the part of the Personnel Board itself, should have sufficed. That might even have pacified Bill Bullitt, who was often as generous as he was short-tempered.

Brooding about these things in my cubicle surrounded by the Good Neighbors, I concluded that President Roosevelt's diktat was temptingly vulnerable to ridicule. I decided to take a poke at it. Thus was invented my articulate protégé, a fictitious bureaucrat named J. Sediment Peachpit, with the obsolete but impressive title "vice and deputy consul, at large."

J. Sediment Peachpit helped me to concoct an article for the *Foreign Service Journal,* the house organ of the Foreign Service. The president was accused of fomenting immorality among his commissioned officers by encouraging them to lead foreign maidens up the garden path of romance, past the violets by a mossy stone, beyond the bluebells, and into the soft, inviting heather. There, the junior diplomatist found himself encouraged by his chief executive to declare to his inamorata, "Look, darling, I love you madly. I want to marry you, but the president of the United States says that I can't marry you. I love you, darling, so let's pretend . . . ."

The piece was not destined to see the light of day. The head of Foreign Service Personnel got wind of it in time to convince the editor of the *Foreign Service Journal* of the unwisdom of lampooning the chief executive of the United States, who did, after all, personally sign our commissions. Possibly that was fortunate for my careeer as a Foreign Service officer. I reluctantly discarded the article. In the event, the Roosevelt ban, as insulting to two hundred alien-born wives of American diplomats as it was undeserved, remained in effect for several years.[1]

President Roosevelt's other contribution did the Foreign Service more lasting damage than his matrimonial tantrum. By equating Foreign Service officers with draft dodgers, he undermined the morale of the entire organization.

During World War I the members of the then separate diplomatic and consular services were discouraged from joining the armed services on the grounds that they were already officers commissioned by the president, and that their training and experience in foreign affairs would be especially valuable in the wartime performance of their duties. It was pointed out that the five hundred diplomatic and consular officers of 1917 represented an insignificant drop in the manpower bucket, and that each individual would be more useful continuing to serve the Department of State than he would be in uniform.

In 1941 there were twelve hundred Foreign Service officers, an even smaller proportional drop in the World War II military manpower bucket than the 1917 contingent had been. Most officers assumed that the practice followed during World War I would be continued. Most were in agreement that the sensible as well as patriotic duty was to remain in the diplomatic service. A few officers with military service antedating entry into the State Department made the switch. Others, including several service academy graduates who were exceptionally competent as Foreign Service officers and certainly were not lacking in patriotism, likewise remained with the Department of State.

The announcement came as a shock, therefore, that Foreign Service officers within the eligible age bracket were required to register for the draft, their individual status to be a matter for decision by the corresponding draft board. That meant that a Foreign Service officer whose number was drawn had to plead his own case for deferment before a local board whose members might not have heard of the Foreign Service or might not have any understanding of the duties performed by the officer under his presidential commission. The State Department was prohibited from intervening with a draft board on an officer's behalf.

---

1. A generation later the State Department had become so cowed in its relations with "grievants" — in practice, almost any petty bureaucrat whose sense of self-importance outweighed his sense of responsibility — that a regulation was issued prohibiting reporting officers from making any mention whatsoever either of wives or of the husbands of female officers. Spouses have been banished from diplomacy — as far a cry from one end of the spectrum of common sense as was the Roosevelt/Bullitt order from the other.

The matter was taken up with the White House, but there is no record that anyone with sufficient authority influenced a president who was not favorably disposed toward professional diplomacy, and who himself had three sons in uniform.

To the credit of the common sense of local draft boards, few Foreign Service officers were drafted, but the registration requirement, plus the procedures for waivers and deferments that had to be applied for as individuals, were humiliating to personnel proud of their Foreign Service heritage, who had anticipated that their wartime status would be a matter of State Department responsibility and intervention.

At the same time this was going on, with diplomatic personnel immobilized while cases were being processed, a State Department trying to cope with the mounting pressure of war-related business found it necessary to establish an Auxiliary Corps, and then to compete with the draft boards in finding people to staff it.

Morale among Foreign Service officers was further impaired when the Personnel Board began transferring officers from one foreign post to another without returning them to the United States. At the end of his tour of duty in Karachi, say, an officer was transferred to Montevideo. But instead of bringing him back to Washington for the customary consultation and indoctrination between assignments, he was shipped directly from Asia to South America, thus avoiding the possibility of being drafted.

Parallel with these developments Foreign Service officers were being exposed to most of the hazards of war, barring only combat duty itself. They were torpedoed at sea, they were crash-landed in airplanes, and they were exposed to the bombing in London and other capitals. Many were interned with their families in enemy countries.

As to the personal safety aspects of diplomacy as a career, the following item is pertinent. When the American Foreign Service Protective Association, a private organization for insuring Foreign Service personnel, was established several years before World War II, the underwriter placed those insured in the "extra-hazardous risk" category, a classification then shared with tightrope artists, policemen, balloonists, parachute jumpers, and "soldiers and sailors in wartime."

President Roosevelt himself utilized the services of few Foreign Service officers. The case of Robert Murphy, who negotiated with the French prior to the 1942 African landings, was so unusual as to seem remarkable. More typical of the president's attitude was his treatment of his consul general at Casablanca and his minister in Tehran during the wartime conferences at those cities. In each case Prime Minister Churchill, aware of the connection in foreign affairs between prestige and performance and of the inherent fragility of the former, saw to it that although the British resident might play no substantive role in the deliberations, he was included as a member of the official delegation. At Casablanca the American consul general, an experienced and capable officer, did not even have a pass admitting him to the official enclosure. In Iran the American minister was evicted from his own legation.

To the failure to make better use of the Foreign Service during the war was added Roosevelt's diplomacy by "special representative with the personal rank of ambassador." Those emissaries, often with no prior experience in foreign affairs, descended upon American diplomatic missions like the locusts of old, arriving with little or no advance notice to the president's resident representative or with terms of reference incomprehensible even to the special representative himself. The confusion they created was immense, and in most cases the information they brought back to Washington was already available there.[2]

The Foreign Service emerged from the war with its influence and self-confidence considerably shaken. Worse days were ahead, and some of the later problems had their roots in the Roosevelt era of diplomacy-charmed-with-the-sound-of-its-own-voice. As chief executive, Roosevelt seriously damaged the foreign affairs apparatus of the American government; he eroded its strength, and he diminished its ability to serve the American people.

2. Toward the end of the war there was invented the position of political adviser, a senior Foreign Service officer accredited not to a country or to a post but to an American commanding general or admiral who, it was conceded, might be in need of advice in dealing with allies, neutrals, and, later, the civilian officers of the vanquished. The position of political adviser still exists.

{ P R O U D   S E R V A N T }

The young Briggs in 1925, about to begin his career.

Foreign Service Class of 1926 (second and third rows).
Ellis Briggs is second from the right, second row.

Lucy Barnard Briggs and Ellis O. Briggs aboard ship, December 1928.

Ellis and Lucy pose in front of their residence in Lima, Peru, 1928.

At home in Lima.

The Santa Rosa, *first of its kind in South America, was commissioned in August 1929.
It was the first of five similar aircraft used for the Talara-to-Santiago mail and passenger run.*

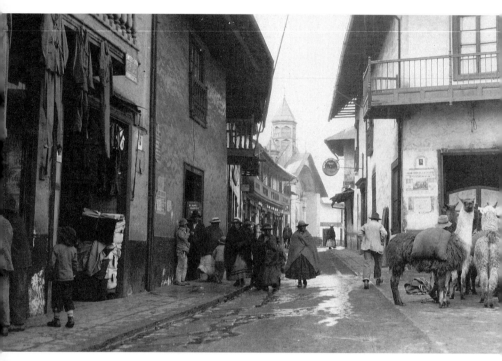

*Cerro de Pasco during a snowstorm.
Note the llamas huddled together at the bar doorway.*

(opposite top)
*In 1944, Ellis Briggs presented his credentials to Rafael Leonidas Trujillo Molina,
president of the Dominican Republic.*
(opposite bottom)
Ellis O. Briggs, U.S. ambassador to the Dominican Republic, 1944.

Briggs is interviewed upon his arrival at LaGuardia Airport from Montevideo, Uruguay, September 1947.

Lucy and Everett Briggs join their parents at the U.S. Embassy in Montevideo, June 1949.

The Briggs family in full hunting regalia in Uruguay, July 1949.

A weekend hunting trip with the family dog, "Cartucho" (Cartridge).

(top) *Ambassador to Czechoslovakia Ellis O. Briggs presents his credentials to Klement Gottwald, 1950.*
(bottom) *The new ambassador is escorted past troops, Prague 1950. (The Communists kept the top hats!)*

(top) *At home, Petschek Palace in 1951 (the U.S. Embassy residence in Prague).*
(bottom) *The Briggs family in Prague: Lucy T., Ellis, Lucy Barnard, and Everett (Ted).*

Adlai Stevenson (center) speaks to guests at a reception held by
the American embassy in Korea in his honor, March 15, 1953.
Left to right are Brigadier General Homer Case, General Wang Pung-Yuan
(Nationalist Chinese ambassador to Korea), Mr. Stevenson,
Brigadier General Lionel C. McGarr, Brigadier General Lewis Hamblen,
and the Honorable Ellis O. Briggs.

(opposite) U.S. Ambassador to Korea Ellis Briggs poses for an informal photo with
General Mark W. Clark, commander in chief of Army Forces Far East, during
the general's visit to Pusan in January 1953. (Courtesy U.S. Army)

Lucy Briggs meets with PFC Daniel Sugure on April 18, 1953, upon his release after two years as a POW. He is dressed in the clothes the Communists gave him. (Courtesy U.S. Army)

Ambassador Briggs talks with newly released prisoner of war Corporal Harold Humphries, August 18, 1953. (Courtesy U.S. Army)

Gathering in Seoul in 1953 on the occasion of the signing of the Mutual Assistance Treaty were (left to right) Mrs. Briggs, Mrs. Rhee, President Syngman Rhee, unidentified man, Secretary of State John Foster Dulles, and Ambassador Briggs.

A time for celebration: the Mutual Assistance Treaty signing.
Shown left to right are Ambassador Briggs, President Rhee, and General Maxwell Taylor

*Posing aboard the
USS* New Jersey *on
September 15, 1953, were
(left to right)
General Maxwell Taylor,
Ambassador Ellis Briggs,
President Rhee, Mrs. Briggs,
Mrs. Rhee, and
officers of the ship.*

*U.S. Ambassador to
Korea Briggs and officers
of the USS* New Jersey
*review troops, September
1953.*

*Ceremonies welcoming
U.S. Vice President Richard M. Nixon
to Korea, November 12, 1953, were
attended by (left to right) Ellis Briggs,
Mr. Nixon, General John E. Hull,
Lieutenant General S. E. Anderson,
and General Maxwell Taylor.
(Courtesy U.S. Army)*

*On the first day of his visit to
Korea, November 12, 1953,
Vice President Nixon called on
South Korea's president Syngman Rhee.
At left is General John Hull;
Ambassador Briggs is at right.
(Courtesy U.S. Army)*

With the aid of a translator, Ambassador Briggs speaks at the ROK Marine Corps' fifth anniversary celebration, April 15, 1954. President Rhee is seated at left. (Courtesy U.S. Army)

The President of the United States of America, authorized by Executive Order July 6, 1945, has awarded the Medal of Freedom to

THE HONORABLE ELLIS O. BRIGGS, AMERICAN CIVILIAN

for meritorious service:

The Honorable Ellis O. Briggs distinguished himself by exceptionally meritorious service as United States Ambassador to the Republic of Korea from 25 November 1952 to 12 April 1955. Mr. Briggs served with distinction in the solution of many complex problems of lasting importance to the United Nations and Far East Commands. In December 1953, he materially assisted in the formulation of plans for the establishment of a basic economic agreement which set up the mechanism for United States aid to the Republic of Korea. Equally noteworthy was his prominent role in negotiating the United States-Republic of Korea mutual assistance treaty, recently ratified. Mr. Briggs' notable achievements, characterized by forceful leadership, astute judgment, rare diplomacy and outstanding cooperation with the Commander in Chief, Far East Command; Commanding General, Eighth Army and Economic Coordinator for Korea, enhanced the prestige of American foreign policy, furthered the missions and objectives of the United Nations Command, and reflected credit upon himself and the United States Government.

Presidential Citation for Briggs for his accomplishments in Korea.

Ambassador Briggs (seated second from right) received an honorary degree from Dartmouth in 1955.

Assistant Secretary of State Henry Holland congratulates Ellis Briggs
on his appointment as U.S. ambassador to Peru.

Ambassador and Mrs. Briggs, off to Peru in 1955.

*Met at the Hotel Bolivar by the Chief of Protocol, U.S. Ambassador to
Peru Ellis O. Briggs prepares to depart for the Presentation of Credentials.*

National anthems are played at the beginning of the Presentation of Credentials.

Introductions are made at the Presentation of Credentials.

On home leave in New York in 1955, Ellis and Lucy Briggs were guests of honor at a banquet given by Ambassador Spruille Braden, Briggs's old chief from Cuba and the Department of State.

Ellis Briggs congratulates his daughter, Lucy T. Briggs, on becoming a Foreign Service Officer in August 1957. Lucy became the third member of the Briggs family to join the career Foreign Service, as her brother Everett had joined the previous year.

Mr. and Mrs. Louis Armstrong were entertained by Ambassador and Mrs. Briggs in Rio de Janeiro, 1958.

Ellis Briggs with his daughter, Lucy, and son, Everett, all career Foreign Service officers.

U.S. Ambassador to Greece Ellis Briggs attends a ceremony in Palzia in 1961, in which the town honored its native son Nick of the Gotham (next to Briggs). The honoree, a humble man, had saved all of his money to rebuild the village church.

Taking a break from duties, Ellis Briggs enjoys the scenery near Athens, December 1962.

Ellis O. Briggs in 1968, after his retirement to Hanover, New Hampshire, where he continued to support his alma mater, Dartmouth College.

The Secretary and the Undersecretary

When in 1933 the president-elect announced that he proposed to name Cordell Hull to be his secretary of state, the country applauded the appointment of the dignified Tennessee senator to the number one Cabinet position. Hull liked being secretary of state of the United States, even though President Roosevelt repeatedly undercut his authority. For most of his eleven years at the State Department, Hull's political position was impregnable, so we used to wonder why he took so little action on his own behalf. It was true, as Drew Pearson was to point out, that "the Tennessee Mountaineer often got his man" — referring to the various people foisted on the State Department whose tenures were comparatively brief — but the record nevertheless showed a procession of incidents indicating something less than enthusiastic support in the one place where confidence most counted in Washington: the White House.

We in the State Department concluded that Hull stayed on because he loved his job, because the work fascinated him, and because the prestige of the office attracted him even if the corresponding power was sometimes withheld.

In the summer of 1940 Secretary Hull invited me to accompany him to the Havana Conference, with the title of personal assistant. For those ten days I lived down the corridor from his suite in the Hotel Nacional on four or five hours of sleep a night, while my chief was mobilizing the hemisphere against the rising menace of Hitler's Germany. His entourage consisted of his office director, Joe Gray; his secretary, Milly Asbjornsen; a handful of senior advisers; and Mrs. Hull. I acted as a sort of diplomatic caddy, counting strokes, chasing lost balls, interpreting here and there, and doing chores and errands that my familiarity with the city supposedly facilitated.

Whether it did or not was perhaps debatable, although I did manage to attract the favorable notice of the press by finding a small restaurant two blocks away in the Vedado where the American correspondents in town to cover the proceedings could eat a breakfast of fruit, scrambled eggs, bacon, coffee, rolls, and butter — all for forty-five cents. I waged an uphill battle against my Cuban friends who, seeing my name on the official list, rallied around with hospitable intent, unable to understand why fun and games did not figure prominently on the agenda of an international meeting staged in the capital city of the Pearl of the Antilles.

I was gratified when former Sergeant Batista, now president of the Republic, greeted me at the inaugural reception, and several members of his Cabinet added, "Qué tal, chico; qué te pasa?" I was less gratified when in the hotel elevator I encountered a Cuban friend of my wife, wearing conspicuous quantities of makeup, whose welcoming *abrazo* ended in a squeak of fright as she identified the gentlemen I was escorting. My attempt to present the secretary of state to the lush and lively Gloria ended when the elevator reached the lobby. "My God, Ellis. Love to Lucy. So sorry . . ." and Gloria fled in a cloud of lily-of-the-valley by Houbigant.

Mr. Hull made no comment until we were in the automobile taking us to the *Capitolio*, where the official sessions of the conference were held. "You seem," he said, "to know a lot of people in Havana." I mumbled something about four years in our embassy with Ambassador Caffery. "If I were you," continued Mr. Hull, "I'd rub off that lipstick before we get to the meeting."

The conference got under way with speeches made one after the other by the heads of the twenty-one delegations, most of whom were foreign ministers of their respective countries. Their orations were mainly for sound effect or for home consumption and publicity, and Mr. Hull endured them with remarkable fortitude. He sat in the front row beside a placard reading "Estados Unidos de América," and I sat directly behind him, assisted by Dr. González, a Cuban lawyer on the staff of our embassy in Havana, who was bilingual. Behind us were the rest of the American delegation, including Harry Dexter White of the Treasury Department, a quarrelsome type whose nocturnal altercations from his bedroom included shouted insistence that he, Harry Dexter White, was "the world's greatest expert on monetary gold." What else he was I did not then find out, because I caused the hotel desk to order him either to pipe down or else close his transom. He chose the latter.

During a pause between opening speeches at the *Capitolio*, I heard Dr. González explaining to the secretary that when Chief Justice Hughes headed the American delegation at the 1928 conference, he told González not to bother to translate anything that was said before a speaker's first "but." After the first "but," Mr. Hughes instructed him to begin summarizing in English translation. Mr. Hughes's theory was that prior to "but," nothing of importance was likely to occur in a speech delivered in Spanish, whereas afterward something of substance might be said.

Secretary Hull expressed interest. Behind the lectern the Argentine delegate, immersed in the perfidy of Albion in the matter of "Las Islas Malvinas,"[1] was clearly some distance away from his first *pero*.

As Chief Justice Hughes had predicted, so it turned out. Following the first *pero* there was enough substance so that when the applause died down, Secretary Hull got the floor to declare that the statement of his eloquent colleague constituted a further proof of the necessity of having the American republics stand united for their individual and collective security. That was hardly what the Argentine foreign minister meant, but it was useful to Mr. Hull to say it.

When we were not attending sessions at the *Capitolio,* Mr. Hull went calling on his fellow delegates, seeking to line them up in favor of his "an attack on one is an attack on all" thesis. At Mr. Hull's first Latin American conference, at Montevideo in 1933, with a number of delegations gunning for the United States over Cuba, the secretary had disarmed hostile critics by making personal calls on them, beginning almost as soon as he disembarked in Uruguay. He had emphasized the importance of the new Good Neighbor Policy as an antidote for the ill-advised actions of a less enlightened era, and he assured foreign officials that the Roosevelt administration would not be averse to a resolution declaring that intervention by one country in the affairs of another country was sinful. The Latinos lapped it up.

Similar tactics at Lima five years later fortified Mr. Hull's belief that person-to-person diplomacy was a sound way to do business with Latin American officials, so we were hardly ashore in Havana before I was on the phone making appointments.

Our arrangements were simplified because nearly all the delegations were housed with us in the Hotel Nacional, along with the newspaper correspondents, who found out what was up as soon as Mr. Hull's visits began. They wrote friendly cables about the down-to-earth initiative on the part of the American delegate.

---

1. Argentina signed with reluctance, after much kicking and screaming. For a diverting account of the conference from the River Plate point of view, the reader is referred to *La Esposa del Embajador* (The Ambassador's Wife [Buenos Aires, 1967]), written by the American-born wife of Ambassador Felipe Espil, one of Argentina's most distinguished representatives, who served in Washington from 1933 to 1943.

Repeating to the secretary of state the gist of what a foreign minister said presented no great problem. But putting into intelligible and reasonably accurate Spanish the remarks of the secretary of state to a foreign minister proved a task of another order, requiring a heavy infusion of mental agility.

Interpreting for him on those occasions was filled with pitfalls because of the secretary's penchant for relapsing, in moments of personalized diplomacy, into Tennessee idiom.

Secretary Hull and I were received by the foreign minister of one of the Central American republics who, as a result of Nazi activities in his country, seemed filled with equal parts of indignation and apprehension. In fact, on the eve of the Havana conference the German minister had told the foreign minister that the latter's behavior at that meeting would be closely monitored, and if it were not marked by a spirit of "friendly collaboration" with Germany, he and his government might regret it as soon as the victorious Reich had disposed of its remaining enemies in Europe.

The secretary of state was all solicitude. "Tell the foreign minister," he ordered me, "that the German fella seems to be trying to treat you like a houn'-dawg chasin' a rabbit." The secretary eyed me while I struggled with that one. "Tell him," he went on, "that what we've come here to Havana to do is to get ourselves together and fix up a hemisphere briar patch where that houn'-dawg will wish he hadn't."

Out of such ingredients did Mr. Hull fashion, with hard work and persistence, what has since been known as the Declaration of Havana — Resolution 14. That resolution declared that "Any attempt on the part of a non-American State against the integrity or the inviolability of the territory, the sovereignty or the political independence of an American State, shall be considered as an act of aggression against the States which sign this Declaration."

The Declaration of Havana was a clear warning to Nazi Germany to stay out of the New World, and Cordell Hull rightly regarded it as one of his most important contributions to inter-American affairs.

As these threads of history were being woven, I found myself heavily involved during the last few days of the conference not in the formulation of policy but in the care of one of the foreign delegates — the foreign minister of Paraguay. That came about because Washington forgot to repeat to Mr. Hull a telegram whose original went to Asunción.

Unbeknown to Mr. Hull, Undersecretary of State Sumner Welles and President Roosevelt decided to invite the Paraguayan foreign minister to make an official visit to Washington immediatley after the Havana Conference. The Chaco War, which had drained the resources of both Paraguay and

Bolivia, had recently been settled. A Bolivian official had already visited the United States, and Roosevelt agreed with Welles that to even things up, the Paraguayan foreign minister should receive a similar invitation. There was in addition the matter of a highway across Paraguay and southern Brazil that might make Paraguay less dependent on the River Plate; Export-Import Bank credits for that project needed discussion.

So the invitation was extended, but through an oversight in the State Department the telegram that went to the American legation in Asunción, telling the American minister to extend the invitation, failed to be repeated to Havana for information of the secretary of state. Mr. Hull was thus in ignorance both of the invitation and of its acceptance by the Paraguayan government when he went to call on the Paraguayan foreign minister.

We found Dr. Salomoni bubbling with excitement and delight, but the reason for his enthusiasm was not immediately apparent to the American callers. When after several minutes of talking at cross purposes the reason finally became clear, a bewildered Secretary Hull was inwardly fuming. On our departure he spoke his mind in the pungent idiom of his boyhood hills. At our office in the hotel a telegram to the acting secretary of state presently came smoking from the keys of Milly Asbjornsen's typewriter.

It turned out that Dr. Salomoni had never been in the United States. An unassuming, friendly little man, he was somewhat alarmed at the prospect. Since I knew the routine for official guests in Washington, I was able to reassure him and to answer most of his questions. He wanted, I remember, to visit the Rock Creek Zoo and the Library of Congress. When I inquired why, he said so he could "tell his children about the elephants."

"And the *biblioteca*, the Library of Congress?" I persisted.

"Oh, that," said Dr. Salomoni shyly. "It is that I have heard that they distribute the books asked for by *clientes* from a considerable distance, employing a pneumatic machine. Through a long tube come the books — whoosh! *Una cosa fantástica . . . .*" I marveled over the minister's having picked up that unlikely bit of intelligence, and I made a mental note to have someone phone the Library of Congress ahead of Dr. Salomoni's visit, requesting that special air pressure be applied to the pneumatic tubes in his honor.

In contrast to the secretary of state, Sumner Welles was a different proposition altogether. Cordell Hull and his undersecretary were almost grotesquely ill-matched in the important arena of national policy and international affairs.

Hull, elected to the Tennessee legislature at twenty-two, was a captain of volunteers in the Spanish-American War — a time when Welles was preparing for Groton, Harvard, and the diplomatic service, which he entered in 1915, eight years after Judge Hull first came to Congress. Hull had no money beyond his salary as secretary of state — $15,000 a year in 1940; Welles inherited wealth and married more of it. Hull lived in a hotel on Sixteenth Street; Welles had a town house on Massachusetts Avenue and a country estate at Oxon Hill, Maryland. Hull was a politician who specialized in economic matters and trade — he was a leading expert on tariffs — whereas Welles was a professional diplomat far more at home than his chief in the maze of international maneuver.

If "rugged" described the secretary of state, *Time* magazine's "patrician" was applicable to Hull's undersecretary. Both men were tireless workers, but there the similarity ended.

It was perhaps inevitable in those circumstances that Hull and his ranking deputy would not be close, and that the secretary from time to time would be suspicious of his able and elegant subordinate, with whom President Roosevelt often transacted foreign business over Cordell Hull's head. Young men in the State Department were well aware of this situation, which did not render their work any easier; in fact, it sometimes required considerable nimbleness not to get caught in the crossfire.

Notwithstanding his condescending manner and his occasional frosty formality, I found Welles the easier man to work for — possibly because I did not have to translate for him — and since the undersecretary's first specialty was Latin America, I was more often in his tidy office than I was in the secretary's cluttered one.

Soon after I reached the American Republics Division I had the temerity to wake Mr. Welles at 2 A.M., when Ambassador Norman Armour needed an immediate answer to a River Plate problem. Cutting through my apology, Mr. Welles said sharply that he would be the judge of what phone call was superfluous; thereupon he approved my proposed reply to Embassy Buenos Aires and bade me a gracious good night. Again, when the Division of Foreign Service Administration took a carping view of my having routed out the Navy Department to send a plane from the Canal Zone to Buenaventura, Colombia, Mr. Welles not only endorsed my decision to move an ill vice consul to Gorgas Memorial Hospital but also later supported the recommendation that the consulate in unhealthy Buenaventura be closed, something the American Republics Division had been trying for a decade to accomplish. Welles was, in short, a highly dependable chieftain.

One of Mr. Welles's idiosyncrasies was his persistent belief that Cuban diplomats could do no wrong. This notion perhaps stemmed from a feeling that his own mission to Havana in 1933 had left something to be desired; or maybe, as a man of sophistication, Welles merely found certain capering of representatives from the island a relief from the tiresome predictability of less uninhibited statesmen.

Under his direction I was twice involved in getting Cuban diplomats in Washington out of holes they had dug themselves. One involved persuading an ambassador, who had not bothered to pay local tradesmen, to settle his debts — without involving the State Department. This was done by having a delivery truck brightly painted "Bill Collector" park beside the embassy, with ensuing publicity that did the trick. The second was bailing out a high-spirited young diplomat who took on the Brooklyn Dodgers on the New York, New Haven and Hartford Railroad and was put off the train, and into jail, at Bridgeport. Few police outside of Washington know the meaning of diplomatic immunity. A telephone call on Mr. Welles's behalf settled the matter.

The Division of American Republic Affairs also had problems of representation created by some of our own chiefs of mission, and Mr. Welles played a key role in a campaign to get rid of some of the more offensive examples spawned by the American spoils system. The undersecretary of course recognized the strength of the forces leading to politically inspired diplomatic appointments, but he went along with Larry Duggan and me when we advanced the proposition that by the middle of a second presidential term, political debts had been paid, and if a minister or ambassador still proved unfit for the job, it was high time to replace him. As an earnest of our good faith, Larry engineered the resignation of two marginal professionals who were approaching retirement age, and after considerable maneuvering we were able to get rid of a disreputable ancient, the protégé of a senator, who for several years had been impairing the relations between the United States and one of the smaller South American countries.

The senator was a strong sanctity-of-the-family man — at least in the *Congressional Record* — and he capitulated when we produced proof that the old goat he had sponsored had become the principal patron of a local bordello where, too decrepit for other indulgences, he used to get drunk and beat up the girls of the establishment. Several times the Guardia Nacional had intervened. Exit that American representative.

There was also an ambassador, a naturalized citizen of Caribbean extraction, who was a scourge to his staff and his colleagues. He spoke native Spanish, which multiplied the number of people he offended in the country to which he was accredited. He was so incompetent that substantive business with his country had to be transacted in Washington. This irritated those of us required to perform the work he was paid to do. Ever since early in the first Roosevelt administration, we had been trying to get him out, but his strength was politico-ecclesiastic, a formidable combination. His wife was related to a churchman who in turn had the ear of an important prelate.

It was with un-Christian glee that one afternoon, toward the end of the second Roosevelt administration, I saw on the front page of the *Washington Star* an announcement that the worthy prelate had died. Five minutes later I was drafting a telegram to the prelate's ambassador, accepting his resignation and instructing him to depart from his post.

Mr. Welles was not in his office, so I gave the telegram to Anne Clarkson, his personable assistant, who read it and was inclined to doubt my chances of getting it signed. Wouldn't it be better if I took the telegram away, returning with it after Mr. Welles got back to his office? When I insisted, she deposited the telegram on the undersecretary's desk, wearing a "you'll be sorry" expression. She was a good enough sport, however, to telephone me later the same afternoon. The telegram had been signed and was on its way to the code room.

In the usual course of events personnel papers were not circulated to the geographic division, but since I was the officer drafting the outgoing telegram, the dossier came back to my desk. "Agree SW" was clipped to the telegram, and Secretary Hull had signed it himself. That was one time when the secretary of state and his ranking subordinate saw eye to eye on how to settle a problem.

Good Neighbors

The Good Neighbor Policy was unveiled by President Roosevelt in his inaugural address in 1933. Roosevelt declared that his administration would be guided by the good neighbor, "the neighbor who resolutely respects himself, and because he does so, respects the rights of others." Roosevelt's prestige remained high in Latin America throughout his years in office.

At that time the Neighbors numbered twenty countries, plus the United States, loosely joined in an organization then called the Pan American Union, with headquarters in an elegant marble palace on lower 17th Street, a few blocks south of the State Department.

The eighteen Spanish-speaking countries, Brazil (half the South American continent), and Haiti were preoccupied with problems of development, social and economic maladjustments, inflation, explosive population growth, and an increasing resentment on the part of the indigenous poor directed against those controlling the wealth of each nation. Local political leaders unable to solve their problems were not averse to blaming the Colossus of the North for alleged sins of omission (called "taking Latin America for granted") and also of commission (called "intervention," and after intervention, "colonialism").

The fact that relations with Latin America during most of our history have rarely been of paramount importance to the United States does not mean that the Neighbors have been neglected. From 1933 until his resignation in 1944, Secretary Hull took a lively if intermittent interest in the hemisphere. He dutifully attended board meetings at the Pan American Union, listening patiently to whispered translations of interminable speeches. He enjoyed heading American delegations at inter-American conferences (e.g., Montevideo in 1933, Lima in 1938, and Havana in 1940). And as his memoirs attest, the problems of such countries — in particular, Cuba, Argentina, Brazil, and Mexico — often engaged his most diligent interest. On routine matters, however, as well as on many fundamental issues, Hull was content to leave decisions to Undersecretary of State Sumner Welles, who spoke Spanish and was diligent, hardworking and sympathetic to many of the Latin American aspirations. In addition, Welles had easy access to the White House; he was personally closer to the president than was his secretary of state.

Another actor on the Latin American stage was Adolf Berle, a precocious New York lawyer who reached the State Department via Harvard and the Roosevelt Brain Trust. An assistant secretary, junior to Welles, Berle dealt in economic matters and communications, and later in security. A protégé of Mr. Roosevelt, he was articulate, argumentative, brash, self-confident, and New Deal in outlook.

In the State Department, Hull, Welles, and Berle were the upper echelon of Latin American warriors in the 1930s. The day-to-day, hour-to-hour work was accomplished by Larry Duggan, and by me as Larry's deputy with the title of assistant chief of the Division of American Republics Affairs. (The equivalent title today is deputy assistant secretary of state for inter-American affairs, but whereas there was only one deputy in 1937, Foggy Bottom now crawls with them.)

Until shortly before my arrival, ours had been the Division of Latin American Affairs. Welles had the title changed to American Republics Affairs as being more caressing to the Latino ego. A similar impulse underlay the Welles/Roosevelt project in the next decade, when all American legations in Latin America were raised to embassies, and all American ministers automatically became ambassadors.

Another New Deal change in the State Department was to absorb the separate Mexican Division, created in the turbulence following the Porfirio Díaz dictatorship a quarter-century before. That sensible consolidation facilitated our operations.

In 1937 the Division of American Republics Affairs had, in addition to its chief and assistant chief, sixteen officers to handle the affairs of twenty countries. Our division occupied the southwest corner of the building, on the third floor, and it extended north along the 17th Street side toward the premises of the secretary of war, Patrick Hurley, in pleasant, high-ceiling rooms comparable to those of the Division of Western European Affairs on the White House side of the building.

When I arrived, fresh from Cuba, Larry Duggan was away and I became acting chief almost before I had located my office. My predecessor, overdue for his vacation, remained long enough to show me the coat rack and to present me to Miss Nina Romeyn, an imposing lady who was the bulwark and mainstay of the division and the guardian of its morale and deportment. My predecessor thereupon fled. One hour later, word reached the State Department of an attempted revolution in Brazil fomented by dissidents, calling themselves Integralistas, who wore green shirts and admired Benito Mussolini's black-shirted Fascisti. Newspaper correspondents, referred upstairs by the secretary's office, converged on the Division of American Republics Affairs. They demanded spot news, of which we had none (because diplomatic telegrams, unlike news flashes of instantaneous transmission, have to be coded at one end and decoded at the other), and background information about Brazilian politics, of which I had none because I had just spent four years in Cuba.

All I remembered, in addition to Brazil's being the New World's largest country and a producer of coffee and samba music, was the residue of Angus Crawford's famous lecture to which I had listened a dozen years before: Brazil had frontiers with every South American country except Chile and Ecuador and, inheriting boundary disputes from Spanish colonial days, settled them all in its favor without shedding a single drop of blood. That achievement was the work of the Baron de Río Branco, trained in the imperial Brazilian diplomatic service, who outsmarted every foreign minister from the River Plate to the farthest reaches of the Amazon. It was impressive information about a great statesman, but not germane to the deadlines of correspondents who were concentrating on the Integralistas.

I summoned Mr. Brazil, who turned out to be an aging professor, with a Ph.D. in history and economics, who as a departmental officer had for twenty years been conscientiously accumulating Brazilian lore and storing it as a squirrel stashes acorns. I later found out he was a competent and meticulous draftsman; his papers were accurate and dependable. He had all the acorns, but he could extract them only one acorn at a time, when what I needed was a decoction of the essence of acorns.

After a struggle with the professor that was painful to each of us, I sent him back to his desk to write me a memorandum. When it came, it was a scholarly effort with references and footnotes, but by the time his paper was finished, the insurrection had been crushed and most of the unapprehended Integralista leaders had fled to Uruguay.

What had promised to be a grim first day for the new acting chief of the American Republics Division was saved by Miss Romeyn, who miraculously produced a junior vice consul named W. Newbold Walmsley, Jr. She remarked that Mr. Walmsley had been in Brazil — perhaps he could help me. It turned out that Mr. Walmsley not only had been in Brazil, he had been raised there, the son of an American businessman in São Paulo. Newby knew half the members of the Brazilian Cabinet, as well as several of the Integralistas, by their nicknames.

By the time Walmsley and I had pacified the press, Ambassador Caffery's telegrams from Rio were being decoded. Sagacious and informative as always, they confirmed Walmsley's projections, thus further enlightening the correspondents.[1]

That was possibly better luck than I deserved on the first day of my Washington assignment. My unkind thoughts about my absconding predecessor were replaced by affection for Miss Romeyn and gratitude for Newby Walmsley, who in due course became Mr. Brazil in his own right in the State Department, always serving with distinction.[2]

There followed three years in Washington that were professionally rewarding as well as personally pleasant, although in discussions I found myself often on the opposite side from my immediate chief, Larry Duggan. Larry, the son of an educator who then directed an endowed foundation, was as attractive a human being as it was my privilege to know. Ours was a firm and lasting friendship unmarred by differences in temperament and outlook that rendered us at times an ill-assorted pair to be working on the same problem, with equal enthusiasm for solving it.

Larry's Achilles heel, as I used to tell him, was his persistent belief that the underdog is always right, an irrational fixation that sometimes impelled him to take the side of the have-nots when in altercation with the haves. That attitude, not uncommon among New Dealers, had serious implications for American business. Having fared well during the Coolidge and Hoover administrations, American business, in the eyes of many Roosevelt appointees, was suspect in the 1930s.

My own view of the Good Neighbor Policy was that Roosevelt had been correct in emphasizing *respect* as the cornerstone of the inter-American relationship. However, in the same way that the United States respected, say, Nicaragua, Nicaragua ought to respect the United States, including the legitimate interests of United States citizens in Nicaragua. The Good Neighbor Policy was not a one-way street to be traveled penitently by Uncle Sam,

1. President Kennedy faced the essence-of-acorn problem a quarter-century later and complained about it. By that time the State Department had become so overstaffed and unwieldy that it could no longer function effectively.

2. Ambassador Walmsley (1904–1974) retired in 1963, after forty years of service. To my regret, he never became ambassador to Brazil, a post for which he had unique qualifications.

walking barefoot and alone, but a two-way thoroughfare with the rest of the Neighbors as much obligated to respect the United States as the United States was obligated to respect them.

Larry conceded the correctness of my interpretation of the Good Neighbor Policy, but his private sympathies lay so strongly with the "downtrodden" that it was often hard for him to be objective about a given case. I myself had scant patience with the "downtrodden." Many of them, I believed, were the way they were mainly because, in terms of human potential, they represented inferior raw material. In all societies throughout recorded history there has been an able minority at the top of the pyramid. To be sure, the minority often included some of the most ruthless and unscrupulous along with the ablest, and those beneath had frequently been oppressed, sometimes cruelly oppressed, by their emperors, monarchs, tetrarchs, and tribal chieftains, long before the advent of *caudillos* and *jefes políticos* in Latin America.

The most effective kind of government, it seemed to me, was one that protected the fumbling incompetent from the grosser forms of exploitation while equalizing opportunity, so that the superior individual, regardless of his origins, could rise by right of his demonstrated ability. I agreed with Larry that in terms of hemisphere development, the destruction of indigenous cultures, followed by the colonial heritage of exploitation, had produced too high a proportion of "downtrodden" for society to sustain indefinitely. Pressures were building that, if not relieved, must lead inevitably toward an explosion.

The colonial heritage was an albatross around the neck of several of the Good Neighbors, but it was *their* albatross and not *our* albatross. While an understanding heart in the breast of Tío Sam might help, the most potent influence the United States could exert was through the example of a functioning democracy. The American democracy was not a commodity to be put in a lift van, neatly packaged for export to the *pelados* of Latin America. I doubted then, and still do, whether certain of the Good Neighbors were capable of learning to dominate the instruments of representative democracy. A Washington bureaucrat did not, however, proclaim such notions aloud in 1937.

When I joined the division, the Good Neighbor Policy was already four years old, and I thought it had, in various particulars, already become a one-way street with Washington mistakenly encouraging the Latinos to dwell on their rights and their grievances instead of on their opportunities and their obligations, such as the defaulted dollar loans. Several of the American republics had borrowed heavily in the 1920s, and then gone broke. No doubt some of the loans had been unwise, for frivolous purposes. No doubt some of the bankers had encouraged imprudence on the part of their clients. No doubt the bankers had made handsome profits while unloading on the public the bonds they had floated. No doubt corruption marred the record. No doubt.

But the fact remains that the money had been borrowed from American investors and that the money had been spent on public projects in Latin America. I believed that it behooved the American government, as representing those investors, to bestir itself more vigorously on behalf of its citizens. Instead, President Roosevelt in effect washed his hands of those transactions, and the feeble best the State Department could do was to encourage the establishment of a private Bondholders Protective Council whose representatives were already being brushed off by unrepentant debtors.

The case of Panama also had one-way street implications. In 1933, Panama had a legitimate complaint when it demanded payment of the Canal Zone rental in gold dollars, as specified in the treaty. It had been a shabby move by the United States, after Roosevelt repudiated the gold clause, to offer depreciated currency. When Panama rejected the offer, the least uncomfortable solution was to negotiate a new treaty, establishing a rental that took into account the depreciation of the dollar. That was done, but the United States did not stop there. The negotiations with Panama, in which Larry Duggan participated, went far beyond the annuity.

The new treaty granted a series of fresh benefits to Panama. The tenor of those arrangements, as well as the discussions that led toward them, implied that the United States was belatedly "righting wrongs" inflicted by the original agreement. As a result, the Panamanians — that is to say, the microscopic segment of people who controlled political power, and hence the wealth, of the isthmus — were nourished in their belief that the way to get results in dealing with the United States was to behave badly, to the end that Washington would soon pay Panama to stop screaming.

Paying Panama to cease misbehaving thus became United States practice, and for the next several decades Panamanian politicians, in conjunction with groping American idealists, established the proposition that by building a canal across the isthmus, a nonextinguishable debt to Panama was created. That was a truly splendid revelation. No downtrodden ever had it any better.

Larry Duggan also took a relaxed view of some of the tribulations of American business, which he examined from the shelter of his liberal as well as his academic background. American public utilities were especially vulnerable. As insolvent governments resorted to inflation, utility costs in terms of local currencies skyrocketed. When the American companies sought to increase the rates to offset the rise in local costs, accusations of "foreign exploitation" followed. The companies were accused of impoverishing the people in order to swell North American profits. Facts were ignored, and ill will blossomed in their stead. To get the flavor of the problem, one has only to imagine that the New York subways were owned by the British at the time when raising the traditional nickel fare was being debated. Duggan's attitude was that by the mid-1930s, foreign ownership of public utilities had become an anachronism, and that trying to salvage those utilities via government good offices went against the drift of history and exacerbated foreign relations.

Although I recognized that Latin America was replete with interwoven and difficult economic and social problems, I did not believe their solution should be sought at the expense of American investors who were simultaneously being urged to go on spending money abroad. It seemed to me ironic as well as illogical to expect American business to continue supplying credit and capital unless existing American enterprises were receiving equitable treatment.

Discussion of these subjects did not take place all at once, and Larry's and my differences were not such as to impair our friendship or our enthusiasm for tackling the government's business. We each recognized that changes, whereby a larger proportion of the people of Latin America had a better existence, were overdue, and we agreed that in various countries mounting pressures in antiquated political boilers might soon blow them apart. But whereas Larry believed it was Washington's business to accelerate changes, especially those that favored the "downtrodden," I remained doubtful both of Washington's ability to do so and of the propriety of our making the effort.

That, however, was not the attitude that prevailed in the 1930s, an era simultaneously witnessing an energetic drive by Nazi Germany to increase Hitler's political influence in Latin America. Partly to counter that drive, but in larger measure in support of the forces of altruism, Summer Welles and Duggan cooked up a program that turned out to be the progenitor of foreign aid, a world phenomenon eventually costing the taxpayers billions of dollars.

The Program of Cooperation with American Republics was born in Larry Duggan's office. Welles sold it to Hull and then to President Roosevelt, who issued a directive to a dozen other government agencies, calling on them to report to a newly formed committee, of which Welles was chairman, on projects, plans, and proposals within their jurisdictions that might be of interest to Latin America. The theory was that we possessed a variety of talents and experience that, if identified and mobilized, could be useful in the development of the hemisphere, *provided the countries concerned expressed the desire to participate in the services (called "cooperation") in question.* (The italicized phrase was my contribution; I was still peddling my two-way street conception of the Good Neighbor Policy.)

In Washington in 1938 we were surprised at the amount of material our Committee of Cooperation with the American Republics discovered. From the Census Bureau to the Coast and Geodetic Survey, and from the Library of Congress to the Smithsonian Institution, projects, plans, and personnel came to light and were for the first time laid out on a single table. The Smithsonian, for example, hoped to complete its *Handbook of the South American Indian* as a companion to the standard reference work on the Indians of North America. The Census Bureau had requests from countries interested in population and demographic statistics. The Biblioteca Nacional in Caracas wanted a librarian to work on documents dating from the days of Bolívar. Our committee became so busy that our sessions proved too much for Mr. Welles, who transferred his duties to Larry, who then shared them with me. We soon had to enlist a departmental desk officer to keep our papers in order.

To initiate our program, we needed two things from Congress: first, a law authorizing the assignment of officials from other agencies to the State Department for temporary service abroad, and second, an appropriation to cover their expenses and travel plus a limited amount for program investment. Each measure was forthcoming, although not all congressmen were sold on the idea of helping cure Latin American ills by collaborating with governments. I remember a representative from the South who heckled a Smithsonian witness, a gentleman preeminent in his field, whose project I was supporting on behalf of the State Department. The point at issue was the salary of a second anthropologist to assist in the exploration of Mayan temples. Guatemala, I had just testified, had expressed enthusiasm.

The congressman listened with hostile impatience. Presently he interrupted, waving a minatory forefinger at the Smithsonian witness. "You want another anthropologist, do you?" he snarled. "What did you do with the old one?"

Our budget for inter-American cooperation of $95,000 was prepared with the help of Charles Hosmer, a canny Maine lawyer in the office of an assistant secretary of state, who handled fiscal matters in the State Department. Our budget passed Congress with little debate, partly on the somewhat dubious premise that the proposed activities, harmless in themselves, might counter the increasingly aggressive penetration of Latin America by Nazi agents. But when the State Department started to operate, we encountered a snag in an unlikely quarter, the White House.

President Roosevelt's penchant for injecting himself into the details of government business was now illustrated by his attempted dictation of the conditions under which, responsive to a request from Venezuela, we could lend a Miss Anita Kerr, bilingual in Spanish, to the Biblioteca Nacional in Caracas. She was regularly employed by the Library of Congress at an annual salary — not inadequate three generations ago — of $3,000. Under our new legislation she would continue to receive that salary, and the State Department proposed that she be paid an additional $8.00 a day because of the expenses she would necessarily face in the Venezuelan capital.

In the late 1930s Caracas was one of the most expensive capitals of the world. It cost more to live there than in either Rio de Janeiro or Buenos Aires. Venezuela, with its vast petroleum resources, was the only country in the hemisphere still on the old gold standard; the bolívar was the equivalent of the gold franc on which many European currencies had been based before devaluation. The bolívar exchanged for 33 American cents in 1939; 1 bolívar bought two eggs in the Caracas market.

President Roosevelt, intrigued by our program, asked Welles to show him the papers. When he reached the per diem of $8, he snorted. Back came the file, with an abrasive and disapproving message to the effect that at $8 a day, Anita would be raking in an extra $2,950 a year, approximately doubling her salary.

Mr. Welles, who knew Caracas, told us to get our statistics and prepare a fresh memorandum, reiterating that Miss Kerr needed a per diem of $8 if she was to live decently in the Venezuelan capital. Back from the White House came the papers a second time, with another abrasive note addressed "Dear Sumner." Welles, who knew his FDR, said we would have to bide our time. Fortunately, the bide was short. A few weeks later the head of the Creole Petroleum Company was a White House guest at dinner, along with Sumner and Mrs. Welles. The question of living costs in Venezuela arose, and the president remarked that he had heard the most extravagant things about Caracas; someone, he said, had recently told him that it cost twice as much to live there as it did in Washingotn, D.C. "Tell me," said the president, with a sly glance at Mr. Welles, "what does it really cost to live in Venezuela?" Miss Kerr sailed the following Friday for La Guaira, her per diem endorsed by the president of the United States. The Biblioteca Nacional was delighted to get her.

A related program, for which Larry Duggan almost alone was responsible, was in the field of cultural relations. Duggan was convinced that diplomacy was neglecting the intellectuals, with whom liaison could be a fruitful source of improved understanding. He even went so far as to predict that success in winning them over might influence the attitudes of certain hemisphere governments in directions favorable to the United States.

I took a neutral stand on culture, but privately I was not convinced. The intellectuals of Latin America seemed to me to be, with a few notable exceptions, rather a seedy lot, many already so far steeped in anti-Americanism that I doubted the ability of government academicians, however earnestly intentioned, to sway them. Even if they were swayed, it was by no means sure that they were in positions to influence the governments. And I doubted whether American cultural leaders of sufficient maturity and prestige could be recruited for attaché service. Junior-grade American intellectuals, armed with shiny new Ph.D.s, might make little impression on the Latino targets. Furthermore, the Nazis had already made "cultural attaché" a suspect title.

As a long-range proposition, influencing foreign cultural leaders seemed to be a legitimate goal, but one to be approached circumspectly and without expectation of immediate dividends. It could be undertaken as a peripheral operation supplementing the regular tasks of diplomacy, which had to do not with people-to-people or professor-to-professor programs but with government-to-government business. In short, I went along with the cultural project, but I told Larry that it reminded me of the old jingle about Nellie and the cow: "The cow kicked Nellie in the belly in the barn; didn't do her much good, didn't do her much harm."

For some reason Larry regarded that as faint praise, but he went ahead, Mr. Welles assenting, and presently arranged for the appointment of Dr. Richard Patte, a serious-minded Catholic layman fluent in Spanish, to handle the Washington end of our intellectual undertaking. Cultural relations officers soon began to appear in hemisphere missions.[3]

3. Experience across succeeding years has done little to change my original view that in certain countries a competent cultural attaché can be a useful *adjunct* to embassy operations. But he should never be the tail wagging the diplomatic dog. In the so-called underdeveloped countries, government-sponsored cultural activity is often worthless. In more sophisticated nations the problem is to attract an American cultural wizard of sufficient magic to impress foreign intellectuals, and then to fit his sleight of mind to embassy operations. That sometimes takes considerable doing.

{ P R O U D   S E R V A N T }

Our activities in the fields of aid (still labeled "cooperation") and of culture did not consume a disproportionate amount of the division's time. Most of this continued to be spent in our bilateral relations with the other twenty republics and on various inter-American enterprises emanating from the Pan American Union and the conferences held under its auspices. Larry Duggan was an innovator, but his idealism had a practical side that caused him to feel his way, seeking firm terrain as he took each step forward. Our ventures in aid and culture were thus cautious and exploratory rather than headlong, and with that I was in agreement.

The situation was changed dramatically after the outbreak of war in Europe. At a special conference held in Panama in September 1939, a few days after the conflict began, an American-sponsored hemisphere "chastity belt" proposal was adopted whereby the belligerents were enjoined from fighting in the New World. That might have been a good thing if the belligerents had accepted the injunction, but they did not, and the attempt to keep the war out of the hemisphere blew up along with the Nazi pocket battleship *Graf Spee,* in December 1939, off the port of Montevideo. When the so-called phony war ended the following spring, with the fall of France and the disaster of Dunkirk, Secretary Hull again summoned the nervous Good Neighbors. He succeeded in securing adoption of the Declaration of Havana, providing that an attack on one would be an attack on all, a safeguard aimed at the possibility that the Germans, now astride Western Europe, might soon turn their attention to the New World.[4]

Although several countries were comforted by the Declaration of Havana, others remained restive and apprehensive. What preoccupied them as much as the prospect of subversion or even attack was the dislocation of their economies: loss of markets, stifling of trade, supply uncertainties, plus the maritime dangers to which their commerce was soon exposed. While the American government worried about the safety of the Panama Canal, what with German commercial pilots flying for Colombia almost within sight of the isthmus, the Neighbors worried about their bread and butter. Dealing with those matters with the standard instruments of diplomacy (such as generous assurances by the United States regarding food supplies, and taking up the slack occasioned by the loss of European

---

4. Several Latin American countries harbored powerful and unassimilated German populations (notably Brazil, Chile, and Guatemala). In Argentina, throughout practically the entire war, the sympathies of the government — as distinct from the Argentine people — lay with Nazi Germany.

markets) pushed into the background less pressing Latin American affairs, including aid and culture.

In Latin America nervousness and apprehension continued. Unhappiness was fed by the realization on the part of the Neighbors of their inability to control events and, as usual, there were those who complained that Uncle Sam was doing too little about it. That view was presently seized upon by volunteer critics at home. The Roosevelt administration was soon implored to redouble its efforts "to make the Good Neighbor Policy a reality." Washington was also instructed "to render the Monroe Doctrine multilateral."

In the technical sense the Declaration of Havana had already done just that with respect to the Monroe Doctrine. The reality, of course, remained: the preponderant power of the United States.

The State Department, a handy scapegoat because, unlike other departments, it lacked a national constituency or lobby, was accused of failing to rise to the emergency. Demands were heard that Washington bestir itself and "adopt new policies to meet the new challenges of the 1940s." Those still believing in the merits of traditional diplomacy were soon to lose out to a youthful peddler of revelations.

I first met Nelson Rockefeller, then thirty-two years old, at a stag supper in Georgetown given by Dr. Herbert Feis, the economic adviser of the department who was one of Secretary Hull's principal lieutenants. The talk was largely about the effects of the war on the hemisphere and about inter-American relations. Primed by someone with ideas (I later suspected Bill Benton), the youthful Nelson was all for an activist role by the United States and for adventurous diplomacy in areas hitherto untouched by government action. I later told Larry Duggan that Rockefeller, a personable young man, had displayed no lack of self-confidence but that he obviously knew very little about Latin America. I thought that after seasoning he might make a fairly competent vice consul — provided, of course, that he could pass the examinations. Although I had a high opinion of the perspicacity of Dr. Feis, who generally did things for a reason, I was inclined to attach little significance to the evening. My own impending transfer from Washington curtailed speculation. Busy with preparations to go to Chile, I did not take seriously the rumors soon circulated by the capital gossip factory to the effect that the youthful Republican millionaire had offered his services to the White House, preferably for duty, in Latin America.

The appointment of Nelson Rockefeller to the newly invented position of coordinator of inter-American affairs, when it penetrated to Chile a few weeks later, astonished me. So did the news that he had been given $5 million with which to make friends, with a job description that, to the extent it was intelligible, appeared to duplicate the functions of the Division of American Republics Affairs in the State Department.

The appointment was well within the genius displayed by President Roosevelt for disorderly administration and for pouring sand into the machinery of foreign affairs. After three years on the rim of the New Deal bureaucracy, I could understand that. And, in terms of the money being spent by a government preparing for war, $5 million was popcorn, even though it was more than *fifty times* the amount Duggan and I had so painstakingly budgeted for the first cooperative program with Latin America.

What did surprise me was that Secretary Hull had apparently acquiesced in, or at any rate had not objected to, the idea of having an inexperienced outsider invade an important area of his own responsibilities. The position of Hull at the time was impregnable, and the political leverage at his disposal was correspondingly great. Had the secretary of state wished to make an issue of handing Latin America over to Rockefeller, the White House would have backed down, and Rockefeller might have been offered Greenland instead, with a mandate to teach Eskimos to ride round and round their igloos on kiddie cars — a program that would have served the national interest just as well as turning him loose on the Good Neighbors. But Hull, for reasons that remain unexplained, chose not to object. Larry Duggan, a peaceable individual who himself suffered from ultraliberal impulses, decided to make do with the situation confronting him. In point of fact, his personal relations with the coordinator were friendly. Within a short time, however, Duggan resigned from government service.

Not so the ex-assistant chief of the American Republics Division. Presently transferred from Chile back to Cuba, this time as number two in a large and busy mission, I was soon on the receiving end of messages emanating from the coordinator, whose staff included a number of young men who had tried to get into the Foreign Service but had failed to do so. These officials began popping up in Latin American capitals with automobiles at their disposal and expense accounts that dwarfed those available to professional diplomats whose elbows they proceeded to jiggle. Few of them were in sympathy with what they described as the old-fashioned methods of diplomacy.

A detailed history of the activities of the coordinator of inter-American affairs awaits the further attention of researchers. Unless my written observations were summarily destroyed by the recipients, future scholars may be regaled by prose originating over my signature describing some of the coordinator's projects. It should be noted, however, that the Neighbors were at first fascinated by the fact that one of the richest urchins in the world was now courting their attention, admonishing them in comic Spanish, giving them awkward *abrazos,* and, for all the lack of dignity of his behavior, intimating that a gravy train was being assembled with himself the engineer.

Had the coordinator's been a cynical government enterprise, deliberately designed to take the Latino mind off mostly insoluble wartime preoccupations, there might have been some small merit to it. Knowledgeable operators with an understanding of what they were doing and the kinds of people they were doing it with might have avoided some of the more ludicrous efforts. But such was not the case. High purpose poured from the coordinator's premises like lava from a volcano, and so did the first $5 million.

For example, it was decided that inter-American sports had been neglected, although it was common knowledge that international games often foster violent nationalism and as frequently produce outbursts of ill will as they do friendly feelings. A girls' basketball team appeared in Cuba, chaperoned by a padre. A nine-goal polo player was dispatched to hospitable Argentina, but the Argentine government continued holding hands with Hitler while lavishing attentions on the crew of the scuttled *Graf Spee,* one thousand of whom were guests of the Republic. The same durable polo player was equally popular in Chile, but the Chilean government went on worrying about the German ships interned in their harbors, and what to do with a year's supply of frozen mutton overflowing from the freezers in Patagonia and Tierra del Fuego.

A handsome motion picture star was sent around the continent, generating much popular acclaim. It was not clear what area of inter-American relations he was supposed to enrich. Shortly thereafter Walt Disney was commissioned to make an animated Good Neighborhood cartoon. It was designed to show that the American cowboy and the *gaucho* descendants of Martín Fierro were brothers under their jeans and *bombachas.* The same picture featured a sweet-tempered Donald Duck making fraternal noises at a talking parrot called Joe Carioca, supposed to represent the spirit of Rio de Janeiro.

Still another project was to have each American diplomatic mission in Latin America — all twenty of them — send to Washington by diplomatic pouch a sample of water drawn from the principal river of the country in question. These twenty samples, plus an infusion from the Mississippi, were to be ceremoniously mingled in the patio of the Pan American Union, in the presence of the twenty applauding Latino ambassadors. The libation was then to be poured over the roots of a Tree of Inter-American Understanding. Those dreaming up this patriotic number were apparently unaware that although the Rimac flowed through Lima, and the Mapocho through Santiago, it was over one thousand miles from the embassy in Rio de Janeiro to the nearest watering hole on the Amazon. It was likewise several hundred miles from Caracas to the Orinoco in Venezuela, and in Panama the principal river was mostly in the Canal Zone. Several Central American countries had no principal rivers at all, and trying to pick one in Bolivia could quite easily start a revolution. (In Havana we filled the flask in the chancery washroom and returned it to Washington with our congratulations.)

A few of Nelson Rockefeller's projects, including those in public health and related fields that demanded professionals, produced tangible results. The malaria campaign in Brazil started with a 95 percent United States contribution; it was still operating fifteen years later, by which time the American contribution was down to 5 percent of the total cost, with Brazil subscribing the remainder. And the *servicio* concept, whereby the host officials were restrained from frittering away the United States contribution on Valdivieso *extra sec* or nightgowns for their *queridas,* was an ingenious and practical device adopted in various aid programs of the succeeding era.

Others, like rubber gathering in the upper Amazon, produced recognizable latex suitable for automobile tires, but at a cost matched only by the solid gold Cadillacs of Arabian emirs, and the cryptostegia rubber-from-milkweed program almost wrecked the fragile economy of Haiti.

Watching Nelson Rockefeller during World War II was an educational experience. His program of adventurous diplomacy demonstrated the folly of good works unleavened by experience. It likewise proclaimed the difficulty inherent in persuading developing societies to abandon their untidy habits in favor of Kleenex, antiperspirants, and bingo on Saturday evenings.

Those were valuable pieces of intelligence even though attempts to advance them during the last dozen years of my career earned me few friends among later purveyors of the New Revelation. It has taken the general public, and their representatives in Congress, many decades to arrive at the conclusion I reached in the 1940s: that an effective foreign aid program is one of the most difficult projects in the world to manage, and that the more backward and "underdeveloped" the beneficiary country, the less chance there is that the program will be successful, or appreciated.

It is not necessary to abandon foreign aid altogether, but it should be conducted on a restricted, selective, and pragmatic basis, a country at a time and a project at a time, never a hemisphere or a continent at a time, and never at the whim of a paladin of progress imbued with a crusading spirit.

Expropriation Is Stealing

The most important issue facing us in our relations with Latin America in the period just before World War II resulted from the seizure by Mexico of American petroleum properties. That occurred in March of 1938, six months before Munich. Both Larry Duggan and Sumner Welles were out of town, so it fell to me to make the initial recommendation, which was that the United States should take a strong stand in defense of the violated rights of its citizens.

The basic facts were not in dispute. The oil companies, British and American, had invested heavily in developing the petroleum resources of Mexico. Petroleum is a high-risk business. The Mexican fields proved profitable, and the Mexican government soon argued that its share of those profits ought to be increased. Out of that altercation, which had grown increasingly bitter, came the expropriation of the properties. No restitution was made for them.

The applicable principle of international law was reasonably clear: a government has a sovereign right to take private property for the public good, but adequate compensation should be paid. The catchword is "adequate," which soon proved as elastic as a rubber band, with the Mexican government pulling one end and the oil companies the other. Another word was presently added. It was "prompt," which was taken by Washington to mean, if not "simultaneous with," then at least "very soon thereafter."

These semantics were extensively debated in the second floor office of the secretary of state, the same large, untidy room with its view across the park where five years before I had listened to Secretary Stimson on the subject of Liberia. Those present now included Dr. Herbert Feis, Mr. Hull's economic adviser with a shock of unruly white hair; Dr. Leo Pasvolsky, a Russian-born Ph.D. from Brookings with a strong accent and a round head stuffed with erudite tokens (as special assistant he did much of Mr. Hull's drafting); and the leftward-learning Adolf Berle, an assistant secretary of state. Mindful of my modest rank, I did more observing than talking. I was shortly replaced by Larry Duggan, but not before I had concluded that Secretary Hull, if his initial view had prevailed, might have taken more serious note of the man-handling of American rights than did the White House under President Roosevelt. I retain a picture of Mr. Hull, seated behind his cluttered desk, dangling his glasses at the end of a black ribbon and declaring in his Tennessee drawl that "Expropriating property without paying for it is stealin'." The United States would be better off today if Hull had made that simple declaration stick.

Words of admonishment were in due course dispatched to Mexico. That nation was informed that the American government, while not contesting the right to expropriate, expected that "adequate, effective and prompt compensation" would be paid. But whereas Great Britain presently broke relations with Mexico over the latter's failure to pay such compensation, Washington, its vision distorted by "continental solidarity," went rolling down the one-way street of the Good Neighbor Policy.

Seven months after expropriation, not a *centavo* having been paid, Mexico agreed on the eve of an inter-American conference to set up a commission to determine the amount of compensation. Thus, as Mr. Hull later observed in his memoirs, argument at that conference over the "difficult question of expropriation" was avoided. That is, proceedings at the conference were not ruffled by the intrusion of a contentious substantive issue.

At the same time, Secretary Hull hailed the American effort to be friendly in keeping with the Good Neighbor Policy. The tone of the secretary's observation implies that he thought this was a victory for the United States, even though by that time Bolivia — rarely a very responsible member of the community — also had expropriated petroleum properties.

It was not until September 1943, more than five years after expropriation, that Mexico finally was induced to make a payment of $30 million, including interest. That settlement was uneagerly accepted by the petroleum companies, which pointed out that such a reduced amount, after sixty-five months, hardly constituted "adequate, effective and prompt" action by Mexico with respect to their interests.

An evaluation of the reluctance of the Roosevelt administration to stand up more valiantly for the rights of U.S. citizens abroad must of course take into account the unfolding panorama of world events, on which the Mexican behavior was a relatively minor smudge on a wide and menacing canvas. Notwithstanding his statement that "expropriation without compensation is stealing," Secretary Hull set even greater store at that time on the mainte-nance of the facade of hemisphere unity as an obstacle to Nazi penetration. Mexico in the end did pay something, and throughout World War II—in sharp contrast to its earlier attitude — did in fact collaborate with the United States in the war effort, as well as in most inter-American undertakings in which solidarity was at stake. It can be argued that had the United States adopted a tougher or more uncompromising stance, Mexico's attitude toward wartime collaboration might have been different.

The issue of expropriation without compensation was therefore in effect shelved for the period of World War II. But if the American public took little note of that, the comparative ease with which Mexico had swindled the oil companies was not lost on the rest of Latin America. Seeing Mexico get away with it set in motion a process of despoiling American companies that continued for years to come.

The termination of hostilities in 1945 found most of the Neighbors solvent for the first, and for some of them the last, time. Their economies had been strained, but they were undamaged by the struggle that had gutted Europe. They were one and all hungry for capital, and that capital was available only from the United States. It was a unique and splendid opportunity for the American government to raise the issue of expropriation, and to have adopted a forthright stand in defense of the proposition that the taking by a government of the private property of foreigners is legitimate only when adequate compensation is promptly paid.[1]

Nothing was done. There followed a period of drift. Secretary Marshall was preoccupied with European reconstruction, Soviet intransigence, and the Far East. He had little time for the Good Neighbors. Dean Acheson, for all his brilliance in many directions, also took a very relaxed view of Latin America, for whose problems he professed to have little stomach. His *Present at the Creation* bears out that conclusion; hardly one page in fifty even mentions Latin America.

John Foster Dulles, Eisenhower's secretary of state from 1953 to 1959, was a strong sanctity-of-contracts man and could have done much to defend the rights of private investors. Instead, Dulles allowed himself to endorse, in the guise of protecting those interests, one of the most misguided of projects — the "investment guarantee program" — which did more to jeopardize American enterprises in Latin America than it did to protect them.

Nevertheless, the expropriation racket, off to a flying start in 1938, developed comparatively slowly in the first dozen years after World War II. There

1. Such a position was in fact advocated by the then assistant secretary of state for Latin American Affairs, Spruille Braden (1945–1947). Unfortunately, he left office (over an unrelated issue) before his views could be adopted as policy.

were two reasons. In the first place, Mexico proved so incompetent at running the stolen properties that production diminished alarmingly, and before long, Mexico found itself importing oil to meet domestic requirements instead of exporting it.[2] Second, during the early post–World War II period (and, in fact, well into the Alliance for Progress euphoria of the 1960s), various of the Neighbors still cherished the hope (and under the Alliance, the expectation) that eventually the American government would agree to their tenaciously held formula for success: the proposition (a) that by being underdeveloped, a country had a right to be developed with capital provided by a developed country; and (b) that it was therefore the duty of the United States, an eminently developed establishment, to allow the Neighbors to keep an acquisitive paw in Uncle Sam's bottomless pocket. And as long as that was in prospect, the temptation to expropriate American property was held somewhat in check.

But presently in Cuba, Castro swept $2 billion worth of American property into his treasury. Nothing whatever was paid. No compensation. Most Americans applauded breaking relations with Havana, although some professed to see not much wrong with taking private property, provided it was accomplished in the name of rising expectations on the part of the have-not sector. Other commentators (e.g., Ambassador Philip Bonsal, in the concluding chapter of his book on Castro) argued that "business statesmanship" ought to be content with the successful operations over a period of years of a given enterprise, after which the host country — regardless of existing covenants — ought to be allowed to take over. "In the case of public utilities," Bonsal wrote, "a generation or so [sic] ought to be enough to satisfy the most avid operator and investor . . . ."

It is of interest, in that connection, that when, in the early 1960s the governor of a Brazilian state, in defiance of an existing provision in the Brazilian Constitution, expropriated without compensation an American utility company, and when, in reply to a press inquiry, an assistant secretary of state agreed that the confiscation would indeed be among the factors taken into consideration under the Alliance for Progress, President Kennedy so abusively berated that honest official that he asked to be transferred from Washington.

With those kinds of friends of private initiative manning the home ramparts, the surprising thing is that *any* American investments survived in

2. Only in the mid-1970s did Mexican oil production suddenly burgeon, and Pemex overcame its earlier reputation for incompetence.

Latin America, or that American capital continued to venture among the Good Neighbors, several of whom developed the expropriation technique to the point where they not only seized without compensation but then publicly declared the stolen enterprise to owe the host country money. That was done by the unsupported declaration that the original contract or concession, which was almost always negotiated with a predecessor government, had been obtained through fraud, corruption, or other extraconstitutional means, and hence should be void ab initio. Or else the government would announce that insufficient taxes were paid over the years — regardless of how many valid tax receipts were produced — or that exchange regulations, or labor legislation, or the sanitary code had been violated. No proof would be given, merely the unilateral statement of the government doing the expropriating, which government, controlling the apparatus of denunciation, would not find it difficult to invent nationalistic excuses.

The case of Peru is instructive. In 1968 the Peruvian government expropriated the International Petroleum Company, a subsidiary of Standard Oil Company of New Jersey and valued, according to the company, at approximately $100 million. Peru offered to pay $30,000, but made that "offer" contingent upon payment by the company of *$670 million* (an indemnity allegedly due for "forty-four years of illegal operation" of the properties. That is, Peru seized without compensation an enterprise that had operated for a generation and a half, with great benefit to Peru and Peruvian workers (a company that never had more than a handful of non-Peruvian employees), and then billed the company for over $600 million.

The action of the Chilean government under the Marxist President Allende, with respect to the five American copper companies, followed a pattern similar to that in Peru, except that the amount of "reparations" demanded by Chile came to *$1 billion*.

In neither of these acts of larceny did the country seizing the property agree to have its actions submitted to impartial arbitration. To do so, according to the ritual response, might be derogatory to the dignity or the sovereignty of the country concerned.

In broad context, these and other troubles involving torn-up contracts and trampled rights were the inevitable result of what, for lack of a more precise definition, might be called the tolerance by developed nations, including the United States, of immorality on the part of relatively weak governments. Every time a dishonest act on the part of one country against the citizens of another country goes ignored or unpunished — or, worse, is applauded by furry-tongued "liberals" — the effect has been to strengthen the forces of disrespect for law, for order, for the contractual relationship, and for the pledged official word. The appetite of the derelict country is sharpened, and it is encouraged to commit further acts of international irresponsibility. Neighboring countries, as well as those that regard themselves as similarly situated elsewhere, are tempted to follow suit.

The disease, which, had it been properly dealt with in the beginning might have been cured, for a time became epidemic.

In the post–World War II period of growing tolerance for government lawlessness, the Soviet Union played an unwholesome role by seeking to raise bad behavior to the status of government policy. In so doing, Moscow encouraged a wide range of reprehensible acts whenever the Kremlin — itself an amoral entity with little compunction about violating agreements — believed those depredations might embarrass or harass a non-Communist country.

It remains to consider the part played by American companies and the extent of their responsibility for the situation they faced. Few would argue that American capital in the first three-quarters of the twentieth century — that is, after the Spanish-American War — did not have a major, probably a decisive, impact on progress in certain countries of Latin America. It has accurately been observed that the inhabitants of several of those countries might still have been crossing their arroyos on burros and reading their *manifiestos* by whale oil lamps had it not been for the initiative of private American companies. And if social progress in various places did not keep pace with material developments, that was hardly the fault of American capital.

In those two and a half generations there were cases of rapaciousness on the part of American operators along with callousness in dealing with sensitive people. There were instances of lack of comprehension or sympathy on the part of distant home offices in the United States. There unquestionably were occasions — for instance, in the Caribbean during the first third of the century — of attempted manipulation of a weak and often irresponsible foreign government by an American company whose legitimate operations seemed threatened.

Professional belittlers of the role of private capital have made exhaustive studies of what went on here and there, and they have come up gloating whenever they have discovered one bad apple in the orchard. Those things should, however, be placed in their proper perspective.

It is time that those with some knowledge and experience of the operations of American companies in Latin America speak out on their behalf.

The truth is that over the years the vast majority of American businessmen in Latin America have been honest, decent, hardworking, and diligent, and that as a class they have often been more scrupulous in conforming to local laws and regulations governing their operations than some of their competitors, citizens of the host country or representatives of European firms. Moreover, those American businessmen and the companies they represented by no means were unsympathetic toward the aspirations of the peoples with whom they were working.

The achievements of American companies in Latin America should be viewed with the satisfaction that comes to those who have tackled hard and complicated tasks, and have overcome obstacles of geography, climate, and alien culture. Those achievements, as well as the conduct of American businessmen abroad, merit deep and patriotic pride on the part of their fellow countrymen.

American companies, almost without exception, bore a minimal responsibility for the difficulties that befell them in Latin America. The original blame should fall on the Roosevelt administration for allowing the Good Neighbor Policy, an excellent policy, to become a one-way street with traffic regulations applicable only to the American pedestrian. A mounting share fell upon successive Washington administrations for inattention — not, as it has been fashionable to say, to the "developing needs of the hemisphere" but to the developing hazards facing American businessmen in a period of rising nationalistic irresponsibility. The American government frequently gave the impression that it was more important not to *offend* the government of a "developing nation" than it was to *defend* the rights of American investors abroad.

Cordell Hull supplied the prescription for the remedy more than three decades ago: "Expropriating property without paying for it is stealin.'"[3]

---

3. Congress eventually took note and imposed the kinds of sanctions successive administrations opposed, thereby contributing to resolving the problem.

False Calm in Chile Before Pearl Harbor

Although Chile measures nearly three thousand miles, south to north, it is only one hundred miles wide, and the snow-capped Andes are often visible from the coast. The northern third, the nitrate pampas, is desert. The southern third is chill, tangled rain forest, ending in the windswept plains of Patagonia, excellent for sheep but inhospitable to man. Only the middle part of the country — the fertile Central Valley — can support an appreciable population.

In the State Department in the autumn of 1940, we were mostly interested in the efforts of Nazi Germany to convert the German segment of the Chilean population into an instrument responsive to Berlin. The Chilean government was staunchly democratic, but the Nazis were nevertheless making a determined effort to dominate the country. Germany was represented in Chile by Baron von Schoen, an experienced envoy whose mission in Santiago was more active than most foreign establishments in the capital.

Also of interest was the presence in several Chilean ports of German merchant vessels that had taken refuge there in the early days of the war. Their crews were still aboard, the ships were victualed and fueled, and they were capable of making a dash into the ocean at any moment. Their presence was a matter of hourly attention on the part of Allied representatives serving in Chile, and of almost equal interest to the United States.

I was well content with my new assignment as deputy to Ambassador Claude Bowers. After fifteen years the number two slot in Santiago seemed appropriate to my rank and experience, and following Peru, Liberia, and Cuba —all in the tropics — I was glad to be stationed farther from the equator. Except for earthquakes, the Central Valley of Chile was a good place to live. Our children were ten and six, and schools were available. The few Chileans I had met were excellent people, not gaily irresponsible like the Cubans but sound and hardworking. American government relations with Chile in the decade since the settlement of the Tacna-Arica dispute had been uneventful, and if the war in Europe should spread to the New World, Chile was expected, notwithstanding its influential German element, to be on the side of the Allies. Ambassador Bowers was regarded in the State Department as amiable and talented, if not an unduly energetic representative.

Undersecretary Welles gave me to understand that my assignment would probably last three years, and that I was expected to shake up the somewhat somnolent embassy organization. I sailed south alone, thirteen months before Pearl Harbor, in good spirits. My family followed in time for a summer Christmas in Santiago. By New Year's Day of 1941 we were busily house-hunting.

It was not until the Chilean autumn (spring, of course, in the United States), three weeks before I departed on an official visit to the Strait of Magellan, that we finally moved into a house in the suburb of Los Leones. We were near the Plaza Pedro de Valdivia, which had been the scene of much patriotic hoopla a month earlier in honor of the four hundredth anniversary of the founding of the capital by the aforesaid conquistador, a short time before he was killed by the Araucanian Indians.

Ours was a commodious house, with a garden boasting a grape arbor and a duck pond, and with tall, shredding eucalyptus and fine chestnut and walnut trees. The last were bearing at the time of our arrival, the heavy walnuts dropping with a clatter on the cement walk; the children rushed out every morning to salvage the night's accumulation. Fresh walnuts for breakfast became a standard item of diet.

We moved in for the expected three years and each room was repainted, thus disregarding a Foreign Service superstition that if you paint, you move.

My chief, Ambassador Bowers, was the most unambassadorial figure ever to present credentials. He suffered from bunions so painful that in the office he wore shoes with holes cut out to accommodate his affliction. He kept another pair under his desk into which he planned to slip when a visitor was announced. But often he did not bother — he cared little for appearances.

Mr. Bowers smiled often, but he had never bothered to catch up on his dentistry and there were gaps where lower teeth were missing. On one of the remaining stubs a dead cigar was often impaled. I never saw him relight a cigar. He chewed it down, a process of slow demolition through which his words, if one listened carefully enough, were both articulate and pungent. A newspaperman and the author of authoritative books on the Jeffersonian era, Ambassador Bowers, hunched over a typewriter, could produce compelling prose with two fingers. He had written the speech with which Franklin D. Roosevelt accepted his nomination for the presidency at the

Democratic Convention. In appreciation of that and other services to the Democratic Party, Bowers was appointed to Madrid, and when the Spanish Civil War broke out in 1936, he declared so heartily in favor of the existing Republican regime that there was no question of leaving him in Spain following the defeat of the Loyalists by Franco three years later. The Chilean appointment came next, to the annoyance of that government, which deplored the simultaneous transfer to Buenos Aires of the exceptionally popular Norman Armour.

Clearly Bowers did not look like an ambassador. He looked — and he would have hated the comparison — like a pixieish and slightly unkempt version of Doctor Goebbels, the propaganda minister of the Third Reich, but I very soon concluded that Ambassador Bowers would in fact have put his right hand in the fire if he thought that by doing so he could contribute to the preservation of democracy.[1]

His years in Spain notwithstanding, Ambassador Bowers did not speak Spanish. At the time of my arrival, his business was largely transacted through his personal secretary, Biddle Garrison, who used to accompany the ambassador on calls at the Foreign Office and interpret for him, to the frustration of the rest of the staff, who, unless the ambassador then dictated a telegram or a dispatch, rarely found out the subjects discussed with the foreign minister or what developed about them. Bowers was essentially lazy about what did not catch his imagination — embassy operations included — and he used to desert the capital altogether in midsummer, spending the weeks between Christmas and Easter at Zapallar, working on another book. Since Zapallar was a beach resort without telephone service, Bowers would drive to Viña del Mar on occasion and Garrison would meet him there, carrying an accumulation of official papers for his perusal.

That proved a difficult time for his ranking subordinate, who, because the ambassador was still within the country, could not assume responsibility as chargé d'affaires. All outgoing telegrams continued for three months to be sent over the name "Bowers," and mail was signed "for the Ambassador," followed by the name and title of the drafting officer. Furthermore, one never knew until Ambassador Bowers had scanned the papers whether he would accept the actions taken in his name.

---

1. The Chilean government intimated that it would welcome a change in American representation. If that initiative reached President Roosevelt, he ignored it. Bowers remained in Chile for fourteen years, until the end of the Truman administration in 1953. By that time his good qualities had long been recognized by the Chilean government.

Bowers was, however, so easygoing that he gave most matters only super-ficial attention. He was not interested in routine, and he rarely criticized de-cisions taken on his behalf. An exception was anything that had to do with freedom, democracy, or the rights of man, including the attitude of the Chilean government toward those developments. About such things he was in a state of perpetual alertness and suspicion.

I respected his courage of convictions, even though his suspicions re-sulted in two of the very few altercations I had with my chief during my tour of duty in Chile. The first occurred only a few days after my arrival, when I received a call at the chancery from the widow of the man who had been counselor of embassy a dozen years before in Lima, under Alexander P. Moore. The counselor had gone from there to Nicaragua as minister and then retired; he did not long survive his retirement. His widow, Gustava, whose American pension was small, had for several years been living in Chile, where her dollar stretched farther than it did in the United States. The lady herself had been a Prussian baroness whose family fortune was wiped out by the inflation following World War I. In 1928, soon after Lucy and I re-ported for duty with Uncle Alec Moore, Gustava had tangled with the am-bassador. She had launched several darts in our direction in the ensuing skirmishes.

Gustava was still thin, chic, cosmopolitan, and bubbling. The words she spoke were the words of cordiality: And when was dear Lucy arriving? We had two children now? How charming! She looked forward so much to re-newing our friendship. Presently Gustava suggested that it would be helpful if she could have an occasional package from the United States sent in the embassy diplomatic pouch, addressed to my wife. Oh, nothing much, of course, but silk stockings, for example, were so frightfully scarce and expen-sive in Chile. She was still an American citizen. She was the widow of an American minister, even if the State Department, which she said was becom-ing stuffier every day, had stupidly lifted her diplomatic passport.

I said I would have to look up the pouch regulations. We parted amicably, with Gustava reiterating that I must be sure to let her know the moment Lucy reached Chile. She expressed satisfaction that, as she put it, there was now a career man running the embassy.

On her way out, Gustava passed Ambassador Bowers in the hall. A mo-ment later the ambassador was in my office, demanding to know what "that woman" was doing in the embassy.

Shucking off my explanation of our past association in Peru, Mr. Bowers was afire with patriotic indignation. Gustava was, he insisted, "one of the most dangerous Nazis in Chile." She was an intimate friend of Ambassador von Schoen and his American-born wife, and she was hand in glove with leaders of the German community who were plotting against Chile. Yes, the ambassador knew that technically she was an American citizen, but that only made her the more dangerous. He would hold me personally responsible that she did not contaminate the personnel of the American embassy.

Mr. Bowers percolated on that stove lid for some time before he calmed down. He was still muttering when he departed. Gustava, in addition, reportedly had not been polite to Mrs. Bowers, a dignified but unpretentious lady whose extreme deafness greatly handicapped her life in Santiago. I concluded that Gustava still talked too much, in too many languages, but I was sorry for her even if we could not give her diplomatic pouch privileges for silk stockings.

The ambassador possibly remembered that incident when a few weeks after he reached Zapallar, he suddenly accused me of "publicly fraternizing" with the German ambassador, the formidable Baron von Schoen. This time Bowers was so upset that he made the uncomfortable automobile trip to Viña del Mar, whence he summoned me by phone to discuss what he called "a very serious matter." Mystified, I caught the next train to Viña, where I discovered that what had set my ambassador off was a photograph in a Chilean weekly, taken a few days before in the Santiago cathedral. There the foreign chiefs of mission had been attending a *Te Deum* in honor of the late King Alfonso of Spain. All the ambassadors were invited, and since Mr. Bowers was at Zapallar and the Chileans wanted the United States to be represented, I was included as his ranking assistant. I was seated as if I were the chargé d'affaires ad interim, and by a vagary of protocol, the seating arranged by the Foreign Ministry placed me directly behind the German ambassador.

By a freak of lighting and angles, the published photograph looked as though I were seated *beside* the German ambassador instead of *behind* him, and my fraternizing smile was actually directed not at von Schoen, who had greeted me civilly enough, but at the Venezuelan representative (not visible), who had just whispered that the next time the Chilean government cranked up a *Te Deum* for a dead Bourbon, he proposed to have a flask of live bourbon in his pocket, or at any rate to bring along a novel by Ramón Gallegos.

All of which I explained to Mr. Bowers, and he, being a fair-minded man, was convinced. He said he ought to have realized that newspaper photographs were often unreliable evidence. He was good enough to apologize to me. And what else, he inquired, had been happening in the capital during his absence? He was delighted to have missed that long ceremony in the cathedral, but it reminded him of the impending visit to Chile of Cardinal Daugherty of Philadelphia with Jim Farley, former postmaster general.

The ambassador said he could guess what the prelate was peddling, but how about the former postmaster general, who had, so he understood, broken with President Roosevelt? When I said "Coca-Cola," Mr. Bowers hooted, but he observed sagaciously that the embassy "ought to get some legitimate mileage out of the cardinal." He would return to Santiago for that affair. He would put on his cutaway coat and high hat and would want me, with a showing of the other members of the staff and the attachés in uniform, to greet His Eminence on arrival. After all, Chile was a Catholic country, and what was more, some of the Chilean churchmen were not averse to throwing an occasional brickbat at the "heretical United States." It would do those Chilean padres good, by God, to take note that the first prince of the church to visit Chile in years was at the same time a loyal American citizen. Mr. Bowers (a Protestant Hoosier) was a strong separation-of-church-and-state man.

I was instructed to arrange a reception at the embassy residence, to be given by the ambassador in honor of the cardinal. Cecil Lyon (a Catholic member of our staff) should act as liaison with the archbishop of Santiago and with the Foreign Office to make sure that the program, while not overdoing it, did not fail to recognize the American connection.

Mr. Bowers did not think that he, personally, would take Jim Farley to call on the president of Chile, but I could set up an appointment with Don Tinto Aguirre if Farley wanted one, and take him to the Presidential Palace. The idea of promoting a Coca-Cola concession from a president who in his private capacity was the owner of extensive vineyards was, said the ambassador, right out of the believe-it-or-not cartoon series. But I was to be sure to invite Farley to the reception for the cardinal.

His good humor restored, Ambassador Bowers sent for drinks, and later we washed down the Valparaiso *congrio* eels with a flagon of chilled Undurraga. During the meal I obtained Mr. Bowers's authorization to try my hand at reorganizing chancery operations, provided, he admonished, I finished the job before he returned from Zapallar in April; he didn't want to find the place in an uproar. He also agreed that after he got back, I could take a trip, already cleared with the State Department, to inspect our recently reopened consulate at Punta Arenas on the Strait of Magellan. Until the opening of the Panama Canal in 1915, there had been an American consulate at Punta Arenas ministering to American vessels making the long voyage around South

America to get from the Atlantic to the Pacific. The presence in 1940 of German vessels, plus concern lest the Panama Canal be damaged, led to reopening the office with a young Annapolis graduate assigned there as American vice consul.

The cardinal's visit, coming on the eve of the national celebration of the founding of Santiago in 1541, was a fine success, and Cecil Lyon did himself proud with the arrangements that emphasized, discreetly, the American presence. Most of the staff, dressed formally and sweating in the summer sun, were present when the presidential train bearing the prelate from Valparaiso reached the capital. There was a minor hitch when the cardinal found he was too wide for the steps of the German-built Pullman car; he finally descended backward, his bright red sash and generously sculptured rear an attraction for the flashbulbs of newspaper correspondents.

Outside the station, with a large crowd in attendance, the ceremonial coach with the coat of arms of Chile on the doors tilted and sagged perilously behind the four horses when the cardinal mounted it. Seated, he waved benevolently at those congregated in the plaza, and they cheered in return. And as soon as the cardinal discovered that he and the archbishop could make conversation in Latin, my services as interpreter, perched on the jump seat facing the prelates, became limited to supplying such words as had not occurred to Roman lexicographers. Presently, when the visitor wanted to ask why there were so few skyscrapers in so impressive a city, Latin failed him. "*Rascacielos*," I offered in Spanish. The archbishop replied to the cardinal in Latin: "Earthquakes, Your Eminence."

Cardinal Daugherty must have weighed over three hundred pounds. His great round face was pink as well as beatific after three weeks of voyaging aboard the Grace Line's *Santa Elena*. He had the well-nourished look of a genial and highly successful contractor. The *chilenos* were impressed by their visitor, whose robust Americanism testified to Mr. Bowers's astuteness in climbing, as he put it, aboard the celestial bandwagon.

The amiable Mr. Farley, contrary to the predictions of those pointing out that a nation with one of the world's highest per capita consumptions of wine might be a reluctant soft-drink client, proved to be a persuasive salesman; the familiar red emblem soon blossomed on the Chilean scene—and wine consumption remained undiminished.

Not all invasions from the United States were so well received. That Chilean summer, the last before the United States was at war, the embassy was nearly inundated by enthusiastic carriers of The Word, not a few of whom traveled under the sponsorship of the coordinator of inter-American affairs, Nelson Rockefeller. These earnest volunteers, as well as many of the crackpots and busybodies whose schemes for fomenting goodwill had already been studied and rejected by the State Department, converged on the self-confident coordinator. Many came away with commissions for all sorts of bizarre undertakings, from building privies guaranteed to be odorless above ten thousand feet to reviving the rubber boom in the upper Amazon to lowering the illiteracy rate by educational movies to be shown (at American expense) in every slum and *favela* from the Texas border to Tierra del Fuego.

More and more of the embassy's time was devoted to looking after these superfluous emissaries, making appointments and accompanying them to call on bewildered and often irritated Chilean officials, and endeavoring — not always successfully — to keep their depredations from impairing relations. Soon the embassy was swapping imprecations with neighboring American embassies that joined us in complaining to Washington and pleading for relief. No one paid the slightest attention.

Preoccupations over visitors were not my principal concern in downtown Santiago, where the chancery occupied two floors that swayed alarmingly whenever a *temblor* shook the city. A *temblor* was a minor earthquake, a mere wriggle on the unstable crust of Chile, but they occurred frequently in the vicinity of Santiago. A real earthquake, the dreaded *terremoto,* from time to time devastated the area. The trouble was that no one could predict when a *temblor* was going to turn into a *terremoto,* and apprehensions mounted accordingly. The rumblings of war in Europe likewise shook the country, and much of our activity was aimed at lessening, to the extent that diplomacy was able, the impact of the conflict on the fragile Chilean economy. The Germans mounted a powerful campaign of propaganda, including broadcasts in Spanish from subsidized stations in Chile. The tenor of each message was the inevitability of German victory, a prediction the news from Europe that year did little to contradict.

The Chilean government became jittery. It required frequent reassurances by the embassy plus proof of support from Washington. The effectiveness of the latter was not always borne out by incidents in the field of bilateral relations, such as a foolish debate over rival claims in Antarctica. The Chilean claim rested largely on the fact that Cape Horn is closer to the nearest finger of that continent (the Palmer Peninsula) than Little America is, say, to New Zealand, with which the American Navy had established an air link for Admiral Byrd. The argument at that juncture seemed singularly futile. Whatever there was in Antarctica would hardly melt or dribble away overnight, and there seemed to us no reason to start singing "America the Beautiful" in the capital of Chile. Washington eventually agreed, and the argument was deferred "until a more appropriate occasion."

Of more serious moment was the embassy's effort in defense of the American light and power company caught between price control and the rising tide of inflation. The difficulties of this American enterprise, established when Chile was still using whale oil, were increased by a fiat contravening the contract between the government and the company about the repatriation of the company's dwindling profits. Our efforts to bring about an equitable solution received little encouragement from the State Department.

It was during this period that I turned my thoughts to the face-lifting job on the organization of the embassy suggested originally by Mr. Welles and authorized, albeit with little enthusiasm, by my ambassador. I decided to try it.

Man for man, our embassy in Chile in 1941 had as high a proportion of talented officers as any mission in which it was my privilege to serve. Several in addition to Cecil Lyon became chiefs of mission. The brilliant but irascible Jim Flexer, who had been a colleague in Cuba, would have become an ambassador if he had worked at it. Jim was a rare judge of political crosscurrents and the best draftsman of official prose I ever encountered, but he marred his chances by deliberately and repeatedly singeing bureaucratic whiskers. He admitted to one departmental inquirer that he had used a certain unanswered instruction to keep his office window from rattling. He told another, who had sponsored an inquiry into the market for American toys outside the capital of Chile, that he was too busy measuring the market for brassieres in Santiago to investigate the market for dolls or roller skates in Antofagasta. Jim was a lovely, uninhibited character. Ambassador Bowers recognized his worth and ignored his irascibility, but Washington rewarded conformity.

Our economist was Clarence Brooks, recently of the Commerce Department, who was experienced, *simpático* with businessmen, and hardworking. He was seconded by the sensitive Charles Knox, bright, young, with literary ability, and by Shelley Mills, a serious-minded Foreign Service officer who was being wasted on routine operations. Our small contingent of attachés and Air Mission personnel in the next few years produced one lieutenant general and two major generals. The naval attaché, who as far as I know did not make flag rank, was equally effective as an embassy officer.

The embassy secretarial staff was superior. It included the daughter of an American ambassador in Europe, sophisticated in matters of representation; the daughter of American missionary parents in Chile, who was an invaluable Who's Who of local personalities; and the incomparable Lucy Lentz from North Carolina, who combined the sharpest eye for an injustice, and the lowest boiling point until that injustice was righted, of anyone I ever served with. With Lucy Lentz as protector of the faithful, no mission needed a guardian angel.[2]

On the eve of World War II a diplomatic mission of one dozen officers (counting the ambassador) was a medium-sized American embassy, even though such an insignificant number might not have been considered adequate for a consulate ten years later, or for a Peace Corps administrative unit in Ouagadougou in the 1960s. Had it not been for the uninvited visitors poured upon us by Washington, our complement would have been ample to handle matters arising between the United States and Chile.

The trouble with the embassy in Santiago was lack of direction under a chief of mission who was a specialist in an early era of American history and who was interested in democracy, liberty, and the four freedoms but not in the tools required to make diplomacy function. Consequently there was inertia. There was haphazard osmosis between one and another of the various components and individuals. The establishment drifted rather than navigated.

Being for the first time in a position to grasp the tiller and move the levers, I found the experience stimulating, although I tackled the problem with caution. While pondering how to go about things most humanely, I received a valuable assist from the State Department in the form of a complaint to the ambassador about a specified shortcoming on the part of the embassy. The next time Ambassador Bowers made one of his pilgrimages from Zapallar, I journeyed to Viña del Mar and persuaded him to sign the following chancery order:

To all Chancery Officers (except Attachés)

The State Department's telegram No. 124 peremptorily requests a report on material called for last November. From the tone of this message, our mission may be the only one among the twenty American Republics which has failed to report. Other instructions, of a similar tenor, have been received in the past few months.

2. A few years later, when I was in Czechoslovakia, it was my good fortune to have Lucy Lentz as a neighbor, first in Frankfurt and then in Munich. In the days of the occupation and the High Commission, Lucy had four-star generals ready to jump through hoops at her bidding. She took on innumerable chores on our behalf that made life in Communist-dominated Prague less unpleasant.

The failure to report more promptly, or to inform the Department within a reasonable period concerning inability to comply with instructions received, reflects discredit upon the efficiency of this mission, and I shall hold each officer personally responsible that no similar case occurs in the future . . . .

The final paragraph of this abrasive scrubbing brush, which I put together on the train between Santiago and Viña, directed that each officer report to me within five days concerning matters within his jurisdiction. Mr. Bowers blinked, but he signed the order without protest when I showed him the telegram from the State Department, which was evidently calculated to remove the cobwebs from the ceiling, if not the paint from the boiler.[3]

Thus fortified, I was able to engineer various changes that I conceived to be in the public interest, although I am not sure all my colleagues agreed with me. They possibly heaved a sigh of relief when, shortly after Mr. Bowers's return from vacation, I departed with my wife to inspect the vice consulate on the Strait of Magellan, an expedition requiring ten days by ship from the railhead at Puerto Montt to the roadstead at Punta Arenas, and ten days back again to Valparaiso after waiting three weeks for a vessel. The actual inspection — the vice consul had little to do except help his British colleague keep tabs on a German merchantman — was conducted in twenty minutes, not counting the time it took to verify the fee stamps and ledger. For the rest, we visited *estancias* grazing thousands of sheep and, shotgun in hand, collected geese, ducks, snipe, and upland plover. The wind blew a steady forty miles an hour, and the whiskey we drank came from barrels laid down at the turn of the century by the thrifty ranch managers, most of whom came from the land of kilts and heather via the Falkland Islands.

What Ambassador Bowers thought of my chancery efforts was not immediately apparent. Some two years after my departure from Chile, I received a small group of congressmen, members of a subcommittee on Latin America, who had come up the west coast of South America. They spent a week in Santiago. The chairman, a tough and genial veteran, said that the embassy

3. Through private correspondence I soon ascertained that for the telegram of reproof I was indebted to Mr. Chile in the Division of American Republic Affairs in Washington. He was my young friend Bob Woodward, whose ability I spotted two years before, when he was on home leave from Buenos Aires, his first post. Bob was then, and many times thereafter, an invaluable confederate. Woodward's career ratified his early promise. His posts as ambassador included Uruguay, Chile, and Spain, as well as assistant secretary of state. He retired in 1965.

was a smooth-running office, and he understood I had had something to do with revising the operation. He had asked Mr. Bowers, but he had received an ambiguous answer. The ambassador said I had shaken things up, but that I sometimes made him uncomfortable by insisting that official inquiries merited precipitate answers. Maybe that is a fair summary of my service in Chile.[4]

At all events, instead of spending three years there, as predicted by Undersecretary Welles, I spent only eight months. A few days after returning from Patagonia, I learned that I was being transferred to Havana, where I had worked as second secretary for four years ending in 1937. I was being assigned as number two to Ambassador George Messersmith, in a much larger office than Santiago. Since it helps describe my new chief, I conclude this chapter by quoting a letter he sent me on May 26, 1941 — Lucy's and my thirteenth wedding anniversary.

Havana, Cuba
May 26, 1941

Dear Briggs:

I had word on Saturday that you have been assigned here to replace Beaulac. I am sorry that I cannot write you at length this morning as I should like to, but I want to send you this word to tell you that I am highly gratified that you and Mrs. Briggs are coming here. When the Department told me it wanted Beaulac to go to Madrid, I naturally made it clear how important it was that the number two man here should come with adequate background and capacity. There is, of course, thorough understanding of this in the Department. Your name, I think, occurred to all of us. It was realized that transferring you from Santiago after so short a time was undesirable if it could be avoided, and that it would be a serious inconvenience to you and, I am sure, to the Ambassador.

You and Mrs. Briggs will hardly have gotten settled before you must move again. I think, however, that in these days when everything, literally everything, is at stake, we have to consider the public interest first. I am sure that although you and Mrs. Briggs would have preferred to remain at Santiago . . . you will understand that it is one of those things which are an incident to the Service which we cannot avoid especially these days, and it must be gratifying to you that everyone thought you were the one to come here for this important assignment. I need not tell you that our

---

4. Shortly after Pearl Harbor, Chile declared its support for the Allies.

mission here in Havana is, and will be for the foreseeable future, one of the most important we have. You will be glad to know that things are going along well here, but it is just as important now to keep them going well as it was to get them on the right track. . . .

The Department wanted Beaulac to proceed to Madrid with as little delay as possible and under the circumstances I could make no objection. He is leaving tomorrow. I shall be very much handicapped until you get here, for I fear I am keeping up my old habits of doing a little bit too much and naturally my burden will be heavier until you arrive. I shall be glad to have you let me know what your plans are and, of course, the sooner you can arrange to get here the better it will be. . . .

Thus goaded, we caught the next Grace ship north. It was our seventh transfer in fifteen years. By midyear we were back in Cuba.

Everything, Literally Everything, Is at Stake

PART ONE: GEORGE MESSERSMITH

It used to be said that there were two kinds of Foreign Service officers: those who had always heard that Ambassador Messersmith was difficult, but had not served with him; and those who had served with him, and were sure of it. "Forty Page" George had few qualities that endeared him to his subordinates. Humorless, opinionated, and sly, Messersmith lorded it over his chancery like the schoolteacher he had once been — a teacher perpetually suspecting misconduct on the part of his students. He was not averse to playing favorites or making it hard for others.

It would be unwise, however, to dismiss Messersmith merely as the vain and preposterous character that in many particulars he was. He had worked hard and diligently, starting as vice consul, in a long career. In Washington, before being assigned to Havana, he had been an effective administrator of the departmental budget. He was dedicated to the Foreign Service as the instrument of the president in the conduct of foreign affairs, and it was largely due to his efforts that the State Department had been able to absorb the commercial attaché service, which for years had been duplicating many State Department and consular commercial functions. Getting rid of the separate Commerce Department service was a genuine achievement for which Messersmith deserved an ample slice of the credit. His service as American consul general in Berlin and later as minister to Austria unquestionably strengthened Washington's awareness of the menace of Hitler and his movement long before the Munich crisis made the world see the ugly face of German National Socialism. Messersmith in his way was as staunchly pro-West as my previous chief, Claude Bowers. In the last months before the Japanese attack on Hawaii, Messersmith tried hard to galvanize the easygoing Cubans and to stiffen their spines against the hardships to come.

Messersmith was correct in his belief that in capital cities the time had come to join the consulates general with the embassies. That lowered to some extent the prestige of the consular officers concerned, each of whom became merely one of several senior members of an ambassador's staff, but it raised the efficiency of the government operation as a whole. The amalgamation in Cuba was accomplished shortly after my arrival, and that arrangement — Messersmith's handiwork — worked smoothly.

Lacking independent means, the Messersmiths conscientiously entertained the right people with dignity, if not vivacity, and there were invariably tables of bridge after dinner. Their limited resources were invested in doing their government job to the best of their ability.

There were a number of reasons why I was prepared to get on with my new ambassador and why I was not overly intimidated by him. Messersmith himself was responsible for my transfer to Havana after a considerable hassle within the State Department. Friends in Washington had described the tug of war that developed between the Latin American Division, which wanted to keep me in Chile, and the Personnel Board, of which Messersmith had been chairman during his Washington service. The matter finally reached Undersecretary Welles. He sided with Messersmith, reportedly on the grounds that Cuba was more important to the United States at that time than was Chile. Even if he had regarded me as a failure, to admit that I had fallen short of his insistently expressed expectation might have reflected adversely on Messersmith's own judgment. Realization of that fact hardly weakened my position.

Second, Messersmith did need someone who knew Cuba. Although I had left Havana for Washington four years before, I had participated in most of the intervening negotiations except for the few months spent with Ambassador Bowers. I had accompanied Secretary Hull to Havana in 1940, and at one time or another I had dealt with practically all of the officials in the Cuban administration, including, on numerous occasions, President Batista. Even though Messersmith bragged about doing most of the work himself, an exception was sugar, which was all-important to Cuban-American relations but excessively complicated. The ambassador would continue to make the major decisions, but he wanted an assistant who understood the sugar problem and on whose recommendations he could rely. With Beaulac going to Spain and Doc Matthews occupying a key job in Embassy Paris, I was elected. Last, Messersmith wanted a hard worker. My dossier, to which he had access, indicted that I was.

In point of fact I got on remarkably well with Messersmith during the months we were together. I even acquired during that period — and was later to lose — a kind of wry admiration for my indefatigable and unjocular chief who, if he had not been so addicted to bridge, might have spent fifteen hours a day in the office, Saturdays and Sundays included. The American ambassador inescapably had social demands to fulfill, and with the office day ending at 5 P.M., by 6 or 6:30 the ambassador had to go home to dress, regardless of the unread documents still before him.

Messersmith was a glutton for work who rarely delegated his authority. As soon as a piece of business became lively or interesting, he would snatch it and spend hours duplicating the work already accomplished. The file would disappear into his desk. A favorable outcome would be a personal triumph for which he took the credit, while some of his associates, including those whose files were in his desk, sat on their hands. One casualty was the American consul general, whose hitherto separate office was about to be merged with the chancery.

This consul general was an expert on everything that had to do with immigration. Called to the State Department after the enactment of complicated new legislation, he had drafted the so-called General Instructions Consular that implemented the legislation. He had served with distinction in Naples, the most difficult American consular post insofar as visa problems were concerned. He had been transferred to Havana because of the flood of European refuges reaching the island, most of whom desired to settle in the United States. In matters within his professional competence the consul general needed supervision as little as a portrait painter or a concert pianist needed to have his elbow jiggled.

Ambassador Messersmith had not handled immigration matters for years, but he insisted on reviewing pending Havana cases, bottling up the files, dictating long, repetitive memoranda, and directing the consul general to investigate this or that aspect of a given case and to report to him before issuing the visa. He announced that many of the individuals concerned, now fleeing Hitler's bloodthirsty purges, had been persons of consequence in Central Europe. That made their cases political, and hence within the province of the chancery, even though he was well aware that by law it was the decision of the consular officer whether or not to issue a visa.

The consul general stood it for several months with mounting fury and frustration. He took to spending more and more time out of his office, visiting and sailing and drinking with Ernest Hemingway. Meanwhile, he was privately seeking an early retirement. He and his wife left Havana within a few days of our arrival, and we were sorry to see them go, even though we were able to take over their excellent house in the Vedado.

Messersmith dictated for hours each day, turning out despatches and long letters to officials in the State Department whose respective areas of responsibility he remembered from his years as assistant secretary of state. Copies of these letters would be sent to other officials, each under an explanatory covering letter that often was longer than the main document itself. The Messersmith prose had a steamroller quality about it that used to numb as well as crumple the recipients, including the president of the United States and the secretary of state. They of course possessed assistants who at the outset were required to make summaries of these mountains of prose. Later the letters went automatically to the geographic division concerned — the American Republics Division — which was allowed to keep on hand a supply of White House and secretary of state stationery on which acknowledgments were typed and then sent downstairs or across the street for signature. One divisional officer was kept busy devising slightly different replies for the signature of the various recipients of the Messersmith messages. Those replies used to be prepared on different machines in order to suppress the evidence that one man had dictated all of the answers. It was a complicated system, wearing on the participants.

Because he kept himself so busy, Ambassador Messersmith was often tired, and when he was tired, he worried about his health. He used to cite the demands made upon him by his official position "in these days," as he put it, "of extraordinary stress and danger, when everything, literally everything, is at stake."

One of his petty tyrannies had to do with promptness in the morning. He himself reached the chancery at 8:45, and he would wait until exactly 9:00, when he would start dialing his staff, making notes of those who did not answer their phones. It made no difference how late an officer might have worked the night before, or how much information he might have picked up at a party. My friend Bob Joyce ran afoul of this. Bob and his vivacious wife, Jane, were the most popular couple in the embassy with Cubans of the beach and country club set, who included many of the Cubans who were running the Republic. They were always in demand at parties, where they behaved with gaiety and discretion. Bob was a first-rate political officer, trained by Jim Flexer in Panama. He and Jane were constantly picking up bits and pieces of useful — at times uniquely useful — information. They were healthy and young, they stayed up late, and they hated to punch a time clock in the morning. Bob did not punch a time clock, growls from the ambassador notwithstanding, and Messersmith — even when conceding the value of Bob's contributions — held it against him.

The Messersmith office hours produced our first competition. As a matter of principle, I decided I ought to reach the chancery before my ambassador did, no matter when he arrived. I started coming in at 8:35, ten minutes before Mr. Messersmith. Discovering this, Messersmith switched his arrival time to 8:30, whereupon I came in at 8:20. When he arrived at 8:15, I was there at 8:05. This idiotic game persisted until we were both arriving *before* 8 A.M., to the consternation of the cleaning women.

Mrs. Messersmith, a sensible person, summoned my wife. They agreed that the ambassador would resume his 8:45 arrival, and that I could come in ten minutes earlier if I wanted to. It was a noble victory for somebody.

We reached Messersmith's jurisdiction on the SS *Veragua,* on a sizzling Havana morning in mid-July 1941, eighteen days from Valparaiso, after a change of season at the equator and a change of ship in Panama. A number of Cuban friends were on hand to welcome us back and to invite us to start the day's drinking without further delay.

Having bought off the welcoming committee with promises of early collaboration and having installed the family in temporary quarters, I lost no time presenting myself at the chancery. As I did so, I could not help thinking of the reception at Rio de Janeiro of my friends Jack and Elizabeth Cabot, who were told by Ambassador Morgan, with his twenty years of Cariocan experience, to stay away from the chancery for several weeks. They would need that time, he said, to find a house, learn their way about the city, start taking Portuguese lessons, and join various clubs under the ambassador's sponsorship. In short, they should meet some Brazilians and start absorbing the local atmosphere. "Get settled. Come back in a month," Ambassador Morgan suggested. "By that time you can start being useful."

Mr. Messersmith's Havana, I surmised, might be a distant cry from Rio de Janeiro. I already knew my way around and did not need to learn Spanish. The clubs I once frequented would doubtless reinstate me. Nevertheless, moving a family was not an overnight job. Getting settled, wherever you were, took doing. Today was Wednesday — perhaps the rest of the week would do it.

At the embassy I was greeted by Ildefonso and González, our two kind and loyal Cuban policemen, and by Amalia, the plump telephone operator, who gave me an adhesive *abrazo*. It was good, they said, to have me back again "en su casa."

Ambassador Messersmith was, for Ambassador Messersmith, affable, almost cordial. Between burps he said he was relieved to see me "at long last" — implying that we might have come by air, in order to arrive sooner.[1] He added that I was badly needed. His important and exceptionally busy office required a number two in order to function properly. He had been doing too much for his own good ever since the departure of Beaulac.[2] Mr. Messersmith then proceeded to give me a playback of the letter quoted in the last chapter. His health, he observed, had not been improved by the additional workload. It had been an exhausting experience. No, he remarked — they were not hiccups; he had an intestinal problem. A burp gave testimony. "In Cuba," he warned, "avoid oysters. But I forget. You've lived in Havana."

With the expression of one conferring an unprecedented favor, the ambassador invited me to take the rest of the afternoon off "in order to complete any pending personal arrangements." He would expect me at the chancery the following morning. Nine o'clock was the hour the office opened.

Since my departure in 1937 the chancery had moved from the park facing the Presidential Palace. That building was now the office of the prime minister of Cuba, my friend Carlos Saladrigas. The embassy had rented the vast Miguel Mariano Gómez house on the Prado, available since Colonel Batista evicted Miguel Mariano from the presidency in 1936. It was an impressive place, but few private residences are suited to embassy purposes. I was relieved when the next year Messersmith's successor agreed to move farther downtown, to an office building that had previously housed the consulate general. Later still, the American government was to build its own vast

---

1. Before the war, an officer could travel by air only with special permission, obtained in exchange for a waiver of responsibility by the State Department in the event of an accident. In South America, in 1941, passenger planes flew only by day. It might have taken four or five grueling days from Santiago to Havana, with uncertain overnight accommodations at such way stations as Arica, Talara, Guayaquil, and Buenaventura — a difficult journey for an officer with a family.

2. Willard Beaulac, a contemporary, had been vice consul in Chile when I was vice consul in Peru. After four years in Havana, he had been transferred to Madrid. An able officer, he held a number of ambassadorial posts after World War II, and he wrote a book, *Career Ambassador*, that is full of advice to those contemplating diplomacy.

chancery near the Malecón beyond the Hotel Nacional, on land made available during World War II by President Batista.

Our business with the Cuban government went smoothly enough, notwithstanding the gathering storm, and I slipped back easily into dealing with officials with many of whom — Cuba being the most informal of countries — I was already on a first-name basis. It was not so carefree a life as I had enjoyed as second secretary under Caffery — our officer complement was not as competent in 1941 as it had been then — or with Bowers in Chile, but there were compensations commensurate with my rank and authority, not to overlook the satisfaction of observing a diplomatic mission that had leadership, no matter how narrow or cramped that leadership might be.

Not the least of the benefits that fell to the new deputy was to regain the services of Dorothy Watson, one of the ablest of the outstanding secretaries it was my good fortune to have. Dorothy had worked for me in Havana in 1933, but she was soon preempted by Doc Matthews after I had incautiously bragged about how good she was. She remained in Havana, becoming a "local" when she married a young Scot who worked for the electric company. I counted myself vastly fortunate to have Dorothy back again.

Most things went along about as I had foreseen, but with the tensions resulting from the war growing each day tauter and more strained. There were, however, incidents of hilarity, such as the affair of King Carol of Romania.

King Carol was of course *ex*-King Carol, who had abandoned his country one jump ahead of Nazi occupation. This, for Messersmith, was a mark in his favor. He was accompanied by his strikingly attractive mistress, Magda Lupescu, who owned several spaniels, and by his chamberlain, a sinister Balkan character named Count Udarianu, who used so much Bucharest perfume that Jane Joyce quickly dubbed him Count Odorono. They moved into a suite at the Hotel Nacional, and the more exclusive of the clubs in Havana sent guest cards made out in the name of His Majesty, Carol, King of Romania. Such was the influence of the conservative Havana matrons, however, that guest cards were omitted for Magda Lupescu. This so incensed the royal visitor that he tore up the cards sent to him and shunned the clubs altogether.

The royal exiles went for their nocturnal relaxation to such public establishments as Sans Souci or the newly opened Tropicana, the latter in what had been the pleasant gardens of Mina Truffin, the widow of Senator

Thomas J. Walsh, whom Roosevelt had appointed to be his first attorney general. Thereafter the Tropicana became one of the most popular night-clubs in Cuba.[3]

Along with nine-tenths of the refugees reaching Cuba from Europe, King Carol wanted to go to the United States, and he had a better reason than some did: in a New York bank there were Romanian funds that the ex-king needed to defray the expenses of his exile. Those funds had been frozen by the Treasury Department in order to keep them from falling into the hands of Nazi Germany. Carol wanted to get them unfrozen, or at least enough of them to cover his hotel bills and living expenses, including those of Magda Lupescu, Count Udarianu, and the spaniels.

To that end, Carol approached the American ambassador through his chamberlain. Messersmith, at the prospect of a genuine Hapsburg-on-the-half-shell, became more genial than I had ever seen him. I was shortly com-manded to appear at the embassy residence following a family supper that included King Carol, Magda Lupescu, and Count Udarianu. My post-prandial assignment was to converse with Madame Lupescu while the king, the Messersmiths, and the chamberlain enjoyed their evening round of bridge. That game, I had explained to the ambassador on arrival, was not my dish. Neither was it Magda's, so we sat on the screened veranda of the Messersmith house in Vedado, with the yellow light from the card room and the squeaky sound of the little tree frogs in the garden.

During the next hour, while the ex-king was losing $12 (which Count Udarianu paid), I admired one of the loveliest complexions in Europe and one of its liveliest ladies. I learned that not only did Carol wish to go to the United States for a reason that seemed legitimate enough, but that Madame Lupescu planned to go with him for a reason that, from their point of view,

---

3. It still fascinates me to speculate about how certain aspects of American history might have been changed had not the aging senator taken the lusty Mina Truffin as his bride on the eve of the 1933 inauguration. Walsh, politically powerful and close to the president, was reported to have accepted the attorney generalship on the understanding that his first official act would be "to kick that so-and-so J. Edgar Hoover out of the win-dow." In anticipation of which, Walsh repaired to Havana, married Mina Truffin (who was what Somerset Maugham once described as a Healthy Woman, in the Prime of Life), and booked return transportation in a nuptial compartment of the Key-West-to-Washington express. The groom did not survive the journey. Mina Truffin de Walsh, swathed in black, returned to Havana, claiming American citizenship. The Havana Social Register continued to give prominence to her credentials. And J. Edgar Hoover contin-ued, for the next thirty years, to direct the Federal Bureau of Investigation.

likewise seemed appropriate. Privately I doubted whether the Washington bureaucracy would see it that way; they might be reduced, on the contrary, to a tizzy.

If the visas were granted, that act might bring down upon the Roosevelt administration all the alarms and excursions I had witnessed when, during President Hoover's time, it was proposed as a routine gesture to appoint a special ambassador to attend King Carol's coronation. Like the Havana matrons who objected to guest cards at their clubs for Magda, American busybodies had shouted for the scalps of President Hoover and his secretary of state merely because Magda, in negligee, might have been lurking behind the Throne Room during the coronation.

After the departure of the guests I was asked to remain briefly to consider the position. Messersmith recalled that he had once been presented to the king at a formal reception in Vienna, but he had exchanged only a few words with him. Now Carol proved to be "so informal and friendly, so *democratic.*" And the chamberlain paid his bridge debt. Mrs. Messersmith wondered whether royalty always had someone standing by to avoid the nuisance of carrying money. And what, as an afterthought, had I talked about with Madame Lupescu?

I told them. I also communicated my misgivings about their proposed American visit.

"Nonsense," exclaimed the ambassador. "That coronation occurred ten years ago. The furor has been long since forgotten. They make a handsome couple."

My remarks made no impression whatsoever upon a man who, I concluded, was a member of that substantial minority to whom adultery, if the participants are rich enough or powerful enough or prominent enough, becomes merely an adjunct to picturesque behavior.

Furthermore, Mr. Messersmith pointed out that it was not adultery because former Queen Helen had already divorced her husband. They were now merely an unwed couple. It was an arrangement widely accepted by sophisticated people.

The next day the ambassador asked me to look over the drafts of two telegrams he had dictated. They were long messages with an abundance of reasoning. The first dealt with the frozen Romanian funds. It recommended that the entire amount, several million dollars, not be made available at once but that the chamberlain be invited to submit a budget indicating in general terms His Majesty's requirements, and that funds then be released $50,000 or perhaps $100,000 at a time. That would ensure that King Carol kept in touch with the American government, which could in turn keep a friendly eye on the king. The ambassador emphasized that Carol had not abdicated — legally he was still the king of Romania — and once the Nazis had been defeated, he might well remount his throne. Carol's goodwill was accordingly worth cultivating, aside from the equity of the matter of the Romanian money.

I thought it a good message and said so. It produced the desired result, but not before I had received a private visit from the manager of the Hotel Nacional, who admitted that the royal guest was several weeks behind with his rent, and what were the chances?

The second telegram, of a higher security classification, was addressed by the ambassador personally to an official of the State Department. It urged for a variety of reasons, some of which also appeared in the frozen funds message, that diplomatic visas be granted to King Carol and to "the accompanying members of his suite," and that "appropriate courtesies" be extended during such time as they were in the United States. The name of Madame Lupescu was not mentioned.

To Messersmith's credit, he showed me the reply to his second message, which was a thumping turndown in the rasping tone of "George, are you out of your mind?" And it left the ambassador no choice but to instruct me to pass on the bad news to Count Udarianu. Shortly thereafter, their hotel bill paid, the Romanian entourage moved to Mexico City. It was given out that the humid climate of Havana had not agreed with Madame Lupescu's spaniels — which I suppose was her way of getting back at the Havana matrons.[4]

The most unsuccessful Messersmith undertaking, however, had nothing to do with royalty. It concerned a conference he arranged for Foreign Service

---

4. The Carol-and-Magda affair had a romantic ending. From Mexico City they went to Rio de Janeiro, where they installed themselves — Count Udarianu and the spaniels still present — in the Hotel Copacabana Palace on the famous beach facing the Atlantic. Presently Magda fell ill, and her condition became so serious that a priest was summoned and last rites seemed in order. Asked if she had a final wish, Magda spoke of marriage — whereupon the padre quickly shifted gears and a wedding took place, then and there, on the deathbed.

At that point, so the story was told me when I reached Rio several years later, the bride sat up in bed, called for a Dubonnet, and said she felt better.

Magda, now styled "Princess Helène," survived her husband by several years. King Carol, whose country was seized by the Communists, never did get his throne back. As a widow, Princess Helène moved to Estoril, outside Lisbon, where the hospitable Portuguese accorded her royal status and privileges.

{ PROUD SERVANT }

personnel serving in the Caribbean area "to consider the political implications of the war raging in Europe." This meeting, which had the blessing of the State Department, brought together a large aggregation of officers from Venezuela, Colombia, Santo Domingo, Haiti, Panama, and the Central American republics, plus consuls from British and French island possessions. Washington was also represented.

The idea was a good one, but the execution was faulty. No ambassadors were invited — that might have detracted from the prestige of the host ambassador, who was chairman — but even so, there were far too many people present and the agenda covered pages. Most of the posts represented were in cities lacking the facilities of Havana, a fun capital dedicated to the entertainment of American visitors. Several, including Barranquilla and Maracaibo, were rather grim places to serve in. Many of the Foreign Service officers, while conceding the meeting's serious purpose, regarded themselves as entitled to at least a minimum of recreation even if they did not qualify as tourists.

That was not at all the Messersmith prescription. To him, life was earnest, and in November 1941 the shadow of Mars lay heavily across the doorsill. The ambassador reverted to his schoolmaster past. He organized the meeting as though the chancery were an academy with reform school overtones and he were the headmaster.

Things began auspiciously with a reasonably brief welcome by the ambassador, followed by an address by the foreign minister of Cuba, who spoke no English.

Four morning hours plus four afternoon hours equals a huge chunk cut from the all-too-brief visit to Havana. Released at last, the delegates streaked out of the chancery like firemen from a firehouse when the siren is sounding. The next morning, those who did appear at 9 A.M. — barring a handful of prim characters who had obviously taken a good book to bed with them — were casualties not yet fit for duty.

Mr. Messersmith made an effort to keep to his agenda, which called for political reports on the situations prevailing in Costa Rica, Nicaragua, Honduras, El Salvador, and Guatemala, but since there still was no quorum, the ambassador called it a day. He declared that with everything, literally everything, at stake, the Foreign Service had failed him. He handed the conference over to the ranking representative from Washington and stalked from the classroom.

A few days later, the Messersmiths departed from Cuba, ostensibly on home leave, and I became chargé d'affaires ad interim. A few days after that came the Japanese attack on Pearl Harbor.

President Batista promptly declared war on the Axis, and he offered to raise a Cuban division to fight side by side with the Americans wherever the High Command might deem them most useful. Batista was proud of his army, which he himself had headed for seven years before he became president of the Republic. Prime Minister Saladrigas, practical as always, declared that the greatest danger would come from Nazi submarines preying on vessels carrying sugar to American ports and bringing supplies to Cuba. He urged that an American warship be dispatched to Havana, representing that a show of the flag would do much to fortify the people and to demonstrate to them the validity of the alliance.

Havana got no American warship — after the destruction at Honolulu, the United States had none to spare — but we did dispatch a small flotilla of yachts and fishing craft from Florida, hastily commissioned in the Coast Guard Reserve and now a part of the navy. They had fifty-gallon drums lashed over the stern, depth charges that, had they been detonated at sea, would probably have blown the American vessels out of the water while not seriously inconveniencing the U-boat.

But the vessels did fly the flag and the uniformed personnel took up some of the slack occasioned by the lack of tourists. The Cubans were grateful, especially the proprietors of such establishments as Dos Hermanos Bar, the Eden Concert, Jiggs' Place, and La Floridita.

My first piece of wartime negotiation took place on behalf of the navy, not at Havana but at the other end of the island at Guantánamo — six hundred miles east of the capital — where the importance of protecting the Panama Canal from the vantage point of Cuba was suddenly recognized.

The naval station at Guantánamo Bay existed by reason of the 1902 treaty, but the station had long been starved by a parsimonious Congress and by a Navy Department with its eye on nearer objectives. Service at Guantánamo was rarely sought. One of the principal discomforts was the inadequate supply of fresh water. For years a trickle had been supplied by Cuban railway tank cars from Guantánamo City to Caimanera, and by navy barges towed to the station. With a procession of warships now crowding into the harbor, and the Panama Canal in mind, a freshwater supply became a high priority item.

I flew to Guantánamo in a Grumman piloted by Major Hayne Boyden, an eccentric marine. On land he was not to be trusted with a Model-A Ford, but in the cockpit of his airplane, with a baseball cap on backward and his waxed mustache bristling like a cat's whiskers, he was one of the best pilots in his service. We lit down four hours from Havana, following the Carretera Central most of the way to Santiago. The admiral laid out the problem: there was absolutely no water within the station. But one mile east, running parallel to the station boundary, was the Yateras River. His engineers had surveyed it. The flow diminished during the winter, but for nine months a year it was ample even with the navy's expanding requirements. With the construction of a few storage tanks a satisfactory annual supply could be assured.

The catch was that the land around the river was privately owned, and if the owner made trouble or demanded an extortionate price, the admiral wanted to have my assurance that the Cuban government would intervene on his behalf. What the admiral needed was the right to construct a pumping station on the Yateras with a pipeline to connect it to the naval station, and the right to take the water. There was no engineering difficulty involved, but the water itself was needed — not today, but day before yesterday. The admiral furnished a station wagon — this was before jeeps — and I went bumping over the dry, unfertile terrain, with Major Boyden along for the ride. It was dark before we returned to Havana, where the major set down the amphibian as softly as putting a carton of eggs on a pillow.

President Batista was sympathetic — more, he was immediately helpful. He summoned his friend Amadeo López Castro, soon to be his secretary of agriculture, and instructed him in my presence to do anything required to make the desired water rights available. "Prepare a decree expropriating the land, if necessary. But I think it would be better if the American Navy makes a contract direct with the landowner, whoever he is. And keep in touch," he concluded, "with Amigo Briggs."

Much as one is tempted to report that a Herculean labor was involved, with abstruse and difficult negotiations in Havana and Guantánamo, and with the intervention of numerous authorities and the drafting of complicated papers, this was not the case at all. Amadeo and I left the president's office together. We agreed that the first step was to check the Registry of Property to ascertain who owned the land on either side of the Yateras River, and whether there were any rights at the source or downstream from the proposed pumping station that might be affected by the taking of water. Amadeo said he would find out and phone me. But it proved even simpler than that, and the speed with which the arrangement was effected so gratified the astonished Guantánamo admiral that it was all I could do to keep him from rushing to Havana overnight to trumpet his gratitude through a megaphone.

Amadeo started his inquires, but before he could report to me, I had an unexpected visit from one Pepín Bosch, president of the Bacardi Rum Company, a man of substance and a prominent fisherman, whose house in Country Club Park was close to the new American embassy residence, then abuilding. I knew Pepín fairly well, as Lucy did his wife, Enriqueta, but I was puzzled when Dorothy brought in his card, on which he had scribbled "Un asunto particular — urgente" (A personal matter — urgent). "Show him in," I told Mrs. Watson.

Pepín came in laughing. He said he didn't know what was up, but that he could guess. And what did I myself think about it?

"About what?" I replied, baffled. "You're going into the soft drink business maybe . . . ?"

"Hell, no." he said. "Not unless someone steals our rum formula. But my lawyers tell me that the Cuban government is looking into a certain real estate title in Oriente Province. Guess where? Guess whose?" He paused while light began to dawn upon me. "Didn't you know I own the land east of your naval station? That is, Enriqueta does. She inherited it. Practically worthless, which is why we haven't sold it . . . ."

My visitor went on to say several things, among them that he made enough money selling rum to navy personnel, to say nothing of oceans of Hatuey beer, that he didn't need extra income from the American government. "Rum and beer — sure, the more I sell, the better I like it. But I am damned if I'll make any money on water. Besides," Pepín went on seriously, "you may not remember what I myself owe to the American Navy." He tapped his knees. "These legs," he said, "instead of crutches or a wheelchair." He went on to tell me that two years before, when his fishing boat exploded in Santiago harbor and he was critically burned, the United States Navy had flown him all the way to Boston, where emergency treatments certainly saved his legs, and probably his life.

"So you can have your Yateras water," he concluded, "for one centavo the million liters, or whatever the *técnicos* mean when they say a token figure. Suppose I send my lawyer to see yours. You write your own ticket: I'll sign it."

It was that simple. I thanked President Batista and I thanked Amadeo. The Navy Department thanked the Cuban government and it thanked me. At my suggestion the navy also thanked Pepín Bosch. And the State Department, catching up after a while with their man in Havana, affirmed that "at the instance of another agency" a note had been entered in my dossier.[5]

5. Soon after Fidel Castro seized Cuba in 1959, he demanded the abrogation of the

During those first days after Pearl Harbor, I expected momentarily to hear from Ambassador Messersmith, and when I did not, I concluded that a transfer was probably cooking. A letter from Mr. Messersmith confirmed this. He explained that he was too overwhelmed with work to write except briefly, after which he dictated seven pages, single-spaced, containing detailed instructions, including what to do about the reprehensible behavior of an American textile manufacturer in Cuba who, against Messersmith's better judgment, had persuaded him to obtain export clearance for certain scarce American machinery under a gentleman's agreement that the manufacturer would then purchase American cotton, which was in surplus supply. As soon as he received the machinery, what had the manufacturer done but place his cotton order with Brazil, at a much lower price. The ambassador was outraged. His efforts to block shipment from Recife had not succeeded, so would I please take up the matter with the government of Cuba?

It took a smart man to get ahead of Gangrenous George (as he came to be known by colleagues), and I resolved to keep an eye on that manufacturer, even though it was clearly out of the question to block his Brazilian cotton transaction.

Messersmith concluded by telling me, confidentially, that he was being transferred to Mexico City — a larger country, to be sure, and of vital importance to the United States. He personally felt that the job in Cuba needed to be kept on the right track, where it now was, because sometimes, for all their good points, the Cubans were not always a serious people. But with a war on and with everything, literally everything, at stake, individual feelings must give way to the duties imposed by the public service. So, Messersmith said, he was going to Mexico. He enclosed a memorandum — four more single-spaced pages — concerning the packing of their effects in the rented embassy residence in Havana. He was arranging to have them shipped to Veracruz, and he hoped the ship wouldn't be torpedoed.

In the meantime, Messersmith said, he was recommending that I remain in charge in Havana. That reminded him that he had run across an assistant secretary of the navy who claimed he knew me in college; the man said I had done a good job for the navy at Guantánamo. That showed, Messersmith commented, the wisdom of his own action in bringing me back to Cuba

---

treaty under which the United States occupied Guantánamo. When told by Washington, belatedly, to go climb a palm tree, the Bearded One retaliated by seizing the Yateras pumping station and cutting off the water supply, thus reducing the naval station to the arid condition that existed from 1902 to 1941.

from Chile. His successor, he informed me, would probably be Spruille Braden, now ambassador to Colombia, where, Messersmith somewhat patronizingly observed, he had shown commendable energy in coping with the local Nazi problem.

PART THREE: SPRUILLE BRADEN

It was some weeks before the Braden appointment was made public, and several months before he reached Havana, during which time the government's business had to move forward. To that end, I was as fortunate in my Mr. Cuba in the State Department as I had been when the same Newby Walmsley saved my Brazilian bacon at the time of the attempted Integralista revolution (see chapter 11). In addition to being an expert on Brazil, Newby had served with us in Havana during the Caffery era. He was invaluable at a time when the State Department was being trapped between its own anachronistic procedures — ill fitted to the pressures of wartime — and Roosevelt's conviction that he, as chief of state, was God's great gift to diplomacy. Although special emissaries often found it more exciting to visit Europe, not a few started popping into Havana. Fortunately, many of them were en route to South America, but enough remained to waste our time and occasionally compromise our efforts.

One of our acute problems was rapid mail communication. The State Department's arrangements for handling paper, and especially its archives and filing system, soon became so clogged that they were almost paralyzed. I remember a phone call from Walmsley: he wanted a copy of such-and-such an embassy recommendation, which he identified by date and number. I said, sure, I recognized the paper, why not get the original, stored within a hundred feet of him? My friend laughed sourly. "If you put a copy in an envelope addressed to me personally, I'll have it by air mail tomorrow. But it might take two weeks to get the original out of the archives." So I mailed him a copy.

We resorted more and more to the telephone until we started to run afoul of the American censors in Miami. The subjects we wanted to discuss were, inevitably, the ones that caused censorship hackles to bristle: shipping and convoys, tonnage requirements, whereabouts of vessels and dates of arrival; submarine losses; stevedoring facilities, from Bahía Honda to Nipe Bay and from Santiago to Cienfuegos — each and every one a forbidden topic. It was in vain that I angrily used to call the chief censor, reminding him that no radio diffusion was involved. Ours was a submarine cable to Key West, and the local telephone company was American, with United States personnel monitoring the Havana end of it. It was comparable, I insisted, to a domestic call within the United States, and such calls were not censored.

I then took to flying to Miami in the naval attaché's plane, calling Washington by telephone from the Opalocka Naval Air Station, and then flying back to Havana — 600 miles round trip at 150 miles an hour — with never a pause on Biscayne Boulevard. But it was better than being repeatedly interrupted by a censor while trying to transact urgent business.

Our satisfactory relations with the Cuban government undoubtedly contributed to the effectiveness of the embassy. We were also fortunate in developing close liaison with the important American business community, some of whose members had upward of a generation of experience in dealing with Cubans. Years before, businessmen had organized themselves into the American Chamber of Commerce, with a professional staff and competent legal counsel; all the embassy had to do was to gear their talents and their willingness to help into our official establishment. This we did through a special committee that became a most effective cog in the machinery of our operations.

One unpublicized type of collaboration, which had nothing to do with the rest of the American community, was conceived in the patriotic brain of Ernest Hemingway and elaborated between him and Bob Joyce. It was what Ernest called his Crook Factory, an effort to exercise surveillance over potential enemies in Cuba, especially Fascists, whom Ernest hated. I am not sure how many Fascists he frustrated — possibly quite a number — but we all had a wonderful time. Certainly the corps of sleuths, informers, and coconspirators recruited by Hemingway represented as strange an assortment of priests and waiters, jai alai players and prostitutes, commercial fishermen and club members, as was ever collected under one aegis — which was personal loyalty to Ernest himself.[6]

Later, when Ambassador Braden merged what remained of the Crook Factory into the FBI section of the embassy, we were able to keep Alvaro González Gordon off the blacklist by proving from Crook Factory sources

6. For an account of the Crook Factory the reader is referred to Carlos Baker's monumental and authoritative biography of Ernest Hemingway, *Ernest Hemingway: A Life Story* (Scribner's, 1979). The book includes material supplied by Bob Joyce and me, as acknowledged in footnotes. Unfortunately, the Crook Factory records disappeared from Embassy Havana and, as far as I know, have never been recovered.

that, although he was not exactly a liberal activated by devotion to the Four Freedoms, Alvaro had no more malign purpose in wanting to go to the United States in wartime than to encourage Nena Velasco, his wife, to spend impressive amounts on gowns at Bergdorf Goodman's. Another beneficiary of the notion that war could be conducted humanely with respect to non-combatants was an Italian-born orchestra conductor, who at the time of Pearl Harbor was in Cuba under contract with the Havana Orquesta Filar-mónica, a reputable organization. His crime against the free world consisted in having worn a black turtleneck sweater while conducting rehearsals. To a witnessing denouncer this made him a black-shirted villain, a supporter of Benito Mussolini, and an enemy of democracy — in short, a Fascist, whose application to reenter the United States must ipso facto be fraudulent. Once again, drawing upon sources whose roots tapped the Crook Factory, we were able to persuade the authorities that Massimo's case was legitimate. He went to the United States, where he became an American citizen.

Such episodes, we liked to imagine, helped justify some of our exertions if not our existence.

In due course I had a letter from Ambassador Braden, who was still in Bo-gotá. Then began a lifelong correspondence with a man who became not only my chief for two years in wartime Embassy Havana but a treasured friend, a man who was to share with me a long succession of encounters with entrenched bureaucracy, some of which we won and some of which we lost — but never from dodging an issue.

Ambassadors Braden and Messersmith had one thing in common: each was an indefatigable toiler in the government vineyard. Each was capable of successive fifteen-hour days while looking around for more terrain to con-quer. There resemblance ended. Messersmith, for all his application to business, was a puny creature, forever contemplating the wonders that lay beneath his navel. Braden was impervious to such preoccupations: he had been a Yale water polo player and later an amateur heavyweight pugilist, a dancer whose tango belied his 260 pounds, a mining engineer turned highly successful businessman, a diplomat who singlehandedly and against the sustained hostility of an Argentine foreign minister had achieved in the 1930s a peace treaty between Bolivia and Paraguay, after a bitter and frustrating struggle.

Braden loved parties and was often the last guest to leave, to the dismay of his less durable associates. Messersmith, cherishing his duodenum, needed seven or eight hours of rest before 8:45 A.M., when he tackled his next paper dragon. Braden, no matter how few hours of sleep he had, came bustling in at 10 A.M. — clear-eyed and pink-cheeked, eager for business. That 10 A.M. arrival was a godsend for his deputy, who was able to organize the day's work and to have things laid out for his ambassador's inspection while Mr. Braden was still at home with his newspapers and coffee.

Messersmith could no more delegate his authority than he could have a substitute take his place in the bathroom. Braden was that rarest of bosses, the man who says what he wants to have done, leaving the details to a subordinate to accomplish, and then backs the subordinate to the limit. The result: a rare commodity called morale, fortifying an office.

At forty-eight years of age, Braden, in addition to his experience in dealing with Latin Americans, possessed an instinctive feel for the intangibles, the obscure and often hidden factors that are difficult to describe but essential to the conclusion of a negotiation. He based his actions, moreover, upon principles that, once defined, he relentlessly pursued, no matter what the odds were against him.

Braden arrived in the spring of 1942 with a brand new embassy residence to move into. He immediately plunged into business and at once was at loggerheads with two ranking officials in the State Department, Larry Duggan and Philip Bonsal. The dispute concerned a project, initiated by Harry Dexter White of the Treasury Department, that would have severed the Cuban peso from the American dollar, with which it had been at par ever since independence. I had resigned myself to the project, to which the Cubans seemed agreeable, and which, after all, seemed within the expanding area of Cuban sovereignty. Not so Mr. Braden, who reached the conclusion that the scheme was unnecessary and inopportune, and that it might impede monetary transcactions at a time when they ought to be operating smoothly. With characteristic energy he proceeded to block it, to the annoyance of Treasury Secretary Morgenthau and Harry Dexter White, and what seemed to me a quite disproportionate irritation on the part of Larry Duggan. Braden had apparently stepped, at the outset, on the toes of Duggan's liberal tendencies; thereafter Larry was not always helpful to embassy Havana. Later Larry apparently conspired to have Braden removed from office.

General Marshall's rejection of President Batista's offer of Cuban troops to fight in the war had been conveyed to the president. Seeking to soften the decision, Marshall had suggested that the American Army would welcome Cuban volunteers who might come to the United States and enlist as individuals, an idea that Batista regarded as insulting. Batista, nevertheless, believed that Cuba should play a part in the war, which in 1942 was not going well for the Allies. The answer to that was a single word: sugar.

The most important task facing the new ambassador became the negotiation of the sugar agreement whereby Cuba would expand production to the limit of its capacity, with the United States agreeing to purchase the entire succeeding crops, whatever size they might reach, minus only the amount needed for local consumption — that is, the sugar requirements of the people of Cuba. That amount had been running at about 150,000 tons a year, a small proportion of the total crop that was soon to exceed 5 million tons. All the rest would go to the United States, which would provide transportation and would undertake to meet the sugar needs of its allies — a large order. In fact, it was to run into hundreds of millions of dollars.

Harsh things have been written about Fulgencio Batista, some of them undoubtedly true. They should not be permitted to erase either his wartime contribution or the fact that his policy, across all the years that he was in power, was based on close and friendly ties with the United States.

That is not to say that Batista was willing to give away his country's sugar, as "Cuba's contribution to the war effort." Braden and I encountered some tough bargaining and had to agree to various concessions, but in a remarkably short time we had an agreement to buy Cuban sugar at 3.25 cents a pound (this was later increased to 3.50 cents). If Batista had insisted on holding out and demanding all the traffic would bear, he could have had several times that amount, a difference that by war's end would have meant not millions but *billions* of dollars.

The agreement provided that the United States would furnish certain essential supplies to Cuba, hardly an unreasonable requirement, since many sugar vessels would otherwise be reaching Cuban ports in ballast. President Batista should receive full credit for appointing, as Cuban price control administrator, Carlos Hevia, whose scrupulously honest administration of a graft-susceptible agency deserved the highest praise.

It was not all molasses and jasmine. Successive Cuban governments did contain individuals, Batista included, who used their political power to build up their bank accounts. Corruption in high places, inherited from more years of colonial administration than other Spanish-American countries had experienced, was a problem the embassy was continuously aware of and was constantly fighting. Our sugar agreement, for example, included one masterly sleight-of-hand gimmick: Cuba insisted, and insisted successfully because of American eagerness in wartime to get on with business, that for local consumption she needed not 150,000 tons, which was statistically defensible, but 250,000 tons — and long tons at that. The higher figure won, and the result was that whereas at the time of Pearl Harbor there had been six Cuban distilleries producing potable rum (headed by such old and reliable firms as Bacardi and Arechebala), one year later there were *fifty-three* Cuban distilleries established in as many of the island's sugar mills. Rum produced a vastly higher dollar return on the sugarcane consumed than did raw or refined sugar. Furthermore, the conversion of cane juice or molasses into alcoholic spirits is one of the simplest and cheapest of chemical miracles, as the farmers of western Pennsylvania discovered with their corn before the Bill of Rights was ten years old. *Alambiques,* the distilleries were called in Cuba, and they sprang up from one end of the island to the other, utilizing allocations, reached after political deals, of those extra one hundred thousand tons set aside for "local consumption."

Nor was rum the only dividend of that modest bonanza. As liquor supplies within the United States dwindled, the *alambiques* obliged with cane-juice gin and then with cane-juice whiskey. Last, the Cuban candy manufacturers rose nobly to the occasion: you could earn the equivalent of 25 cents per pound of sugar selling it in the form of bonbons, as against 3.25 cents under the American contract. All this went under the caption "local consumption."

Corruption in various quarters continually plagued us, and attempts to curb it produced a lengthy, and at times acrimonious, struggle with various Cuban officials. It was Braden's thesis that any extralegal payment was a form of intervention, and that since intervention had been outlawed by agreements to which the American government was a party, such payments — by American firms, for example — ought to be discouraged. He likewise believed, on a more mundane level, that once a company had paid graft, it was forever on the sucker list, and that while the initial payment might produce a short-term dividend or favor, in the long run the company lost more than it gained when it allowed itself to be shaken down. He accordingly summoned the leaders of the American business community in Cuba and laid it on the line that irregular payments and political contributions were out.

Since all firms, domestic and foreign, were solicited for funds by Cuban politicians, this ukase did little to build up the personal popularity of the American ambassador. Meanwhile, Saladrigas had been replaced as prime minister by one Mongo Zaydin, a loud and gaudy character with a religious taint: he always contributed at least 10 percent of his graft to the church. He said it was like an insurance policy.

We soon locked horns with Zaydin over the rights of an American sugar company. That company owned two immense and profitable mills in Oriente Province, Chaparra and Delicias, and a marginal western mill called

Tinguaro, which caught fire and was seriously damaged. The company accordingly planned to dismantle it, using such machinery as could be salvaged for spare parts elsewhere and having the Tinguaro cane crushed at one or another sugar mill nearby. Thus the cane producers themselves stood to lose nothing by closing Tinguaro and the efficiency of the overall Cuban production would be increased.

At that point someone got through to Zaydin with the notion that a sugar mill, once built, became a part of the national patrimony (like Morro Castle or the monument to Máximo Gómez) and that it was the duty of the state to preserve it, regardless of the rights of private ownership or the economic factors involved. Zaydin accordingly demanded that the company rebuild the mill and that it prepare to grind the 1943 crop, regardless of the results of such an order. The company appealed to the embassy, and a battle was joined in which the State Department gave the embassy so little help that anyone except ex-pugilist Braden would probably have thrown in the towel. The Cuban government itself finally bought the mill — at a greatly reduced price — but the rights of the private company were sustained and an important principle vindicated.

The State Department not only gave the embassy scant credit, but when Batista was later persuaded to instruct his Washington ambassador to observe that Ambassador Braden was perhaps being somewhat zealous, that remark was twisted in the Division of American Republics Affairs into a Cuban demand for Braden's dismissal. Research into this unpleasant episode indicates that Ambassador Concheso was terrified by the instruction from Havana and that he approached the State Department upon metaphorical tiptoes, looking around apprehensively for the nearest exit to use when his remark produced the anticipated explosion. Instead, he incredulously heard his American listeners declare, "Very interesting, indeed. Tell us more!"

The upshot was a message from Secretary Hull to Ambassador Braden indicating an intention to remove Braden from Havana "as requested by the Cuban government."

Ambassador Braden's reply, sent as a personal message to Secretary Hull after several days of careful investigation (in a country where very little long remains secret) was an eloquent defense of what he had been attempting to do on behalf of legitimate United States interests, and an equally cogent demand that the secretary of state investigate the facts of the Concheso interview.

The ambassador remained at his post, his position strengthened rather than weakened by the incident. Thenceforth, however, we had to rely more heavily upon our Mr. Cuba in the State Department — Newbold Walmsley — than we did upon his immediate superiors.

A matter more directly connected with hostilities concerned a crash program for the construction of airports. It had been decided that the best protection against German submarines, which were now taking a toll on American shipping in the waters surrounding Cuba, was escort planes plus search-and-destroy operations conducted over waters, like the Yucatan Channel and the Old Bahama Passage, through which submarines had to pass. The Airport Development Program, known as ADP, used a commercial company as a cover for government-subsidized construction. There were immediate difficulties. The company was either out of its depth on that sort of construction or perhaps was eyeing certain postwar possibilities.

President Batista designated his minister of agriculture, the honest Amadeo López Castro of the Yateras River water supply, as liaison with the embassy on the ADP. Soon Amadeo and I were flying down the island to a place near the western tip of Cuba called San Julián, where the ADP brethren proposed to move an entire hill into a large swamp, using bulldozers not then in Cuba, to facilitate patrol of the Yucatan Channel. It did not take long to discover that within one mile of the hill there was a long, level, sandy corridor that required no bigger investment to convert it into a landing strip than the mobilization of a score of Cuban farmers armed with machetes. That trip alone saved the American government hundreds of thousands of dollars.

We had a far worse time much nearer Havana, where Washington decided to build an immense aviation complex at San Antonio de los Baños, twenty miles from the capital. If the American contractor concerned had ever before built anything, anywhere, that fact escaped us. Before long we detailed Garry Ackerson, a competent officer of the embassy, to work full time with the Cubans, trying to reduce to manageable proportions the crises resulting from the incompetence, stupidity, and irregularities spawned not only by the contractor but also by uniformed personnel turned loose by Washington in our midst. It was not until the fortunate assignment of Colonel Leigh Wade that we could go to bed without expecting to be awakened in early hours by frantic appeals from San Antonio de los Baños.[7]

7. Colonel Wade was one of the famous round-the-world fliers of the mid-1920s. After the war he was to see distinguished attaché and air mission service, retiring as major general.

It was about this time that the embassy acquired Bill Yuni, a Japanese-language officer, and we bethought ourselves of the Japanese internees on the Isle of Pines, and how we could utilize Bill as an undercover agent. Yuni was a second-generation Finn, born in the United States and bilingual almost from birth. Entering the diplomatic service, he chose to study Japanese and became proficient in that language. After Pearl Harbor there were more Japanese specialists floating around than were immediately needed, and Yuni, a solemn and conscientious youth, was sent temporarily to Havana, where an assignment in the Consular Section was obviously a waste of his training and talents.

One embassy project, shortly after Pearl Harbor, had been the rounding up of several hundred Japanese citizens inhabiting the island and interning them in the model penitentiary on the Isle of Pines, thirty miles off the south coast of Cuba. This was done with the Cuban government's cooperation and an enthusiastic assist from the Chinese legation in Havana. The American government provided Cuba with a special fund for subsistence that I turned over to Prime Minister Saladrigas.

Word of the harsh treatment of Americans interned by Japan, as well as American POWs from Bataan, had by now filtered back to the United States. Should our few hundred Japanese internees in Cuba not be receiving fair treatment, it occurred to us that it might, in some way, militate against humane treatment of American prisoners in Asia. It was embarrassing to express those thoughts to the Cuban government, which was being subsidized by Washington for the upkeep of the Japanese on the Isle of Pines. One way of dealing with this was to cook up with Cuban authorities an intelligence operation, the ostensible purpose of which would be to identify secret agents among the internees, and if possible find out what they were up to.

Bill Yuni was the perfect candidate for the project. He was docile, unimaginative, and diligent. We decided that he would be a stranded Finnish seaman who got drunk in Havana, had a fight, and missed his ship. A Finnish vessel had in fact called recently at Havana with lumber, and we had in fact repatriated several belligerent seamen. For a week we kept Bill out of circulation. Mariano Faget of the Cuban police obliged with a Finnish seaman's outfit. We then kept Yuni in the Havana jail for a couple of days, so he could acquire a beard and additional patina. We flew him to the Isle of Pines with a batch of prisoners to work out his sentence. He was not, of course, to admit to anyone that he understood Japanese. His chore was to listen.

A week later we had Bill Yuni back, and after fumigation and laundering, this was his story:

It was not until a Japanese turned up who could speak Finnish that Bill's status as a jailed Finnish seaman was accepted. Before that, conversation with him had been conducted in a mixture of bad Spanish and worse English, and among themselves the Japanese had expressed in their own tongue contempt, not unmixed with pity, for his plight. Their attitude derived, he added, from their belief that Finland was a weak and feeble power that would be unable to assist him in his extremity. Unlike the Japanese, who were members of a superior race that would soon vanquish their enemies — whereat Japanese prisoners would be released in triumph — a wretched Finn might languish in jail indefinitely, perhaps forever. He said he had been closely questioned by the Finnish-speaking Japanese, and once over that hurdle, his jailmates became kind, friendly, and solicitous. As to the Japanese feeling toward their Cuban jailers, they said the food was monotonous but they did not go hungry. The model penitentiary, built of Isle of Pines marble, was not an altogether bad place; there were certainly worse prisons.

Signs of plots? Whispers of secret agents? Not a dime's worth, said Yuni.

A few days after that, we allowed Bill to make an official inspection of the Isle of Pines. In his white sharkskin suit and his Panama hat, diplomat Yuni looked not at all like seaman Yuni. The warden of the prison accompanied him, explaining to the internees assembled for the purpose that here was an American official, who could speak their language, come to inquire about their welfare and treatment. Bill reported that his Finnish-speaking Japanese friend was pop-eyed with astonishment — absolutely pop-eyed. Everyone crowded around, and for a few minutes everyone forgot the grim business across the Pacific. It was, Bill concluded, a cheerful interlude. No spies. No secret agents.

We did not always draw blanks in the domino game of espionage. Hemingway's Crook Factory had given the embassy a good running start that Ambassador Braden extended by prevailing upon J. Edgar Hoover to assign three operators to our mission; they became integral parts of the embassy, responsible to the ambassador.

Hoover needed little coaxing to extend his operations to Cuba. He was soon to make a deal whereby the FBI was responsible for certain intelligence operations in all the countries in the New World while the OSS took all the rest of the real estate. This had results not then anticipated by Hoover. When the Central Intelligence Agency succeeded the OSS in 1947, it opened its ranks to FBI men in Latin America in order to staff its new offices in the hemisphere. Hoover was furious. He sent word that anyone accepting a CIA commission would be regarded as personally disloyal.

Nazi espionage in the New World was more than hearsay or gossip. Centered in Argentina, where a certain Colonel Juan Domingo Perón and other pro-Axis officials gave covert assistance, and where one thousand sailors from the scuttled *Graf Spee* had been accorded hospitable asylum, the German network extended throughout Latin America and into the United States itself. Shipping was the principal target, and Allied losses were unquestionably multiplied as a result of German espionage. It was a feather in the cap of our embassy FBI unit when, following the cracking of a spectacular case in Chile, one of the threads thereby exposed led to Cuba and to the apprehension of a German agent in our bailiwick. That spy was tried, convicted, and executed by a Cuban firing squad — the only German agent in all Latin America to suffer the death penalty during World War II. Of interest in connection with later charges of Batista's alleged bloodthirstiness is the fact that in 1943 President Batista was extremely reluctant to have the court's sentence carried out. In fact, we were so doubtful about whether there might be some last-minute stay of execution that one of our embassy officers, Ray Leddy, was detailed to be present. We in the embassy believed that making an example of a convicted spy might have an effect on espionage activities elsewhere in Latin America.

Thus passed two tense and active years in close association with a fearless chief of mission. I have no doubt we made mistakes. A marginal case may have been put on the blacklist or we may have been too lenient in the face of civilian or military incompetence. But we prevented innumerable costly — if often well-intentioned — lunacies, and we prevented the establishment in Cuba of a vast Board of Economic Warfare office, which would have duplicated in the ratio of ten men to one the commercial operations conducted with rare efficiency by our own economic man, the experienced and imperturbable Al Nufer.[8]

Finally, the embassy in Havana operated as an integrated unit. There was never a doubt about who was in charge or what was the direction in which we were moving. In the light of Foreign Service developments elsewhere,

---

8. We accepted two BEW men and gave them desk space in Nufer's section, where under his direction they did useful service. Some Latin American capitals had BEW and other types literally by the hundreds. So much so that Dr. Oswaldo Aranha, the foreign minister of Brazil, observed at this time that if the United States sent any more volunteers to Rio, his country would have to declare war on ours.

then and thereafter, ours was not a bad record. It was a record on which I look back with pride and satisfaction.

One night in early 1944, Dorothy Watson, who had the code room duty, telephoned to ask me urgently to come to the office. No, the message was not susceptible to telephone discussion, although the cable was slugged for me, personally. This was Secretary Hull's message: "Confidential for Briggs. The President desires to appoint you Ambassador to the Dominican Republic. Before submitting your nomination, however, he wishes to know whether you are in a position to accept the appointment. Please telegraph reply. Signed Hull."

My apprenticeship — eighteen years climbing the rungs of the diplomatic ladder from vice consul in Callao to deputy in Havana, was ended. I was being appointed chief of mission.

Fulgencio Batista Zaldivar (1901–1973) died in exile in Spain, fourteen years after falling from power. This chapter may serve to remind historians how much the United States and its allies owe to the man who was president of Cuba during World War II, and who caused his country to declare war on the Axis while American ships were still burning at Pearl Harbor.

15

Dominican Republic
Here Today, Gone Tomorrow

My service as ambassador to the Dominican Republic lasted eight months. That period may be likened to a culvert, with President Trujillo poised with a machete at one end and Nelson Rockefeller armed with a shotgun at the other. Any enthusiasm for either man is likely to be accidental.

The Dominican Republic occupies the eastern two-thirds of the island of Hispaniola, which is separated from Cuba by the Windward Passage; the western one-third is Haiti. Columbus named Hispaniola on his first voyage. His bones — or what pass for his bones among the Dominicans — are buried under the aisle of the cathedral of Santo Domingo, the first Catholic diocese in the New World.

Of all the peoples of Latin America, few have shown less aptitude for self-government than those of Hispaniola. Dominican history from independence until 1930 produced a tragic pattern of dictators who looted the treasury, *golpes* overthrowing the dictators, revolutions, more dictators who looted the treasury, followed by more *golpes* and more revolutions.

The United States intervened from time to time to stop bloodshed, or to protect lives and property. An American loan would thereupon underwrite fiscal reform, or sanitation, or public works, and the premises, under the diligent eye of United States Marines, would be tidied up and again made fit for the Dominican people to live in. The Americans would then withdraw, and soon the dismal cycle would be resumed. Those who crave details are referred to *Naboth's Vineyard*, by Sumner Welles, who served in the Dominican Republic in the 1920s.

In 1930, partly as a result of his discovery by these same United States Marines, who were on the lookout for military talent with leadership potential, Rafael Leónidas Trujillo took over his country. For the next generation — until his assassination in 1961 — everything in the Dominican Republic was different and everything was his. It was, as he soon named it, the era of Trujillo.

The tragedy of the situation was that Trujillo was perhaps the ablest man born in the Caribbean since the Spanish colonization. The energy and confidence recognized by the Marines were qualities that fed upon themselves and multiplied when Trujillo became chief of state. He was an indefatigable worker, a tireless administrator who mastered details, a decision maker who saw to it that his fiats were carried out. As thinker and doer, as schemer and dreamer, he dominated his environment and every individual in it. Trujillo could, in short, have converted his country into a garden of prosperity and content. Instead, he made of it a penal community, a nation of trembling sycophants who not only lacked freedom and liberty but also were denied dignity as human beings. Rafael Leónidas Trujillo ruled his country by fear, including fear of the consequences of anything short of instant, cringing obedience.

Trujillo also identified himself with the state. Under his strong hand the state prospered. Efficiency was the word. Production went up, streets were paved, water was piped, schools were built, milk became drinkable, and the foreign debt was extinguished — whereupon the president added to the title "Benefactor of the Fatherland" that of "Restorer of the Financial Independence of the Nation." He required both titles to be used every time his name appeared in the local press. I once counted thirty-seven such repetitions in a single issue of the government paper *La Nación*. Always the military man, Trujillo soon appointed himself generalissimo, and tailors were recruited to devise the gaudiest uniforms seen in Hispaniola since the imperial days of Haiti, more than a century before.

Had President Trujillo been merely a vain man — or a weaker man — these manifestations of self-love might have been ludicrous, but if you were a Dominican citizen within the borders of the Dominican Republic, there was little ludicrous — and nothing weak — about a chief of state whose critics began disappearing without trial, and often without a trace, shortly after his era began. His known enemies who survived took refuge abroad.

In addition to an ego so inflated that it required massive and continuous doses of adulation to keep it taut, what blocked Trujillo from greatness were avarice, cruelty, and lust.

He absorbed the resources of the Dominican Republic like a sponge, utilizing its treasury as a private bank. Not satisfied with unlimited access to state funds, he soon invaded private business, using the power of the presidency to acquire assets and to stifle competition. Within a few years of the dawning of the era of Trujillo, the president in his own name, or through various rapacious members of his family, had a stranglehold on the economy of the nation. The family owned or controlled everything from construction to banking, from cigar making to prostitution, from aviation to horse breeding.[1]

To the excesses perpetrated upon those suspected of less than total fealty, Trujillo added the shame of psychological torture. That became known as "la técnica de la perrera" (the doghouse technique). Deciding that someone had enjoyed position or prosperity long enough — a senator, Cabinet member, ambassador, business leader, palace eunuch, or whatnot — President Trujillo would without warning remove that individual from whatever he was doing. Often there was no public accusation, no denunciation, no trial — just removal, followed by an intimation that it might be well if his associates joined in boycotting the individual in question. Whereupon that individual became an outcast, an unperson, shunned by his former friends and even by members of his own family. Prevented from leaving the country, the pariah vegetated almost as if in solitary confinement. Possessions, income, credit, colleagues, friends — all gone, all evaporated at the snapping of Trujillo's fingers.

Sometimes the president might relent after a period he considered sufficient to ensure future good conduct. A former favorite might generously be permitted to emerge from the darkness of the doghouse. As suddenly as he had been thrust into obscurity, he ceased to be an unperson; his name would again appear in a social column of *La Nación*. He might even be permitted to resume his former office or position.

A lusty man in the prime of life, Trujillo was a sensational lecher. Few Dominican women — wives, matrons, daughters — were immune once the ardent presidential eye focused upon them. While making a to-do in public about Family Life and the sanctity of the hearth (his mother had by now been given the title "First Mother of the Republic"), the president engaged in innumerable affairs and maintained numerous mistresses.

President Trujillo wanted to found a dynasty, but in that he was doomed to frustration. Throughout history dictatorships have often proved incapable of germinating the seeds of succession, and in Trujillo's case the

---

1. An exception was the sugar business, then largely in the hands of Americans. In the early years of the Era of Trujillo, American citizens were generally not molested.

father's competence went mostly to a daughter, Flor de Oro, instead of to Ramfis, the heir apparent.[2]

In foreign affairs the Trujillo formula was pragmatic and simple: do not quarrel with the United States and be on the winning side. Respecting power, Trujillo paid it heedful and envious attention. His attitude toward other international problems was a blend of self-interest and a desire to share the limelight when pictures of the victors were taken. His country was one of the first to establish a public relations apparatus in the United States separate from the diplomatic and consular offices, and to accord it a generous budget. It is reported that Trujillo paid a prominent American politician with access to the White House *ten times* the salary of the American ambassador to the Dominican Republic. This arrangement was designed to exploit news favorable to Trujillo emanating from his propaganda factory at home, and to stifle Washington projects deemed inimical to his interests, including those confected in the Department of State.

This, then, was the Dominican Republic to which my family and I traveled in 1944. Nazi surrender was still one year away, but with the successful Allied landings in France, the war in Europe was clearly grinding toward a predictable conclusion. No one cheered more loudly than the president of the Dominican Republic, whose "spontaneous demonstrations of anticipated victory" often featured El Benefactor, in his generalissimo uniform, surrounded by suffering, dutifully beaming diplomats.

2. Flor de Oro Trujillo matured in the 1930s. Sexy in a sultry Caribbean way, she was appointed counselor of the Dominican legation in Washington. Her name duly appeared on the Diplomatic List issued by the State Department. Thereafter Flor de Oro was involved in several spectacular marriages and divorces. An American husband burned up in his bed, amid considerable speculation.

Ramfis Trujillo was commissioned a colonel in childhood. In his teens he had his own apartment atop the Hotel Jaragua, where he entertained friends and contemporaries, including girls from Miami. A general in his twenties, Ramfis voluntarily reverted in rank to colonel in order, so it was given out, not to outrank his American colleagues at the Staff School of the United States Army at Fort Leavenworth, Kansas, to which he had been admitted for training. The Dominican press dwelt ecstatically upon this refulgent example of humility and abnegation. Meantime, the presidential yacht sailed to California. Ramfis soon found that state so much to his liking that he abandoned his lessons in Kansas for a series of Hollywood lovelies, with whom he was photographed aboard ship in unmilitary postures. At the end of the course, the Leavenworth command, showing unexpected sturdiness, declined to give Ramfis his diploma, to the rage of his generalissimo parent. Ramfis's interests remained sports, girls, and the abundant life, rather than learning how to administer a country. He did not long survive his father.

In his capital, now renamed Ciudad Trujillo, my wife and I found awaiting us a new and spacious embassy residence with cascades of purple, white, and brick-red bougainvillea, screened verandas, and a view across tropical greenery toward the blue Caribbean. The grounds were ample and well tended; there were several fine mahogany trees and clumps of croton and brilliant hibiscus. Below our air-conditioned suite on the second floor, feathery bamboo and a gigantic flowering tree shaded the swimming pool.

Opening an eye upon our inherited opulence on the morning after our arrival, my wife remarked cheerfully, "Good morning, Mr. Ambassador. And to think we get paid for living here . . . ."

The pay was $10,000 a year — we were not destined to collect it very long — but that did not detract from the pleasure of our first morning swim in the Dominican Republic.

"Great and Good Friend" was the formal salutation in the letter by which I was accredited ambassador by President Roosevelt, who added that he "reposed special trust and confidence" in his new envoy to the Caribbean. Stirring words, but as I look back upon them, I doubt whether my first official suggestion lived up to the implications of that prose. Remembering a Roosevelt-Churchill agreement that for the duration of hostilities formal attire would be laid aside, I dispatched a reluctant deputy to the Dominican Foreign Office with the suggestion that the new ambassador would welcome presenting his credentials in a tropical business suit instead of in a cutaway coat, striped trousers, a black waistcoat, and a high hat, none of which articles had been devised for use in the Caribbean.

In retrospect, that was a silly aspiration on my part. President Trujillo would sooner have fulfilled an oath of chastity than forgo an opportunity to don fancy dress and parade before cameras, no matter what the temperature. So formal regalia it was. In the horse-drawn coach on the way to the Presidential Palace, with the windows closed against the afternoon downpour, the new envoy and the chief of protocol sweated in our woolens while the aroma of wet horse vied with that of the moth balls in which our garments had been stored.

My first interview with the dictator went smoothly enough. Although upholstered to suffocation, I suppose each of us was on his good behavior. One readily sensed the power of Trujillo. As his fellow citizens oozed fear, so from the president flowed the strength of a man born to lead, a man now accustomed to the exercise of absolute authority. The president made affable observations about inter-American solidarity. He invited me to call on him whenever I believed that he personally could be of assistance. He pledged continuing collaboration in the war effort, reminding me that soon after Pearl Harbor, Washington had informed him that the most valuable contribution the Dominican Republic could make would be in foodstuffs and in sugar, the production of which he had accordingly caused to be substantially increased. He inquired about the health of Secretary Hull, which he had heard was failing, and in friendly fashion about my predecessor, whose appointment as ambassador to Panama he had noted.[3]

The cordiality did not survive for long. Soon after I arrived, I sought to force Trujillo to comply with the terms of a contract under which the American government bought surplus Dominican foodstuffs for distribution to the food-deficient islands of the Caribbean, and the Dominican Republic obligated itself to publish the prices paid for each commodity bought by the United States. The purpose of the provision was, of course, to prevent Trujillo from buying from his peasants at starvation prices while selling at double or triple those amounts to the United States.

After irritating days of procrastination and unkept Dominican promises, during which crops were being harvested and pitiful prices paid to the Dominican farmers, the embassy solved the matter by buying space in the local newspapers and publishing the price schedule, "in accordance with paragraph so-and-so of the contract." President Trujillo's agents were forced overnight to raise the amounts paid to the Dominican producers.

The embassy decision to publish the price schedule was not taken without debate, although I do not recall that the matter was submitted to Washington for prior endorsement. It was an action that, my colleagues accurately predicted, would be regarded by President Trujillo as a declaration of war by the new ambassador — since it affected both Trujillo's pride and his pocketbook — but it seemed to me that, if so, it was not a problem of my making but one inherent in the situation Trujillo had created. A contract was a contract, and a relationship based on performance by one party and of nonperformance by the other was not to be tolerated. My chancery colleagues applauded, especially Bob McArdle, a fine New York Irishman who as representative of the Board of Economic Warfare had earlier negotiated the agreement, but they were not wrong in interpreting this show of embassy independence as a watershed dividing prior and subsequent relations between the chief of state and the American representative.

3. Avra Warren (1893–1957), a Foreign Service officer who subscribed to the "butter up the dictator" school of diplomacy. Avra's son, a contemporary of Ramfis Trujillo, accepted an honorary commission in the Dominican air force.

Although remaining outwardly correct in his behavior, Trujillo gave increasing priority from that time forward to replacing the United States envoy. Broadly speaking, there are two ways a chief of state can get rid of an unwanted envoy. He can declare him persona non grata — an unwelcome person — in which case, out he goes. International law provides for no debate on the merits of such a case. Alternatively, the host government can promote a whispering campaign of innuendo and abuse in Washington, catching the ears of officials hostile to the administration and even of members of the State Department. The idea behind this more subtle approach is to create a situation in which the initiative appears to come from Washington, which decides to make a change "for the good of relations."

A decision whether it is or is not in the national interest to maintain relations with a disreputable government is a policy matter decided in Washington. Based on my own experience both as performer and as observer, I conclude that there are indeed times, including wartime, when as a practical matter it is desirable to deal officially with a country whose government we may deplore.

When I went to the Dominican Republic, the *attitude* of the United States was one of sympathy with the exploited Dominican people, but at the same time the American government felt no compulsion to throw out Trujillo because his conduct toward his own fellow citizens was bestial. The *policy* of the United States called for formal — but not cozy — relations with the Trujillo dictatorship, whose support for the war effort was useful to the Allied cause. But that dictatorship, Washington held, should not be permitted to misrepresent acts of routine official collaboration as endorsement of the enslavement of the Dominican people; much less should El Benefactor be allowed to utilize the normal courtesies extended by the resident American ambassador for the aggrandizement of the tyrant himself. These are easier prescriptions to write than they are to put into practice.[4]

Granted that the foregoing oversimplifies the problem and that while it may be the primary responsibility of those who are oppressed to exterminate their oppressor, that task is rendered no easier when the dictator (as a wartime ally) is supplied with arms. A machine gun solicited by Trujillo to

4. This was recognized later by Ambassador Charles Yost, an astute career officer, when he was United States representative to the United Nations. Yost suggested redefining the term "free world" to confine it to countries with democratic governments. For strategic reasons the United States might need to ally itself with a dictatorship, but dictators should not be identified as friends.

defend the Dominican coast against German submarines was equally capable of being turned on local citizens. Moreover, merely having official dealings with a Trujillo — or a Stalin — even upon the most disinfected basis conceivable, is bound to affect to some degree the credibility of American support for such lofty war aims as the Atlantic Charter or — later — the Charter of United Nations. Even the best-intentioned declarant cannot, if he hops into bed with a polecat, escape the redolence associated with *Mephitis*, whose perineal glands are impossible to represent as responsive to the Four Freedoms.

The problem of the Washington representative in a dictatorship is further complicated by his having to play on the home field of the opponent, which football coaches say is often worth a touchdown a game. That may be debatable, but recognition of those and other hazards led to the wise Washington decision to leave *tactics,* as well as day-to-day decisions, to the man on the spot, who was instructed to operate within the general framework outlined above: that is, official relations, yes; arms around the neck — no.[5]

The fact that every move of the American envoy was scrutinized and then assayed for political content, in the hope that something of local advantage could be extracted, was illustrated soon after my arrival, even though I did not become aware of it until sometime later. I had as my guest one weekend in Ciudad Trujillo, Gustavo Durán, a member of Ambassador Braden's staff in Havana. Gustavo, who had become a naturalized American citizen, had fought on the Loyalist side during the Spanish Civil War. He had been recommended to Ambassador Braden by two such disparate sponsors as Ernest Hemingway and Nelson Rockefeller. He served with Braden in Cuba, later in Argentina, and in 1945–46, when Braden was assistant secretary of state, in Washington.

It was during the Washington association that Durán was publicly accused in the Senate of Communist affiliations in Spain, where it may be recalled that the Loyalists received important support from Moscow while Berlin and Rome were aiding Franco.

Durán's visit to me in the Dominican Republic in 1944 had no political content whatever, but no sooner had he been accused in Washington of hav-

---

5. In all of this I was greatly assisted by Jack Cabot (with whom Sam Reber and I had rented a house in Peru in 1927). Jack's next post after Lima had been Santo Domingo, in the days when Trujillo was whetting the blade of his guillotine. To have a competent and sympathetic colleague in the home office in Washington was of inestimable value when I was in Trujillo's lair.

ing once had Communist ties than Trujillo issued a pamphlet declaring that during Durán's "secret visit" to Ciudad Trujillo in 1944, "Briggs and Durán had plotted to establish a Communist party in the Dominican Republic." Few were impressed by these charges, but the fact that they were made, two years after I had left the Dominican Republic, is illustrative of the closeness of the tabs that must have been kept on the American representative, his comings and goings, his callers and friends.

Matters at first proceeded on a relatively stable keel. Although El Benefactor kept a baleful eye on the activities of the American ambassador, I was beyond the reach of his predatory claw, a comfortable feeling. Thirty years ago diplomats were still scrupulously accorded the immunities that a careless State Department allowed to crumble away after World War II — and that State has since been frantically attempting to reestablish, not, it may be noted, for the comfort or well-being of the diplomat in person, but because without those immunities from local jurisdiction it obviously is impossible for the foreign envoy to function effectively. In 1944 diplomats were literally the only persons in the Dominican Republic who could not be touched by the chief executive or his agents.

Hispaniola in 1944 was a fertile land with spectacular scenery and a benign climate. It offered the same good bird shooting I had enjoyed in Cuba, and with my shotgun as my excuse, I was soon exploring the country and exchanging gossip with farmers in out-of-the-way corners, a more profitable exercise than town life, which involved listening to speeches by officials owing allegiance to the chief of state and seeking to curry favor by extolling the miracles accomplished during the Era of Trujillo.

I was pleased with my small wartime establishment, which was sufficiently compact for intelligible operations. (That can be said of almost no diplomatic mission today.) My deputy was Bob Newbegin, a young man from Massachusetts, serious of mien, who had not lacked the courage to tell his new chief what would happen to his suggestion that credentials be presented in a business suit.

There were two political officers: Andy Donovan, a friend my age who was in fact a spare; he suffered from an obscure service-contracted ailment that rendered him miserable in cold weather. I gladly took him on, in hopes that the Caribbean sunshine would improve his health. It did not, but in the meantime Andy, a competent bridge player and an insatiable gossip, found out everything that was happening in the diplomatic corps.

My second political officer grew up on the coast of Ecuador, the son of Protestant missionaries, and married a devout Catholic from one of Ecuador's leading families. Harry and Germana Reed mixed conscientiously with what passed for society in Santo Domingo. What intelligence there was in that sector they acquired, and it was through Germana that I first recognized what a mine of information is possessed by members of the church hierarchy, even — or perhaps especially — in places like the Dominican Republic.

My embassy economist was bright, studious, and, as far as my comprehension was concerned, might just as well have been writing in Hindustani. Ascertaining that his graphs and abstractions were nevertheless pleasing to Washington, I left him largely to himself, seeking out my Board of Economic Warfare representative, Bob McArdle — who had spent years in business in the Caribbean — whenever I wanted to know, for example, why the market for tobacco had shown such sudden signs of instability.

My air attaché was a navy two-striper enjoying a tropical respite after tangling with Japanese and williwaws around the Aleutian Islands. A competent pilot, he was almost embarrassingly loyal to his new profession of diplomacy, as witness his response to a too casual marine at the air station at Opa-Locka. After landing there, we borrowed a car for our business in Miami. At the gate, after a lackadaisical salute for the lieutenant, the marine inquired rudely, "And who is that civilian bird with you, Lieutenant?" It turned out that my two-striper came from the Southwest, where his father held a post in Indian affairs and his mother had been a pure-blooded Yaqui Indian, the tribe whose ancestors had not been intimidated by the appearance of Coronado four centuries before. Around the head of the marine the Florida air now crackled and blistered.

"This civilian bird," concluded my lieutenant, "ranks a four-star admiral. Now let's see you salute again before I get you busted back to private." And we drove out the gate, diplomacy ascendant.

That may have been a prophetic incident, because during the balance of my service in Santo Domingo, I had almost as many problems with the American military as I did conducting affairs with the government of Trujillo. The reason was that by the latter part of 1944, the war had moved away from the Caribbean, where the United States military establishment had been hastily organized to protect the Panama Canal and to counter the submarine menace. It had also been used to service our planes on the long, roundabout route through the West Indies to the shoulder of Brazil at Natal, and thence across the Atlantic to Dakar. This presence had remained intact long after the military reason had ended. In consequence, we had more generals floating around than Washington knew what to do with.

The majority of these senior officers were patriotic servants who schemed for jobs closer to the heat of the conflict. Some succeeded, and not all of them returned. Others, including some who, had it not been for Pearl Harbor, might have had honorable retirement as lieutenant colonels or commanders two decades after leaving West Point or Annapolis, found much to commend in the quarters of commanding officers, such as 15 cent beer, hearts of palm salad, and mess boys at attention. Most diverting of all for them was an abundance of airplanes to buzz around in, visiting colleagues and calling upon West Indian officials with whom — the German submarines having departed — they had in fact very little legitimate business; this could, in any case, have been transacted for them by the resident American diplomatic or consular representative.

Like my naval attaché, but with more years of experience to back it up, I also was loyal to diplomacy. I took seriously those lines about the responsibility of the chief of mission as the personal as well as the official representative of the president of the United States, and about the ambassador's being the number one United States official in the country to which he was accredited.[6]

In the special circumstances surrounding the Trujillo despotism it seemed singularly improper for ceremonial deference to be promoted by our military in Trujillo's direction, since it invariably resulted in publicity that El Benefactor could misrepresent to his own advantage. There was one American general in particular who was so captivated by the achievements of the Era of Trujillo, and by the attentions of El Benefactor to himself, that he could scarcely contain the sawdust stuffing beneath his bemedaled tunic. The behavior of this general led before long to a collision with the ambassador in residence. Although I did not realize it at the time, that was the last piece of business to bring me to the personal attention of Secretary Hull.

Incongruously, the encounter began with the death of the Peruvian ambassador, Juan de Osma, who bore an illustrious name. He was a bachelor, and his embassy was maintained by his sister Belén, a lady renowned for her piety and good works. She reported to me, in tears, that Juan's dying wish had been to be buried in the family ground in the City of Kings in far-off Peru.

---

6. In retrospect, I was perhaps slow to recognize the situation wrought, de facto, when the United States became a belligerent; but after hostilities ended, I fought a bitterly contested and not always losing battle during the final decade of my service against the attempted ursurpation of diplomacy by the military.

My telegram to Washington was sympathetic. I reminded the State Department that the war had long since absorbed the steamship service to the Rainless Coast. It would be a compassionate gesture, within the scope of Peruvian-American friendship as well as the appropriate manifestation of the President's Good Neighbor Policy, for the army air force (which certainly had planes available in the Caribbean theater) to provide transportation for the ambassadorial remains from Ciudad Trujillo to Lima.

Through the slipping of a bureaucratic cog, my message went directly from State to the Pentagon, without the usual State Department notation of assent or disagreement. It was received by an officer who conceived it to be his duty to lecture the ambassador upon the exigencies and sacrifices of war. Among the circumstances flowing from belligerency was one specifying that military aircraft were not to be diverted from their martial occasions, or to be sent upon frivolous or nonmilitary errands. The current cliché of that period — "Doesn't the ambassador know there is a war on?" — was politely omitted, but that was the gist of the message.

By a coincidence these events took place at a time of yet another visit to Ciudad Trujillo by the footloose general, who arrived in his B-17 bomber called *The Swoose*. There was military jollity that night in the general's honor. One motor of *The Swoose* stuttered the next day, so a second B-17 was quickly mobilized and flown to the Dominican Republic from Puerto Rico to return the general to his command. Repaired, *The Swoose* departed empty, only to return to Ciudad Trujillo forty-eight hours later with the general's aide bearing a color photograph of the American general inscribed with a message of esteem to Generalissimo Trujillo from his recent guest.

This souvenir was duly delivered to the Presidential Palace by the aide, who then, in accordance with regulations, made a call upon my military attaché, Major Burns, in the course of which he gave the major a clipping describing the general's latest trip and his return to his command, on which occasion the general had made a statement to the local press. In it he eulogized the Era of Trujillo and praised the progress and tranquillity prevailing in the Dominican Republic under its progressive leader.

I considered this intelligence in the light of the Pentagon telegram about Ambassador de Osma. Two messages thereupon smoked from the ambassadorial typewriter to the Department of State. My first telegram had to do with the general problem created by these superfluous and indiscriminate military visits, rarely cleared with the embassy in advance, and the effect of those visits on our policy of "correct official relations, yes; embraces, no," under which I was endeavoring to conduct relations with the Dominican

Republic. The telegram concluded with the calculation, worked out by my naval air attaché, of the amount of fuel consumed in the past few days by the two four-motor B-17s in transporting the general, his aide, and the general's photograph between the post he was supposed to be occupying and the capital of the Dominican Republic.

My second telegram was brief: it reiterated my recommendation that the remains of my Peruvian colleague (which were being preserved in the refrigerator of the local brewery by special dispensation of the archbishop) be transported by air from Ciudad Trujillo to Lima, for reasons stated in my original message.

By this time my colleague Cabot, on the Dominican desk in Washington, was firing on all of his Beacon Hill cylinders. With the help of Hugh Cumming in the secretary of state's office, my telegrams were among those on Mr. Hull's desk when he reached the State Department that morning. As I got the story from Cabot, Secretary Hull was so aroused that he seized his telephone and called his predecessor, Henry Stimson, who was now the secretary of war.

Several results flowed from that Cabinet-level conversation. The first was the arrival of an army C-47 with comfortable accommodations forward for Señorita Belén de Osma and her maid, and with cargo space aft for the remains of His Excellency Dr. Juan de Osma, late ambassador of Peru to the Dominican Republic. Another result was a message from the secretary of war to the footloose general, who thereafter became less footloose and gave no more interviews to the press about the political affairs of countries within the perimeter of his operations.

The third and most important result was to fortify me in the belief — reckless though it turned out to be — that an ambassador was, as his copybook declared, the official responsible under the secretary of state for the relations between Washington and the country in which the ambassador served. The incident gave me a warm feeling of loyalty to the old gentleman now preparing to leave his beloved State Department, but it did little, I am afraid, to prepare me for the events of the immediate future.

Secretary Hull had been in declining health for several months. A few days later he resigned his office. For twelve years he had been secretary of state, almost two-thirds of my entire career as a Foreign Service officer. Often wondering at his patience under provocation, I admired the old gentleman. I never doubted his integrity, his honesty of purpose, or the validity of the principles that he espoused; they seemed to me then, and still do, to be legitimate objectives of the United States. Nor did it occur to me, so long had

Mr. Hull been in office, that a policy carefully elaborated with respect to an area of the world or one country within that area was likely to be modified, without careful and thoughtful deliberation and debate, at the whim of a successor. In short, I did not immediately comprehend that with Hull out of office, Briggs might be out of luck.

I knew little about Mr. Hull's successor, Edward R. Stettinius. He had been borrowed from the United States Steel Corporation for Lend-Lease, was a Harry Hopkins protégé, and was considered in some quarters to be not very bright. Through marriage he was related to Juan Trippe, the founder of Pan American Airways, with whom I had had many things to do over Pan Am's relations with a German Colombian airline called SCADTA, whose German pilots were flying too close to the Panama Canal for our 1939 comfort. On the whole I took note of the Stettinius appointment with more regret for the departure of Cordell Hull than with the idea that the policies with which I myself had to do had been rendered vulnerable by the change, or that the status of one executing those policies might also be affected.

In Ciudad Trujillo I went about my business as usual, taking note without enthusiasm, but without surprise, of the reelection of Franklin Delano Roosevelt to an unprecedented fourth term. In that connection a few days after the election I duly forwarded, as tradition and usage required, my pro forma resignation as ambassador, a document that would remain on the table until the president either acted upon it following his inauguration or — as in the case of most professional appointments — took no action, which meant that the incumbent continued in office.

There were storm clouds to which, as I look back upon them, I ought to have paid apprehensive attention. With the approach of Thanksgiving 1944, I received a telegram that, while I did not regard it as an added cause for thanksgiving, I first assumed to be a routine matter. The message informed me of a twenty-four-hour visit to Ciudad Trujillo, beginning Thanksgiving morning, by the coordinator of inter-American affairs, Nelson A. Rockefeller. He apparently was on a tour of some of the projects conducted by his office. The message did not inquire whether the visit would be timely, or convenient, or likely to be useful, but merely that it would take place and that certain arrangements had already been made through the Dominican embassy in Washington for the coordinator to interview "various Dominican officials."

I did not care much for the sound of that, but again attached no special importance to the visit. The position of the coordinator was incongruous per se, inasmuch as what President Roosevelt had created, possibly to irritate Sumner Welles or Cordell Hull, was a second and free-wheeling Latin American division, whose head was supposed to receive "policy guidance" from the secretary of state but who in fact operated with his own budget, concocting all manner of odd projects. Some of these (like the anti-malaria campaign conducted by professionals in Brazil) were useful, but most were superfluous, impractical, wasteful of public funds, or downright lunatic.

My personal acquaintance with Nelson was slight. I regarded him as a well-laundered and housebroken Eagle Scout from Pocantico Hills, but I found it hard to take seriously most of his operations. From private correspondence with Washington I was aware that some of my comments on some of his projects — observations made to colleagues in the State Department about the grammar school thinking and high school prose in which they were conceived — may possibly have found their way to his attention. I shrugged that off. Nelson was nine years my junior and had little practical experience in dealing with Latinos — except, of course, as a handout artist — whereas I had served fifteen of my nineteen Foreign Service officer years in rough-and-tumble dealings with four different Latin American countries, plus a tour in the Latin American section of the State Department in Washington.

Nevertheless, Thanksgiving Day was Thanksgiving Day, and I was prepared to be as hospitable as I could to a fellow alumnus of Dartmouth College who, I assumed, would be a good if somewhat self-assertive presence. Maybe all he needed was a swim in our pool and a fistful of martinis. I wired back an invitation for Nelson to stay at the residence and also asked him to accompany me to the Thanksgiving Day American church service, at which I would read the president's Thanksgiving Day proclamation. He accepted.

Intimations that all might not be serene began at the airport on Thanksgiving morning, where, before Nelson's arrival, I found awaiting him the foreign minister, one Peña Battle, who for some time had enjoyed the favor of President Trujillo. From the number and rank of accompanying stooges, it promised to be a full-dress welcoming affair, following which, the foreign minister informed me, he proposed to transport the guest to the Presidential Palace. The American ambassador apparently was not expected to figure in these events.

Politely I declined the suggested arrangements. I indicated that Señor Rockefeller, an American official, would be my guest while in Ciudad Trujillo. After his journey he would doubtless wish to freshen himself, to have breakfast, and perhaps to relax a bit, following which he would accompany me to a service at the Protestant church, since the day happened to be a national holiday in the United States. Thereafter, Señor Rockefeller would, of course, be at the disposition of the foreign minister, and I remarked that I would be happy to accompany him to pay his respects to President Trujillo should *el Señor Presidente* desire to accord Señor Rockefeller an audience.

Very correct, very protocolaire, and I gave the glowering foreign minister no choice. When Rockefeller arrived, the minister made a second effort, which again I frustrated. My guest gave the impression, however, which was not lost on Peña Battle, that if left to himself, he would have accepted the foreign minister's invitation with alacrity. There was a session of handshaking and arm patting with many photographers in evidence before Nelson and I drove away in the embassy sedan. He remarked upon the courtesy of the foreign minister in offering transportation. It was not an auspicious beginning.

The foreign minister was waiting for us at the embassy when we returned from the Thanksgiving Day church service, and it immediately developed that a schedule had been arranged for the visitor about which I had received no previous information. It was to culminate in a special extraordinary session of the Dominican legislature, followed by a banquet in Nelson's honor, hosted by *el Señor Presidente* himself. My wife and I were invited to be present. All this was pursuant, I gathered, to arrangements discussed in Washington, although I had received no word about them from the State Department; if I had, I assuredly would have objected. I had no personal prejudice against my guest, but his official status was not compatible with an extraordinary legislative session in his honor, even if the legislature had not been known with derision for a dozen years throughout the hemisphere as the prototype of a rubber-stamp congress of a dictator. As for the presidential banquet, here the propaganda objectives were ridiculously clear. Nelson, in short, was being had for the benefit of El Benefactor.

When I indicated, with all the tact I could summon, that these arrangements seemed a trifle lush in view of the status of American relations with the Dominican Republic, and that the beneficiary was not likely to be either the guest of honor or the American government, but the most disreputable ruffian in the New World, the firecracker that had been fizzling ever since Nelson's plane set down that morning went off with a bang in the smoky aftermath of which it was not easy to mince words.

In the view of my guest, I was a stiff, unsympathetic, and unbending representative who had made no effort to befriend the chief of state, much less to appeal — as had my predecessor — to his better nature. I retorted that Trujillo had no better nature to appeal to, and offered to cite chapter and verse to prove it. I reminded Nelson that Washington had agreed, when I took the job, that relations would be "official and correct," but would go no further than that.

Nelson said that might have been the obsolete Cordell Hull policy, but that now a fresh wind was blowing through the State Department. He intimated that Ed Stettinius might have other and more progressive ideas. Recognizing that our argument was not getting us anywhere, I reminded Nelson that fresh wind or stale wind, I was still the American ambassador. He could call as many shots as he liked, but the finger on the trigger would still be mine.

Since it was too late to cancel the legislative session or to take sick leave of the presidential banquet, I thought the damage might be minimized by a deliberately low-key response to the legislative oratory, to which few would be listening anyway, plus a carefully fumigated acknowledgment of the president's toast at the dinner. I said the Rockefeller answer to the toast would be the important thing, for people would be listening to that, and the president's own toast would be a carefully rehearsed act of baiting the hook. The way to regurgitate the hook, I advised, was to emphasize the inevitable connections that lie between all material achievement and such human values as are specified in the Atlantic Charter. There was still time to get some ideas along that line on paper.

That provoked a reiteration of the statement that as coordinator of inter-American affairs, Nelson was not under the jurisdiction of the State Department. Furthermore, he proposed to speak extemporaneously, and in Spanish — at which I winced — and therefore no prepared text was necessary.

Ours was not a pleasant exchange. Our positions were irreconcilable. Short of arranging to have my Yaqui Indian naval attaché tap my guest on the head with a hammer (a project that I admit crossed my mind), there was nothing for it but to allow Trujillo to have his fun and then — as so often happens in the Foreign Service — to pick up the broken pieces and try to fit them together again.

The sharp edges of that evening have long since been softened by time. There remains the now amusing memory of the incongruity of the most vicious and unprincipled tyrant of the hemisphere fraternizing with Our Hero, and of his utilizing the name, title, and naiveté of his guest, with one jovial and intimate pose after another following the dinner. Trujillo's photographs never had it so good.

It was said later, but this is untrue, that during the banquet in question President Trujillo deliberately attempted to insult the American ambassador by downgrading him at the banquet table, and that the ambassador created a stir by demanding and occupying his rightful place. Trujillo was too smart to waste time on pinpricks of that sort (unless he had first poisoned the pin), and anyway, he was concentrating on the principal business at hand, which was focusing the light on Nelson Rockefeller and then basking in that light to his heart's content.

"Well, Old Man, how did it seem to go?" asked Nelson genially at breakfast the next morning. From his tone, the previous evening might have been a joint undertaking, successfully accomplished by two harmonious participants.

"About the way I expected," I replied soberly. Nelson and I shook hands in the embassy doorway.

That day Rockefeller's Dominican friends accompanied him all the way from Ciudad Trujillo to the Haitian frontier, "so you can see something of the development of our country," as President Trujillo had put it. Foreign Minister Peña Battle, plus a police escort, arrived for the journey across the country to Montecristi.

The night of that same day, as I heard, when Nelson had reached the American embassy in Port au Prince and was installed as the guest of the Orme Wilsons, he received a phone call from Harry Hopkins in Washington. Would Nelson, Hopkins wanted to know, accept a position in the administration of Secretary Stettinius as assistant secretary of state for Latin American affairs?[7]

I have often speculated whether, since Trujillo's extensive Washington sources were good ones, he may not have had some advance intimation of the Rockefeller appointment and have been astute enough to recognize his opportunity. If Nelson himself was aware of the prospective appointment, he gave no indication of it while talking with me; on the contrary, most of

---

7. Nelson Rockefeller lasted as assistant secretary a short three months after Truman became president of the United States, and he was dropped even more summarily than I had been. As assistant secretary his principal achievement was the end-of-the-war Chapultepec Conference, held in Mexico City in the spring of 1945. Its accomplishments included forgiving Argentina for pursuing a pro-Nazi policy throughout almost the entire period of World War II (a decision, defended on the basis of hemisphere solidarity, that was to enrage former Secretary of State Hull) and cranking up an elaborate project to change the name and character of the Pan American Union to the Organization of American States, with a second Latin American ambassador per country resident in Washington, accredited to the regional international organization. This duality of ambassadors has produced almost endless nonsense and confusion in the period since Chapultepec.

his chatter was about the importance, and the alleged independence, of the coordinator of inter-American affairs, who owed no allegiance to the American ambassador.

That I was due to be bounced by Rockefeller became evident several weeks before the telegram accepting my resignation was received in Ciudad Trujillo, although that message arrived almost as soon as Roosevelt himself had taken his fourth oath of office. When it became known that Nelson was appointing Avra Warren, the "Butter-up-Trujillo" man who had preceded me in the Dominican Republic, to be his deputy, an effort was made by some of my friends to sew up Warren's vacated Panama ambassadorship for me. That elicited a statement by the ex-coordinator that in no circumstances was former Ambassador Briggs to have "any post, anywhere in Latin America." Perhaps some of my barbs had penetrated deeper than I thought.

Fortunately for me, I had friends in Washington in the echelons below what are now called the "policy making level," including several in the key Division of Foreign Service Personnel. They were responsible for adding, at the end of the telegram informing me that the president no longer required my services as ambassador to the Dominican Republic, a sentence inviting me to come to Washington for a discussion of future arrangements. Having started packing soon after the news of the Rockefeller appointment as assistant secretary of state became public, I appeared in Washington within seventy-two hours — my wife and two children returned to Havana to await developments.

All this was in January 1945, with the Yalta Conference, which would open so many Pandora's boxes affecting the next decades, only a few days away. That was how I found myself, at the time those fateful Yalta decisions were being made, transferred to Chungking, China, as the principal aide to Ambassador Patrick Hurley.

Trujillo was exterminated in 1961. A period of confusion followed, at the end of which one of the first acts of the first freely established Dominican government in more than a generation was to award me a decoration — the Grand Cross of the Order of Merit of Duarte, Sánchez, and Mella. The accompanying citation took note of my efforts on behalf of human values during the period of my ambassadorship in the Dominican Republic. By that time I had retired from active duty, but I am proud to remain a member of that fellowship.

16

Pat Hurley's China

My new official card read "Minister Counselor of Embassy," which was a comedown from "Ambassador of the United States of America," but perhaps I was lucky, after the Dominican vendetta, to have a job at all. In those days, when a Foreign Service officer was promoted to chief of mission, he automatically ceased to be a Foreign Service officer. He was then paid from a separate appropriation, and although his name was carried on the books as an officer of career, his legal separation was complete, so that if he was subsequently fired (or, in my case, if his "resignation was accepted"), he was out on the sidewalk — finished.

This was repaired by the Foreign Service Act of 1946, but in 1945 the only way to get back into the Foreign Service was for the Personnel Board to persuade the secretary of state to recommend to the president that the former officer be nominated all over again, with his individual name sent to the Senate for confirmation — a process that could take several months. Fortunately for me, there existed a piece of wartime legislation providing for what was called the Auxiliary Service. Nathaniel P. Davis, who was then head of Personnel, arranged for me to be appointed an auxiliary officer, at the same pay I had been receiving as ambassador to the Dominican Republic, while the process of my reinstatement unwound. No Senate confirmation was required for an auxiliary officer.

The American ambassador to China was visiting Washington in January 1945, and I called on him after the Personnel Board had arranged for me to become his deputy in our wartime embassy in Chungking, one thousand miles up the Yangtze River, in the interior of China. I saw Pat Hurley only that once before we met again in Chungking.

Considering Hurley's mistrust of the Foreign Service, my interview with him was remarkably amiable. He showed little interest in chancery operations, indicating that he dealt personally with Generalissimo Chiang Kai-shek (to whom he invariably referred as the G-mo) and with such leaders as T. V.

Soong, the foreign minister, and his brother-in-law, H. H. Kung, the finance minister, and that he himself reported directly to President Roosevelt.[1]

Ambassador Hurley told me that I would be expected to keep his chancery office and the State Department itself "out of my hair." He referred disparagingly to the new secretary of state, and he reiterated that the kind of business he dealt with went straight from him to the White House. Clearly my job would be to keep his fairways from being cluttered with extraneous golfers, including the secretary of state and the Division of Far Eastern Affairs.

Weeks later, in Chungking, I asked Ambassador Hurley why he had accepted as his number two an officer who had never before set foot in China and who had been bounced from his last post. I was favored with the fine Hurley smile. He was a handsome fellow when his humor was good; in fact, with his athletic frame, his immaculate silk suits, his flashing blue eyes, his mane of gray hair, and his carefully tended gray mustache, Hurley was a splendid figure of an ambassador. Vainly conscious of his good looks, he was never unkempt or untidy in an environment that rarely lent itself to elegance of attire.

He replied that there were several reasons why he had let Pen Davis sell him a bill of goods with my initials on it. First, Davis had assured him that I was one of the hardest working officers in the Service. According to my dossier, eighty-, ninety-, or hundred-hour weeks were my dish, but when things slacked off, instead of hanging around the office and punching the time clock, I liked to relax or to get around the country and see things for myself.

Second, I "wasn't afraid to slap down bureaucrats, including military bureaucrats, who tried to interfere with my work." That observation puzzled me, for I was aware that Hurley, a former secretary of war and a "retread," as he used to call himself, from combat service in World War I, was as proud of his recent military promotion and the second star that went with it as he was of the title of American ambassador. It turned out that what he meant was that there should be only one boss speaking for the United States in a foreign

---

1. When I reached China, I found out that this meant not only "directly" but also "not through the State Department." Hurley's classified messages were transmitted through an undercover naval organization, by that time uneasily affiliated with the Office of Strategic Services, known as SACO (for Sino-American Cooperative Organization). Hurley imagined he was plugging leaks in both State and the Pentagon. It also meant that Embassy Chungking had no copies of Ambassador Hurley's classified despatches.

capital, and that boss should be the ambassador, who personally represented the president. From what he had heard of my Dominican service, he gathered I had the same idea.

"Anytime President Truman wants to replace me," I remember Hurley saying, "all he has to do is send out one — just one — goddamn kibitzer from Washington to report over my head." I found this a refreshing declaration from one who had been dispatched to China by President Roosevelt the year before on just such an errand, but Hurley was often oblivious to things that no longer claimed his attention. He was correct, though, in his belief that with multiple persons reporting to Washington on policy matters, confusion was compounded and the interests of the United States were seldom advanced.

Finally, the smile reappearing, Hurley said that he had satisfied himself that I did not know one damn thing about China and so did not carry around a trunk full of prejudices. I could look at problems with an open mind; I was less likely to bother him with endless contradictory reports, most of them critical of Roosevelt's policy to lend all possible aid and support to the Nationalist government now temporarily established in Chungking. A part of that policy, he conceded, was to obtain more effective performance from Generalissimo Chiang Kai-shek's administration — the very rock on which General Joseph Stilwell's craft had foundered. Another was to bring the Nationalist government and the Communists together, to the end that the Communists, holed up in Yenan, would cooperate in fighting the Japanese.

"Those Yenan bastards," Hurley declared with rising heat, "spend more time planning how to bitch the G-mo than they do going after the Japs." The trouble was, he continued, China was a big place, and the Yenan Communists were a couple of thousand miles away. An urgent problem was to get their leaders together with the Nationalists here in Chungking under a safe conduct he hoped to arrange.

This, in essence, was also the objective of the Marshall Mission, one year later.

I was often to compare that conversation with the difficulty I encountered in Washington trying to pry something useful out of the Far Eastern Division before I left for Chungking. That division, then in the charge of stately, stuffy Stanley Hornbeck, was demoralized. Small wonder. Riven by those who regarded Chiang Kai-shek as the only salvation of China and those who were almost as virulently anti-Generalissimo as Stilwell himself, the State Department was further shaken by those who wanted to deal with the Yenan "agrarian reformers" and those who, like some of their frontier ancestors who fought Indians, believed that "the only good Communist is a dead Communist." The division's position papers, when finally put together in the State Department, were often ignored by the White House.

China policy in fact was being formulated in the Pentagon and in the Treasury Department, in the Lend-Lease Administration, and in a dozen different cubbyholes in the White House itself — almost anywhere except in the agency theoretically responsible for the conduct of foreign affairs. Small wonder, indeed, that I did not find the Far Eastern Division in a jubilant mood. In addition, my going to Chungking had not been their idea in the first place.

In Washington I was shown few reports. No mention was made to me of the Chungking embassy telegram, sent in Ambassador Hurley's absence, that was to contribute so much to inflaming the relations between Hurley and his staff. Instead, I was given a bibliography of volumes that would have taken me the next ten years to absorb. My homework, they told me. I was also told — this after the door into the corridor had been closed — that it would be a useful thing if a greater degree of order could be brought into the intelligence-gathering in China, an assignment that I quickly discovered was as unlikely of achievement as persuading Mme. Chiang Kai-shek to invite Mao Tse-tung to her next Wellesley College reunion.

I thus went to China not only with an open mind but also with a blank one. I would have given a great deal for a volume as knowledgeable and compact as Barbara Tuchman's account of the early decades of the century. (That is not to say, however, that I agree with her castigation of Ambassador Hurley. A tidying of that record seems overdue.)[2]

My flight priority with Air Transport Command got me to Calcutta somewhat winded, even though I stopped in Cairo with a Foreign Service friend, Cecil Lyon, at whose house I found another self-invited guest, Ed Flynn, the Bronx politico (who for no intelligible reason had just attended the Yalta Conference); and with George Merrill in New Delhi, where, when I walked in, an exuberant Australian colonel, by way of after-dinner greeting, cut off my necktie with a pair of shears.[3]

---

2. *Stilwell and the American Experience in China, 1911–1945* (Macmillan, 1971).

3. Lyon was chargé d'affaires in Egypt. He appears in chapter 13 as my colleague in Chile, where he was later to serve as ambassador. George Merrill, another Foreign Service officer, was acting high commissioner in New Delhi. The title had been devised to flatter the Indians in advance of their independence in 1947.

The over-the-Hump flight in a new C-54 was uneventful. I spent that night with Bill Langdon, our consul general in Kunming, whose pessimism was equaled only by the austerity of his living arrangements. It was my first night in China, cold at six thousand feet, with the roar of motors revving up and of planes taking off and landing around the clock. In a single month the air force was to bring in seventy thousand tons of cargo, Burma to South China, which was vastly more than the supplies that came in over the Burma Road.

The next morning I had my first view of Chungking from a dilapidated C-47. The city is built on a steep, red sandstone ridge at the junction of the Yangtze and Chialing rivers, each as wide and as muddy as the Mississippi where it joins the Missouri. The Chialing was low at the time and we set down on a dry strip along the shore, which meant a climb of some three hundred steps to the nearest vehicle. George Atcheson, the outgoing chargé d'affaires, met me. We were friends from Washington service in the 1930s. Our ascent of those red sandstone steps, with pauses for breath, reminded George of Vice President Wallace's mission to China the previous year, an account that fitted readily into my recollection of the adventures of that statesman in Latin America.[4]

When I reached Chungking in the late winter of 1945, George and the other senior officers of the chancery lived in a house on the Chialing side that threatened after each rain to slide into the river. They existed in circumstances that I soon came to recognize as luxury, compared to the cramped and wretched facilities of most of the Chinese people. The city was bursting with refugees and government officials. Much damage from Japanese bombing was still unrepaired, and inflation was undermining the poor and the

---

4. The ostensible purpose of the Wallace mission, like many another special visitation, was to persuade the Nationalists and the Communists to join forces in fighting the Japanese instead of fighting each other. A collateral Roosevelt purpose was probably to keep Henry away from the 1944 Democratic Convention, so someone else — it turned out to be Harry Truman — could be nominated vice president.

On his arrival in Chungking, Wallace was met by Chinese dignitaries and by the elite of the Guild of Chair Bearers, mobilized to honor the vice president by carrying him up the hill. Looking them over, and sizing up the situation with his genius for folly, Henry announced that he never yet had allowed another human being to carry him as a burden. Up the three hundred steps he charged — followed, of course, by all the greeting dignitaries. If the guest of honor walked, they had to walk. Thus, with a single stroke, Wallace alienated the senior officials of the Nationalist government and the deans of the Chair Bearers' Guild, an important labor organization, who lost face as well as revenue.

middle class alike. Muddy and wet and chill in winter, Chungking was suffocatingly hot all summer, with no nearby resort to escape to.

Up the hill from us was the Chialing Hotel, housing foreign diplomats but boasting few of the amenities to which most of them had been accustomed. The Chinese Foreign Office was at the top of the ridge, on the saddle between the two rivers. Adjacent to it was the wooden American embassy chancery. It had burned down a few months before I arrived and had been rebuilt to the identical specifications, at some fifteen times the original cost — a measure of the plummeting depreciation of Chinese currency.

One of my first acts as chargé d'affaires was to persuade K. C. Wu, the deputy foreign minister, whom I saw on an almost daily basis, to let his American neighbors pay for constructing a gate in the wall separating the Foreign Office from our chancery. That gate allowed us to go back and forth without descending the seventy-six steep steps from our chancery to the road, walking a few yards up the road, and then climbing back to the level we had just quitted. That was possibly the most useful contribution I made to Chinese-American relations.

George Atcheson dutifully arranged my round of official calls. I remember being much interested in the bone structure of the Generalissimo's shaved head, and in the way in which — even in translation — Chiang Kai-shek exuded an optimism few of my embassy colleagues shared. Chiang talked a splendid game of cooperation: "Now I have Americans with whom I can work" — meaning Ambassador Hurley and General Albert C. Wedemeyer (successor to General Stilwell and commander of American Army forces in China). There was much nodding and "ding-howing" when I told the Generalissimo that Mme. Chiang had been a neighbor of my family in a New York suburb. No substantive business was transacted.

In contrast, Mme. Sun Yat-sen, the widow of the first president of China, had much to say, little of it complimentary of the way in which she thought things were heading. She and George had long known each other, and she spoke with remarkable frankness. The dominant impression was of a strong woman saddened by large events that she expected to become worse before they became better.

The only substantive business on my round of courtesy calls was with Mme. Sun Yat-sen's brother, T. V. Soong, the foreign minister — who left the Foreign Office to K. C. Wu in much the way Ambassador Hurley left the chancery to me. It was business created not by the American government but by my Cuban friend Pepín Bosch, of the Bacardi Rum Company, the man who had given the Yateras River water to the naval station at Guantánamo. Pepín wrote me that in token of his admiration of the way the Chinese people were resisting Japanese aggression, he was taking the liberty of sending to me, via the Cuban consul in Calcutta — there being no Cuban representative in China — a small shipment that he hoped could be delivered to Generalissimo Chiang Kai-shek by "Amigo Briggs." At the bottom of his letter Pepín had scribbled that there were three cases: one for the Generalissimo, one for me, and one "to help defray transportation expenses." A simultaneous message from the American consul general in Calcutta ended in a slightly waspish tone; he enclosed an aide-mémoire from his Cuban colleague. How, the American consul general wanted to know, was he going to hornswoggle the air force into lugging that shipment of liquor over the Hump, in violation of military rules, regulations, and proprieties?

The answer to that one proved as easy as getting fresh water for the navy in Cuba: George Atcheson invited the air force colonel commanding Pai Shih Yi, the main airport of Chungking, to supper. The colonel in turn produced a captain scheduled to make a round trip flight to Dum Dum Airfield, outside Calcutta. Within ten days I had thirty of the original thirty-six bottles — the balance going one to the colonel, and five to the captain and crew, in lieu of air freight charges.

T. V. Soong was amused by this episode. He informed me that the Generalissimo did not drink. But, he said, "I do." He volunteered to have drafted a letter of thanks to be signed by Chiang Kai-shek himself and turned over to me to forward to Cuba, where he hoped it would impress the members of the Chinese community on the island. Soong and I ended by splitting the order: a full case to him, with labels and seals intact; the balance to the American chargé d'affaires, who added it to the household supply. On the parched black market, with genuine scotch bringing as much as $100 a bottle at the Pink Elephant Club, Pepín's Bacardi could have netted us a tidy sum. Instead, we used it at our mess in lieu of Chungking gin and Chungking vodka, which were distinguishable one from the other only because the vodka had more sediment in it. Both were potable, else the Western representation would have perished en masse, but countless Allied livers were scarred and Allied duodenums bruised by recourse to the two local products.

My impression of T. V. Soong confirmed chancery reports that he was a formidable operator, so Westernized in idiom and attitude that you could easily forget you were dealing with one of the most sophisticated of Oriental leaders. The same could be said of his brother-in-law, H. H. Kung, who controlled the finances of Nationalist China.

{ *Pat Hurley's China* }

Two unrelated happenings punctuated my early weeks as chargé, before the return of Ambassador Hurley. The first was the unexpected appearance of my friend Lt. Winston Guest, United States Marine Corps, complete with uniform and equipment, including an oversized parachute, cut to the dimensions of the wearer. The last time I had seen Wolfie was at a ceremony in Havana in honor of Ernest Hemingway.

Winston had just reached China, under auspices not immediately explained, but they were sufficiently elastic so that I added him to our house, sharing quarters with him on the third floor of our rickety barracks and, a few days later, appointing him honorary aide to the chargé d'affaires. Neither project elicited enthusiastic support from my serious-minded housemates, even though Wolfie spent much of his time away, in arduous, unrehearsed travel. The fresh air billowing around the person of Lieutenant Guest, aloft or grounded, proved too heavily charged with ozone for some of my chancery associates, although Wolfie quickly became a favorite with Ambassador Hurley, to whom he reported on a visit to Yenan and on his dealings with Communist leaders.

The other event during my chargéship was the death of President Roosevelt on April 12, 1945, and the competition among groups in Chungking desiring to take the lead in honoring the deceased chief executive. George Atcheson, whose advice I could well have used, had by then departed. The news of the president's death reached me on the morning of April 13, a morning that brought endless hordes of condolence callers. They included Chiang Kai-shek's personal aide, several members of the Chinese Cabinet, Kuomintang leaders of all sizes, practically all of the Allied diplomatic chiefs of mission, including Sir Horace Seymour (Ambassador Hurley's British opposite number), the Soviet counselor (who said his chief could not walk up all those stairs), and old Count Potocki, the Polish ambassador (who had already, although neither of us knew it, been sold out at Yalta). The count should never have attempted those seventy-six steps, but when the old gentleman caught his breath, he made a speech of such eloquence that he wept.[5]

5. Of all the tasks of that summer, the most ignoble followed receipt of a circular telegram from the State Department on July 4, instructing the embassy immediately to inform "the former Polish representative" of the withdrawal of United States recognition from the London Polish government-in-exile in favor of their Communist-dominated enemies in Lublin. To have to comply with that betrayal on our Independence Day made the duty doubly sad and ironic.

At the chancery callers included missionaries of various faiths and denominations, some of whom had lived in China for decades. They knew exactly what should be done by the newly arrived American representative: turn over the Roosevelt memorial arrangements to them. The missionaries were especially insistent that "since Generalissimo Chiang Kai-shek is a Christian, too," they — the missionaries — were the ones who ought to take over.

Stilwell's rank-conscious successor, General Wedemeyer, sent an aide, and he phoned to say that his headquarters and the embassy "ought to coordinate our efforts," from which I deduced that the military would gladly preempt the entire enterprise, complete with a saluting battery and a riderless horse, flown from Burma. Everybody, in short, wanted to get in on the wake. My head throbbed with conflicting suggestions.

During a lull I summoned my staff to consider the problem and, I hoped, give the chargé d'affaires sound advice. But no president since Harding (in 1923) having died in office, which event was before the time in China of any of those present, there was no precedent for them to fall back on. My colleagues were stymied. Why not cable Washington, they suggested, requesting instructions? Instead, I called a time-out for luncheon.

The solution came to me a few minutes later while Winston Guest was mixing a *presidente* cocktail, which seemed an appropriate drink for the occasion. Our sole guest was an old China hand with no ax to sharpen on anybody's sepulcher. He was L. K. Little, an American civilian a dozen years my senior, who had spent most of his adult life in the Chinese customs service.

"The thing to do," advised L. K. Little, holding his *presidente* up to the light, "is to turn the whole show over to the Nationalist Government. The generalissimo knows that without President Roosevelt he might already be pushing up cabbage leaves beside some forgotten rice paddy. The gov-

---

The Potocki estates had been overrun in 1939 and 1940. Except for a few dollars banked in the United States and the jewelry Countess Potocki had with her, the couple was wiped out. They were stunned and bewildered. "Where can we go?" they asked. "Why has this blow fallen upon us?"

Within the hour I had returned to their house with the embassy seal in my pocket, along with the inked pad and rubber stamp with which we issued visas. Thanks to the inertia of one of our clerks, the record of visas issued in June had not yet been tabulated, and the diplomatic visas I stamped on July 4 were backdated. That was enough to get the Potockis into the United States when they applied for admission some weeks later. Never have I signed my name and official title with greater satisfaction. When informed the next day, Ambassador Hurley applauded.

ernment has a hall in Chungking that seats several thousand. They can rig up some sort of altar. Make a Chinese ceremony out of it, with you as chargé d'affaires representing the American government. The hall's big enough to accommodate the whole Kuomintang party, plus the diplomats, the military, the missionaries — the works. My guess is Chiang Kai-shek will be flattered if you ask him, and that gets you off the hook with everyone else."

"After all," he concluded, "nobody can complain if the chief of state of China wants to take personal charge of rites in his own country honoring an American president."

I reached K. C. Wu by telephone at once. In fifteen minutes he called back to say that Chiang Kai-shek not only was delighted, but would personally conduct the memorial service.

It was an impressive affair. We used the military as ushers. Half of them were Chinese. The rest included Americans and officers of the Allied powers. The generalissimo did himself gracefully and simply and well. The only decorations were flowering locust trees, ten to twenty feet high and in full, fragrant bloom. They had been dug up, roots and all, and used to cover both wings of the stage. In the center stood an altar of sorts, consisting of two uprights and a crossbeam. On it, facing the audience, was an enlarged photograph of President Roosevelt. Nothing else. No other ornament.

Having been exposed to official mourning ceremonies from Liberia to Chile, I was apprehensive lest something untoward occur, lest it go on and on, or lest some extraneous mourner, overcome with emotion, manage to seize the microphone and soar out of reach, in uncontrollable oratory. Nothing of the sort occurred. Although the words and gestures of the generalissimo were unintelligible to me, they sounded sincere, and whatever he performed in front of the altar — whether Christian or Buddhist or pagan —seemed dignified and in tribute to Franklin Delano Roosevelt, the only American who had ever taken the presidential oath four times, who died on the eve of the triumph of American arms.

My participation ended the ceremony. It was limited to reading the Twenty-third Psalm, a nonsectarian message I chose as combining both beauty and hope, and embodying principles difficult to claim as exclusive to any specific religion.

Meanwhile, with the results of the Yalta Conference in mind — including the secret agreement that within ninety days of the Nazi surrender (which occurred on May 8, 1945) Soviet Russia would attack Japan — Hurley prepared to return to Chungking. His absence had already extended beyond the time he had expected to be away. Nevertheless, the ambassador flew via London, in order to confer with British leaders about the China-Burma-India theater, and Moscow, to learn whether Premier Stalin had anything new to say about Mao Tse-tung and his "agrarian reformers."

Ambassador Hurley returned a few days later, and I learned what it was to go from number one to number two, from the responsibilities of "Mr. United States" to being deputy to an ebullient and hot-tempered ambassador, one of whose favorite exclamations was "If it is a day old or an inch high — I'll fight it!"

His return in a White House plane confirmed my belief that Ambassador Hurley liked to travel first-class, and that it is appropriate for a presidential envoy on important assignment to do so. Following the death of Roosevelt, Hurley said he considered resigning, but that President Truman urged him to stay on. He had troubles enough, the new president said, without tangling at the outset with the difficulties of China. Existing orders and policy were endorsed: continue to support the Nationalist government of China; continue to try to persuade the Yenan dissidents to carry the war against the Japanese.

Hurley's staff in Chungking, except for those of us working in the chancery (which Hurley rarely visited) were his own acquisitions. Their names did not appear on the Foreign Service List of the State Department, although they were the most influential assistants he had. In practical terms, the most important of those was a Sergeant Jones, who in peacetime had worked as a shipping clerk in a mail order house in his native Brooklyn. Jones could take dictation and do stenography. He did the Hurley accounts. He made appointments. He kept files, including pounds of highly classified documents, most of which he could remember and retrieve but few of which, according to the regulations, should have been left outside the chancery. Jones was used to being routed out at all hours and to working ten or twelve hours at a stretch, whenever "the General" — he never called Hurley "the Ambassador" — demanded it. He was hard-boiled and cynical and ungrammatical; he had little use for foreigners of any nationality, and he was not above an occasional bender. Hurley tolerated the benders, considering them to be outweighed by other qualities, but on occasion he would berate Sergeant Jones without mercy.

I recall a Sunday afternoon meeting in the residence with several high-ranking Chinese. Presently Hurley wanted a paper that Jones, who had the appearance that day of a soldier sufffering from a hangover, was unable to find. Five minutes later the ambassador, remembering the need for the document, again shouted, "Jones!"

Sergeant Jones reappeared and came to attention. He confessed his inability to locate the desired paper. Hurley's denunciation almost peeled the sergeant's uniform off his back, along with patches of skin underneath. Brought up in Oklahoma at a time when the art of invective still flourished, Ambassador Hurley was an accomplished performer. The sergeant set himself, took it, and managed a subdued "Yessir" on his dismissal. Our discussions proceeded without the document, and after a while the Chinese departed, leaving only a disgruntled ambassador and his minister counselor.

Sergeant Jones reappeared. "General, Sir," he said, "you hadn't oughta done that to me. You *hummilated* me, in front of all them Chinese. You hummilated me."

Ambassador Hurley glared, while I awaited an explosion that would either incinerate Jones or blast him across the Yangtze River. The ambassador rose, a menacing figure. He advanced toward Sergeant Jones, who looked as though he expected to be thrown to the lions. Hurley put a hand on Jones's shoulder.

"Sergeant Jones," he said mildly, "forget it. I'm just a bad-tempered old bastard. Forget it."

Jones gulped, his Adam's apple working. "Yessir. I mean Nossir, General, Sir." He executed an about-face and departed. He returned a few minutes later with the missing paper, found in the ambassador's dressing room.

Sergeant Jones, the office man, was assisted in the residence by Sergeant Hovey, the housekeeper. Hovey was a country boy from a village in North Dakota. He was the antithesis of Jones. He neither smoked nor drank; he was unsophisticated; and he had large, outstanding ears and big, scrubbed paws. The ambassador occasionally used to brag about him when Hovey, doubling as waiter, his hands looking enormous as he passed around canapes, would turn pink with self-consciousness. "And this," Ambassador Hurley would say to his guests, "is Sergeant Hovey, from Itching Springs, North Dakota. He's a farmer. He's the only man in China who knows the difference between a yam and a sweet potato."

Hovey supervised the larder and cellar. He was responsible for keeping the Chinese staff (who knew more English than Hovey did Chinese — but not much more) tidy, alert and — one hoped — virtuous. Hovey, honest to the penny himself, tried to keep the inevitable Chinese squeeze within bounds. His ideas about dinner arrangements were strictly from his army experience. They included having the bottles of catsup, Worcestershire sauce, chutney, and Tabasco in a straight line down the center of the table, interspersed with pepper and salt and with an occasional glass tumbler stuffed with parsley or romaine, leaves up, by way of decoration.

The residence itself contributed to Ambassador Hurley's antipathy for the Foreign Service. When Ambassador Clarence Gauss lived there — until the previous November — various Foreign Service officers who had managed to salvage this or that piece of personal furniture in the flight upriver to Chungking, and who had no need for the extra chair or table or mirror in the furnished staff houses they now occupied, put them in Ambassador Gauss's residence, where they were shortly spread around, it being more practical to use them than to store them.

Gauss was a product of the old Far East consular service: he was hardworking, incorruptible, unimaginative, knowledgeable about various aspects of Chinese affairs, and fiercely addicted to the consular regulations. He had little presence and no sparkle. Although he kept the loyalty of his subordinates, some of whom shared his background, Gauss was uncomfortable with officials of high rank. He quarreled with General Stilwell, although they saw eye to eye on the Kuomintang, the generalissimo, and the failure of Chinese arms to play a larger role in fighting the war. Gauss found it rasping to have some of his Foreign Service officers comandeered by the army, reporting thereafter through military rather than State Department channels.

A number of Foreign Service officers, old China hands, resented what they regarded as the scuttling of Gauss. They blamed Hurley for his departure, and they unwisely made little attempt, when General Hurley became Ambassador Hurley, to disguise their sentiments, much less to make the new appointee welcome. Hurley told me that when he reached the residence, there was not even a bed in the ambassadorial bedroom for him to sleep on. The bed Gauss had been using was the personal property of a member of the staff, who moved it out when Gauss departed. Back in 1944, there was no embassy administrative officer with personnel to supervise putting the premises to rights in advance of a new chief of mission.

Ambassador Hurley, whose boiling point was lower than that of an egg cooked at the altitude of Tibet, was not pleased by his reception. Moreover, he was not one to suffer in silence. His indignation did the reputation of the Foreign Service no good. Thenceforth the new ambassador regarded his State Department staff not as colleagues but as enemies.

These personal antipathies were multiplied by the dispatch by George Atcheson, as chargé d'affaires during the ambassador's absence the previous February, of his famous "boys on the burning deck" telegram, which urged that the entire existing American China policy — which had been endorsed by President Roosevelt — be scrapped and reconstructed. When I saw that message after my arrival in Chungking, I interpreted it as having been conceived in honesty by the China hands who joined in approving it. It was, however, transmitted to Washington in reckless and irrational folly, because the writers must have known that Hurley would be furious. Even if the recommendations were approved in the State Department, they would probably be ignored in the White House and the Pentagon. That message put the finishing touches on Ambassador Hurley's determination to have as little as possible to do with his own chancery when he returned to Chungking.

Another point that caused Ambassador Hurley to hold his American colleagues in low esteem was Clarence Gauss's lack of what Hurley might have termed "ambassadorial prestige." Gauss was not a man of private wealth nor was he one to push himself forward. While perhaps taking wry note of the ostentation within the prevailing poverty of certain Chinese officials, and of the shining motor cars of certain foreign representatives of countries being supported by American Lend-Lease, Ambassador Gauss was content with the two ancient and battered sedans of the American embassy that anywhere else would have been condemned as scrap. One car had been driven over the Burma Road and the other flown in, surviving a crash landing on arrival. The doors on one side could not be opened. The glass in the windows had been cracked and repaired with tape, so the windows could not be lowered. The springs poked through patches in the worn-out upholstery. They were museum pieces rather than transportation units, and when they were in the repair shop — which was often — Ambassador Gauss hired a rickshaw, as he had been accustomed to doing since his vice consular days in Chefoo a quarter-century before.

It was the inadequate Chungking transportation that caused Ambassador Hurley almost to disrupt relations with the South East Asia Command. Lord Louis Mountbatten, whose youthful charm had failed to captivate Hurley when they met, now had his SEAC headquarters established on Ceylon, where almost as much pomp prevailed as had been enjoyed by the viceroy of India in the days of Lord Curzon. Hearing that Lord Louis was about to receive a Lend-Lease Cadillac limousine, Ambassador Hurley — who could move fast and quietly when he wanted to — arranged a small change in the routing of that automobile. The C for Candy and Ceylon was changed to C for Chungking and China, and the limousine was flown over the Hump in the largest cargo plane then in service. It was landed at Pai Shih Yi as softly as a crate of eggs beside a neighborhood grocery.

No maharajah ever mounted the howdah of his ceremonial elephant with any greater satisfaction than Ambassador Hurley climbed aboard that Cadillac. He instructed Sergeant Jones to destroy, unanswered, the messages that soon started to arrive from the State Department and from Lend-Lease, and from points as far separated as Detroit, London, and Ceylon.

His proved a short triumph. The Cadillac of that era had an automatic drive that was meant for highway travel. Protracted operation below a certain minimum speed spelled disaster, and ten miles an hour was extravagant progress through the packed and twisting streets of Chungking. Outside the city the roads were designed for oxcarts whose drivers did not have to worry about their transmissions. Shortly before Ambassador Hurley was summoned to Washington, the gearbox burned out.

When I reached Chungking, George Atcheson told me that no matter what I left undone before Hurley's return, the repair of that automobile must be accomplished. This was the embassy's number one priority.

Figuring that a man with a nine-goal polo handicap would know where to find a Cadillac mechanic, I turned the problem over to Winston Guest. That was a good choice. Through his connections with the Office of Strategic Services, Wolfie learned that the same motor that powered the ambassadorial automobile propelled a light tank then in production. I refrained from inquiring how many light tanks were cannibalized to keep the American ambassador mobile.

In addition to Sergeants Jones and Hovey, the members of the Hurley menage who counted most with the ambassador were a pair of ex-newspaper men: Major Parker La Moore, who wore an insignia that looked like a steering wheel and denoted, I think, some sort of transportation unit he had long since abandoned; and Lt. Commander Lacey Reynolds, who boasted that he was the only man in the United States Navy who did not know starboard from port. When I explained the origin of "posh" (for "port out, starboard home"), thinking it a helpful mnemonic device, Lacey insisted on associating "home" with the United States, and "out" with a westward Pacific crossing, which left him no better off than before.

Ambassador Hurley did not explain how he had acquired these two officers who, like me, had not previously been in China. I suspected that Hurley had greater need of companionship than he admitted, for being ambassador can at times be a lonely job. What those two supplied in the way of public relations advice was supplemented by their acting as a critical and sympathetic audience for a man who prided himself on his self-sufficiency but who, like many loners, may have found it hard at times to be alone.

The relations of the ambassador with the resident correspondents, on the other hand, were rarely cordial and often the reverse. The correspondents lived, grubbily, in a tumbledown building called the Press Hostel, and their requirements were theoretically met by one Hollington Tong, a glib Westernized Chinese who was later to be ambassador to Washington. Almost to a man the resident correspondents were anti-Kuomintang and anti-Chiang Kai-shek, and hence critical of United States policy. Hurley, with his fine airs and his low boiling point, was an inevitable target. Nearly all of the Chungking reporters were sympathetic toward the Yenan "agrarian reformers." Others were a mixed and changing crew, from transients like radio reporter Eric Sevareid to Mary Jean Kempner, the lively and sophisticated war correspondent of *Vogue* (whose tailored uniforms were a delight to observe). They included columnist Henry J. Taylor, who endeared himself to the turbulent ambassador by a stage-whispered aside, following a deliberately nasty question at a press conference. "Pat," he cautioned, "don't let them get your bowels in an uproar!"

One of the most articulate of the resident correspondents, both in dislike of Hurley personally and of the policies he represented, was Theodore White. With a Mrs. Jacoby, the widow of a reporter lost in a flight over the Hump, White represented the Luce interests in Chungking. Once a week, when the airmail edition of *Time* reached China, one of the standard diversions was to witness the hysterics that followed perusal by White and Mrs. Jacoby of the paragraphs on the Far East, which were often the antithesis of what they had written. Their stories were pro-Yenan and pro-"agrarian reformers" — often lyrically so — and anything good the Nationalists might have accomplished was regularly downgraded.

Henry Luce, China-born and esteeming himself for his Oriental as well as his oracular wisdom, used to switch the words around in favor of the Nationalists. The effect of the *Time* reporting, as published, was as favorable to Chiang Kai-shek as the original Chungking version had been adverse. To observe Teddy White's weekly tearing out of tufts of his hair became one of the pastimes of those frequenting the Press Hostel.

Another writer occasionally in evidence was Captain Joe Alsop, who as aide to General Claire Chennault wielded more influence than his rank implied — as noted with repetitious animosity by Mrs. Tuchman. Joe was anti-Stilwell and pro-airpower, especially if the power was wielded by Chennault, but since Stilwell had departed before my arrival and since airpower was not within my bailiwick, our relations were not affected. Anchored to

Chungking by chancery minutiae, I envied Joe's mobility, to say nothing of his pipeline into the White House.

Another visitor whose presence gave the ambassador much pleasure was Paul Patterson, publisher of the *Baltimore Sun*. He, however, was a guest rather than a resident of the Press Hostel, and I do not recall that he greatly influenced local reporting.

Thus the spring of 1945 moved toward summer, with the weather daily growing hotter, more humid, and more uncomfortable. Nazi Germany had surrendered. Okinawa, after one of the bloodiest campaigns of the war, had fallen. The Philippines were liberated. All over the Pacific the area of Japanese hegemony was shrinking under the blows of Nimitz and MacArthur. But in Chungking, chancery morale continued low. The Foreign Service officers who had participated in the February telegram demanding a change of China policy either had departed or had applied for transfers. If they had been there long enough, they did so by official despatch, otherwise by personal appeals to such colleagues in the Far Eastern division as Maxwell Hamilton and John Carter Vincent, the latter a friend of Dean Acheson, then assistant secretary of state. In the chancery there seemed to be a feeling of rodents deserting the ship of state. Whenever word arrived that John Doe was due for a swim abroad, there was feasting and celebration on the part of the crew. Not a happy atmosphere in which to work.

In those circumstances I thought of the suggestion conveyed in Washington that I attack the problem of fragmented and redundant intelligence operations, with too many people and too many agencies engaged. When I informed the ambassador that during his absence I had tried to make a start on that job, Hurley hooted with derision. He said it could not be done — at least not during the war — with the military top-heavy with unvouchered funds, spare noncombatants at headquarters, and an unshakable conviction of their own prescience. (Former General Hurley could be critical of the military when he had a mind to.) The ambassador wished me luck and invited me to report from time to time, or whenever the bruises and contusions became too painful to endure in solitude.

Hurley was right. In happier circumstances the political section of the embassy should have been the repository and clearinghouse for intelligence. But since we were in a war area, the military believed themselves supreme in that sphere. I was invited to attend the daily briefing at military headquarters, but after a few exposures I bowed out because the fare dispensed was either so detailed or so esoteric, or else demanded so much specialized military background, that it seemed of little practical value to diplomacy.[6]

The embassy attachés were up to their ears in intelligence activities, with large staffs, large purses, and a vast accumulation of data, much of it superior to that acquired elsewhere. There was simultaneously a hugh G-2 apparatus in General Wedemeyer's headquarters, together with other G-designation units. They and the embassy attachés acted as competitors rather than colleagues, eager as hungry quail in a cornfield and as likely to take off suddenly in all directions.

Then there was Admiral Milton Miles[7] and his navy contingent, bivouacked outside Chungking in a place called Happy Valley, where nearly two thousand Americans were training with Chinese guerrillas under the aegis of a General Tai Li — otherwise known as "the Chinese J. Edgar Hoover." The nearest salt water, as the army never ceased to emphasize, was one thousand miles down the Yangtze River. They regarded General Tai Li as a sinister character.

Admiral Miles's SACO Command had an additional and still more distant tentacle that the army found equally obnoxious. Two thousand miles *west* of Chungking, behind the back of beyond in Central Asia, a handful of nautical weather specialists were engaged in observing atmospheric conditions along the rim of Tibet. The rationale of the Happy Valley enterprise just outside Chungking, which the army called Miles's "Rice Paddy Navy,"

---

6. General Wedemeyer, in conjunction with the Chinese and utilizing the Chinese Division, was mounting Operation Coronado — a drive to capture Canton. It was scheduled to begin in late August. Had it taken place and succeeded, that might have gone some way toward restoring the morale of Nationalist arms and the spirit of Nationalist leadership, even though most of the Japanese in the south, whom they hoped to cut off, had already moved north of Canton. The operation was canceled in mid-August when the Japanese surrendered.

7. Milton Miles, Annapolis '22, was a character out of Richard Harding Davis and W. Somerset Maugham. Hurley used Miles and his SACO communications facilities to transmit his classified messages to Washington. Hurley remarked that it was a relief to discover one American who, instead of constantly complaining about the Chinese, not only cooperated successfully with them but enjoyed doing it — and, moreover, believed that together they were accomplishing something useful. Students of the distracted Chinese scene, exhausted by General Stilwell's vituperative sonnets or tired of the laments and alibis of other observers, should not miss Admiral Miles's account of his mission, *A Different Kind of War*. Based on the papers he left, it was published in 1967 by Doubleday, with a foreword by Admiral Arleigh Burke. Miles died a vice admiral in 1961.

was that the guerrillas trained by Admiral Miles kept an eye on the Chinese coast (where at one time American naval landings had been considered), helped downed American flyers (Winston Guest's project), and harassed the Japanese whenever and wherever the opportunity offered. Miles's "Sinkiang Camel Corps" of weather watchers operated on the theory that world weather moved from west to east, and that to define and transmit what went on at, say, Tihwa could be of importance to American fleets in the Pacific by permitting their weather specialists aboard ship to plot the prospects a few days later off Tinian, or Saipan, or the Ryukyus.

There was also the Office of Strategic Services, which, like its postwar successor, the Central Intelligence Agency, engaged in gathering intelligence and interpreting events (thus duplicating a primary State Department function), and in operations including espionage. Obviously Miles's SACO and Donovan's OSS overlapped. I was able to dodge most of the flak from these operations partly because of Miles's talented liaison officer, Commander George Berger, with an assist from Winston Guest, and partly because of John Whitaker, a former *Herald Tribune* correspondent who appeared in China at about the time I did, wearing the eagles of a colonel as well as the mantle of the OSS. An able citizen whom I had known elsewhere and a delightful companion, John explained his presence by declaring that all his European covers had been blown and "Donovan wanted some fresh ideas on the China Theater." We got on well, as I did with young Quentin Roosevelt, his deputy, but OSS was never viewed with enthusiasm by General Wedemeyer's headquarters, in some measure because it consorted with SACO and Admiral Miles.

Altogether there must have been a dozen different American agencies collecting so-called intelligence in China, each jealous of the others' and none of them willing to discuss pooling their material, much less amalgamation. My efforts were a waste of time except as experience, which was subsequently valuable in attempts in other countries to see to it that the "intelligence community" (as they called themselves) did not become the tail that wagged the diplomatic dog. I reported to Ambassador Hurley that is must be an unenterprising Chinese who, assuming he wore a jacket and could speak a few words of English, could not get on the payroll of at least three or four of these intelligence groups by selling the same bit of gossip to each of them.

Of the numerous things that the ambassador was against, nothing galled him more than Lend-Lease, especially the giving without strings attached, on the theory that if all requests were met, even Stalin would become benevolent. Hurley regarded that as nonsense. While admitting that some parts of the program were better than othes, and that our Western allies had at least used weapons against the now vanquished Germans, he saw that a gigantic boondoggle was developing. With it he identified a giveaway philosophy on the part of the Washington bureaucracy, abetted in China by the Kuomintang plutocracy. It irritated him that local leaders went about in new Buicks while his embassy — except for his purloined Cadillac — had to make do with those two decrepit sedans, together with such jeeps as Hurley had cadged from the army.

Hurley remarked that if he were in charge, "The first thing I'd do would be to cancel Lend-Lease. Next, I'd use the first million dollars saved to straighten the bent axles in China. Then perhaps the Chinese could get on with the war." While continuing to subscribe to the proposition that the Nationalist government of the G-mo was a better bet for the United States than the "agrarian reformers" of Yenan, Ambassador Hurley was sufficiently a quid pro quo advocate that, had the conflict with Japan been protracted, he might have had some stormy sessions over the use of American matériel in China.

Meanwhile, the ambassador was trying to arrange a further meeting between the Nationalist and Communist leaders. On this subject he met frequently with the generalissimo. Now that Mme. Chiang Kai-shek, with her fluent command of English, was back from the United States, his visits with them were more relaxed. The interpreters, on the other hand, trembled in fear when working with Hurley and Chiang Kai-shek in Mme. Chiang's presence, precisely because of her competence in the ambassador's language. The extrovert Hurley thrived on these visits to a degree never approached by Ambassador Gauss, but politically the results were meager, hedged with reservations or involving unverifiable contingencies.

The Oklahoma lawyer was too smart not to recognize procrastination when he saw it. He likewise chafed at the restrictions on what he could say about Yalta. There his Washington instructions gave little leeway; Chinese security had proved so defective in the past that it was feared a premature disclosure in Chungking of the Soviet promise of intervention ninety days after the Nazi surrender might leak to the Japanese, whose Kwantung Army in Manchuria was long believed by our military to be stronger than it was.

In fact, it was the military who persuaded the ailing Roosevelt at Yalta that it was worthwhile, even essential, to bribe Stalin to attack Japan. In my opinion it should have been the other way around; an exorbitant payment should have been exacted for letting Soviet Russia into the Far Eastern theater.

Thanks to the campaigns in the Philippines and across the islands, Japanese fortunes of war had declined steadily since before Yalta. Even without the bomb, Japan was finished. In February 1945 the Allied military were guilty of a monstrous and costly miscalculation at Yalta.

The Chinese Communists proved amenable to attending the Hurley-promoted parley in Chungking that summer. Protected by a safe conduct guaranteed by the American ambassador, they had nothing to lose. Chou En-lai and his leader Mao Tse-tung came to Chungking. They talked, they listened, they said various things, and they departed, probably more convinced than before that the Kuomintang tree that shaded the Nationalist government of China was ripe for the felling.

Inasmuch as the ambassador liked to do his own upper-level negotiating, the part I played in that unproductive confrontation was minor. I remember being more impressed by the massive eyebrows and the expression of tough, uncompromising alertness of Chou En-lai (whom Hurley addressed, phonetically, as Joe N. Lie) than I was by his burly companion. Chairman Mao Tse-tung wore a pair of vintage golf knickers, a Sun Yat-sen jacket, and a floppy plush cap shading a conspicuous wen. He did not look like the potential leader of millions of his fellow men, tens of thousands of whom he would slaughter in the Communist rise to power. Ambassador Hurley addressed the chairman, likewise phonetically, as Mr. Mouse Dung.

The lack of progress during this meeting fortified Ambassador Hurley's growing suspicion that the men of Yenan would "cooperate" only on terms unacceptable to Chungking. It was a preview of "what's mine is mine, and what's yours is negotiable." What Hurley had hoped might be a major achievement, perhaps the breaking of the logjam of Chungking-Yenan relations, served mostly to emphasize differences. Recognition of this was, I suspect, an underlying cause of Hurley's resignation.

On August 6 an atomic bomb was dropped over Hiroshima. Soviet Russia leaped gleefully into the fray two days later. The Japanese, after argumentation over the status of their emperor, surrendered. Their formal capitulation took place on the USS *Missouri,* off Tokyo, on September 2, 1945.[8]

8. Saving the emperor from the vengeance of the victors was one of the few contests won by the diplomats. It was gained almost single-handedly by former Ambassador Joseph C. Grew, who remained as undersecretary of state until August 15 — just long enough for statesmanship to prevail.

The global war was over. In Chungking the emphasis, the thrust of our operations, our entire perspective changed suddenly and dramatically — literally overnight. It was instantly replaced by a new set of preoccupations: How to keep North China from falling into Communist hands. How to move enough Nationalist troops into the area ahead of the Soviets and the Yenan "agrarian reformers." How to make it possible for the Nationalists to take Japanese surrenders, at the same time acquiring their arms. How to reestablish the authority the Nationalists had not exercised for a decade, not only in North China but in the great coast and river cities held throughout the war by the enemy.

These preoccupations were to occupy the American government's attention for the next eighteen months, or until recognition by General Marshall of the failure of his own yearlong mission, the aches and pains and disappointments of which neither Ambassador Hurley nor I was destined long to experience.

This chapter can, I suppose, be compared to a leaf pulled from the creeping vine of history, but it is also a segment of my own career in the Foreign Service, which at that moment was involved with certain officials whose movements are now relevant to my story. President Truman had allowed Stettinius, his inherited secretary of state, to remain in office through the San Francisco Conference that established the United Nations. Stettinius stepped down on June 27, 1945. James F. Byrnes, whose talents and wide experience as a politician had come close to gaining him the vice presidency in 1944 (in lieu of Harry Truman), took over the State Department on July 3. He found present various members of the "team" of his predecessor, to whom Ambassador Hurley used to refer as "the pearly-toothed Brainless Wonder."

Byrnes wanted Dean Acheson to be his undersecretary, and Ambassador Grew (1880–1965) on reaching retirement age, after an exceptionally distinguished career, was eager to relinquish that office. On lower levels, however, fumigation was in order. Several officers resigned in the wake of the Stettinius dismissal. Others were handed one-way tickets from Washington. The departure of Nelson Rockefeller as assistant secretary of state for Latin American affairs was announced on August 17, while Nelson was making a speech in Boston. Secretary Byrnes had decided to offer the post to Spruille Braden, then serving as ambassador to Argentina, whither he had been moved from Havana the previous April, two months after I had gone to China.

Braden accepted. The first I knew of these departmental changes, less than a fortnight after Hiroshima, was a personal cable from Buenos Aires, shortly followed by an official one from Washington, informing me of my appointment to be director of American Republics Affairs.[9] Pursuant to these orders, I left Chungking the last week in August.

Pat Hurley was remarkably gracious and cheerful about my defection. China, he said, was no lifework for either of us. Let someone else try to straighten out all those bent axles. He declared I had been a help to him at a difficult time, and that he would so report.[10] At that point Sir Adrian Carton de Wiart, the British prime minister's personal representative in Chungking, invited me to join him in accepting the Japanese surrender of Singapore. I was greatly tempted, and I did in fact ride with him — in notable luxury — as far as Kunming, in South China. There, in accordance with the urgent tenor of my orders, I reluctantly parted from that eminent warrior, whose Belgian cousin was to be my colleague in Prague four years later. I flew east to Manila, then a city of rubble, and thumbed island-hopping rides across the Pacific in a series of converted bombers, the conversion consisting of sealing the bomb bay doors; passengers stretched out on the metal floor of the fusilage, their teeth rattling. A week later I was in Washington and in the State Department. The first five friends I met said, "What? You back! We didn't expect you before the end of September."

Without taking leave, I wound up my Chinese business by preparing for the Personnel Board various delinquent administrative reports and by endorsing the appointment of Walter S. Robertson to be chargé d'affaires in Chungking when Ambassador Hurley abandoned the city. As I recall it, the ambassador did not request leave; he announced he was going.

Busy with my new duties and trying to catch up with the shifting Latin American scene, I had little contact with Ambassador Hurley, who was visiting his family in New Mexico. However, he invited me to attend the Press Club luncheon in his honor on November 25. At that time he announced his resignation in an explosive speech denouncing the State Department and the Foreign Service in general, including those in China, some of whom had, he declared, been covert supporters of communism. (He excepted me.)

Ambassador Hurley's resignation produced a furor, coming as it did when the press was baying loudly on the Stilwell trail and while the news

9. Today the title would be principal deputy assistant secretary.

10. Ambassador Hurley did so. That was useful when, a few years later, disgruntled demagogues launched unguided missiles against many of those who had served in the Far East. Those unfortunates were automatically suspected of contributing to the "loss" of China as well as of harboring sympathy for communism.

from China itself daily grew more confused and less reassuring. The continuing clamor caused by Hurley was one of the factors that led President Truman to dispatch the Marshall Mission, a final convulsive, all-out American effort to achieve the unification of China under the National government of Generalissimo Chiang Kai-shek — an impossible undertaking.

In assessing the role of Ambassador Hurley in wartime China, it must be conceded that he was hardly the prototype of the diplomat's diplomat. Diplomacy is (or should be) a profession employing various talents, among which are patience and self-effacement. "Skill in handling affairs without arousing hostility" is a secondary dictionary observation, the qualifying clause of which Hurley would have regarded as largely irrelevant.

Hurley sought results — let the chips fall where they might. Moreover, the dictionary definition failed to conform to his favorite slogan, implying readiness to square off at whatever opponent: "If it is a day old or an inch high." But it was that same self-reliant pugnaciousness that had raised Hurley from the obscurity of his Oklahoma beginnings to combat service in World War I, to wealth and prestige as a corporation lawyer, to political power in the Republican Party, and to the important Cabinet post he occupied in the last administration before Roosevelt.

Hurley would have seen nothing incongruous in Gilbert and Sullivan's advice:

> If you wish in the world to advance
> Your merits you're bound to enhance
> You must stir it and stump it,
> And blow your own trumpet —
> Or trust me, you haven't a chance.

The contrary notion — that he merits approbation who is "diffident, modest and shy" — would have aroused Hurley's contempt. In some respects Hurley was a sort of Cyrano de Bergerac who, "marking the manner of those canine courtesies," would exclaim, "Thank God! Here comes another enemy!"

No, Pat was not the ideal copybook diplomatist. He would have been the last to claim that distinction. He was too hot-blooded and unpredictably explosive. He was intemperate in his public declarations and too sweeping in his charges against those who opposed him. He was scornful of routine and impatient with the slow unwinding of events. Alexander disposing of the

Gordian knot would have appealed to him, but not the fable of Robert Bruce and the spider.

On the other hand, those critics who would dismiss Hurley as "all sound and no substance" could be mistaken. If Hurley was not a diplomat, he should not be rated (or berated) as if he had claimed to be one. He was a political diagnostician and a troubleshooter who, during his short stay in China, accomplished with two sergeants and one Cadillac more than his predecessor had done in three years, and probably as much as his successor, General Marshall, did in 1946 with the entire resources of the victorious United States government behind him.

Notwithstanding the confusion prevailing in 1944, it took Hurley only a few weeks to decide (and to persuade Washington of the correctness of his decision) that General Stilwell, for all his courage and other admirable characteristics, had by his spleen and venom disqualified himself for further usefulness in the China theater. Ambassador Gauss, outweighed and outreached by those with whom he had been sparring, and on almost equally bad terms with both Generalissimo Chiang Kai-shek and General Stilwell, had registered few accomplishments, notwithstanding his long years in China. His retirement was in order.

In the period between that mission and Hiroshima, Hurley again correctly estimated the situation, concluding that there was scant prospect of genuine collaboration between the Nationalist government, which he was under instructions to support, and the Communists, who were soon to dominate all of China. Hurley did not unify China, but unification on the basis sought by the United States was impossible.

It was soon to be declared in the United States, already exposed to Moscow's Cold War, that our country had "lost" China. The true explanation, apparent today as it may not have been at the time Chiang Kai-shek fled to Taiwan, is that the United States never "had" China, and therefore China was never ours to "lose." The Kuomintang lost China, because not even the United States, with its tremendous power and World War II victory, could breathe spirit or strength into a corrupt and incompetent regime that did not possess the confidence of the Chinese people.

It was wrong of Hurley to denounce the Foreign Service and the State Department so intemperately. His charges were not true. The majority of the officers concerned had no more admiration for communism than a raccoon has for a porcupine in estrus. The fact that so many "China hands" were anti-Chiang Kai-shek and against the policy of their own government did not make them Communists, but it did make some of them bad public servants.

One notorious case illustrates the point. The officer in question believed so strongly that Washington policy was wrong that, heeding the call of what he apparently interpreted as Duty — a duty higher than his own oath of office — he caused classified documents to fall into the hands of a magazine editor who happened to be pro-Communist. The officer was disciplined by the State Department, not for his alleged communism but for his deliberate violation of security, for which he should have been dismissed from the Foreign Service.[11]

Furthermore, Hurley did have a legitimate grievance against certain Foreign Service officers for their behavior upon his appointment and for sending to Washington in his absence from Chungking, which he regarded as "his office," the telegram denouncing the policy he had been instructed by the president to follow. Moreover, most of the Foreign Service officers who criticized Washington policy had nothing more constructive to offer. To support the Communists instead of the recognized government of China would have been lunatic even if politically feasible for the United States government (which of course it was not). To have withdrawn from China in 1944 or 1945 might, in the clarity of "after the event," have been a better choice, especially if it had been combined with keeping Russia out of the Far East struggle. It would have saved the United States hundreds of millions of wasted dollars. However, it would certainly have facilitated an earlier Communist takeover; I do not recall that that choice occurred to those dissident officers, although it apparently did to the bitter and disillusioned General Stilwell.

The trouble with some of the "old China hands" was not that they were disloyal to the United States but that they were not fully competent to serve it. A proportion of them never got over the 1926 abrogation of their extraterritorial rights, and they longed for the return of the days described by Ann Bridges in her novel *Peking Picnic,* when "boy" meant an immaculate servant who for the equivalent of a few cents a day would do anything from pressing his master's cummerbund to mixing his third or fourth drink. Other old China hands could not keep pace with the tempo of the times; they were no longer geared to the problems of war or to the acceleration it demanded.

---

11. Instead, his career was allowed to peter out in a series of dead-end assignments. Curiously enough, in subsequent years he became something of an icon to the career service for his alleged ill treatment during the McCarthy era.

I had been twenty years a bureaucrat at the time of the Hurley denunciation. My Far East experience, although brief, left me with the depressed feeling that, compared with officers I had known elsewhere in the world and during several years in Washington, many of the Oriental specialists — with notable exceptions like John Paton Davies — simply did not measure up to the standards of colleagues elsewhere.

Hurley may, therefore, have been both right and wrong, a situation more often encountered than recognized. He was wrong to denounce all professional diplomats and to try to fasten upon some of them the responsibility for the failure of his mission. He was right in criticizing a group some of whose members had been anything but helpful to him during a period of Chinese history that would have proved sufficiently difficult even if everyone had pitched in and tried hard to help him.

With me, a neophyte in China, Pat Hurley was genial, amusing, a stimulating companion and a considerate chief of mission. He was a patriotic public servant who worked indefatigably to advance the interests of his country as Washington then saw those interests. Patrick J. Hurley (1883–1963), soldier, Cabinet member, international troubleshooter, lawyer, and politician, returned to his family in New Mexico, a state he sought to represent in the United States Senate. It is a pity he was not successful, for he could wear dignity with distinction, and he would have lent color as well as sound to the Upper Chamber. In fact, Patrick Hurley looked more like a senator than do many members of that body. Had he been a candidate from his native Oklahoma, he might have been elected by acclamation; instead, in deference to his family, he remained in New Mexico, where the local machine was too firmly entrenched to be ousted by a newcomer.

The State Department Struggles with Peace

PART ONE: THE ARGENTINE PROBLEM — PERÓN, BRADEN, AND MESSERSMITH

I served as director of American Republic Affairs (ARA) from September 1945 until the middle of 1947. Our family was together again after seven months of separation, and our two children — still bilingual in Spanish — were in American schools for the first time since 1940. Our rented house in Georgetown had a cheerful if microscopic garden. I was enthusiastic about the new job and eager to get on with it.

From my two periods in Washington in the 1930s I had many friends among the permanent staff of the State Department. Notwithstanding the battering of diplomacy during the long Roosevelt administration, the old State Department in its quarters beside the White House in 1945 was still reasonably intact.

Secretary Byrnes, recognizing the importance of access to the center of power, clung doggedly to his old high-ceilinged office on the second floor of the State War Navy Building, one minute's walk from the White House. With the war ended, diplomacy, we believed, would soon return to its own, as had happened after previous wars. The soldiers had come home; the volunteers had gone back to their peacetime occupations; the professional military had resumed life in their barracks; and the diplomats had taken over the tasks of diplomacy.

The secretary, searching for a Latin American hand callused by fieldwork, summoned Spruille Braden, who had only just arrived in Buenos Aires, to be assistant secretary of state for Latin American affairs, succeeding Nelson Rockefeller.

So my immediate chief was Braden, my old friend who had been my ambassador for two years in Cuba. We probably saw eye to eye on nine-tenths of the problems affecting — and afflicting — the Good Neighbors.

Since being appointed in 1933 as a delegate to the Montevideo Conference, Braden — a mining engineer with much prior experience in Latin America — had worked continuously in diplomacy. Almost single-handed he had achieved the peace treaty that ended the Chaco War. His service in Colombia (1938–1942) and in Cuba (1942–1945) had been distinguished by straight talking and fair dealings. This had culminated in a short and bitter exposure in Argentina to Juan Domingo Perón, whom Braden accurately identified as an anti-American demagogue with limitless political ambition (shared by his consort Evita) but with scant competence except as a rabble-rouser.[1]

If Braden and I had set out, in 1945, to write a credo for dealing with the other twenty republics, it might have run something like this:

1. Juridical equality exists in international law and thus is entitled to deference. But in practice the power of states is unequal. It is silly to act as though the voice of El Salvador carries as far as the voice of Brazil.
2. During the twentieth century the predominant power of the United States will remain a major factor; envy of that power on the part of some of the Neighbors will inevitably result. Since he who is envied is rarely loved, it is futile and a waste of time for the United States to pursue popularity.
3. *Respect* — not popularity — is the element that should be sought by the United States. If this fosters an "Uncle Sam takes us for granted" syndrome, those with inferiority complexes may be unhappy. That is too bad, but it is not a reason to reshape a policy.
4. The Good Neighbor Policy, as originally expressed in 1933, emphasizes respect and the mutual fulfillment of obligations. It provides a sound basis for international relations.
5. As Cordell Hull observed, "Expropriation without compensation is stealing." The most serious failure of the American government in its

---

1. During an interview with Braden in Buenos Aires, following a speech in which the ambassador had extolled democracy before an enthusiastic Argentine audience, Perón observed blandly that it might not be possible for his government to protect the person of the new American ambassador from "the fanatics who adore me." These were Perón's *descamisados*, his famous "shirtless ones," whose larcenous passions Perón was to dominate for a decade.

relations with Latin America during recent years had been the supineness of Washington toward the protection of legitimate United States interests.

Having subscribed to these propositions, Braden and I might have added a few private scribblings, out of experience picked up here and there:

1. Latin America is important to the United States, and in the future will become more so. For the next generation, however, it will probably not be so important as the reconstruction of Europe, or the stabilization of relations with the Soviet Union, or the solution of the problems of Asia.

2. In dealing with foreign officials, always give an honest answer. That does not mean, however, that having said, "Yes, I do hold the ace of clubs," it is essential to spread the other twelve cards face up on the table.

3. Countries that do not accord fair treatment to American interests should expect no favors from the United States.

Having the postwar tribulations of twenty American republics to cope with, ours was a busy schedule, crammed with daily incidents, many of which stemmed from causes diagnosed but still unresolved. It was a period when democratic self-government, while not exactly enjoying universal acclaim among the politicians of the Good Neighborhood, was nevertheless doing better than it was destined to do in the (then) predictable future. In 1946–1947, notwithstanding the stench of the late Juan Vicente Gómez still contaminating the Venezuelan air, or the activities of Perón in Argentina, or of Trujillo in the Dominican Republic, both Braden and I were more hopeful of the future of free institutions than we would be thirty years later.

We in ARA spent a good deal of time trying to get down on paper some short and comprehensible formula that would truly represent the view of the people of the United States toward the existence of democracy elsewhere. Irrational, even fatuous, as the idea may seem today, we worked hard at it, but the closest we were able to come was not wholly satisfactory. First, we could not agree on a final clause, and second, our formula inevitably skirted the quicksand of an assumed moral superiority, which seldom has a proper place in international affairs. Our formula went like this, and although we failed to get it into the vocabulary of the secretary of state, we ourselves used it twice, with 50 percent success:

The government and people of the United States have a warmer feeling of friendship for, and a greater desire to cooperate with, governments that rest on the periodically and freely expressed will of the people . . . .[2]

The first time we used the formula was on Anastasio Somoza, the boss of Nicaragua, and the second time was on Trujillo, the Dominican tyrant.

Tacho Somoza had been running Nicaragua most of the time since the departure of the United States Marines, a dozen years before. Intelligent, amusing, and sagacious in the ways of the United States, where he had been educated, Somoza had developed into a benevolent Central American dictator who, while not impoverishing the clan of Somoza (which was numerous), had nevertheless given the Nicaraguan people, including his political adversary Emiliano Chamorro, a fairly decent run for their money.

By 1946, Somoza decided to relax for awhile from the rigors of governing the country. His wife's brother, the portly and amiable Guillermo Sevilla Sacasa,[3] was ably representing Nicaragua in the United States, and an old gentleman named Doctor Argüelles was duly elected president of Nicaragua with instructions to hold the fort while the Somozas recharged their batteries (an idea that had been tried with success a decade before by Rafael Leónidas Trujillo in Santo Domingo). The trouble was that Tacho misjudged his man, who, having been sworn in as president, had the presumption (and the bad judgment) to act like the president. A few weeks of that sufficed, and then Tacho unceremoniously threw old Argüelles out, the pretext being as flimsy and transparent as one of his wife's Fifth Avenue nighties.

Here was a clear case of high-handed anti-democratic behavior, which in no circumstances could be said to conform to the "freely expressed will of the people." Into our high chair facing the wall went Tacho, whose government (now rudely referred to as his "regime") remained unrecognized for some time by the United States.

There had been a time during the first decades of the century when non-recognition by the United States spelled the early demise of an offending, invariably insolvent, Central American administration. Further credit was denied by bankers, who in those days wanted no part of an establishment

2. The architect of this noble prose was my colleague and friend Paul Daniels, a year or two junior to me in the Foreign Service. Then in ARA, he was later ambassador to Honduras and to Ecuador. But we were unable to agree on "warmer than *what*" or "greater desire than what."

3. Guillermo Sevilla Sacasa was dean of the Washington diplomatic corps longer than any ambassador in history.

lacking Potomac favor, but by the end of World War II, Central America had changed. The Somoza family was far from broke, the economy of Nicaragua was in good shape, and while the Argüelles tribe was not exactly clapping hands or emitting loud cheers, none were in jail and not even the ferrets of the left-wing press could produce evidence of fingernails pulled out or solitary confinement in rat-infested dungeons. Furthermore, other American republics, observing that things in Managua were orderly and moving along about as before, began extending recognition to the reestablished Somoza government, regardless of the moral high horse prancing under an increasingly uncomfortable Uncle Sam.

In brief, the State Department climbed down and went back to dealing officially with the Somozas, who continued to give Nicaragua (again, at no lack of profit to themselves) as efficient a government as that small but aggressive republic had enjoyed.

We had better luck with our formula when we tried it out on the Benefactor of the Dominican Republic, who wanted a fresh supply of arms and ammunition. After some procrastination, during which we listened to the Pentagon argue that if the United States failed to supply what Trujillo wanted, he would take his business elsewhere, we dusted off the Paul Daniels formula and quoted it to the Dominican ambassador in an official note that declared: "The government and people of the United States have a warmer feeling of friendship for, and a greater desire to cooperate with, governments that rest on the periodically and freely expressed will of the people." In the next paragraph we turned down the request for arms. We did so in good conscience, the record of the excesses of Trujillo by that time being a matter of world-shaped repugnance. Trujillo promptly bought his hardware elsewhere, as the generals had predicted.

We wound up doubting the efficacy of moral preachments as instruments applicable to foreign affairs. Moreover, it does not necessarily affect one's private belief in the democratic process in, say, New England to doubt the ability to handle the slippery and complicated machinery of self-government of countries we are inclined (often with offensive smugness) to describe as "emerging" or "underdeveloped."

We also spent a good deal of our time listening to the complaints of our Latino friends to the effect that the prices of their raw materials had declined with the reopening of world trade, whereas the cost of manufactured goods had risen. After Pearl Harbor, most of the Neighbors (except Argentina) followed the United States into World War II. They did so out of conviction, or out of what they interpreted as their own self-interest. Nevertheless, they had been prodded and propositioned by the United States, with resulting American responsibilities. Commitments were made concerning the purchase of raw materials and supplies to be furnished in return. Considering the magnitude of the American war effort, its record in those particulars was good but not outstanding.

Many of the charges by the Latinos were true. A buyer's market prevailed for sugar, coffee, petroleum, and copper — each of vital importance to the economy of one or more countries of Latin America, none of which had it within its power to control prices. We were sympathetic and did the best we could. Raising the price of foreign raw materials is not, however, a popular Washington enterprise or a feasible one for the State Department. About all we could do was to assist in the sale of American products on reasonable terms through Export-Import Bank and other credits.

During these various exchanges we diligently promoted the Cordell Hull dictum that "expropriation without compensation is stealing," and without engaging in hypothetical correspondence with other republics on the subject, we made it clear that countries seizing United States property without making arrangements for "prompt and adequate compensation" could expect few favors from Washington.

Cuba proved a case in point, with the ironic result that at the Bogotá Conference in 1948, the United States was accused of "economic aggression" for having attached a provision to its sugar legislation that unless American interests received *fair* treatment — not special treatment, nor treatment more favorable than anyone else, but *fair* treatment — that fact might jeopardize the preferential tariff on Cuban sugar. The reason for this provision was that Cuba, while benefiting to the extent of millions of dollars per year from the sugar preference, was in fact treating certain other United States interests, including claims long since adjudicated by Cuban courts in favor of American creditors, in a most cavalier fashion.

What blunted Braden's and my efforts and betrayed our premise was the problem of Argentina — or, perhaps more accurately, the problem of convincing the hemisphere that during almost the entire period of the war, Argentina had been a bad rather than a good neighbor; and of convincing the American people that the conduct of Argentina during the war still mattered.

After consulting with Cordell Hull (retired and living in Washington), Braden decided to assemble the facts of the Argentine record and to make them available for the information of the hemisphere, including the Argentine people. That decision was a key one in terms of unlocking future developments.

The outline of Argentine behavior was not generally known. When the German pocket battleship *Graf Spee* committed suicide beyond the Montevideo breakwater in December 1939, the crew of more than one thousand men had already disembarked, and they were taken across the River Plate to the Argentine side. There, instead of being interned, they were treated as guests, forming the nucleus of a vast Nazi espionage network in the hemisphere. During the next five years that apparatus cost the Allies heavily in torpedoed ships, drowned sailors, and lost cargoes.

In addition, the Argentine government dragged its feet in nearly all hemisphere matters involving defense against Nazi penetration. Cordell Hull's anger at Sumner Welles for not bearing down on Argentina at the Rio Conference in 1942 is one of the sharpest passages in his memoirs.

Following a 1944 coup d'état that backfired, the United States withheld recognition from the ensuing regime, and Ambassador Norman Armour — an outstandingly able professional — was withdrawn. Six weeks before Hitler perished in his Berlin bunker, Argentina belatedly broke relations with the Axis and was rewarded by a Rockefeller arms-around-the-neck reconciliation at Chapultepec (again to Cordell Hull's disgust).

Spruille Braden was appointed ambassador to Argentina and began his short River Plate encounter, which ended with his return to Washington to be assistant secretary of state. He presented credentials in Buenos Aires on May 21 and returned to Washington on September 23, 1945.

Padding the skeletal outline with the details of the behavior of the Argentine government was not a job that could be accomplished in minutes. An able task force was assembled under the chairmanship of Carl Spaeth, later dean of the law school at Stanford University. Spaeth had served on an international commission functioning in Uruguay during the war, and he was well qualified for the work. Assembling the data took time, however, and it was the end of January 1946 before the State Department Blue Book (*Consultation Among the American Republics with Respect to the Argentine Situation*) describing the wartime activities of Argentina was ready.

That turned out to be almost six months too late. In the interval between the Nazi surrender the previous May and the winter of 1946, when the Blue Book was ready, the preoccupations of the American people had shifted to the atomic bomb, to the increasingly offensive behavior of Stalin, and to bringing the boys home. Braden was convinced, however, that as a matter of principle the story ought not to be suppressed, although messages from Cabot, the chargé in Buenos Aires, warned that releasing the text *at that time* might play into the hands of Perón by permitting him to convert his presidential campaign into a "Braden versus Perón" issue with xenophobia — seldom in short supply in Argentina — triumphant.

Secretary Byrnes, who often relished a fight, took up the matter of Blue Book publication with President Truman, who sided with Braden. The Latin American ambassadors were duly invited to Blair House, where, with Acting Secretary Acheson as host and with Braden and ARA personnel in attendance, copies of the Blue Book were distributed to the assembled diplomats. The text was thereupon released to the press.

The election of Perón as president of Argentina a few days later, after he had blanketed Buenos Aires with posters depicting himself as a handsome candidate oozing machismo, versus an unflattering cartoon of the former American ambassador, was a severe blow to Braden. It took moral courage on his part to insist on publication, and he remained convinced that by showing the unsavory Argentine record he had done the honest thing; that if he had failed to do so, he would have been an object of scorn among the many patriotic Argentines who believed in democracy and who had tried in vain to support the Allies during the war. As for contributing to the Perón electoral victory, Perón probably would have won anyway, such being the hold that he and Evita then had on the *descamisados* of the country.

The incident did, however, materially weaken Braden's political position in Washington, especially among certain influential senators. It played into the hands of his critics among the correspondents, as well as arousing that vocal segment in and out of academe that is ever eager to interpret as "intervention" any American action more positive than ruefully rubbing a shin kicked by an unrepentant Good Neighbor.

There is no question that the Argentine episode contributed to the troubles of Braden a year later, following further River Plate developments that reflected more credit on him than on his detractors. These troubles were precipitated by our having dispatched Ambassador George Messersmith to Buenos Aires in the hope that the toughness he had displayed toward the Nazis in the 1930s would not be lost on Perón, and that some sort of workable, if not amicable, arrangement favorable to United States interests might follow.

That was not to be, first, because such was the personal enmity of Perón toward Braden that as long as the latter occupied a position of authority in Washington, a hostile glare illuminated the River Plate; and second, because Messersmith himself, while in Washington between posts, apparently reached the private conclusion that since Perón had been elected president of Argentina "in spite of Braden's Blue Book," the Potomac days of Braden were numbered. The result was a classic attempt at double cross that ended the State Department careers of both officers.

Messersmith presented his credentials to Perón in May 1946. Although his instructions were explicit, before long the word started to drift back that far from treating the *platense* demagogue with reserve, a relationship of almost fraternal warmth was being promoted in the American mansion on Avenida Alvear, with growing signs of reciprocity in the Casa Rosada. These rumors of conviviality were at first discounted as being the antithesis of the ambassador's instructions. But soon they reached the cocktail circuit in Washington, where the Latino representatives, a kind of wheel within a wheel in the diplomatic corps, were both indefatigable canapé chasers and galloping gossips. Moreover, their fiestas were invariably attended by members of the press, not all of whom were friendly to the outspoken Assistant Secretary Braden. We had also to contend with certain former New Dealers whose ideas about the Good Neighbor Policy included the belief that the Neighbor is always right.

By the time Byrnes had been replaced by General Marshall, Washington was buzzing with the story of how the American ambassador to Argentina, sent south to be severe and uncompromising, was instead in and out of Perón's pocket like a tame *vizcacha*, and only slightly less cozy with Evita. Argentine sources in the United States fathered additional stories to the effect that a new day for American business would dawn as soon as Braden was eliminated.

Messersmith was in fact trying to play both ends against the middle, perhaps having ambitions to replace Braden in Washington. His game was defeated by his uncontrollable passion for writing letters, including letters highly critical of Braden, to several members of Congress. Even before proceeding to his post, Messersmith had begun to criticize Braden's stewardship. Armed with incontrovertible proof of Messersmith's duplicity, Braden went to the White House.[4]

American diplomacy could no longer contain both officials. The resignation of each was to be accepted. But whereas Braden returned with relief to his private business in New York, Ambassador Messersmith, whose profes-

---

4. For an account of that meeting, see Braden's autobiography, *Diplomats and Demagogues,* chapter 32.

sional career still had more than a year to run, was permanently and prematurely retired. He left Buenos Aires, almost literally kicking and screaming, on June 21, 1947, a week before the announcement of Braden's resignation.[5]

The termination of the services of such an exceptionally capable, upright, and experienced public servant as Spruille Braden was personally distressing to me. The nation was the poorer except that through the following three decades the Braden voice — nothing impaired by the passage of time — still echoed in the land, denouncing the failure of Washington to defend more vigorously the rights of American citizens, violated time and again in the name of sovereignty.

PART TWO: THE PENTAGON, PANAMA, AND ALGER HISS

It might have been assumed that the United States, having achieved a great world victory, would have sent its military back to polishing their sabers and oiling their muskets. This proved to be a short-lived illusion. Trouble for our Latin American sector was already brewing in the Pentagon, which had two sets of demands for our urgent consideration. One had to do with the establishment of military missions, and the other, the acquisition of bases. The former, although a more complicated problem, proved the easier to handle.

Before the Second World War there had been a profusion of missions operated in various Latin American countries by European governments as well as by the United States. There had been a French military mission and a Spanish police mission in Peru; a German military mission in Bolivia; an American air mission in Chile; and, ever since shortly after the First World War, American naval missions in Brazil and in Peru.

The Pentagon's arguments for the replacement of European missions by American ones were several. First of all, uniformity: in the event of another world war, it would be greatly to the advantage of the United States to have

5. It is with regret that I must report that the account of this altercation, appearing in Secretary Acheson's *Present at the Creation,* is not in accordance with the facts. Acheson reports, for example, that Messersmith went to Mexico *after* Argentina, implying that the transfer was part of an arrangement that terminated the services only of Braden. In fact, Messersmith served in Mexico from February 24, 1942, to May 15, 1946. He was chosen for Argentina, unwisely as it turned out, by Braden himself. Messersmith served in Buenos Aires from May 23, 1946, to June 21, 1947.

the weapons of its (presumed) allies standardized. That was an argument we did not attempt to refute, although it seemed fairly clear that the popularity of a given mission was likely to depend upon its success in obtaining arms for the host government, so that the presence of missions (of any nationality) was as likely to promote unnecessary or uneconomic military competition as to reduce it.

Second, the Pentagon maintained that "since in the United States the military defers to the civilian authority, and since the armed services of the United States are the most democratic in the world," exposure of our Latino friends to American training both in the home countries and through attendance of picked officers at American staff schools would reduce the prospect of military coups d'état and the establishment of military dictatorships in Latin America. Furthermore, through the operation of the Inter-American Defense Board in Washington, on which all the Neighbors would be represented, an exchange of information about plans and requirements would of itself "tend to reduce tensions," an assumption that sounded as if it meant something until you tried to analyze just what.

Finally, the total of all this would result in added protection for the Panama Canal, although when the Pentagon was pressed for details about the precise roles to be played by — say — Paraguay, Honduras, or Haiti in preventing a potential enemy from committing a nuisance in the Culebra Cut, a convincing answer was not immediately forthcoming.

Spruille Braden and I viewed this entire Pentagon initiative with skepticism. It did seem to be to the advantage of the United States to have all twenty republics standardize their weapons, and it was possible in theory for the various United States missions (which were under the operational control of the commanding general at Quarry Heights in the Canal Zone) to reduce rather than inflate the ambitions of our Latino allies to compete with one another in attempting to acquire the latest — and most expensive — military gadgetry. Nevertheless, we shuddered against the day when, notwithstanding all the talk about promoting the spirit of democracy by studying at Fort Jackson or Fort Leavenworth, the inevitable revolutionary attempt would come, when American airplanes and American machine guns acquired through our American military missions would rake the Plaza de la Independencia, massed with local citizens whose blood would fill the gutters.

Furthermore, we apprehended that as time passed, these proliferated missions might have increasing difficulty in attracting the best American military talent to head them. They could become the dumping grounds for second- or third-rate officers or for superannuated wearers of old school ties, rather than posts professionally sought by ascending colonels and captains. As the years slipped by and as the Pentagon continued to exercise a disproportionate influence on the conduct of foreign affairs, several of our concerns turned out to be valid. But in the circumstances prevailing in 1946 and 1947, it was manifestly impossible to derail the Pentagon train. We had to be content with applying the brakes when we could, and with instructing our respective ambassadors in the other republics to keep a sharp eye out for flying cinders.

At the time the missions were under debate, the Pentagon was lusting with equal fervor after military bases, not only in Latin America but also in so many other nooks and corners of the world that the effort soon attracted the attention of Secretary Byrnes himself, who was heard to remark that if he had to buy all the foreign real estate labeled by the joint chiefs as "essential for national security," he would have to loot Fort Knox to pay the bill.[6]

Since much of Secretary Byrnes's time was occupied in coping with major problems outside Washington, he invited a friend to take a temporary job as special assistant to look into the base problem, worldwide, and to advise him what to do. The man chosen was Fred Searles, an engaging eccentric who headed an important American mining company and (happily for us) knew a good deal about South America. An idiosyncrasy of his was carrying uncut emeralds in his pants pocket — he said he liked their feel on the tips of his fingers.

I well remember an occasion when I took Searles to luncheon in Washington. Norman the Doorman, who had been with the Metropolitan Club a quarter-century, accepted the Searles cap, which might have been borrowed from Mao Tse-tung, with the expression of one handling something found in a trap under water. He gave me a look of sadness and reproach as he handed me the pen to sign in my guest. I found this diverting, since Fred Searles could probably have paid off the club mortgage overnight, with enough left over to buy a house on Massachusetts Avenue.

Searles quickly got the idea that some of the plans of some of the generals were strictly stratospheric. It was not easy for the Pentagon to make a case with him for "defense from possible Soviet aggression" by laying down a runway in the middle of the Paraguayan Chaco, or trying to keep permanent

6. When President de Gaulle evicted the United States from France some twenty years later, we gave up over *fifty* separate pieces of land in that country.

possession of a corner of Brazil, or of retaining an airport fifty-five miles west of Havana, where in 1942 Braden and I had restrained a particularly incompetent construction company from bulldozing the graveyard of the adjacent village in order to add an extra thousand feet to a bomber runway — which could have just as readily been extended in the opposition direction.

Two sites gave us special trouble. Each related to the alleged protection of the Panama Canal. One was the Galápagos Islands, which lie seven hundred miles west of Guayaquil and over one thousand miles south of Balboa. The military were on the point of offering $20 million to Ecuador for the Galápagos Islands before Braden and I, with a nod from Fred Searles, invited a just-retired and much-bemedaled four-star flying general to give us an opinion, having in mind the projected development of military aviation in the postwar decade.

Our general was a splendid character: articulate, profane, and specific. "Off the record — hell," he declared. "You can quote me. I wouldn't take those goddamn islands as a gift. Not even if you threw in the giant land iguanas and the sea turtles, plus that crazy German couple who went there before the war. You remember? They had all their teeth pulled out and got themselves dentures of stainless steel so they could chew stewed cactus and chomp on clam shells. After Pearl Harbor we evacuated the poor bastards as enemy aliens. Far as protecting the Panama Canal is concerned, the Galápagos Islands are worthless. You can quote me."

By a coincidence I was off to New York that afternoon, to make one of those superfluous speeches demanded of my position, and as the Congressional Limited pulled out of Union Station, whom should I encounter but Galo Plaza, the ambassador of Ecuador. As soon as we were safely coasting through Maryland, we sought the club car, where over drinks I broke the news that Quito had better not start spending that $20 million. Galo took it in stride.

Panama was a harder nut to crack — a nut that continued to defy the efforts of our successors. In 1946 the Pentagon requested us to arrange for the acquisition, outside the Canal Zone, of no less than 112 "defense sites." The majority were five- to ten-acre plots on some of which the military had already, through informal wartime arrangements, mounted machine guns or anti-aircraft batteries. Although no threats had occurred during World War II, the generals called it "preparing for possible contingencies."

We finally succeeded in whittling down the number of sites from 112 to approximately 30, including the large air base at Río Hato, seventy miles west of the Canal Zone on the Pacific side (protection against an air attack from Costa Rica, perhaps). But thirty pieces of land, outside the ten-mile-wide Canal Zone, was still quite a sackful of Panamanian soil for us to ask for. To our surprise, the initial response of the Panamanians was restrained. The reason, we discovered, was that the farmers and peasants in the little villages adjacent to the base sites had prospered as never before. Not only had a steady market developed for the fruits and vegetables and pigs and chickens raised in the vicinity, but the village maidens had been exposed to nylon stockings from the nearest PX, American cigarettes, and cosmetics less abrasive than those dispensed by the local stores. Several up-country villages sent emissaries to Panama City to testify to that effect.

These proposed arrangements were not, in the end, accepted by the Panamanian Assembly, although they did get as far as a draft agreement signed ad referendum by both parties. Before debate could begin, there stepped upon the stage a new figure not hitherto involved in the affairs of the isthmus. His name was Alger Hiss. The poisoning of United States–Panama relations may be said to date from his initiative.

Alger Hiss was a drafting officer — as distinct from a Foreign Service officer — whose tenure in Washington was limited to four years per assignment. Hiss had arrived young, and risen rapidly. A Harvard graduate with an excellent law degree, he was fluent, articulate, and possessed of considerable personal charm. Attached to Dean Acheson's office, which was now handling international conferences, Hiss specialized in international organization affairs. At the San Francisco Conference he had served as secretary-general of the American delegation and when the United Nations was formally established, Hiss was promoted to the section in the State Department that dealt with the General Secretariat of the United Nations.

Hiss's section was initially viewed as a liaison office to facilitate the handling of matters arising in the geographic divisions of the State Department that went to specific areas of functional offices of the fledgling U.N. But like other bureaucratic enterprises, his section soon developed powers and policies of its own, and it began to take initiatives in areas of substantive operations. The office nevertheless was instructed to clear all its proposed communications to the UN with the office in the State Department having primary responsibility for the country or the issue in question — in the case of Panama, the Division of American Republic Affairs.[7]

7. The act of "clearance" consisted of getting the initials of the responsible officer in the geographic division on the blue file copy of the proposed document. In urgent cases clearance was granted by phone, and the drafting officer would so note on the permanent file copy.

The document that was to cause the trouble with Panama was the most mundane and nonconfidential of government papers — the Annual Report of the Governor of the Canal Zone. Available from the Government Printing Office, it was filled with statistics of each year's operations: number and tonnage of vessels transiting the canal; tolls collected; cubic yards of earth removed because of slides; personnel employed; etc. All the data, in short, that a private company would issue for the information of its stockholders, who, in the case of the Panama Canal, were the citizens of the United States — whose genius and whose taxes built the canal in the first place, opened it to international traffic in 1914, and thereafter operated it for the benefit of the world.

The Canal Zone was territory leased from Panama "in perpetuity" under the Treaty of 1903, for the purpose of the "construction, maintenance, operation and protection" of the canal. And in order to avoid argument about who was running the enterprise or whether a given vessel should swap pilots at the Continental Divide, the same treaty wisely provided that the rights of the United States within the Canal Zone were those it would "possess if it were the sovereign."[8]

Hiss, pondering his United Nations Charter, decided (as far as is known, on his own initiative) that the Canal Zone was a "non-selfgoverning territory" under Chapter XI, Articles 73 and 74, of the charter, and that in accordance therewith, the United States had assumed a whole series of obligations and "sacred trusts" with respect to the inhabitants of what, in effect, would have to be presumed to be a colonial possession, and a backward one at that. To this end, Hiss drafted a third-person transmitting note to the secretary-general of United Nations, in the name of the secretary of state of the United States, and forwarded a copy of the Governor's Annual Report. Hiss thus equated the leased Canal Zone, with a population at the time of approximately thirty-five thousand American citizens (not counting the military), with Guam and Samoa.

The first I knew of this time bomb ticking under my chair was when Murray Wise, the Mr. Panama of ARA, came into my office waving the blue file copy of the Hiss transmitting note. This had not been cleared by anyone in ARA, in violation of standing instructions. As a so-called third-person

8. The treaty was amended twice — in 1936 and in 1955 — in each case in Panama's favor and in order to iron out operational problems not foreseeable before the canal was opened. Panama had publicly declared, sometime before the Hiss episode, that all pending problems had been settled to the satisfaction of the Republic.

communication not requiring the signature of the secretary of state, the original bore the initials of Alger Hiss.[9]

Failing to reach Hiss by phone, I barged downstairs to Dean Acheson's office — he again being acting secretary while Byrnes was attending United Nations meetings on Long Island. Dean, as usual, was genial. "What," he wanted to know, "is all the excitement about? Is Evita Perón pregnant, or has Nicaragua declared war on Venezuela?"

"No," I told him, "but Panama is about to declare war on the United States." I handed Mr. Acheson the blue file copy of the note to the secretary-general.

The acting secretary read it in seconds, noted that it bore no concurring initials of ARA, and reached for his copy of the UN Charter. One of the stimulating things about working with Dean Acheson was that you did not have to waste time on explanations.

"And you think the Panamanians are going to be stuffy about it? Hmmm . . ." Dean summoned Alger Hiss to join us.

Hiss professed astonished chagrin at the oversight that had permitted the document to be sent without going through ARA. He apologized to me for any seeming rudeness, which he assured me was unintentional, and to the acting secretary for his violation of departmental regulations. Having thus freshened the atmosphere, Hiss delivered a crisp legal argument that sought to place the Governor's Report (and the Canal Zone) within the purview of Chapter XI of the charter. It was neatly done, but I gathered from the smoothly flowing presentation that the transmission had not been a routine or haphazard affair, such as might easily occur when dealing with a multiplicity of papers, but one deliberately concocted with a defense position already prepared.

Acheson, no amateur himself when it came to legal interpretations, engaged in several minutes of technical debate, with Articles 73 and 74 being batted back and forth like Ping-Pong balls and Panama only casually mentioned. It was erudite and decorous, but I did not think it was getting us anywhere.

"Gentlemen," I remember saying, "I'm not a lawyer, but if I were, the last people I'd take on would be two such eminent performers. But this is not a

9. Third-person notes at that time began as follows: "The Secretary of State of the United States presents his compliments to His Excellency the Secretary General of the United Nations, and has the honor to . . . ." There followed whatever the sender might have up his sleeve for the delectation of the UN bureaucracy — and this is the important point — in the name of the secretary of state.

legal question. It is a loaded political question, and if we don't recall that note before Ricardo Alfaro gets a copy, there's going to be the damnedest explosion beside Lake Success since Sperry invented the gyroscope."[10]

Our conversation in Mr. Acheson's office then became less amiable and likewise less legal. It was a routine communication, reiterated Hiss. Chances were that the document had already been marked "File" by the secretariat. To recall a message officially sent might end by calling attention to it, rendering more likely to occur those dire things of which he implied I was unduly fearful. Hiss repeated his apology for having inadvertently bypassed ARA, but might I not be magnifying his molehill?

Unfortunately, the problems of Latin America bored Dean Acheson. He did not regard the area and its squabbles as of primary importance, and spent little time studying what took place. He found the speeches of its delegates at international meetings tedious, often irrelevant, and interminable, which they were. During previous years he left most decisions on Latin America to Sumner Welles and Adolf Berle (neither now present), or to Larry Duggan (also departed), who was a friend of Alger Hiss.[11]

The acting secretary gave Alger and me two minutes apiece to recapitulate our arguments, and then decided to do nothing. That is, he decided in favor of Hiss, and he cheerfully dismissed us.

When I reported my rebuff to Assistant Secretary Braden, he took the phone to ask Acheson, urgently, to reconsider. Dean, who did not care greatly for the outspoken Braden, was inclined to be frosty, and turned him down.

The explosion, when it came, rendered my prediction an understatement. The Panamanian representative at the meeting of the General Assembly outdid himself in vindictiveness and abuse. The tenor was that the Canal Zone was not a colony but Panamanian territory — more, it was "sacred soil of the Republic" — leased to the United States by an unfair, obsolete, unclean agreement, etc., etc.

10. Ambassador Alfaro, a leading critic of the United States, was the Panamanian delegate to the United Nations, then meeting at Lake Success while the architects did blueprints on First Avenue.

11. In Acheson's otherwise magnificent account of his stewardship, *Present at the Creation*, a volume of one thousand pages, scarcely fifty contain references to inter-American affairs. Acheson's account of his differences with Assistant Secretary Braden is inaccurate, and some of the rest has to do with socializing with a Brazilian millionaire friend in Rio de Janeiro. No statesman can be an expert on everything, but Acheson's mistake was his failure to encourage knowledgeable officials to call the Latin American turns.

This field day of vituperation got an outraged if bewildered Secretary Byrnes, still in New York, on my telephone in Washington. I listened for several paragraphs to straight South Carolina cussing — directed, to be sure, primarily at his Panamanian colleague at Lake Success, but with an ample share that rubbed off on the listening director of American Republics Affairs. I was then ordered to get on the first plane or train I could catch to New York, because he damned well was not going to take all that abuse lying down and he was going to ask for time to reply. At which point Mr. Byrnes hung up, leaving my secretary very pink-eared because, in accordance with standing instructions, she had been making notes of the conversation. That is to say, of the monologue.

I am happy to report that Dean Acheson came promptly and effectively to my rescue. He said he himself had a call in to talk to the secretary later that afternoon, that he would explain what happened — including my prediction of trouble — and that since he himself had made the decision, he would take the blame.

Did I, in those circumstances, want to go to New York, or should he get me off that hook also? I said the man who knew the most about Panama was Murray Wise, who had the Panama desk in ARA. Murray remembered everything since Vasco Núñez de Balboa first sighted the Pacific Ocean in 1513, and if Secretary Byrnes wanted to frame a reply, Wise was the man best equipped to help him. (That remark got a breathless Wise to Byrnes's hotel suite in New York that same night.)

Whether Alger Hiss was a Communist is beyond the scope of this writing. What is not questionable, however, is that no man seeking to impair the relations between the builder and operator of the Panama Canal, on the one hand, and the people of Panama, on the other, could have devised a move better calculated to implant the virus of "colonialism" into the tissue of relations. The immediate excitement died down, but the professional nationalists of Panama City and Colón did not forget the incident. With Moscow's assistance the virus was thereafter spread by left-leaning demagogues elsewhere in Latin America who raised the cry that it was "immoral" for one country to operate a waterway across the territory of another.

The objective — which eventually succeeded — was to weaken the United States by forcing it to turn over the Canal Zone, including effective control of the waterway itself, to the Panamanians. We never had any quarrel with the people of Panama, whose livelihood since the turn of the century has depended upon American enterprise and competence, to the extent that the per capita income of the country is now one of the highest in Latin America.

But it is, and was, naive not to recognize that those same Panamanians, if left to themselves without the benefits of the Treaty of 1903, might still be paddling their dugout canoes up the Chagres River and swatting yellow fever and malarial mosquitoes in their village huts on either side of the isthmus.

A postscript to the Hiss incident was written two decades later by ex-Secretary Byrnes, then a spry and active eighty-six years old. Having turned in my own uniform, I did a stint as visiting professor in 1965 at the Institute of International Studies at the University of South Carolina, and in due course I was taken by the director to make a courtesy call on my former boss. The old gentleman recalled how angry he had been at me over "that damned Panamanian note," as well as how decent Dean Acheson had been in assuring him that I not only had done my best to persuade him to have the note recalled but also had predicted the effect it would have on the Panamanians.

"I see," remarked the former secretary, apropos the riots on the isthmus the year before, and the way in which Washington had almost apologetically accepted the destruction of thousands of dollars' worth of American property by Panamanian hoodlums, "that our enemies are still doing business at the same stand." The ex-secretary wondered how long it would be before the United States had the guts to stand up for its rights and to treat nuisance problems like nuisance problems instead of permitting liberal lunatics, including those wearing the mask of liberalism, to present as a moral issue what in reality was a challenge to the security of our country.

James F. Byrnes, the only man in American history to serve as governor of his state, as congressman, as senator of the United States, as justice of the Supreme Court, and as secretary of state, died seven years later, his question still unanswered.[12]

PART THREE: THE MOVE TO FOGGY BOTTOM

One of the most difficult struggles in which I engaged during my first post-war year in ARA had only peripherally to do with Latin America. When the shooting war ended in 1945, some of the survivors of the propaganda apparatus were blanketed into the State Department, where the dynamic Bill Benton took them in charge and kept them out of our hair, pending the es-

12. The author died in 1976, before the Senate approved the new treaties with Panama, thereby bringing to a close the chapter begun by Alger Hiss's note to the UN secretary-general.

tablishment of the semiautonomous United States Information Agency. This was not the case for a group of veterans of the Office of Strategic Services when that agency was dismantled. It was initially proposed that these individuals be quartered in the respective geographic divisions, meaning an influx of upward of twenty superfluous persons per division, few with any previous State Department experience and some with dubious security records. Dean Acheson thought well of the idea; Spruille Braden uttered immediate and forceful objections.

This squabble occurred before enactment of the National Security Act of 1947, which created a secretary of defense, and established the Central Intelligence Agency and (unfortunately for American diplomacy) the National Security Council. Acheson, as he describes it in *Present at the Creation,* thought it was a good idea to take in these wayfarers, but Braden was able to block their entry into the various geographic divisions, to Acheson's extreme annoyance.

It was finally arranged, again over Braden's strongly expressed criticism, to form them into a separate "intelligence unit" whose numbers would perform liaison functions with the Central Intelligence Agency when that agency was established; in the meantime they would study what was going on in various foreign countries and then interpret the tea leaves for the benefit of all concerned. As Braden vociferously pointed out, the latter function precisely duplicated a primary function of the geographic divisions as well as of our embassies abroad. We lost that ball game, and unfortunately the Braden-Acheson relationship was never repaired, to the extent that Acheson has some sharp and not fully accurate things to say about his colleague's Washington service.

Another activity that absorbed some of my time during that first year, with happier experiences than the Acheson-Braden controversy, ended in the Foreign Service Act of 1946, the first piece of basic diplomatic legislation since the Rogers Act established the Foreign Service twenty-two years before. With a bow to the nonpartisan support received from several key members of Congress, the two officers most concerned with the legislation were Selden Chapin (1899–1963), who entered the service in the first class in 1925, and Andrew Foster (1903–1964). Although successive departmental administrators have whittled down and even managed to nullify some of its provisions, the legislation governing the Foreign Service today remains a monument to the zeal and devotion of those two officers.[13]

13. This was written before entirely new legislation seeking to reduce abrasiveness between the Foreign Service and the Civil Service was enacted in 1980.

Ours in 1946 was still a small and essentially elite service — using "elite" in the sense of superior competence demonstrated in a nonpartisan competitive career bureaucracy (what a college president once described as an "aristocracy of brains"). Such a service was still sufficiently compact that most senior officers who had had an average of eight to ten years of Washington experience along with twice that abroad knew one another, if not personally at least by name and reputation.

With the passage of the act of 1946, five of those senior officers decided to lunch together once a week, in order informally to iron out incipient problems and, when possible, to agree on courses of action. Our group was headed by the first director general, who, appropriately, was Selden Chapin. The remaining members were the directors of the four geographic divisions: Loy Henderson for the Near East; Doc Matthews for the European Division (often represented by his able deputy, Jack Hickerson); John Carter Vincent for the Far East (often represented by Jim Penfield); and me, often aided by Eddie Trueblood, for the American Republics.

We patronized a nearby club where we limited ourselves to one cocktail, oysters or clams in season, a lamb chop with green salad, and for dessert a lethal and marvelous concoction straight out of a drugstore cowboy rodeo — a fudge nut sundae with chocolate ice cream and marshmallow sauce — followed by a large cup of black coffee in order to restore circulation.

Policy matters in foreign affairs were strictly off limits, and kept there by unanimous decision. Our meetings had to do with the administration of the service, using that word in its broad sense to include all the mechanics of operations, from making "selection out" as compassionate as possible, to budgetary problems, the Inspection Corps, and rendering the system of rating as fair and objective as was humanly possible. In theory all this might have impinged on certain "legally constituted authorities" of the State Department, but our whole procedure was in a sense extralegal, resting on the probity of the members of our group and upon our confidence in each other. We took no notes and composed no memoranda, although Selden Chapin sometimes brought an agenda, and our respective secretaries were told not to expect us back on Wednesday afternoons until we appeared at the office.

One of our most spirited debates was an outgrowth of the Welles-Roosevelt action in the early 1940s suppressing the title of minister and the designation of legation (which had been in use for more than a century), and making every American diplomatic mission an embassy headed by an ambassador, whether the capital was Tokyo with its millions of inhabitants or Tegucigalpa with its thousands. No single action has done as much to undermine the prestige of "embassy" and "ambassador" as this action by Roosevelt. The State Department, saddled with that crackpot decision, found its appropriation for ambassadorial salaries and allowances, which had not been correspondingly augmented, too small for its new needs. The director general was instructed to divide the capitals of the world into four confidential categories, to be known as Classes One, Two, Three, and Four, with compensation differentials, notwithstanding the fact that every chief of mission now had the same ambassadorial rank and title.

As originally conceived, this list was to be as hushed and invisible as the wings of a night-flying moth, so that the holder of a Class Three post on a given continent would not develop hurt feelings when he discovered that a neighboring ambassador enjoyed a Class Two or even a Class One post, with a higher salary and a limousine to ride in, instead of a sedan. That list remained secret about as long as the aforesaid moth would have survived in subzero weather.

Initially, Class One posts were to be very limited in number, as ambassadors themselves had been before this project was conceived. The whole New World was to have only four Class One posts, of which one obviously went to Ottawa, which, notwithstanding its New World location, belonged to the European Division. That left me with only three Class One posts for my twenty Good Neighbors. Two were easy: Rio de Janeiro and Buenos Aires, but then the trouble began. Was Havana, capital of a small country with billions of dollars of American investment, to be chosen over Mexico City, capital of a larger and contiguous country but one at that time with a smaller American stake in its future? And how about Caracas, with the gigantic petroleum potential of Venezuela; or Lima, the ancient City of Kings, in Spanish viceregal days the most important city in the hemisphere?

We finally decided on Mexico City as our third Class One post, for reasons that might have been difficult for the professional administrator to calibrate within his statistical tables but that I still believe were valid. Accepting the premise that the Good Neighborhood should eventually have four Class One posts, we chose Mexico City because (a) none of us, especially Selden Chapin, could endure the thought of the hundreds and hundreds of single-spaced Messersmith pages that would soon come marching angrily across the border, explaining why the omission of Mexico City was iniquitous; and (b) we were sure that the occupier of the Havana embassy, hearing about Mexico City, would soon bring such pressure to bear on certain upper echelons in the luckless State Department that enough extra pennies would somehow have to be found to put the Malecón once again on a par with the

Paseo de la Reforma. Which is precisely what happened, much to our amusement.

Heaven knows how many Class One posts there are today, as successive political appointees, hearing that Post A paid more than Post B, invited the Republican or the Democratic National Committee (as the case might be) to turn the heat on Foggy Bottom.

Nor have I any idea how long those Wednesday luncheons continued after the original members of our group were assigned abroad. But while ours existed, we saved uncounted solemn committee meetings, not to forget the piles and piles of equally solemn position papers and memoranda that would otherwise be cluttering up the archives of the Department of State.[14]

Meanwhile, these parochial concerns were being dwarfed by developments on a broader stage — developments likewise inimical to the successful conduct of American diplomacy. James Byrnes, never too happy with his Truman relationship, which many considered might so easily have been reversed, had been appeased by the firing of Henry Wallace from the Cabinet. But as Byrnes describes in his account of stewardship, *Speaking Frankly,* his duties — as the behavior of our Soviet ex-allies grew progressively more obnoxious — became less and less satisfying to an official who for more than forty years had held important positions in state and national politics. Byrnes, in short, decided that he had had it. Turning his back on Washington, he headed for Columbia, South Carolina, where he ended his days.

President Truman announced that General Marshall would be his successor. While his role as wartime chief of staff had earned him national respect, I was by no means enthusiastic over the idea of a soldier in the State Department. I foresaw the establishment of a gigantic secretary's secretariat, manned by acres of ex-colonels in mufti boiling down every document to a

---

14. It may be of interest to historians that of the five original members of that luncheon group, three were to be promoted to the special so-called super grade established in 1955 as the topmost rung of the Foreign Service ladder, that of career ambassador. A fourth member of our luncheon group, Selden Chapin, would undoubtedly have become a career ambassador had not ill health forced him to retire prematurely after serving as minister to Hungary and as ambassador to the Netherlands, Panama, Iran, and Peru. John Carter Vincent (1900–1972), our Far East member, fell upon the evil McCarthy times in the early 1950s, and he was forced by Secretary Dulles to resign in 1953. He departed with dignity, under fire, and it is the belief of his colleagues that his papers, now at Harvard University, will confirm that he was an officer whose loyalty should never have been questioned.

dozen lines with appendices and tabs A to ZZ, all on paper with a Pentagon watermark.

But worse was coming. In his volume *Present at the Creation*, Dean Acheson proudly takes the credit for persuading Marshall (who became secretary on January 21, 1947, resigning a favor of Acheson himself two years later) to move the State Department out of our old building beside the White House. It is true that our old building had become extremely crowded. But the reason for the congestion was the irrational increase in the size of the State Department itself and the equally specious notion that as the comparative stature of the United States among the nations of the world grew apace, so should the number of bureaucrats employed by our Foreign Office. It would still have been comparatively easy to concentrate in the old State War Navy Building all those officials performing substantive functions: the secretary with his spacious, old high-ceilinged room that Cordell Hull and Jimmy Byrnes refused to relinquish; the undersecretary nearby via a connecting door; a small corps of useful assistant secretaries spreading out along the ample corridors; Blanche Halla's invaluable Office of Coordination and Review, which performed with a handful of experienced and dedicated women; and the four geographic divisions in which nine-tenths of the basic work on international relations was accomplished.

There was little need for much of the rest of the apparatus to be within shouting distance, or even commuting distance, of the secretary of state. The Passport Division, for example, is a service unit that might as well be in Chicago as Washington. Much of the burgeoning administrative apparatus could have gone to the suburbs, with everyone else twice as happy. And as for the rest of the peripheral performers — the aid dispensers, the propagandists, the spooks, and even the policy planners — the farther away from the center of gravity they were kept, the less helium was required to enable the eagle to soar around the Washington Monument.

The impending move was debated at one of our Wednesday luncheons. Early opinions were divided. Most of us had surreptitiously examined our proposed new quarters on Virginia Avenue and had come away not unimpressed by the wood paneling, the discreet private johns, and the air conditioning that, while it made it impossible (lacking a sledge hammer) ever to open a window and breathe fresh air, nevertheless allowed the eager bureaucrat to wear his jacket at his desk no matter how high the temperature outside. Moreover, parking in the basement was assured, not to forget the special dining room facilities for those who outranked the immense cafeteria provided for the commoners.

The only strong dissent at our luncheon came from Doc Matthews, my colleague from Havana days with Ambassador Caffery, and now the chief of the European Division. Doc was explicit in his denunciation of the evil effects that he prophesied would flow from removing ourselves from our traditional location, at the very elbow of the president, to Foggy Bottom, where our modest contingent of employees would, he predicted, soon multiply to five thousand, whereupon it would take five times as long to get things done as it had when the State Department was of manageable dimensions and close to the presidential office.[15]

We nevertheless obediently trooped to Foggy Bottom one spring weekend in 1947, and thereafter I never set foot in the old State War Navy Building again.

While this disastrous move was in contemplation, Braden's career came to an end. The timing of my own departure from Washington was not geared to the resignation of Mr. Braden, although they both occurred in the summer of 1947. For some months my service as director of ARA had convinced me that I could be more useful abroad, in charge of a diplomatic mission, than wading in the Potomac reaches. The kaleidoscopic Washington scene fascinated me, as a spectator, but I concluded that I had no great aptitude, much less flair, for bureaucratic in-fighting or for the annual ordeals to which my rank would now expose me before various congressional committees, some of whose members were more interested in the publicity generated by baiting a diplomatic witness than they were in the conduct of foreign affairs, much less in statesmanship.

I had no particular special ambassadorship in mind until I read in the newspaper one spring morning in 1947 of the sudden death of Williamson Howell, a career officer who was en route to New Orleans to take ship to his new post when he succumbed to a heart attack. Here was Montevideo unexpectedly vacant, so that reaching for it myself would result in shoving no colleague aside nor in depriving any worthy rival of fruit suddenly accessible. I had acquired a good deal of information in the past two years on each of the other twenty republics, and while posing as no expert on the River Plate I was aware of the problems of Uruguay. Moreover, I had just chaperoned, most pleasantly, the elderly president-elect, Don Tomás Berreta, who had made an official visit to Washington. The association formed with

15. Doc Matthews erred in his statistics. By the days of Dean Rusk in the 1960s, the fellahin of Foggy Bottom, who by that time had expanded into a gigantic and ugly annex stuck against the original palace of the engineers, approached *nine* thousand persons.

Don Tomás and the members of his official party would be useful if I went to Montevideo.

Secretary Marshall was out of town, but Dean Acheson (not prejudiced by Braden's warm endorsement of my candidacy) readily agreed to present my name at the White House, whither he was on the point of going when the matter was mentioned. He phoned me from his office an hour later. "Congratulations." he said. "You are the new ambassador to Uruguay." President Truman signed my nomination and sent it to the Senate two days later.

For the next fifteen years I served abroad in six countries, by appointment of three presidents, under four secretaries of state. I never again was to hold office in the labyrinth of Foggy Bottom.

Gaucho Interlude

The Good Old Days in Uruguay

My letter of credence was presented to the president of Uruguay on August 21, 1947. The original document was written by hand in the State Department by one of the few surviving masters of the art of calligraphy. It read as follows:

Harry S. Truman
President of the United States of America

To His Excellency

Luis Batlle Berres

President of the Oriental Republic of Uruguay

Great and Good Friend:

I have made choice of Ellis O. Briggs, a distinguished citizen of the United States, to reside near the Government of Your Excellency in the quality of Ambassador Extraordinary and Minister Plenipotentiary of the United States of America. He is well informed of the relative interests of the two countries and of the sincere desire of this Government to cultivate to the fullest extent the friendship which has long subsisted between them. My knowledge of his high quality and ability gives me entire confidence that he will constantly endeavor to advance the interests and prosperity of both Governments, and so render himself acceptable to Your Excellency.

I therefore request Your Excellency to receive him favorably and to give full confidence to what he shall say on the part of the United States and to the assurances which I have charged him to convey to you of the best wishes of this Government for the prosperity of Uruguay.

May God have Your Excellency in His wise keeping.

Your Good Friend

Harry S. Truman

By the President
    George C. Marshall
    Secretary of State
    Washington, July 3, 1947

Except for the addressee and the signatures, this letter of credence is identical with each of the seven such documents that I presented between 1944 and 1962.

Old Tomás Berreta, president-elect of Uruguay, whose presence in Washington I had so much enjoyed, did not long survive the inaugural celebrations. He was succeeded by his vice president, Luis Batlle Berres, a rather bewildered but politically sagacious young man. My departure from Washington was delayed while the trained scribe of the State Department, quill and parchment in hand, laboriously composed a new letter of credence, addressed to His Excellency Dr. Luis Batlle Berres, instead of to the late Don Tomás Berreta.

The ceremony was brief, informal, and in some contrast to the studied stiffness of my credentials ceremony three years before in Ciudad Trujillo. When the president and I were seated on the uncomfortable little sofa for the prescribed five minutes of chitchat, the president, instead of handing my letter of credence to the waiting minister of foreign affairs, continued to hold the square white envelope in his hand.

"What do I do with this?" he inquired.

"Whatever you want, Señor Presidente. The letter is addressed to you."

"So it is," said the president, reading the elaborately inscribed name and address. He pried off the white wafer seal on the back of the envelope and took out the communication, the first such document, apparently, he had seen. "It is in English," he complained. "Would you mind translating?" I did so, stumbling over the opening phrase "I have made choice of" followed by my own name, since I wasn't sure whether *habiendo escogido* was really the Spanish equivalent of the archaic English.

The president wanted to know whether they were the real signatures of President Truman and General Marshall; he appeared pleased when I assured him that they were.

It was my good fortune to inherit from my predecessor, Ambassador Joe McGurk, a fine embassy staff, headed by Edward J. Sparks. Eddy Sparks, after five years in Montevideo, was soon transferred, to my regret but in circumstances that I remember with pride. Hearing of the Sparkses' imminent departure, their Uruguayan friends organized a farewell dinner, a subscription affair. So many wanted to attend that successive restaurants had to be abandoned in favor of larger quarters. When we were finally seated, I counted every living ex-president of the country, and each one made a little speech acknowledging the contribution of this "pareja simpatiquísima" to the friendship of Uruguay and "Norte América."

Through the Sparkses, we were soon to get on personal terms with Luis and Matilde Batlle Berres, and to discover that a way into the presidential heart was via what he called "cintas policiales," that is, cops-and-robbers movies.

An unstuffy human being, much of whose ceremonial duty bored him, Don Luis Batlle Berres liked to escape for a few hours and to "forget the presidency," as he put it. We began such evenings with a family supper, the Batlle Berreses' teenagers often present, one presidential aide (in case something unexpected should come up), and one or two couples from the embassy staff. Fifteen minutes over coffee and a brandy, with occasional piano music from the oldest Batlle Berres child — who later became a professional musician — and then a period of real blood-and-thunder motion picture relaxation.

When the Montevideo American embassy residence was built in the 1930s, some predecessor benefactor — possibly Butler Wright or William Dawson — managed to persuade Washington to include on the second floor a professional motion picture projection room with standard equipment. Through the cooperation of the local representative of the American Motion Picture Association, the embassy was able to borrow, and to show to small and select audiences, prerelease movies, which turned out to be one of the most pleasant as well as officially fruitful forms of entertainment we could have devised.

For my own pleasure, I considered myself fortunate that I was once again in a place where I could walk through open fields, carrying my shotgun. The Cattleraisers' Association, taking note of my weekend visits to the country for quail shooting and my presence on *estancias*, elected me honorary president of the Uruguayan Producers of North American Herefords, a formidable title in English but several times as impressive in *platense* Spanish. Before I could think up a plausible excuse to decline the honor, I was stuck with the duty of attending cattle fairs (while the rest of the diplomats were sunning themselves at Punta del Este), pinning ribbons on winning animals, and even making an occasional speech extolling the virtues of that noblest of creatures, *el Hereford Norte Americano.*

These and other diversions were facilitated by the presence of an excellent embassy staff. As successors to the Sparkses I had Bim and Caroline Brown, good friends from other days. My consul was Charles Whitaker, interned during the war in the Philippines, where he invented a machine to shake the weevils out of the flour supplied by the Japanese to the prisoners for their cooking. He thus acquired enduring fame.

The embassy in Montevideo also included an outstanding "local," an American of Italian background who had chosen to remain in Uruguay, unavailable for transfer to another country. George Vitale and his Uruguayan wife knew everyone. Equally important, everyone of consequence in Montevideo knew and respected George and Sarita Vitale. Numerous American embassies can boast of such assets, and they are worth their weight in gold to the effective operation of those missions.

Among the smallest of the South American states, Uruguay is the size of South Dakota, seventy thousand square miles. The country is geographically an extension of the coast of Brazil, something its three million citizens do not like to be reminded about. Uruguay has no greater natural boundaries with its vast northern neighbor than Arizona has with Mexico. Uruguay was in fact occupied by Brazil in the 1820s, and its independence dates from 1828. It is bounded on the west by the Uruguay River, one of the principal tributaries of the River Plate, with Argentina on the western bank. Uruguay derives its official name — La República Oriental del Uruguay — as the land to the *east* of the river. To the south is the muddy River Plate estuary, twenty-five miles wide opposite Buenos Aires, which lights up the sky over the opposite Uruguayan town of Colonia, and sixty miles wide opposite Montevideo, farther downstream.

The population is the most homogeneous in the continent. The seminomadic Charruas, tough but armed only with spears and bolas, a kind of sling, were exterminated during the early years of Spanish colonization, which began in 1624, a century after Pizarro had raped Peru. The present population of Uruguay, concentrated in the capital and in the towns toward the Atlantic on the east, is almost wholly Spanish-Italian in origin. One of the boasts of the Uruguayans of a generation ago was that in contrast to democratic and progressive Uruguay, Argentina had not had a respectable government in decades, because (they claimed) the Italians of Argentina were quarrelsome and illiterate immigrants from the south and from Sicily, whereas the Uruguayan Italians came from the civilized north of Italy. It was true that the Italians who came to the República Oriental mixed admirably with the existing Spanish population, which included no Indians and only a handful of other ethnic groups.

Nonetheless, the nineteenth-century history of Uruguay was sufficiently chaotic and filled with civil strife to mark its inhabitants as ferociously independent and politically articulate, if not always sophisticated. In fact they did not settle down until the second decade of the twentieth century, when they opted, under President José Batlle y Ordóñez, an uncle of President Luis Batlle Berres, for a series of social and economic reforms that endowed the land with the nickname of the Switzerland of South America.

The United States, in the 1930s and 1940s, had no acute problem affecting the relations between the two countries. Except for the obscene shouting and posturing of the Peróns across the River Plate, which produced a mixture of indignation, apprehension, and contempt on the Montevideo side, Uruguay in 1947 was at peace with herself and with the hemisphere. For the first time since I entered the service in 1925, I found myself in repose and unhurried.

Settled in, the first thing we did was to start examining our new bailiwick during the pampas spring, heady with wildflowers and loud with the bawling of newborn calves and the bleating of lambs. We found it a proud, happy, and open land; a land of gently rolling plains, with few trees except along streams, but with expanding patches of imported eucalyptus, which from the air looked like islands of dark green set in the pale green sea of grass.

Birds were everywhere, and I soon found myself dedicated to amateur ornithology, which went well with my shotgun, since the pastures were alive with the little pampas quail, *la perdiz chica,* which is not a true quail at all but a tinamou. About the weight of the North American bobwhite, the bird is shaped like Al Capp's cartoon schmoo, an easier target than a quail because although fast-flying, the bird flushes one or two at a time instead of exploding in coveys like the American quail, and instead of veering this way and that like a snipe, it usually flies in a straight line. A larger variety, called the *martineta,* was already becoming rare in the 1940s.

In addition to countless and gorgeous songbirds, *ñandú* ostriches abounded, and when we drove inland on weekends, there was always a one-peso prize for the first person to spot one. Rather useless birds, except for feather dusters, they grew arrogantly tame around farms. Being practically omnivorous, they often swallowed a spoon or a thimble or a coin — anything within reach that glittered. To retrieve the object, the bird was tethered with a rope around one ankle, which the ostrich did not like, and its nether area was equipped with a diaper borrowed from the youngest member of the family, which the ostrich liked even less, until the swallowed object was retrieved.

The flightless *ñandues* are capable of bursts of considerable ground speed; I used to clock them up to thirty-five miles an hour ahead of the car, at which point the bird would suddenly veer away from the track. The tiny newly hatched ones, called *charabones,* could take off faster than a man could run, fresh out of the pale eggshell.

Another marvelous Uruguayan bird was the *teruteru* — the spurwing lapwing — a creature quite without fear and highly suspicious of intruding man, around whose head it would angrily fly, shouting "teruteru," and alerting every wild thing within hearing. *Teruterus* regularly invaded the Montevideo golf course, swooping around the players and occasionally moving a ball, apparently under the impression that it was a stray egg, better off in a sand trap than on the fairway. Whenever I think of Uruguay, I remember with affection that fearless bird, black and white, with a dark crest curling insolently from the back of its head. Luckily for its survival, the *teruteru,* a cousin to the plovers, is too tough to eat. Long may its defiant four-syllable call echo over the Purple Land!

The most engaging Uruguayan animal I found was the *carpincho,* the largest surviving member of the rat family, a vegetarian aquatic beast that lives close to streams and weighs up to forty and even fifty pounds. The *carpincho,* rarely seen by day, will, if disturbed at night, leap off the bank in an earsplitting belly flop. The *carpincho's* skin is highly prized for saddle leather, being as soft as chamois but several times thicker and more durable, so few of them survive in Uruguay. In western Brazil, where the animal is called the *capivara,* it is still relatively abundant.

Lucy and I made many trips into the Uruguayan countryside, frequently staying at the *estancias,* the Uruguayan ranches, where hospitality was generous and informal, culminating in an *asado con cuero,* the most typical of all gaucho meals. As the name implies, it is a barbecue with the hide of the animal left on. Some six or seven hours before the event a steer is slaughtered and eviscerated, the head removed, but the hide left in place. The unskinned carcass is then spread-eagled on an iron frame, canted over a pit of glowing coals, and very slowly roasted. This operation takes place during an entire morning, under the supervision of a bevy of gaucho culinary artists, most of whom are somewhat drunk by noon and considerably more so an hour or two later, when the *asado* is finally declared ready for eating. The reason the cooks are unsober is that in order for the meat not to scorch, various liquids, including wine, are squirted onto the roasting carcass. What does not go on the meat side is soaked liberally onto the skin side, to keep the dry hair from igniting. It is also a smoky business, because the coals can be stoked only from the top of the fire in the pit, and as a precaution against fits of coughing, the gaucho cooks subsist during the morning on repeated cups of wine, along with gourds of yerba maté, the Paraguayan tea without which no proper citizen of the Republic would fail to begin the day. Various additional condiments and herbs are used, along with repeated applications of garlic. An *asado con cuero,* with the wind in the right quarter, can be identified at a considerable distance.

The guests seat themselves at trestle tables, and the meal starts with a serving of accessory niblets, all originally pertaining to the cooked carcass. The main course follows. It consists of a plate for each person containing a huge chunk of beef, with the skin (and singed hair) still on. The trick is to be able with your *facón* — the heavy knife of the pampas, used for everything from cutting wood to mayhem and self-defense — to separate the meat from the skin and hair. For an amateur this is invariably a messy and treacherous business, but there is no denying that the meat, so presented, has a flavor unlike any other in the world.

A serious topic that shortly engaged my attention was the future of passenger steamship service from the United States to Montevideo. Moore, president of the Moore McCormack Line, was due to arrive on the SS *Uruguay,* the first of the line's three vessels to be reconditioned after wartime service. With an assist from embassy Montevideo, Mr. Moore had prevailed on President Batlle Berres to attend a gala luncheon on board the *Uruguay,* signaling the revival of the Good Neighbor Fleet.

The *Uruguay,* the *Brazil,* and the *Argentina* had been laid down fifteen years before as the *Virginia,* the *California,* and the *Pennsylvania* for the California-New York trade, via the Panama Canal and Havana. The idea was that motion picture stars, instead of bumping across the continent on the Super Chief and the Twentieth Century Limited, would flock aboard, in circumstances of maximum maritime luxury, felicity, and delight. Instead, Hollywood took to the brand-new DC-3, which flew at more than 150 miles an hour, and pretty soon those three ships, renamed and under new management, were shuttling between Buenos Aires and the Hudson River.

It soon became clear, however, that the return of his rejuvenated Good Neighbor Fleet was not the only reason for Mr. Moore's trip. The principal reason for his presence, and for his many interviews and conversations with foreign and American officials along the route, was to discuss the future of ocean travel in the face of rising airplane competition.

His company was considering, Moore said, replacing the three old vessels with two fast luxury liners, so that approximately the same schedule could be maintained with the two new ones as with the older and slower three. Moore then believed, as did many other experienced steamship operators, that no matter what happened to airplane development, there would still be a substantial demand for steamship travel by people who could afford comfort and a few extra days of unique relaxation before reaching a given destination. As a lover of sea travel, I found it easy to subscribe to that point of view.

Both of us were wrong. Neither the beautiful new SS *Brazil* nor her equally luxurious sister ship SS *Argentina* was proof against jet travel. The Boeing 707, which entered international service within five years after their commissioning, did for transocean steamship service in the 1960s what the old DC-3 had done to the New York-California sea route in the 1930s. The last regularly scheduled American passenger ship has disappeared. The little vice consulate at Callao, where my first Foreign Service responsibility was on behalf of American vessels and American seamen, has long since passed into history. The airplane has wiped out something relegated to the memories of those fortunate travelers of the first half of the twentieth century.

Uruguay proved a lovely country in which to live, but a sad country to contemplate because the process of political disintegration — a generation later far advanced — was even then beginning to show. More and more of the previously individualistic and self-respecting citizens succumbed to the lure of promised easy living, state benefits, and early pensions, with the result that production slumped, featherbedding in government enterprises multiplied, and rich and elaborate retirement projects were successively crippled by inflation.

In contrast to my misplaced optimism about the future of steamship travel, I found myself increasingly pessimistic about the steady drift of events — a drift encouraged by the Colorados, the party of President Batlle Berres. It was a movement toward more and more government operation of what previously had been the private sector, of more and more government intrusion into the economy of the country, and of more and more government interference in the life of the individual — all, of course, with greater promised benefits. It was a drift, in short, toward statism, which if not synonymous with socialism, soon leads to it. The Uruguayan electorate, probably the most sophisticated in all Latin America at the time, nevertheless acquiesced in successive moves leading inevitably to the roller coaster that starts so slowly toward the precipitate plunge that lies around the first few gently rounded corners. And unlike the roller coaster in an amusement park, this one does not stop to let the passengers get off.

Uruguay was so small a country that government operations, often unintelligible on a broader canvas, could readily be followed by a sympathetic foreigner with some experience in watching political machinery in motion. The distribution of imported petroleum products illustrated one aspect of the situation. Uruguay produces no petroleum. The difference between the state-owned gas stations, which were often out of gas or oil — or else the operator was eating lunch or having his yerba maté from across the street — and the privately owned ones was so ludicrous as to be almost pathetic. This did not, however, still the agitation by certain influential politicians for a state monopoly on the importation and distribution of petroleum products, and the consequent enlargement of the bureaucracy.

The pension plans were fantastic; they aimed at retirement for everybody after twenty or twenty-five years, on full pay, with fringe benefits that would have been regarded a quarter-century later with envy by American labor leaders. There was no possible way of funding these resplendent luxuries except by printing money.

The meatpacking business, vital to the economy, was perhaps the most disturbing example of all. Since colonial times the people of that region have been eaters of prodigious amounts of meat. An abundant supply, at a low price, was high on the agenda of every politician in Uruguay. However, with the cost of cattle fodder and other ranching essentials rising, the *estancieros* — politically powerful and employing the bulk of rural labor (whose members as individuals freely voted in every election) — wanted a price for their cattle and sheep that would reflect their rising expenses. Result: fixed minimum prices for animals on the hoof to satisfy the *estancieros* and their ranch hands and fixed top prices for meat sold at retail to satisfy the meat-hungry urban public. Because one-third of the population of the country had flocked to Montevideo, theirs was a potent voice in the latter arrangements.

The quality of meat available at the fixed price promptly declined. Black markets sprang up all around the city limits of Montevideo, where from time to time the only good-quality cuts were available at prices that, while reasonable by later criteria, were considerably in excess of the "legal" ceiling established by unenforceable government fiat.

Here was a problem that could easily have involved the embassy. The American meatpackers (and equally the government-owned Frigorífico Nacional) were trapped between the high government price for the live animals they had to buy and the low fixed price they received for the meat they sold to the market. But whereas the American packers were privately owned, ultimately responsible to their shareholders, the losses sustained by the national plant could be (and were) made up by government subsidy, through taxation or printing more money.

This problem was under constant discussion by the embassy with the American packing interests, with frankness on both sides. That the companies did not then desire official representations derived from a combination of factors, including the much larger investments of the same firms in Argentina, where the Perón administration was systematically and deliberately trying to destroy both the *estanciero* class and the foreign *frigoríficos*, the meatpacking plants. The difficulties of the American companies operating across the river in Argentina dwarfed those in Uruguay, where there was little xenophobia and practically none directed specifically at American interests. Hence deals and accommodations were still feasible, and at the time they were preferred by my compatriots, rightly or wrongly, to official intervention.

Convinced though I became that Uruguay, through these and various other measures, including attempts to industrialize an essentially agricultural nation, was heading for economic disaster, I do not recall arguing about them with President Batlle Berres, no specific United States interest having called for my assistance. Furthermore, experience had taught me that one of the less profitable of diplomatic initiatives is to lecture a foreign chief of state about how to run his own country. I left that kind of extracurricular discussion to my embassy economic colleague, Franklin Wolf, a mature and dignified retired banker, who had many private sessions with the head of the Uruguayan Central Bank, with whom he often saw eye to eye. Tragically, that gifted official of Uruguay, whose wise counsel might have staved off later woes, was lost in an airplane accident not long after I left the country.

From my observations I concluded that the Achilles heel of democracy is the fact that although all men may be "created equal," they are not equal by the time they are old enough to vote. By then the drones, the ne'er-do-wells, the drifters, and the marginally competent inevitably — in whatever manner of society — so outnumber the more sensible and responsible citizens that the former offer an irresistible target for demagogues who, as the twentieth century advances, seem more and more to outnumber the statesmen. I believe it was Winston Churchill who remarked that democracy is the worst form of government except for all the others. This is the essence of his aphorism. "Rather tepid solace," I thought, as Uruguay continued its march, almost like the lemmings toward the fjords of Norway, down the road toward socialism and disaster.

These musings about a country for which I had come to feel a genuine affection were cut short one morning in the Uruguayan summer of 1949 by a phone call from President Batlle Berres. Don Luis suggested I come to his office, where he had an interesting document to show me.

That paper was indeed interesting. It was a dispatch from the Uruguayan chargé (later ambassador in Washington), my friend José Mora, who in a confidential report to his president conveyed the news — almost incredible to me, since I had received no word from the State Department about it — that President Perón of Argentina had demanded that I be removed as ambassador to Uruguay. The alleged grounds, according to José Mora, were that I, as the agent of the hated Spruille Braden (who had long since returned to private life), was plotting in Montevideo with Argentine expatriates and other foes of the Perón regime against the stability of the Argentine Republic.

The story, as the Uruguayan chargé had it, was that an emissary of President Perón, a former foreign minister, had asked for an appointment with President Truman. That meeting was not forthcoming because Dr. Bramuglia was no longer in office. He and the Argentine ambassador then tackled the State Department, where they were received not by General Marshall, who was on the point of retiring, but by Bob Lovett, the acting secretary.

It was my ill fortune that Lovett, an honorable and charming gentleman of many talents, knew as little about Latin America as Dean Acheson, and possibly cared less. Although Lovett may have been surprised at the unorthodox nature of the demand — involving an American official serving not in Argentina but in a different country — the acting secretary reportedly failed to inform his callers that these were serious accusations, or even to inquire what they might possess in support of their allegations. Instead, he apparently said, in effect: "Fascinating story. Tell me more."

Returning to my chancery after my conversation with President Batlle Berres, I composed an inflammatory telegram to the Department of State. No copy of this message is before me — professional diplomats, unlike some of their politically appointed colleagues, rarely violate the official edict against retaining classified documents — but its general tenor was that if the report of the Argentine initiative was correct, I ought at the least to have been informed by my home office about a matter touching my conduct. I added that if anyone was sufficiently naive to believe such nonsense, I should have been fired as an incompetent meddler. Otherwise, I ought to have been defended. The message possibly concluded with a demand for exoneration plus a few teeth to be kicked by the Department of State down the throat of Juan Domingo Perón.

To balance the ill fortune just mentioned, it was my good fortune that, at the time my intemperate blast was being decoded in Washington, Ambassador Jim Bruce, my opposite number in Buenos Aires and a personal friend of Bob Lovett, was strolling into the latter's office in Foggy Bottom to inquire amiably what was cooking on the pampas before he flew back to resume his duties in Argentina. Jim was the older brother of David Bruce, who entered the Foreign Service with me in 1925. David had arranged for his brother and me to meet at the time we were appointed to our respective posts in 1947. We promptly discovered that we shared an enthusiasm for bird shooting. During ensuing seasons we had twice flown together over two thousand miles south to Patagonia and Tierra del Fuego — among the disappearing virgin territories for bird hunters — and in addition we had often hunted bird covers closer to Buenos Aires and Montevideo, each being the other's guest on those occasions. Lucy and I had become close friends of James and Ellen Bruce, and that relationship on opposite sides of the River Plate remains one of the happy memories of our years in the Foreign Service.

Ambassador Bruce, as I learned later, told Bob Lovett what he thought of the Argentine maneuver. He kindly undertook to pacify his still-fuming United States colleague in Uruguay.

There the incident ended, insofar as President Perón's efforts to have me expelled from Montevideo were concerned. It is recounted, however, for two reasons. It so happened that there was a plan afoot to transfer me from the relative calm of Uruguay to one of the hotter spots in the Cold War, a project that had to be deferred in order to avoid giving the impression that the move was made in response to Argentine pressure. In defense of Washington in 1949, it is fair to add that those then directing our government, from President Truman to officials in State and the Pentagon, had more important things to think about than a petty vexation involving a government servant in small and distant Uruguay, remote from the critical Berlin airlift and all the other preoccupations that followed the collapse of Roosevelt's credulous and imbecile Grand Design.

However, in a broader context, the failure of Washington to support its agents abroad more decisively has long been a factor not conducive to morale-building in the Foreign Service. One of the difficulties, too, is that the State Department, which is not always consulted by the president about the appointments of chiefs of mission, has too often condoned the dispatch abroad of ambassadors whose qualifications for diplomacy have approximated those of an amputee for ballet dancing.

Montevideo and our comfortable residence beside the park had been a splendid post for us, but two years were enough for one to whom activity possessed a greater appeal than what the military, in their quaint groping for expression, term R and R, for rest and recreation. It had been a time for more meditation than I had known since I entered the Foreign Service, with friendships made that were thereafter cherished. Our two children, ignoring the fact that vacations in Uruguay meant five successive winters, had been able to join us. Our daughter, now entering college, had "come out" in Montevideo, along with Susana MacEachen, the daughter of a Uruguayan career diplomat. Our son had learned on the pampas, shotgun in hand, the truth of one of Ernest Hemingway's favorite sayings, that every wing shot is different from every shot you ever fired at a flying bird, and the ten thousandth shot gives the hunter the identical thrill as the first one.

Uruguay had provided a respite from the ninety- and one-hundred-hour weeks that had been my fascinating lot during most of my previous assignments, but this was its least important dividend. The notion that long hours are degrading to the diplomatic animal is a part of the less-work-for-more-pay movement that is destroying the effectiveness of so much of American labor. It had no appeal to one whose career still had a dozen years and five more ambassadorships to run.

Thus it was not until well into 1949, during "the little summer of San Juan," as the Uruguayans term their benign and lovely autumn, that I received a telegram informing me of my nomination to be ambassador to Czechoslovakia — a nation gobbled up the year before by Stalin in much the way Hitler had seized the Sudetenland soon after Munich. I was instructed to make for Washington, where new lessons awaited me.

My gaucho interlude in the Purple Land of W. H. Hudson's unforgettable fable had ended. We called it among ourselves "the Good Old Days."

A Turn to the Left
Czechoslovakia

Having an inquiring mind — or perhaps merely one afflicted with curiosity — I was interested to learn why, after so many years in Latin America, I should suddenly have been chosen to go to Czechoslovakia, which Moscow had seized the year before. That aggressive betrayal produced widespread revulsion in the Free World and especially in the United States, with its hundreds of thousands of Czech- and Slovak-American citizens.

When I left Uruguay, I had spent sixteen years — barring the few war months with Pat Hurley in Chungking — either in Latin America or working primarily on Latin American problems in Washington. I was in fact in a fair way to being tagged "Latin American expert," and I was pleased as well as surprised to be sprung from the Good Neighborhood, where the problems — real and acute and absorbing as many of them were — nevertheless were not the main issues confronting our country.

Moreover, the world had moved while I vegetated beside the River Plate. In Europe, 1949 was an exciting year. The Marshall Plan, whereby the recuperative powers of Western nations were teamed with generous American resources, had begun to prove that the misery and devastation of war could be overcome, and that the rebirth of hope was not an illusion. NATO had been organized. The Berlin airlift, whatever may be the verdict on the wider implications of that failure to meet the overt Soviet challenge, had demonstrated that a great city could be supplied by air alone — so long as the enemy did not interfere.

The Czechoslovakia of Tomas Masaryk and Edward Beneš had been gobbled up by Stalin in 1948. Tomas Masaryk, friend of Woodrow Wilson and beneficiary of Wilson's stubborn insistence at Versailles on the dismantling of the Austro-Hungarian Empire, had not lived to witness World War II; President Beneš, surviving both Munich and the Communist coup d'état, had died the previous summer, embittered by the failure of his dream of making Western-oriented Czechoslovakia a "bridge of understanding" between the rest of Europe and the Soviet Union. His brilliant foreign minister, Jan Masaryk, one of the most gifted diplomatists whose talents illuminated the first half of the twentieth century, was found dead beneath his window at the foot of the Czernin Palace wall. His broken body now lay beside those of his father and his American mother in the unpretentious graveyard at Lany, a few miles from the capital.

None of this explained why I had been chosen to man the oasis known as the American embassy in Prague, one hundred miles on the cold side of the Iron Curtain. When I asked Dean Acheson, now secretary of state, he fobbed me off with some vague phrase to the effect that "the president and I decided that you possessed the necessary qualifications, etc.," without specifying what those qualifications were. It was not until after Mr. Acheson left office that I was able to tackle the former secretary and repeat my question.

Dean Acheson grinned. "It was President Truman," he said. "I didn't tell you before you went to Prague, because I thought you might overreact. I remember very well what President Truman said: 'What I want in Prague is a tough son-of-a-bitch, who will stand up to the Commies.'" Mr. Acheson added, "You were elected, but I didn't want you to kick President Gottwald in the shins the first time he tried to spit in your eye. That would have meant I had to start looking for another ambassador. Besides, we were having one hell of a time getting you confirmed in the Senate."

The latter problem had involved my being blackballed for an important mission by one of my own senators. My successor as ambassador to Uruguay, a Foreign Service officer, had leaped to take the oath of office the moment he was confirmed. He thus set in motion a train of bureaucratic procedure whereby it became mandatory for him to reach Montevideo within thirty days, regardless of the convenience of his predecessor, whose early confirmation for Prague he probably took for granted, since I, too, was a Foreign Service officer and therefore (in theory) an unpolitical and non-controversial candidate.

The only flaw in that scenario was that, instead of my being routinely confirmed, Senator Owen Brewster of Maine (my legal residence) objected to my nomination. That blocked the confirmation machinery, because it is a part of "senatorial courtesy" that the Foreign Relations Committee will not consider a nominee until he has been declared acceptable by both senators from his home state. Margaret Chase Smith said yes, but Owen Brewster said no. The noes had it.

Such was the eagerness of the State Department in 1949 to have the Prague post covered that Dean Acheson had gone personally to see Senator Brewster to find out what was the trouble. Brewster assured him that he had nothing against me personally. "I scarcely know Briggs," Brewster said. "For all I know, the bastard may even be a Republican." But the senator had refused to budge. My nomination remained stuck.

This had nothing to do with me. The problem concerned Franco's Spain. Spain was one of the earliest targets of the meddlesome do-gooders of the United Nations. In 1945 Franco was still in the doghouse among liberals for his crushing of democratic liberties after three years of fratricidal civil war preceding World War II. Six years after that many right-thinking people were still venomously anti-Franco. They demanded, via a UN resolution, that member states refrain from appointing ambassadors to Madrid. If you must deal with Franco, went this injunction, do so on the inferior chargé level. Do not fortify the usurper of Spain by accrediting an ambassador in Madrid. The quaint ratiocination behind this resolution was that by thus ostracizing Franco, his doom would be expedited. The United States accordingly for several years had sent no ambassador to Spain, and my old friend Paul Culbertson, with whom I had once shared Room 300 in the Western European Division, had a splendid and protracted assignment as chargé d'affaires in Madrid.

Senator Owen Brewster of Maine did not subscribe to any of this. Unfriendly critics have even accused the senator of being on the Franco payroll. Whatever may have been the intimacy joining a Maine Republican senator to a Spanish chief of state, there seemed little doubt — fortified by the *Congressional Record* — that Senator Owen Brewster was the Franco apologist at the legislative end of Pennsylvania Avenue.

There was not a great deal Senator Brewster could do. In a Democratic administration his political power was limited. In those meager circumstances my nomination to be ambassador to Czechoslovakia, which the Truman administration was actively promoting, was like finding a $50 bill on the back seat of a Washington taxi.

Senator Brewster notified Senator Tom Connally, chairman of the Foreign Relations Committee, that the proposed appointment of Ambassador Briggs was not agreeable, and later, after the Acheson conversation, he reportedly intimated that if President Truman were to appoint an ambassador to Spain, he might be prepared to look more favorably upon my qualifications for Prague.

What finally turned the trick was assistance from an altogether un-expected quarter, one it would not have occurred to me to approach. The man who removed the senatorial roadblock was a recent treasurer of the Republican National Committee, James S. Kemper of Chicago, who — fortu-itously — had been a fellow passenger on a Delta Line ship sailing to Uruguay with Lucy and me two years before. Jim Kemper his wife Gertrude, Lucy, and I had been the only passengers at the captain's table for eighteen days, from New Orleans to the River Plate.

Two years later, hearing through the Republican grapevine of my difficul-ties on Capitol Hill, Jim Kemper descended upon Senator Brewster. A few days later my nomination was unanimously endorsed by the committee, and I was promptly confirmed by the Senate.[1]

The incident illustrates once again that, notwithstanding the boasting of successive administrations about the promotion of diplomats by merit and the nonpolitical status of career officers — largely true as they climb the lower rungs of the bureaucratic ladder — once a successful competitor has achieved a grade entitling him to become ambassador, his professional sta-tus, at the moment when it should be most secure, becomes instead the most precarious. As ambassador, an officer is exposed to all of the variable winds not only of international but also of domestic politics. That is true, more-over, because of the Constitution, which gives the president the power to ap-point but makes him share that power with the Senate. The fact is that the professional status and the security of tenure of a senior Foreign Service officer have not been a defense against the vicissitudes of Potomac politics.

When I went to Czechoslovakia, my book learning as to the circumstances of Communist life was, I suppose, reasonably adequate. After nearly a quarter-century in the diplomatic service I had read — not without boredom — most of the standard tomes as well as the day-to-day emanations of the State Department. I first heard the words Bolshevik and Menshevik during a his-tory course while I was in uniform in 1918, trying to become a second lieu-tenant in the army. The United States had had no official dealings with Lenin (later canonized) or Trotsky (later assassinated), or even with Stalin (later "Uncle Joe" of Roosevelt's Grand Design). Charles Evans Hughes, the one luminous star in the Harding constellation, took an unfavorable view of those who confiscated private property as well as of those whose declared ambition — never to be withdrawn nor repudiated — was to destroy the

---

1. During the Eisenhower administration, Mr. Kemper tried his own hand at diplo-macy. He was ambassador to Brazil in 1954.

Free World. The word "confiscate" was not in the Communist dictionary. Their verb was "to nationalize," which meant that once the Communists had seized a coveted asset, it thenceforth was advertised as belonging to The People. (*Narodni podnik,* meaning "nationalized enterprise" — that is, stolen property — were the first two words of Czech I was to learn.) It was not until the Roosevelt administration, in 1933, that recognition and official relations led to the establishment of embassies in Moscow and Washington.

One important dividend of those fifteen years of nonrecognition of the Soviet Union was the incubation within the State Department during that period of a small group of exceptionally gifted Foreign Service officers who, perceiving the coming need, elected to specialize in Russia. The group included George F. Kennan, who entered the Foreign Service in 1926; Charles E. "Chip" Bohlen; Llewellen E. "Tommy" Thompson; Foy D. Kohler; and Charles E. Thayer. All but Thayer served as ambassadors in Moscow. To each of them our country owes a debt, the dimensions of which would be even greater had their advice been more often followed.

After a belated start, Lucy and I, my secretary, Barbara Eastman, and my pointer pup, Cartucho, were installed aboard RMS *Queen Elizabeth,* then the largest and fastest passenger ship in the world. We were sailing for Cherbourg and Southampton, taking along an automobile for our drive across France and occupied Germany to Czechoslovakia, to the most architecturally romantic capital in Europe, filled with the most unromantic people. We had a smooth October crossing, and though we were headed for Southampton, we were able to put Cartucho off at Cherbourg, to be brought to us in Prague, thus avoiding the long British quarantine.

In Southampton the American consul came aboard with messages from Washington. Most were not reassuring. A phase of mounting harassment by the Communist masters of their newest satellite had already begun. A young staff officer of our embassy, accused of espionage, had just been expelled from Czechoslovakia on forty-eight hours' notice — man, wife, children, and belongings, the latter rudely handled at the border. Another employee, a Czech-American, had disappeared and was presumably in custody. I was instructed, after checking with Embassy Paris, to confer with John McCloy, the American high commissioner in Frankfurt, who would facilitate travel across the American Zone through Nuremberg to Waidhaus, the last American post before the highway disappeared behind the Iron Curtain at Rozvadov.

One message was welcome. At the suggestion of the desk officer for Czechoslovakia in Washington, a junior member of the Prague staff would be sent to meet me in Paris, to share the driving and to handle the passports and paperwork.

It was late afternoon of the last day of October 1949 when the American sergeant at Waidhaus saluted, and we coasted slowly past a brown hayfield toward the bridge over a small brook that marked the Czechoslovak frontier. On the far side, two concrete pillars supported a steel rail, heavily weighted at one end so it could be raised and lowered by soldiers holding machine guns and eyeing the approaching visitors without cordiality. Fifty feet farther on, on the left, was a flagpole with the blue, white, and red emblem about to be lowered for the night. Down the road stood the customhouse, with a police station and barracks showing considerable recent construction on the opposite side of the highway. Beyond this stretched a forest of dark spruces through which the first snowflakes of approaching winter were sifting down, melting on the hood of our car as our Prague staff officer, Jack Armitage, took our handful of passports for their first Communist inspection.

We spent three years in Communist Czechoslovakia. It was a busy, revealing, and instructive period, and a pleasant one in terms of the friendships formed with our non-Communist diplomatic colleagues, with whom we were constantly and soon exclusively thrown. The Communists, at approximately the time of our arrival, began arresting Czech citizens as they emerged from non-Communist diplomatic missions. That soon discouraged relations with citizens of the country, except for bureaucrats bearing documents for official action; they were party members with special accreditation. Soon all private American citizens left Czechoslovakia.

My Czechoslovak experience falls into several clearly defined periods. First was the effort, epitomized by my address to President Gottwald when I presented my letter of credence, to establish, if not an entente cordiale, at least a nonhostile relationship between our two governments. I stressed that our two peoples had unique ties resulting from the presence in the United States of a large population of Czechoslovak origin, most of them now American citizens but all of them cognizant of their roots and of their family ties in Central Europe. I concluded by pulling out a tremolo stop for the part the American government played after World War I in helping to set up the independence of Czechoslovakia, a country whose continued well-being, I assured the president, remained close to the hearts of the American people.

President Gottwald in reply paid lip service to these ideas — with the usual Communist caveat about the alleged imperialist designs of the capitalist world in general and the United States in particular, witness the scandalous behavior of members of the staff of the American embassy in Prague. That was the opening I had been awaiting, because the naturalized American citizen who belonged to the staff of one of the embassy atachés, of whose arrest I had been apprised en route, was still in custody and I had subsequently received some classified instructions to do everything I could to obtain his release.

I told the president that as a newcomer I was not in a position to argue about past events. What I was suggesting, based on the statements I had just voiced in the name of my government, was that we adopt a fresh slate, wiped clean as of today. The best way to inaugurate such a relationship was to erase the pending problem involving a member of my official family, instead of wasting time on an argument over the immunities that, from the United States point of view, had been violated by his detention. I urged, therefore, that the individual be turned over to me, against my assurance that, regardless of my private views about the case, he would be escorted from Czechoslovakia in no more time than it would take to drive him to the border for delivery to the American authorities in occupied Germany.

We batted that one back and forth with some vigor. It was the longest initial interview I had experienced with a chief of state, and one conducted against a background of language difficulty, since I spoke neither Czech nor German, and my French — long years after Bill Dawson and the Foreign Service School of 1926 — had accumulated a thick coating of rust. The unhappy chief of protocol, a holdover from the previous regime (who was himself soon to be liquidated) had a hard time: his English was limited, but fortunately I could understand most of his French. Somewhere along the line he had picked up enough Spanish so that President Gottwald and I were not often bogged down.

Kliment Gottwald was not a prepossessing figure. He had a round head and a face with the puffiness and coloring that often denote the heavy drinker, which he was reported to be. Gottwald survived, however, while many of his colleagues of that period, including the powerful Rudolph Slansky, secretary-general of the local Communist party, were either shot or hanged in the late-blooming Stalinist purge that impended.

In public, Gottwald talked often of "Communist emulation" — part of the standard Moscow gibberish of the era — but what impressed me several years later was his personal performance of what he preached. When Stalin finally died, Gottwald was among those dutifully attending the frigid

Moscow obsequies; there he caught a cold that quickly turned into fatal pneumonia. Within ten days, he, too was the occupant of a coffin. I interpreted that as "Communist emulation" at its most edifying; starting a vogue would have made it perfect.

Whether Gottwald was sufficiently impressed by my representations to give my proposed modus vivendi a try, or because of some more mundane or less statesmanlike reason — like wanting a too-long-deferred drink — the president finally agreed to surrender the prisoner. I bowed myself out with expressions of hope, sincerely expressed if not convincingly held, that such future problems as might arise would prove equally susceptible of amicable solution.

The prisoner was duly released, apparently undamaged, and expelled. A Department of the Army civilian, he had been moved to Germany a fortnight before on suspicion that his Prague cover had been punctured. The fool then sneaked back to visit his girlfriend, whose room was shortly invaded by agents of the secret police. Getting that creature released earned me a gratifying message from Washington, but I doubt he was worth it.

The State Department also expressed the guarded hope that my proposed détente might prosper.

Thus began the first part of my Prague service, which lasted from November 1949 until the following April, when five-sixths of my staff were suddenly declared persona non grata under blanket charges of espionage, and given fourteen days to depart the country. That winter and spring had been a period of almost unrelieved frustration for two unrelated reasons. One emanated from Moscow; its agents in Czechoslovakia, the newest of the satellites, were eager to curry favor with the Kremlin by demonstrating zeal toward imperialists, warmongers, and other enemies of the people, with the staff of our Prague embassy at the top of the list. The second was the responsibility of Washington, which after encouraging me to suggest useful reductions in my Prague staff, failed in the most cowardly fashion to implement my recommendations.

My inherited staff was made up of reasonably competent individuals, but they had too little to do — a temptation to mischief. Moreover, more than half of them owed primary allegiance not to the Department of State but to the Washington agencies from which they received their pay: the Pentagon, Agriculture, Treasury, the Central Intelligence Agency, or whatever. At least two organizations had separate telegraphic communications facilities, and those that did not were accustomed to sending sealed despatches, which might or might not have been scrutinized by embassy State Department personnel before being forwarded in the diplomatic pouch.

The army and air attachés, with separate offices, accounted for over 40 percent of my total roster. This was a system by no means confined to Czechoslovakia. It prevailed generally throughout the world, in spite of the fact that its shortcomings should have been obvious to the most unsophisticated observer. The same problem still plagues American diplomacy.

In suggesting staff reductions to Washington, I was greatly assisted by my deputy, Jim Penfield,[2] one of the ablest of the many associates with whom it was my good fortune to be thrown. We were together in Prague for ten months, during which his wise assistance and that of his vivacious and amusing wife were invaluable assets in the experiences we shared.

Washington had directed that I survey the embassy personnel needs in the light of the Communist domination of the country. My first recommendation called for a 50 percent reduction, from eighty persons to forty, to be borne primarily by the military, whose cut was to be from thirty-three to ten (the ten including the four-man crew of the useful old C-47 then attached to the embassy). In the meantime, I had had to fire two of the military for involving themselves — in direct contravention of orders — in a childish piece of "intelligence gathering" that involved prying up a certain cobblestone in a certain small Prague park at two o'clock in the morning, in order to extract a bit of paper hidden beneath the stone. All went well until the paper was retrieved, the cobblestone still out of place, and the conspirators, including one wife, about to depart in the captain's automobile. At that moment a dozen flashbulbs illuminated the scene, clearly identifying the actors. Fortunately the individuals concerned had with them their Foreign Office diplomatic cards, and accordingly they were grudgingly permitted to be on their way, the paper having first been sequestered by the Czech police.

By fast footwork I had that group over the border and into Bavaria one hour before the Czechoslovak eviction notice, couched in the most abrasive of Communist prose, was delivered to the chancery. The flash photograph,

---

2. James K. Penfield, originally a China language officer, was astute enough to climb off that bandwagon before it plunged into the I-ch'ang Gorge. During the war he manned a frozen consulate at Godthåb, the capital of Greenland, learning Eskimo in his spare time. Later, Jim and the Danish minister to Prague, Peter von Treschow, harassed the Czech censors by having telephone conversations that began in English or French and then, clicks on the line having established that the censors were tuned in, switching to Eskimo.

suitably enlarged and followed by the text of the Czech note, was featured on the front page of *Rude Pravo*. That reduced my military contingent from thirty-three to thirty-one, still three times the quota I had recommended to Washington.

The agencies whose supernumeraries I had named rose up at that point and howled, and the State Department caved in. The loudest denunciation of me came from the Pentagon, which not only boasted a budget several hundred times as large as that of the State Department but also was developing a viselike grip on foreign affairs via the National Security Council and later an octopus called the Defense Intelligence Agency, which became almost as large as the CIA. My State Department desk officer, Harold Vedeler, did the best he could, but the matter was soon out of his hands. I doubt whether my recommendation reached Secretary Acheson or President Truman, but the upshot of my staff-cutting endeavor was an ignominious State Department retreat behind a flimsy barricade of bureaucratic prose, in which, while taking note of my "diligence in the direction of economy," it was left that "suitable reductions" could perhaps be better achieved through a process of attrition — by not replacing certain drones when their tours in Prague expired.

My initial military complement of thirty-three out of eighty was by no means unique. By 1950, our diplomatic missions all over the world were equally top-heavy with uniformed personnel, the attachés all theoretically being a part of the ambassador's staff although in fact their primary expertise turned out to be freewheeling. Those attachés, moreover, were in addition to the American military missions and military assistance advisory groups, the personnel of which in a given country might number hundreds, and in some cases thousands.

By the following April, when the Communists framed my United States Information Service as a prelude to ordering the general exodus of my staff, this Washington policy of attrition had succeeded in reducing my swollen quota to seventy-eight persons — from eighty to seventy-eight in five months.

The Communists could not have been expected to know with what satisfaction, bordering on glee, the forced departure of sixty-five of the remaining personnel would be regarded by the American ambassador whom they sought to insult. It was the best news since I entered the country, making it difficult for me to maintain the sour and angry mien that many of my colleagues believed the situation demanded. The Communists were correct in calculating that various sectors in Washington, including the American press, would be outraged, and that for a few days the Czechoslovak government would enjoy a surge of publicity during which their own reiterated charges of "espionage" would be repeated — if not believed — in areas far removed from Czechoslovakia.

But in every other particular it was a bad bargain for the Communist government. The more the Free World press thought about it, the less plausible it seemed that several score American officials would be engaged in a wholesale subversive movement to overthrow the now firmly entrenched Communist hierarchy. The accusation was preposterous per se. Nor were the "confessions" squeezed out of the pitiful handful of Czechs employed by the United States Information Service convincing in the light of Communist judicial procedure.

Outside the crash of ideology the Communists fared worse still. The United States did not break relations. I strongly recommended that it was worthwhile to maintain the American presence, including the high visibility of the American flag on the hill above the chancery, flying from one of the most conspicuous spots in the capital. We did, however, immediately reduce the Washington personnel of the Czech embassy to the same size as ours — twelve persons, plus the ambassador. The United States having an area of over three million square miles, against fifty thousand square miles for Czechoslovakia, that reduction obviously hurt them more than it did us. And we simultaneously closed all the Czech consulates in the United States, those in Chicago and New York being of special importance in the collection of dollars remitted by Czech-Americans to their relatives in Europe. That alone was a blow to the Communist government, at the point it hurt most — dollar exchange. We closed our one consulate in Bratislava, which was of minimal importance to us, our diplomatic establishment in Vienna being only thirty miles away.

The Czech official directing the American exodus from Prague was a nasty little man named Hajdu, at that time a vice minister of foreign affairs in Czernin Palace, to which he summoned me once or twice during the fourteen-day "period of grace," as he expressed it, in order to check on the number of my colleagues who had already departed and to inform me of the number of days remaining before "my government will have no recourse except to lift the diplomatic immunity of any surplus personnel remaining."

Regarding that as a bluff — the methodical Czechs, including the Communist Czechs, were generally meticulous about diplomatic status — I threw it back in Hajdu's face. That same official, I was happy to see, was on a proscribed list some few months later: he was tried and sentenced to life imprisonment for some alleged deviation involving Foreign Minister Clementis, the only pleasant Communist official I was to know in Czechoslovakia. (He was later hanged.)

It was a scramble, but the last embassy expellee departed within the two-week period specified by the Foreign Office. Choosing the list of those to stay behind was not as difficult as might be imagined, but the anger that arose from the Pentagon when I telegraphed that the military quota in the thirteen persons remaining would be one army colonel, one air attaché (whose C-47 had by that time likewise been expelled), and one sergeant to do for the two officers, was penetrating and inflamed. Three military out of the diplomatic roster of thirteen was not a proportion our high-riding soldiers were prepared to support.

In point of fact, we cheated a bit on our thirteen survivors. The wife of Vice Consul Dick Johnson had been a WAVE communications officer, and she was hired, Washington approving, as a code clerk. Similarly, the sergeant, a towering Irishman in constant terror of his diminutive wife, had in that wife a former WAC sergeant with all sorts of useful talents that we employed. Each of them counted as a dependent, so that our quota of thirteen remained intact.

The senior surviving colonel became so insubordinate over my selection of personnel that I shortly demanded his replacement, as persona non grata to me as ambassador. For once the State Department dug in its heels and behaved like an organization capable of running foreign affairs. It declared that the selection of personnel was a decision for the chief of mission, and the State Department made that stick, even though it took several months to get rid of the offending colonel, whose office employed every delaying tactic it could think of. The officer in question, surly and ignorant in matters of "military intelligence," was a competent fighting man. In Korea he attracted the attention of General Mark Wayne Clark, who in due course replaced his eagle with a star. In fairness to uniforms, I here add that my air attaché, a former fighter pilot, and the army colonel's replacement would have been assets to any diplomatic mission — to say nothing of their shared, ever-cheerful sergeant.

So May 1950 found me in Prague with an official family of exactly one dozen, the pick of our crop. With the excision of the obnoxious but soon-to-leave colonel, it was a wonderful aggregation. It was the most efficient staff I was to enjoy in the seven countries where I served as ambassador. All of the *essential* business of the American government was conducted with dispatch, and even with relative ease, barring the deliberately unpleasant aspects of Communist behavior. Of the messages deluging us from Washington, we did spend a certain amount of time each day separating the substantive from the trivial, after which we would inform Foggy Bottom with a clear conscience that, due to our limited personnel, it might not be possible to reply overnight to the lengthy questionnaire prepared by some obscure slavery in the Department of Commerce about the market for American zippers in Brno.

This second period of our Prague service lasted exactly one year from the departure of our staff, until the arrest in 1951 of the Associated Press correspondent, Bill Oatis. Because of the hostility of the government, which was by this time in process of framing former Czech officials and of holding spectacular "treason trials," it remained impossible for non-Communist diplomats to enjoy any kind of social relations with the citizens of the country, who were learning — too late, for many fine and patriotic individuals — what it is to be faced with the realities of the Communist Utopia. Thus the non-Communist diplomats were thrown, to an extent that one who has not served behind the Iron Curtin might find difficult to understand, into a peculiarly close association with their colleagues, many becoming the best of friends. This was an association that persisted among many of us thereafter.

Edgar Fraga de Castro, my Brazilian opposite number from our time in Havana, and his wife Celina became our close friends.

I owe a special debt to Bob Dixon, the British ambassador (as Sir Pierson Dixon he was subsequently head British delegate to United Nations in New York), whose experience in dealing with the government was more extensive than mine, and whose counsel was invariably sound, cheerful, and generously extended. My first French colleague was Maurice de Jean, a tough politico soon transferred to Moscow. His successor, Jean Rivière, a professional from the top of the basket, taught me how good a competent French diplomat can be — a useful lesson to one whose French colleagues in Latin America were too often drawn from the list of those whom the Quai d'Orsay hoped might ask for retirement.

Count Hubert Carton de Wiart, the Belgian minister, was a cousin of the Sir Adrian Carton de Wiart, V.C., who had invited me to help him take the Japanese surrender of Singapore in 1945. Hubert, and his wife Noelle, who as a member of the French underground had escaped death before a German firing squad by an eyelash, were among Prague's gayest hosts. A frequent visitor to Brussels, Hubert invariably returned with bushels of the world's most succulent snails. They were a first course that was served downstairs in the legation kitchen on a bare wooden table, with implements and sauces handy, and laundry facilities available for each guest, before trooping up to the formal dining room for the rest of the meal.

Having come to Prague from Montevideo, I instantly became the ward of Don Antonio di Pasca, the deaf-as-a-post chargé d'affaires of Uruguay. Don Antonio was married to Doña Aurora, an ample Brazilian lady from Porto Alegre, where her husband had begun his career as a vice consul. Their household was a madhouse of Brazilian Portuguese and *platense* Spanish, shouted and screamed at the top of everyone's lungs to try, unsuccessfully, to make Don Antonio understand. A talented daughter, Carmen, spoke seven languages; she accompanied our two children on a tour of Slovakia they could never otherwise have undertaken. My Brazilian colleague said of the di Pasca family, "the perfect arrangement, Uruguay dominated by Brazil!"

Our Canadian colleagues, Ben and Frances Rogers, were as attractive a couple as it was our privilege to meet — and we met often later, for Ben was appointed ambassador to Peru a few months before I returned there in 1955. Four years after that, when we were in Athens, the Rogerses were serving in neighboring Ankara with pauses in Greece whenever we could persuade them to do so. After my retirement we were their guests in the Canadian embassy in Madrid.

Other strange and wonderful fish swam about in our restricted non-Communist diplomatic pond. The White Russian wife of the Iranian minister could incinerate a Communist with a sentence in any one of a dozen languages, and often did so. The Afghan minister, a handsome brigand who never looked at home in Western clothes but who had in fact an excellent education at a German university, could easily outwit the Czechs. When the local Communists began to infringe on diplomatic privilege by setting up an inspection of the baggage of a departing (non-Communist) diplomat, the Afghan minister remarked to the Foreign Office functionary, "In my country our women are sacred. In my country if a man asked about my wife's clothes, I would kill him." There was no inspection of the Afghan luggage.

Last but by no means least was the bachelor Danish minister, whom I first called on at a nationalized hospital in Prague, where he was recovering from the painful extraction from his rear of a charge of number 6 shot, fired into him from a distance of some seventy yards by the careless Argentine consul general, a fellow hunter whose presence on the diplomatic pheasant shoot had already been protested by von Treschow "because a consul general is not a diplomat." The contrite Argentine sent a case of champagne to the hospital with a solicitous and apologetic note. Both were rejected by the unappeased patient.

"He stupidly shoots me. Why should I drink his silly wine?" was the minister's opening question when I crossed the doorway, seeking to comfort a stricken colleague.

Peter von Treschow was the cherished tyrant of the non-Communist diplomatic corps. He entertained often and meticulously and always on Wednesdays, the day of the arrival of the weekly SAS plane that brought him frozen salmon and iced sea trout and countless Copenhagen goodies. If the flight was canceled, he canceled the dinner. And if a guest was late, no matter what his rank or position, he found the meal already in progress. Moreover, his hospitality ended precisely at 10:15, after the serving of delicious hot chocolate and the passing around of excellent cigars in prime humidor condition. So intolerant did Peter become about the departure of dinner guests that on one occasion he would not allow several to reenter when their car had failed to appear, saying that the rooms were being cleaned. Finally Noelle Carton de Wiart and the pretty wife of the South African chargé d'affaires succeeded, during the minister's absence one Wednesday afternoon preceding a dinner party, in hiding a series of alarm clocks behind books and under tables in the salon where we used to congregate after dinner, preliminary to departure. The clocks were set to go off at three-minute intervals, starting at exactly 10:15. For several minutes the outraged confusion of the Danish minister was great, but when Noelle knelt at his feet in contrition, Peter embraced and forgave her. When his government later appointed him ambassador to Canada, he wept with emotion when the ladies kissed him good-bye, and everybody, except perhaps the Argentine consul general, was sorry to have him leave Prague.

These trivial and often insubstantial incidents illustrate an aspect of diplomacy that is frequently misunderstood or misrepresented. They indicate the value — the legitimate value in terms of one's own country's interest — that is derived from the friendships that develop among members of an otherwise widely dissimilar group who are drawn together because of the identity of the work they are engaged in. Diplomacy is such an amorphous business, the details of which can vary so widely, country by country or climatically or culturally or depending upon the type of government one represents or is accredited to, that it is not easy to describe, for the benefit of those who may have seen mainly the fringes of diplomacy or read communiqués about foreign affairs, the unique usefulness of incidents that taken alone sometimes appear of little weight, but added together can become like cement. The main ingredient of these is confidence: confidence in the honesty of purpose or the accuracy of judgment of someone with whom you have dealt in the past, perhaps a decade ago, perhaps on another continent.

Even in a society like Czechoslovakia, whose masters attempted to make it as hermetically sealed an area as ingenuity, experience at repression, and terrorism could achieve, the diversity and disparateness of our diplomatic group — even Yugoslavs were included — produced a remarkably accurate picture of what was going on in that festering society, enabling us to recognize trends and even to predict without the use of any more magic than experience and common sense, allied with professional training, certain movements and policies and possibilities almost from their inception.

My own experience indicates that covert information — the end product of espionage — though occasionally unearthing a gem of great value (like the atom bomb formula stolen from the United States by Soviet Russia), far more frequently turns up trash or trivia or material that any sophisticated performer might, without all the complicated paraphernalia of espionage, have figured out for himself. That, of course, is what professional diplomacy is about, notwithstanding which successive presidents have succumbed to the blandishments of agencies unrelated to the State Department that not only have tried to wreck the profession in the process but also have landed our nation in a series of almost irremediable predicaments.

In one particular, our personal situation in Prague was unique. Although we were surrounded by evidences of the grinding pressure of a totalitarian regime upon a gentle and intelligent, if now helpless, people, we lived in the greatest luxury it would ever be our lot to experience.

When Czechoslovakia was still free and the United States was trying to bolster the Czech economy by one means or another, Ambassador Laurence Steinhardt, a sagacious New York lawyer who served the Roosevelt administration in various capacities, arranged for the acquisition by the American government of the Petschek Palace. This had been built in the 1920s by a fabulous local Midas whose central idea, apparently, was to make Buckingham Palace look like a Quonset hut. His pleasure dome was erected on an ample private park surrounded by a high iron fence inside which was planted shrubbery so thick that what took place in the open ground within could only be conjectured from the surrounding streets. What actually did take place was baseball and cricket on alternate weekends, with the maharajah of Alirajpur, an Oxford graduate serving in the Indian embassy, as the cricket star; the best baseball player we had, by an equally wide margin, was Federico Mariscal, the minister of Mexico.

Additional lawn space contained our croquet pitch, and we played the game with heavy standard British equipment, which is to the American children's game as the difference between chess and Parcheesi. It is a fierce and ferocious contest. No game in the world can cause angry passions to rise as high, or to burn so hotly, as standard croquet with four contestants, paired in opposing teams, each plotting with remorseless and diabolical glee the destruction of the opponents. It is a game in which superior strategy wins over superior skill, thus giving the dark and devious mind an edge over the player able to strike an enemy ball forty feet across the greensward. In order to minimize arguments ending in homicidal encounters, we obtained a large blackboard and an easel to support it, on which after each play it was the duty of that player to announce which balls were now dead on whom, and so inscribe the situation on the blackboard.

There was a swimming pool at the far side of the park that we shared with the staff and any friends (necessarily all non-Communist diplomats) who wanted to join the club. The Czech employees of the embassy never came. We could not expect them to take that risk. And finally, there were two tennis courts, equally open to friends, that we flooded in winter for skating.

The main palace was built like a fortress, so stoutly that although we installed a first secretary with wife and two small children in a separate apartment directly over our heads, and although they entertained extensively and with sound, no echo of their presence on the third floor, except the occasional squeaking of the elevator at the far end of the hall, penetrated to the master rooms beneath, in which Lucy and Cartucho and I rattled around. My wife's bathroom, a sunken affair modeled on the Roman Empire with marble brought from Italy, had fixtures that were each and every one gold plated. My own shower, on the far side of a master bedroom that overlooked our playing fields, had thirty-four separate nozzles, sprays, flexible hoses, and gadgets too complicated to mention — all apparently dedicated as much to culture (if that is the word) as to the cleanliness of the bather.

The second floor hall measured 150 paces, in a long arc, with bedrooms and dressing rooms and sitting rooms on the outside, and with smaller quarters, nurseries, closets, and such like on the inside. A costly rug, woven for the house, not only extended the entire length of that hall, but then wound its way, still in one piece, down the grand staircase to the main floor, where were located a dining room that could seat one hundred guests, the ballroom, numerous reception rooms, and a vast library still stocked with the Petschek books, gorgeously bound, in half a dozen languages. The cellar contained all sorts of hydraulic and other machinery, capable of converting an outdoor patio into a winter garden. The operation of this machinery was complex and understood only by the gatekeeper, Pokorny, whose knowledge probably saved him from extermination by the Nazis, who used the palace as Gestapo headquarters during the occupation and took excellent care of everything, possibly recalling Hitler's prediction that the Third Reich would last one thousand years.

The furnaces, where in winter the Steinhardts had burned *five tons* of coal a day, were connected by a little underground railroad with a coal dump. Communist rationing of coal turned out to be a trump card in their deck. There was no way of cutting off parts of the house and heating only essential rooms, but by care and parsimony we reduced consumption to one ton a day.

The cellar contained another huge swimming pool surrounded by forty-eight red marble columns and an adjacent gymnasium filled with stationary bicycles and all the athletic equipment found on the great ships of the Hamburg-Amerika Line built for the pre–World War I luxury trade. When I found it would cost the equivalent of five hundred dollars for a onetime use of the special heating apparatus dedicated to regulating the temperature of the water in the pool, we used the place to store the summer furniture, plus the athletic equipment. The gymnasium we converted into a movie theater, using films cadged from our military in Germany.

The property took up an entire city block, and at the far side were two small but well-appointed houses originally constructed for married Petschek children. These we used for various members of the staff, the rest of whom lived in the old Hapsburg palace housing the chancery, which was even larger than the Petschek establishment, about two miles away near the Vltava River.

Lest anyone infer that this outline of the Petschek establishment embroiders the facts, let the skeptic refer to *Life* magazine; the issue of November 15, 1948, is largely devoted to describing the house that for three years was our home away from home in Czechoslovakia. That the place enriched our life and added greatly to the satisfactions of our circumscribed existence is true, but there were drawbacks: the palace must have been a paradise for bugging devices, and although with the aid of technicians intermittently imported from Embassy Paris we uprooted a lot of them, it was nevertheless an eerie sensation constantly to be reminding oneself that what was being said was probably being painstakingly recorded at SNB headquarters. Later consideration leads me to doubt the value of much of such eavesdropping. To monitor it, a huge bureaucracy must be maintained, existing in a gigantic granary where the occasionally useful kernel, perhaps one seed among tens of thousands, is as apt to be overlooked as it is to be misunderstood if it is discovered. Furthermore, the mass of the evidence collected eventually tends to overwhelm the listeners.

Another problem was more practical. The Petscheks, not misinterpreting the writing on the wall during Hitler's rise to power, sold out and moved to the United States, where among other sagacious initiatives they employed John Foster Dulles's law firm to represent their continuing private interests. They left behind most of their household staff, many of whom they cared for generously, but with two or three exceptions like Pokorny, the caretaker, these were not available to maintain the abandoned palace. Moreover, the State Department, while pleased with Ambassador Steinhardt's deal whereby the American government acquired that fabulous property, lacked funds adequate to maintain diplomatic premises of such magnitude.

Fortunately, the place was so well built that during our tenure it had not yet started to decay or fall apart, but trying to operate with a handful of servants an establishment geared for two dozen, not counting gardeners, was not the easiest chore for a housewife trained in New England thrift.

On the whole, however, that tour stands out as providing more satisfactions than sorrow. Our children visited us in the summers and our daughter, taking her Smith College junior year in Switzerland, was with us during the long winter vacation. Our official staff was so small that the State Department had waived the no-employment-of-relatives provision, and our sixteen-year-old son and the son of the counselor became guards and assistant chauffeurs of an army truck used on weekly trips to Nuremberg for supplies, a privilege they would have paid their entire allowances to enjoy and for which they received a small salary from a grateful government. Perhaps most important was our children's witnessing at first hand how a Communist country works: the drabness, the crowding, the cruelties, the lack of intellectual freedom, the pressures, the hopelessness, the deadening of ambition.

Perhaps Czechoslovakia is not the fairest example. The Czechs (who have often been called the "doormats of Europe," notwithstanding the bravery of certain individual citizens) had learned to survive during three centuries of Hapsburg domination as a subject people, while keeping alive in their hearts the spark of patriotism that made the Republic of Czechoslovakia so pleasant and civilized a place for the twenty-eight years of its independent existence in this century. Their experience seems to have taught them that the chances of survival are often increased by turning up one's coat collar, with one's back to the winds of adversity, rather than by leaping to support patriotic causes doomed to disaster, as the Poles and the Hungarians repeatedly do.

Our visitors were few. One welcome exception was the Anglican chaplain of the British embassy in Vienna, a Father Masters, whom Ambassador Bob Dixon used to get in for a weekend, four or five times a year. The Czech government, following the Communist anti-religion lead, forbade him the use of a church, unless he would "assure that no Czechs would take part in the service," so we therefore offered for the service a first-floor room of the Petschek Palace, which on other Sundays served as an interdenominational chapel with lay services and various diplomats taking turns "reading the lesson."

One reason for the paucity of American visitors was the competent Ruth Shipley, a lady who for years operated the Passport Division of the Department of State. Mrs. Shipley was no lover of communism, or of Communist travelers. She responded with enthusiasm to the State Department's injunction to mark passports "Not valid for travel in Czechoslovakia" — except in the special case of dependents of embassy personnel. That means that few outsiders reached us, and no congressmen. While I am a supporter in theory of the value of congressional travel, since World War II, and especially since the jet age, there has been no greater abuse of the taxpayers' money, or of the diplomat's patience and powers of endurance, than that inflicted by the never-ending stream of Potomac visitors, nine-tenths of whom — in terms of the national interest — would be far better off having remained at home. I do not exclude from that majority chief executives, vice presidents, and the swarms of voracious cohorts of each.

It was in this period in Czechoslovakia, however, that I was to win the only encounter with the formidable Ruth Shipley that was ever to grace my record — and few of my colleagues can claim as much. In this case, the altercation involved the issue of diplomatic passports to three young clerks on our staff, the only ones among our thirteen who were without them, and hence vulnerable to Communist abuse or indignity when crossing the border, as they frequently were required to do in the performance of duty.

In the days of Ruth Shipley, as in all the previous days of the Republic, the American diplomatic passport, personally signed by the secretary of state and bearing a special "To whom these presents shall come, greeting" on its first page, was a document of prestige. It was carried by Foreign Service officers to identify them as diplomats and by attachés as members of an ambassador's personal suite for the period of that duty only. The president and vice president of the United States carried it, as did members of their Cabinet. The subordinate members of the Foreign Service — later known as the Staff Corps — as well as traveling subordinates of the Department of State were issued documents known as special passports, which went as well to all other personnel traveling abroad on official business, including members of Congress and the Supreme Court.

The special passport did not imply diplomatic immunity, to which I believed the three young women on my staff were entitled because of the unique circumstances prevailing where they were assigned to serve. That was not the timid apprehension of an overcautious envoy. Shortly before my arrival, the wife of one of our staff members had been stripped at the border by a heavy-handed Communist police matron, who then conducted an offensive examination. It had been a disgusting ordeal.

So I wrote to the State Department, describing our situation in Czechoslovakia and suggesting a special title, "secretary of the American embassy in Prague," be accorded to Brynnie and Mary and Barbara, each such passport to bear a notation that it was valid only during the service of the bearer in Czechoslovakia.

It was a good try, but for all the reasons that have since been discarded by Mrs. Shipley's successors (so that diplomatic passports literally by the tens of thousands have not been issued, with concurrent destruction of the prestige of that document), I was told, politely but firmly, that it could not be done. If a senator was now entitled to a diplomatic passport, declared Mrs. Shipley, she did not see in good conscience how she could issue not one but three irregular passports to three candidates carried on the department rolls as "clerk/stenographers," no matter how bright and efficient I had represented those three young ladies to be. Ruth then wound up, unwisely, with an observation to the effect that even if she prepared the three requested diplomatic passports, she doubted the secretary of state would be willing to sign them. This communication was signed "For the Secretary of State, Ruth B. Shipley, Chief, Passport Division."

I was annoyed as well as disappointed, for I conceived the hazard as real and the requested exception as reasonable. So I decided on an end run, which is a standard bureaucratic ploy, except that for every time it succeeds, there are probably as many occasions, especially when the runner himself is abroad and the scorekeeper in Washington, when the scheme backfires to the detriment of the instigator. I wrote a private letter to Dean Acheson, enclosing the exchange of official amenities and pleading for reversal. I enclosed my communication to the secretary with a note to Barbara Evans, Mr. Acheson's personal assistant, with the request that my piece be brought to the secretary's attention instead of forwarded to the Passport Division for a reply.

Nothing happened for three weeks, at the end of which I received a manila envelope, heavily encrusted with sealing wax, in the diplomatic pouch. In it were diplomatic passports in the names of Brynhild Rowberg, Mary Horak, and Barbara Eastman, each duly signed by the secretary of state of the United States. With them was a small piece of white paper on which was scribbled, "Dear Ellis: You win (this time)." It was signed R.B.S.

These intramural sparklers were nothing, however, compared with the firecracker that the secretary himself was about to place under my ambassadorial chair. The secretary told me that I was slated to go as ambassador to Indonesia — recently the Netherlands East Indies — where an altercation had erupted between the incumbent ambassador and his chief dispenser of aid that appeared insoluble in terms of the personalities involved. A complicating factor was the unstable lecher who was chief of state of the new Republic, one President Sukarno, whose ideas about collaboration seemed somewhat bizarre, even measured by postwar Potomac standards. The aid man, with apparently limitless funds at his disposal, was proposing — over the ambassador's head — everything from indoor privies for the island of Java to brassieres for the girls on Bali. The aid man, concluded Dean ominously, was an outside appointee "with some rather important backing."

"The aid man" was shorthand for the official, theoretically subordinate to the ambassador, who administered the program of civilian (as distinct from military) assistance. The spiritual grandfather of the program was the Lend-Lease of World War II, which conditioned the American public to dishing it out without much prospect of getting much of it back. After the Marshall Plan in Greece and Turkey, a special agency was established in Washington. It was subject, in theory, to "policy guidance" by the Department of State. These handout enterprises have variously been known as ECA (Economic Cooperation Administration) and ICA (International Cooperation Administration) and now Agency for International Development (AID).

In the remainder of his communication, the secretary was good enough to extend congratulations on the job I was doing with my reduced staff in Prague and to say that for that reason, among others, I had been picked for the difficult assignment ahead. Until receiving official word, however, I was to inform no one — repeat, no one — of the projected move.

This was the period immediately after the tremendous success of the Marshall Plan, when (that triumph having been achieved) the illusion prevailed not only in government circles, but also widely throughout the country, that no matter how primitive the culture or how dissimilar the inhabitants from those of Indianapolis or Tallahassee, by joining American money with American know-how, the "emerging" recipients would soon be reciting the Declaration of Independence as they marched happily to the polls, singing snatches of the "Star Spangled Banner." There was added to these lunatic expectations the notion that our aid program would insulate the Bongo of Bugwallo from any temptation to go Communist.

H. Merle Cochran had been appointed American ambassador when Indonesia became independent the prvious year. I remembered that the United States had been at the head of the procession of those jiggling the Dutch elbow and urging the government of the Netherlands to get on with the business of decontaminating itself of the evil of colonialism — a busybody policy the wisdom of which I doubted at the time and have questioned ever since.

Indonesia was now independent — a giant archipelago stretching in a crescent three thousand miles from the Strait of Malacca to the Philippines, with God only knew how many millions of people of all colors, races, religions, and customs, and no experience whatsoever, for three hundred years, in the intricacies of self-government.

If Merle Cochran was having *his* throat cut by his handout merchant, as Dean Acheson's letter seemed to imply, I could almost see the razor approaching my jugular vein, for Merle was one of the genuinely tough and hard-boiled senior officers of the Foreign Service. A financial expert — for years he had occupied the important slot of financial attaché in Embassy Paris — he had also done a distinguished job in the Inspection Corps. My only personal contact with him had been on a special panel investigating extracurricular uses of the diplomatic pouch between Cairo and Athens where Cochran's acquired knowledge of the subject matter and of the intricacies of a Levantine plot, the ingenuity of which was equaled only by its complications, had earned my everlasting admiration and respect. If he could not cope with the situation at Jakarta, he would at least be a hard man to follow. I answered Dean Acheson's note with a handwritten letter saying that I would stand by for further orders.

I must admit that there were aspects that fascinated me. Indonesia, along with Australia and New Zealand, was one of the comparatively few lands I had never visited, and from childhood I had been an enthusiastic reader of Joseph Conrad and Somerset Maugham, not to forget those hair-raising and magnificent tales by John Russell. I discovered in the Dutch legation that my Netherlands colleague, the excellent Wim van Tets, possessed shelves of books on the Indies, many in English. Without arousing suspicion, I managed to borrow some, and my book learning was correspondingly increased.

As it turned out, this was all the benefit that came to me. Sometime later a further note from the secretary informed me (a few weeks after the Oatis case broke but not, I gathered, on that account) that "after further consideration it has been decided to make no change for the present in our ambassadorial representation in Jakarta." Merle Cochran, correctly interpreting developments, got himself ordered to Washington on consultation; there he mended his fences so efficiently that his handout colleague presently tripped and fell on his face. Unhappily, that occurred far too infrequently in the 1950s.

Meanwhile, our life in Prague followed much the pattern of the previous winter, with some of our time devoted to composing messages for the Voice of America to broadcast in Czech for the discomfiture of the Communist oppressors, and with an occasional retaliatory step to annoy our tormentors, such as making Czech officials wait at the border before entering Germany exactly as long as they made us wait at Rozvadov, instead of passing them through in five minutes, which had been the previous practice. We managed occasional trips to Vienna and Bavaria, and once, in a moment of aberration, I authorized a segment of the staff to go skiing in Austria, from which they returned as from the Balkan wars: with casts, splints, bandages, and crutches.

We were concerned during this time for the safety of the American correspondents who had been attracted to Prague by the trials and executions of prominent members of the Communist government. I remember in particular the correspondent of an important metropolitan daily who, after talking big about the "de facto immunities" of the press, on hearing a rumor that he himself might be in disfavor with the Ministry of Information, abandoned the country in a flash. Various Czech employees of United Press, Associated Press, Reuters, and France Presse were arrested from time to time and interrogated about the activities of their chiefs. The Israeli embassy, one of the best informed inasmuch as most of its personnel were former Czechs, passed on to us a rumor that something — nature undisclosed but reportedly involving the American press — was under discussion in Hradcany Castle, where President Gottwald met with his cabinet.

Before long the only American correspondent left was William Oatis, a cheerful extrovert who wore Truman-type bow ties and constituted the single attendee at the weekly embassy "press conference." Bill ably represented the Associated Press, and we heaved a premature sigh of relief when his accreditation papers, with which the Ministry of Information had been playing cat-and-mouse for several weeks, were finally and officially validated, along with residence permit, on April 15, 1951. One week later Oatis disappeared, on a night we expected him at dinner.

The Oatis case has already received extensive reportage, including a book published after his release and a rather lengthy chapter in *Farewell to Foggy Bottom* with the accurate title, "It Cost the Communists Fifty Million Dollars to Imprison Bill Oatis." Bill's case was the principal subject occupying my attention during this, the third and final part of my service in Czechoslovakia, which ended in my going to war-torn, still warring, Korea.

Some of the facts of the Oatis case are worth mentioning again, lest the capacity of communism for evil be overlooked by wishful thinkers. Bill was arrested in April 1951. The Foreign Office, after evasive replies, finally admitted that he was in custody, charged with espionage on behalf of the American embassy. Embassy access to the prison was denied; we had no treaty requiring it. The "trial" was held on July 4, in order to insult the United States, more than two months after Bill had been taken into custody. It was not held, however, until the prisoner had been appropriately "conditioned" — that is, brainwashed — and had become automatically perfect in the prepared "questions-and-answers" role that the accused was destined, in a Communist spy trial, to play.

No foreign correspondents were admitted to the proceedings, but by dint of haunting the Foreign Office practically day and night and engaging in endless frustrating conversations with Vilem Siroky (the foreign minister, and later prime minister, who at one stage tried to extract a steel mill from the United States in exchange for Oatis's release), arrangements were made for the presence at the trial of two representatives of the embassy.

That concession was the Communists' undoing, for one of those two was Mary Horak, who was bilingual in Czech and who had, after graduation from college, done a stint as a court stenographer. Her verbatim report of the proceedings, running to over one hundred printed pages, was subsequently published in full by the Department of State. Her report showed several occasions when the prisoner, apparently confused by floodlights in his face and deliberately deprived of his eyeglasses, gave the correct prepared answer but gave it out of sequence — he replied before the prosecutor put the question!

The formal charges, preposterous on their face, were nevertheless mechanically accepted by the accused. Speaking in a lifeless monotone, Bill Oatis pled guilty after a speech expressing sorrow at the wrongs he had attempted to inflict upon the hospitable and democratic Republic of Czechoslovakia. He was sentenced to ten years' imprisonment, of which he served two before being expelled from the country. By that time I was in Korea.

There are several aspects of the Oatis case that merit being remembered. First, the conduct of the American press in keeping the case alive and in keeping Bill's name and the false charges against him before the American public (in this they were ably assisted by Secretary Acheson and President Truman). Second, the collaboration of the Associated Press, which, having satisfied itself that the government was doing everything it could on Oatis' behalf, could not have been more cooperative or understanding. John Hightower, an ace reporter then covering State, was assigned to daily liaison with Harold Vedeler — not for news stories but to keep abreast of the case. He was shown the messages exchanged with Prague and his own suggestions were solicited. Frank Starzel, the general manager of Associated Press, conferred with me in Vienna, and he maintained daily contact with developments through Hightower. Third, Bill's young wife, a girl from a small town in Minnesota, behaved throughout with dignity and restraint.

As to less obvious lessons to be learned from the case, I would list unremitting pressure, applied at whatever points the arresting power is vulnerable. In the Oatis case, his value to the Communists, once the trial itself had faded from memory, rapidly decreased, so that they were probably glad — at the end of two years instead of ten — to be rid of the prisoner. But $50 million dribbling away from them a day at a time, with the limited exchange then available to the Comrades, was a stiff price to pay for an act of propaganda regarded in the Free World with revulsion and certainly given little credence by the Czech people themselves.

After unremitting pressure, I would list continuing publicity — not damning the State Department for not sending a battleship up the Vltava River to shell Hradcany Castle but the sort of restrained but indignant reporting that keeps a story, and the plight of the prisoner, before the minds of the American people.

And finally — no ransom. The worst solution to a problem of that kind is to be blackmailed into paying an aggressor. I am still of the opinion that I might well have had Oatis set free within a few months of the trial had not the Pentagon — against my shrill and angry protests — at approximately the same time paid Hungary a considerable sum to ransom some American flyers. I do not recall the nature of the escapade that landed the flyboys in the Budapest hoosegow — probably more foolish than discreditable — but I remain convinced that if the Pentagon has used its head instead of its pocketbook, Bill Oatis would have been a beneficiary.

In the late summer of 1952 we were informed of our transfer to Korea — almost as long a jump as the discarded Indonesian assignment. By then nearly all of our "original twelve" had been replaced, although the quota of thirteen persons in Embassy Prague still held. The Penfields had gone to London, Jim's replacement being Tyler Thompson, who likewise went on to ambassadorial rank before retirement. My secretary, Barbara, on whose behalf I had taken on the formidable Ruth Shipley, got small use of her diplomatic passport: she up and married our communications officer — matrimony being one of the principal hazards that faces an ambassador with a competent and attractive secretary — and I gave the bride away in a military chapel in occupied Germany.

Our official farewells to the government of Czechoslovakia proved nonexistent. The customary formal note was dispatched to the Foreign Office, informing it of my impending transfer and inquiring as to a convenient date when I might make a farewell call on the foreign minister and on the president of the Republic. That communication was not acknowledged, a calculated discourtesy duplicated toward the majority of departing non-Communist chiefs of mission in that era. The Czech equivalent of a third secretary was dispatched to the railroad station to make sure we departed, but in other particulars the government of Czechoslovakia took no note of our going.

Not so our friends in the diplomatic corps. We had a struggle of major proportions in seeking to avoid the ghastly business of a farewell dinner party every night for the last weeks of our service in Prague. Finally Lucy had a wonderful idea. Since we were all such close friends and saw so much of each other anyway, why didn't we avoid a farewell party by each chief of mission and instead have a combined, single bang-up going-away dinner?

That having been agreed upon, our friends asked, Why not have the party in the Petschek Palace, since in addition to being big enough to hold everybody who wants to come, the place was originally built for just such celebrations? We, the guests of honor, would stay upstairs until we were officially notified that it was time to appear; then we would march down the grand staircase to meet our hosts and hostesses. Lucy offered to contribute our kitchen staff to help downstairs, but in every other way — food, drinks, music, seating, service, and all the other details and arrangements — the responsibility would be upon our colleagues.

After more discussion than the importance of the matter warranted, the second suggestion was likewise adopted. We were amused to learn that the Yugoslavs, who since Tito's successful defiance of Stalin had been existing in a sort of limbo in Prague, applied for membership in the corps of hosts; more, they donated a case of slivovitz of surpassing smoothness and potency, a couple of surviving bottles of which I slipped into our effects for Korea. There was a banquet (during which there were many speeches), and the junior diplomats put on a cabaret show that would have set the patrons of Zelli's upon their ears.

The party was held not on our last night in Prague but on the *penultimate* evening, thus assuring us of a clear-eyed departure from Wilson Station. It was the perfect farewell, never duplicated or equaled in my thirty-six years in the Foreign Service.

Korea

The First War We Did Not Win

My assignment to Korea was a recess appointment by President Truman in the summer of 1952, when the Senate was not in session. For the first time in my career, I was to be allowed to make a leisurely trip from Washington halfway around the globe to Korea. The armistice negotiations, which were strictly military, had already dragged on for a year (while the fighting continued), and there seemed to be no rush in getting a new ambassador to Seoul much ahead of the termination of hostilities. Then would begin the difficult and complex business of transferring functions back to the civilian authorities, a process in which the embassy was expected to play an important role.

Lucy and I accordingly proposed to drive to California, seeing something of our country in the process, and then to take ship from San Francisco. From Tokyo to Pusan, the temporary capital, we would complete the journey by military airplane, commercial service to the peninsula no longer existing. In addition to Washington, I would have a week chasing woodcock in Maine, plus time in New York to listen to the scheduled UN debate on Korea. The Republican victory at the polls that November not only changed my plans but affected the course of the thirty months I was to serve in Korea.

A brief chronology should help retrieve perspective. In 1945 at Yalta, because of miscalculations on the part of our military as to Japan's military capabilities — which that winter were rapidly coming to an end — Stalin was unnecessarily bribed into entering the Pacific war within ninety days after V-E Day. Soviet Russia thereupon did so in August 1945 — the same week as Hiroshima. Thus the Russians surged back into Manchuria, whence they had been ejected in 1903. Although General MacArthur was able to keep them out of Japan — perhaps the best and most lasting of his achievements — the northern half of Korea (with the major share of mineral resources along with most of the Japanese industrialization) became a Russian zone of occupation following an agreement that in the north the Russians would accept the Japanese surrender, whereas the United States would do so in the southern half of the peninsula below the 38th parallel.

The United States held its southern half in good faith, in trust for the Korean people, who had endured — and by their toughness survived — forty years of heavy-fisted, unimaginative Japanese domination. In 1948 we turned over our zone to the freely elected president, the elderly Syngman Rhee. Rhee had spent sixty years of his life, mostly in exile, struggling with a tenacity rarely equaled for one objective only: the liberation of his country. The Soviets, on the other hand, proceeded to communize North Korea, with the intention of making of it another satellite.

In the process of winding down the American military presence in the south, it became clear that if the Republic of Korea (ROK) was to survive, a substantial United States presence would have to remain at least until the country got on its feet. The ROK had no effective army, little training or equipment, and, so completely had the Japanese dominated every aspect and detail of administration, no bureaucracy. Constructing a government had almost literally to be from the ground up, with foreign-educated Koreans (except those trained in Japan, who remained anathema to Rhee) initially holding many of the key positions. They were the only people available with some knowledge of how to make a government function.

Meanwhile, the Communists in the north continued to demand unification on their terms.

Aware of ROK weaknesses, the North Koreans on June 25, 1950, launched a major offensive across the 38th parallel, which is not a geographic frontier but merely a line drawn on the map. The extent to which a speech six months before by Secretary Acheson, interpreted by some to indicate that the peninsula might lie beyond the sphere of United States interest, may have encouraged that Communist attack is still a matter of debate.

The critical few days that followed, in Washington and in New York, have been fully described by the principal American protagonists, including President Truman and Secretary Acheson. Capitalizing on the folly of the Soviet government in boycotting the Security Council, that body under American leadership was able to function without a Soviet veto. North Korea was named the aggressor. Its government was called upon to cease and desist as well as to withdraw behind the 38th parallel. The same mandate made possible the establishment of the United Nations Command, with its blue and white flag surrounded by the flags of sixteen countries, including the United States, volunteering to come to the assistance of the Republic of Korea.

At the time of the Communist attack the American embassy in Seoul was the largest diplomatic mission we possessed, with some two thousand persons on the payroll — shades of my twelve stalwarts in Prague! With the able assistance of Don McCue (later my administrative officer in Rio), Ambassador Joseph Muccio succeeded in evacuating the lot of them one jump ahead of the advancing Communist forces. The Korean/American military, outmanned and outgunned, continued its retreat through that hot Korean summer until by September 1950 all that was left of the battered ROK was a postage stamp of territory at the extreme southeastern tip of the peninsula. There the exhausted troops, together with such reinforcements as MacArthur had been able to scrape together in Japan, dug in.

There then occurred an amazing succession of reversals, diplomatic as well as military. In September 1950, when it looked as though the "Pusan perimeter" might be overrun at any moment, General MacArthur executed a maneuver so daring that his subsequent fade-out seems the sadder to contemplate: he landed an American army at Inchon, the port to the west of Seoul, an operation unexpected because of the raging tides equaled in height and velocity only in the Bay of Fundy on the opposite side of the world. That invasion caught the North Koreans by surprise. Furthermore, as the Americans advanced across the peninsula, the North Koreans around Pusan were in danger of being cut off. They scrambled north with all the speed of which they were capable. The Americans, with the First Marine Division in the vanguard, were now in pursuit of the fleeing aggressors.

To MacArthur — to whose shining self-esteem as proconsul in Tokyo was now added the luster of the Inchon landings — there was no choice but to pursue the demoralized North Koreans across the 38th parallel and as far into their lair as necessary to annihilate them as a military force. "In war, there is no substitute for victory!" Meeting with President Truman on Wake Island that October, MacArthur so expressed himself, adding that the Chinese Communists, who were beginning to make noises in adjacent Manchuria, were unlikely to enter the fray.

At the United Nations the noble unity of the preceding June was already disintegrating, some of our allies taking the position that once the retreating North Koreans recrossed the 38th parallel, the aggression had been repelled; righteousness had prevailed; the "Korean incident" was over. This left the United States in a difficult position. Washington had so magnified the importance of the United Nations mandate (notwithstanding the fact that more than 95 percent of the military effort was being put forth by the United States) that when that mandate showed signs of strain, President Truman hesitated. In the end, however, he allowed MacArthur the free hand that proved the general's undoing.

Against dwindling opposition, MacArthur continued to move north. He also divided his forces, apparently relying on the conviction — buttressed by the coterie of yes-men and sycophants attracted by his monstrously inflated ego — that once the Invincible Leader had spit in the Yalu River, the war would be won and he could send his victorious American boys home in time for Christmas.

Instead, the Chinese Communists did attack, and by December 1950 the rout of the North Koreans had suddenly become the retreat of the American forces, now overwhelmed by hordes of Chinese "volunteers." It was in those few weeks of approaching arctic weather that most of the American prisoners of war, who were to figure so prominently in the armistice negotiations, were captured.

On the diplomatic front, as 1950 waned, President Truman found himself in further trouble, such was the fear of our European allies lest the "Korean incident" explode into World War III. The Soviet Air Force (apparently a less potent weapon at that time than it was supposed by some to be) was crouched around Vladivostok, ready to leap into the fray along with the Chinese "volunteers."

MacArthur, conceding that he had been misled about the Chinese, now created further apprehension by demanding authority "to bomb across the Yalu" — that is, to have the Fifth Air Force attack the Chinese cities, supply bases, and arsenals in Manchuria. When President Truman vetoed that project, an angry and frustrated MacArthur declared war on his own president. From his majestic perch in the American embassy in Tokyo, MacArthur undertook to destroy his commander in chief. While the surviving American forces, along with what was left of the United Nations Command, were in a retreat that carried them once again across the 38th parallel and into South Korea, MacArthur became more and more intemperate and insubordinate, to the point where President Truman had no choice but to dismiss him. That was in April 1951.

An uproar ensued in the United States, where the citizenry was bitterly divided over China policy, dismayed over the accusations of disloyalty in high places, and confused by the rapid shifts of American fortunes in Korea. MacArthur, the details of whose conduct were not then understood, received a hero's welcome, including an invitation to address Congress. There he proclaimed, amid an unprecedented outpouring of sentimentality, that "old soldiers . . . fade away." He thereupon faded into the Waldorf Towers, where he died in 1964.

To replace MacArthur, President Truman appointed the able and experienced General Matthew B. Ridgway, who with the remnants of those surviving his predecessor's grandiose ineptitude, plus fresh levies from the United States as well as the developing ROK forces, managed to pull things together and once more to start pushing the enemy back across the 38th parallel. In the first nine months of the war, Seoul — thirty miles south of the parallel — changed hands four times; only Warsaw and Manila suffered as much physical destruction.

As General Ridgway progressed, our United Nations allies declared for the second time that "aggression has been repelled; let us call it a day." Only this time the refrain was echoed by an increasing volume of American voices. We were approaching the 1952 election year; the furor over MacArthur had not yet subsided; and the spirit of crusade with which we had entered the conflict had been dissipated by the vicissitudes of war, by incessant and conflicting blasts from Congress and from the United Nations, and by the capture of American soldiers during the retreat from the north in December 1950.

At that point the Soviet delegate in New York, Comrade Malik, proposed that a Military Armistice Commission be established with a view to the termination of hostilities.

It is not difficult, this long after the event, to say that the beleaguered Truman administration ought at that point — Ridgway's military position being strong (otherwise Malik would not have made his proposal) — to have nailed down a cease-fire, to take place at once, prior to the convocation of the Armistice Commission. Also, the terms of reference for the latter should have been spelled out. Instead, the Soviet initiative at the United Nations was snapped up the way a hungry trout gulps a fly. Two solid years of Communist vituperation and acrimony, while the shooting war continued, might thereby have been avoided. (But I was in Czechoslovakia at that time, and it is easy to criticize in the prescient light of hindsight.)

The first of those two years had already elapsed when I was appointed ambassador to Korea, a period of such acute frustration that successive American military negotiators at Panmunjom retired on the verge of prostration. And all the time the Communist negotiators were screaming irrelevancies, the battle line was again slowly approaching the now well-worn 38th parallel.

I reached Washington several weeks before the 1952 election, the campaign in full swing. I attended strictly to my Korean knitting, seeking to learn what had been happening, how it had happened, and what were the prospects. John Allison, the assistant secretary of state for Far Eastern affairs, had been loaned to John Foster Dulles, to whom the Democratic administration had assigned the difficult task of negotiating a treaty of peace with Japan. Both men were in Tokyo, and I was invited to occupy Allison's office and to utilize his staff. Secretary Acheson was at the United Nations, listening to the interminable tirades of Comrade Vishinsky, the Soviet foreign minister, and to the self-propelled preachments of that Indian peacemaker, Jawaharlal Nehru. My immediate mentor was U. Alexis Johnson, later a career ambassador, a solid and knowledgeable officer with thousands of dull facts at his fingertips. The acting secretary of state was my friend of Foreign Service School days, David Bruce, whose brother had been ambassador to Argentina during my Uruguayan service.

To David Bruce I was indebted for keeping me from being fired almost before I had taken my oath of office as ambassador to Korea. I called presently on General Omar Bradley, chairman of the joint chiefs: a fine soldier and a great gentleman. His briefing was frank, helpful, modest, and full of wisdom. I was long to remember his friendly assurance that pending the conclusion of an armistice, which if we did not have to go through the confusion of a change of administration he hoped could be achieved at a very early date, the most useful contribution I could make would be to develop friendly personal relations with the patriotic old president of Korea. President Rhee believed, as General MacArthur had, that the only permanent solution was to defeat the North Koreans and drive the Chinese "volunteers" back to Manchuria. That, said General Bradley frankly, was no longer a feasible operation. Public opinion in the United States would not support it. Rhee, Bradley concluded, could at times be "very difficult." He suggested a low-key approach, adding with a disarming smile that that was merely his personal opinion, and that he would await my views after I had reached Korea.

I then visited Bradley's former colleague, and later David Bruce's successor as undersecretary of state, General Walter Bedell Smith, our first postwar ambassador in Moscow, who in 1952 was head of the Central Intelligence Agency. Another able soldier (he had been General Eisenhower's chief of staff), Bedell Smith was habitually irascible and now more so because of persistent ill health. He nevertheless outlined operations in Korea, one of which within the week had disastrously blown up in his face with a furious President Rhee threatening to throw the whole CIA undertaking — lock, stock, and barrel of spooks — out of his country. That was not the phraseology Smith used, but he was clearly harassed and full of distemper.

What had happened was that by some incredible mischance the little old president, who loved fishing and was never so happy as when bobbing about in a small boat, reeling in the tiny whitefish that abounded off the southern shore, had been fired upon — or at least had his bow fired across — by some overzealous Korean soldiers who were protecting an area where some highly classified monkey business, designed for the benefit of the ROK, was in preparation by the CIA. The president was now demanding that the overzealous ones be turned over to him for punishment. The CIA was thus faced with a choice between possible impairment of local morale if they acceded to President Rhee's demand and possible destruction of their entire apparatus on the peninsula if they did not. A tough decision.

For some reason, the contrast between the elaborate edifice of covert CIA paraphernalia and the fragile old gentleman in his little boat, eagerly catching the small fish he would share that night with Mrs. Rhee, struck me as too preposterous for solemnity. When I was so undiplomatic as to laugh, General Smith exploded in rage and the interview was over. David Bruce told me later that it needed all the diplomacy *he* could muster to mollify the general, who demanded my scalp. In the end, Generals Clark and Van Fleet were delegated to pacify President Rhee, which they finally succeeded in doing; the CIA, in the process, changed its local cover name to hide its chagrin and embarrassment. I was relieved, nevertheless, when Allen Dulles, Foster's younger brother, shortly moved into the CIA front office.

My New York exposure initiated me into the viciousness of the verbal tactics of the Soviet delegate, with more than an occasional assist from Nehru and Krishna Menon, who, for reasons I did not fathom, never appeared so happy as when implying that the United States (without whose donations of foodstuffs literally millions of Indians would recently have starved) was guilty of this or that malodorous practice, unworthy of the democratic principles for which the Indians stood. (The image of Nehru presenting himself to an applauding world as the first immaculate conception in two thousand years was somewhat tarnished by the rape of Goa, which the Indian prime minister later accomplished with a cynicism worthy of Stalin.)

It was also my misfortune to be in New York for the famous Vishinsky speech on Korea, up to that time the longest uninterrupted tirade since the UN was established. The oratory and debates generated at the United Nations were not, however, the controlling factors with respect to the drawn-out negotiations at Panmunjom. The American election of 1952 was more significant even though had Stevenson won, the Korean outcome might not have been very different. The fact was that the American people had become sick of an unwon and apparently unwinnable war being fought ten thousand miles from the United States.

Recognition of that attitude gave the Communists a negotiating edge throughout the two-year talkathon. It may also be remembered that the Republican presidential candidate, in the last week of October 1952, suddenly dragged the hitherto nonpartisan issue of Korea into the campaign via a speech to the effect that, if elected, General Eisenhower would go forthwith to the battlefield and there endeavor to bring hostilities to a prompt and honorable conclusion. (That speech, by the way, was regarded by his Democratic opponent as a blow below the belt.)

The Eisenhower victory not only affected my immediate plans but also was to complicate the thirty months of my service in Korea. The first thing that blew out the window was our project to see the United States by automobile and take a ship to Yokohama.

My farewell call on President Truman was set for Thursday morning of election week — that is, two days after the election itself. Although Truman had not been a candidate, his party, which had been in power for twenty years, had just taken a severe licking. The president would not, I felt, be in a cheerful mood; my cue was to say good-bye to him and get out in rapid, if not record, time.

I could not have been more mistaken. There was the president of the United States sitting jauntily at his desk, wearing one of his more conspicuously gay bow ties, as perky as a chipmunk with a stolen peanut. He spoke pleasantly of my service in Prague and of Dean Acheson's plans to use me in Korea, "once we button up that damned armistice."

The president went on to say that he had just been on the telephone "with the president-elect." A week earlier Truman would doubtless have said "with Ike," whom he did not greatly admire, but now, meticulous about anything that touched upon the dignity of the presidential office, General Eisenhower was "the president-elect." The president said he had offered his airplane, the *Independence,* but that the president-elect had declined, stating that the air force would provide the necessary transportation to and from Korea.

"What did come out of it, though," President Truman told me, "is that the president-elect expects to go to Korea within the next ten days or two weeks. So if you still want that job I picked out for you, you better get there ahead of him. I'll say the same to Secretary Acheson."

So off to Korea we flew. The only thing I was able to salvage, extracted with reluctance from the State Department, was authorization for our daughter, Lucita, who had graduated from college the previous June, to follow us to Korea, notwithstanding the "no female dependents" edict of General Clark. It was the only time in my career when I felt I had the State Department in a vulnerable spot, and the temptation was irresistible. My predecessor had been a bachelor ambassador, and one of the reasons I had been chosen to succeed him was the expectation, or at least the hope, that my wife would find a sympathetic friend in Mrs. Rhee, who reportedly wielded much influence with her husband. Having thus discovered that State was all eagerness to have Lucy accompany me (an ambassadress being exempt from military jurisdiction), I obstinately held out for the presence likewise of Miss Briggs.

It was settled, Personnel grumbling, that Lucita would not accompany her parents, who would, however, "survey the situation on arrival and the State Department would abide by my recommendation." Our daughter, who had whiled away the autumn at secretarial school, was accordingly able to join her family for Christmas in Pusan, shortly after which she was employed as a DAC (Department of the Army civilian entitled to official transportation by jeep but not by sedan, the privilege of field-grade officers and higher).

I spent a morning with General Mark Wayne Clark at his grandiose Tokyo headquarters, whence he directed not only the Korean War but all other United States Army forces in the Far East, including Okinawa, Taiwan, and the Philippines. Six-foot-four, he was an impressive soldier with a retinue of aides, assistants, and acolytes who leaped to attention at the flicker of a Clark eyelash. After his briefing the general placed his second-best airplane — MacArthur's old *Bataan,* a weather-beaten but luxuriously fitted C-54 — at our disposal for the flight to Pusan, where the embassy (and also the Rhee government) was temporarily established. The port was some 150 miles from Seoul, and the idea, I soon found out, was to keep us both — President Rhee and me — out of the hair of the military, since what they called the MLR (for main line of resistance) was then less than fifty miles to the north of Seoul.

Pusan was by no stretch of the imagination a garden spot. Ever since the days of the "Pusan perimeters" in 1950, it had housed thousands upon thousands of refugees in circumstances of indescribable misery. We occupied one of the best houses in the city, on a hillside overlooking the congested harbor, a property that had been the residence and garden of the manager of the excellent railroad system the Japanese had constructed. It was the only American embassy in the world with a built-in Buddhist shrine, which we treated with respect if not with comprehension. Strung out on the hillside beyond us were refugee huts, some of which housed our Korean servants. All were living in such miserable conditions that one of my wife's first concerns was to try to alleviate some of the pains of their existence. The Maryknoll Mission then had a hospital in Pusan, operated by a dedicated group of American nuns, who were shortly importuned to vaccinate the children of surrounding families, including our Korean staff. A sister reported to my wife afterward that several hundred children had appeared (we provided as inducement to each child a bonus of candy from the PX), but that among them one child had not been vaccinated: she was just recovering from an attack of smallpox.

The Maryknoll Sisters were treating over one thousand Korean outpatients a day. Other missionary groups (abandoning for the period of the war their squabbles, the shabbiness of which had so marred early United States relations with the Hermit Kingdom) worked during Communist hostilities with equal selflessness and effectiveness. To this day there are probably more Christians in the Republic of Korea than there are in Japan, with several times Korea's population, or in all of China, with its hundreds of millions.

With the visit of the president-elect of the United States impending, presentation of credentials took place almost at once, not in Pusan but in Seoul, devastated though it was, because President Rhee thought it would have a good effect on the country's morale for the new American representative — and presently President-elect Eisenhower — to be received in the real capital of the country.

We accepted General James Van Fleet's dinner invitation in Seoul the night before the credentials ceremony, but declined to use his military guest house. That may have been a mistake, because the general, recognizing that hordes of Washington visitors would be descending upon him, combed his card index until he found a major who had once been a hotel manager. Van Fleet put him in charge of a very comfortable establishment operated for VIPs.

The embassy had two compounds in the capital, about a mile apart. Although they had been badly knocked about during the fighting, I had the same feeling about a State Department roof over my head that President Rhee had about receiving me in Seoul instead of in Pusan. The first embassy compound contained the lovely old embassy residence, once one of the royal palaces, although it was so small it could have been hidden in a wing of the Petschek Palace in Prague. It had, however, been so badly damaged, as well as looted, that it was not habitable.

Compound Two had a number of staff houses, into one of which Lucy and I moved, surviving a frigid and miserable night following the demise of our space heater, a military contraption burning fuel oil that was capable of converting an igloo into an oven in five minutes, and back again into an igloo faster than that if the burner went out. The pipes had long since frozen, but we got the heater going again the next morning in time to melt water to bathe in.

President Rhee, whose formal regalia had been stolen at the time of the first Communist drive, had kindly suggested business suits for the credentials ceremony, instead of cutaway coats and striped trousers.

The ceremony was pleasantly informal, and I liked the old gentleman on sight. Furthermore, Mrs. Rhee insisted that Lucy come also, and together they watched the official proceedings from the back of the hall.

In 1953, Syngman Rhee was probably approaching eighty, bright as a newly minted coin and amazingly active. He could be humble, furious, wily, unassuming, or gay, depending on the circumstances and the immediate objective, but his ultimate purpose never varied: the unification of a free Korea, which meant defeating the Communists and ejecting them from the country. Since that also was General Van Fleet's private view, they got on better than did Rhee and General Clark. Furthermore, the Van Fleets had lost an aviator son over Korea, and when the Rhees moved back to Seoul, Mrs. Van Fleet was invited to be their guest. Clark, although he was violently opposed to American wives on the peninsula, was unable to prevent acceptance of a presidential invitation.

Beyond having an observer present, Rhee would have nothing to do with the armistice negotiations. Since I was not authorized to discuss military matters, we got on very well, although I listened to a great many lengthy and repetitious declarations about the iniquity of accepting less than victory, which Rhee was convinced meant storing up trouble for the future. Nor was the president an amateur at arguing his case; he had an earned doctorate in international law and years of his life had been spent haunting the League of Nations (where he and Austrian-born Mrs. Rhee first met in the 1930s), listening to debates, pleading his cause with diplomats and international bureaucrats, and observing firsthand the functioning of the League machinery. He was well informed on Marxism and theoretical communism, and he had watched actual communism in action. He wanted no part of any of them.

I returned to Seoul briefly a few days later for the visit of President-elect Eisenhower, who talked to his generals, inspected some troops, reluctantly called on President Rhee, and flew home again. My small contribution to this exercise in futility was limited to urging that Eisenhower not follow his original bent, which was either to avoid altogether a confrontation with President Rhee or else to receive him at Van Fleet's headquarters instead of himself calling on the president, as courtesy as well as protocol demanded.

Interpreting sentiment at home, Eisenhower gave both President Rhee and the high brass of the army, navy and air force no hope of mounting a major new offensive. When this news leaked to the Communists, it probably rendered the conclusion of the armistice more difficult by confirming the eagerness of their enemies to reach an accommodation. The Eisenhower preelection speech on Korea doubtless won him some extra votes unneeded for his victory at the polls, and the visit itself may have given the American people an impression of diligence in high places, but as a practical matter it accomplished nothing.

A few days later, back in Pusan, my wife, daughter, and a houseboy who had once been a tailor were sewing the guestroom curtains when who should appear (to the consternation of the houseboy and the astonishment of my wife and daughter) but President and Mrs. Rhee and Mrs. Van Fleet, who was their houseguest, who had come to pick up some items my daughter had brought for Mrs. Van Fleet from Japan. We served them coffee, and Mrs. Rhee, finding that embassy Pusan lacked a sewing machine, loaned us hers, so that our first official guest, who was Senator Hickenlooper, could dress without being face to face every few moments with the pacing marine guard outside. The same curtains sheltered successively, during our first few weeks in Korea, Helen Traubel and later Marian Anderson of the Metropolitan Opera. Both came to Korea to sing for the soldiers. Other visitors, though not houseguests, included Marilyn Monroe and Cardinal Spellman, but not simultaneously.

As a newly arrived representative I was impressed by the military competence of our first team, most of whom had been merely names to me during the fighting of World War II. Many of them, especially Generals Ed Hull and Maxwell Taylor (who followed Generals Clark and Van Fleet) and several of our navy, air force, and marine commanders, became my close friends — as much perhaps because I could hit birds with a shotgun as because of diplomatic prowess — but that relationship failed to convince me that where international matters were concerned, the majority of them really knew what they were talking about.

In one particular, however, my sympathies were wholly with our military. Here they were, the victories over the Nazis and the Japanese behind them, commanding forces of the richest and most powerful nation in the world and now assisted by an increasingly competent ROK ally whose president hated communism with all of his passionate intensity, prevented by forces outside Korea from putting forth the winning effort that almost every general and flag officer considered both possible and desirable. Our military felt they were being asked to fight with one hand tied behind their backs and with as many glances over their shoulder at Washington as they cast north at Pyongyang.

It was also true that the Korean terrain was no boon to our mechanized equipment, for the country is an excessively mountainous and rugged peninsula. Notwithstanding control of the air by the Fifth Air Force, control of North Korean waters by the Seventh Fleet, an Eighth Army of a quarter of a million men, plus growing strength of the ROK division, Communist soldiers in sneakers, eating handfuls of rice, continued to bring up their ammunition at night on the backs of the men who would fire those same rounds of ammunition at United Nations troops the following day. Those remembering the Ho Chi Minh Trail of a decade later may have less trouble visualizing Korea, which for men trained at West Point and Annapolis — trained, in the tradition of professional fighting men, to win — was (until Vietnam) the ultimate in frustration. And the United States was far away.

I got on well with General Van Fleet, whose great talent was the training of men. Shortly after World War II, almost single-handedly, he had pulled the numbed Greeks together and had succeeded in throwing the Communists out of that country. It was a significant achievement, based on his singular ability to take a heterogeneous mix of recruits, so raw they were unable to walk across a field without stumbling over their own shoelaces, and in record time to breathe something into them that made them soldiers proud of their uniforms, proud of their flag, and eager to tackle the enemy. These same Greeks, albeit with their country ravaged by a Communist war that lasted four years after V-E Day in 1945, volunteered in 1950 to contribute to the UN effort in Korea. They flew a squadron of C-47s, many of which were almost literally held together with chewing gum and baling wire. They were fighting as much for General Van Fleet as they were for Korea.

With General Mark Wayne Clark, on the other hand, I almost immediately tangled. Our relationship, although superficially friendly thereafter, was one of raised hackles. The sufferings of the Korean people, nearly one million of whom were casualties during that three-year war, were much on Lucy's and my minds, and one aspect of their suffering produced my first altercation with the four-star commander from Tokyo. It was over the propriety of using official funds to pave the road connecting Pusan with the principal military airfield, called K-9 (and inevitably known to the GIs as Dog Field).

It was a dreadful road, several miles in length, lined on either side by pitiful and overcrowded refugee huts made of five-gallon oil cans hammered flat, used for both walls and roofing. The climate of Pusan resembles that of North Carolina, but the wind blows harder, straight off the plains of Manchuria. When it rained, this road was ankle-deep in viscous, evil-smelling mud. When it did not rain, which was the case for several weeks after our arrival, the road was equally deep in tainted dust that rose in billows from the military truck traffic flowing day and night between the city and the airfield. It was a suffocating experience to be a passenger, but the effect on the wretched refugees living along the road must have been infinitely worse, with no surcease from round-the-clock operations.

The only time the road was tolerable was on the occasions of the visits of General Mark Wayne Clark, on whose behalf army trucks would hose down the highway, just before the commanding general arrived, and again the next day, before his departure. When I tackled the general, who was our house-guest on one occasion, I received the old "Don't you know there's a war on?" treatment, and Clark declined to discuss the matter further. To this annoyance was added a further provocation because, although my embassy staff included a marine guard detachment who efficiently patrolled the residence premises at night, my army guest, with no prior notification to my wife or me, much less with our permission, arrived with an escort of MPs in Mickey Mouse boots, who tramped about on our gravel all night long. Over breakfast coffee I was constrained to observe that next time he could leave his MPs at headquarters. We parted with some coolness, but that was not the end of my highway project.

With no further reference to the Tokyo Command, I asked the Army Medical Corps to run a series of tests on the incidence of tuberculosis and other respiratory ailments here and there about the city. The results in the vicinity of the highway, in contrast to other areas of the city, were so appalling that a recommendation went forward, without mention of the embassy, for urgent work between Pusan and K-9. The road was asphalted in record time, to the surprise of General Clark on his next visit. He did not mention the matter to me, but some less respectful colleagues referred to it as the Briggs Memorial Highway.

My real row with Clark came as a result of a much more trivial incident that nevertheless seemed to me to involve a matter of principle. One of President Rhee's recurring complaints was "My war is being run from Japan," by which he meant that although the commander of the Eighth Army, General Van Fleet, made his headquarters in Korea, the overall command — the High Command — was not in Korea but in the Tokyo headquarters established in the days of General MacArthur. True, with the conclusion of the Japanese treaty and the appointment of Robert Murphy as the first postwar ambassador to Japan, the military had disgorged the beautiful embassy residence and the adjacent chancery (where MacArthur housed his famous honor guard); nevertheless, the American military headquarters in Tokyo was nothing if not huge and impressive. Nor were the Tokyo residential quarters assigned to General and Mrs. Clark exactly spartan in their simplicity. To put the matter bluntly, it was much more comfortable for our higher military authorities to operate from Japan than it was to camp out in Korea.

None of this appealed to President Rhee, who was aware of the meetings held in Tokyo every two or three weeks, attended by the military high brass, that he — the chief of state of the country primarily concerned — could not in dignity attend.

During my first talk in Tokyo with General Clark, the day he offered the *Bataan* to take us to Pusan, I was invited to be present at one of these military meetings. While I then had no feelings one way or the other about where Clark maintained his headquarters, I agreed that it would be useful to attend them as well as to take advantage of the opportunities to consult with Ambassador Murphy, a most sagacious officer who was by now a friend of long standing. When I accepted the general's invitation, he graciously offered each time to send an airplane to Pusan to transport me to and from the meeting in Tokyo.

It was a four-hour ride, Pusan to Tokyo, in a C-47, passing each way both the burned-out shell of Hiroshima and the glory of snow-capped Fujiyama. The *Bataan* took less time; and Clark's number-one plane, with equipment almost as elegant as that provided for the occupant of the White House, was a Lockheed Constellation, one of the most beautifully designed airplanes ever to fly, which did the trip in two hours and a half.

For the session, a few weeks after my arrival in Pusan, General Clark sent over his Constellation, which in addition to the suite deluxe had seats for thirty-three persons. The passenger list for that trip consisted of myself, my wife, and my secretary. The secretary was a sprite named Iryne Codon, who, after graduating from Stanford and doing a stint in beleaguered Berlin, decided she liked the Foreign Service and landed in Korea. Allan Lightner, my invaluable deputy, learning that because of the matrimonial defection of my secretary in Czechoslovakia I would be arriving without an assistant, stole

Iryne from the public affairs officer, a considerable disfavor to the latter because Iryne, in addition to being able, energetic, and tireless, was cute as a new button wrapped in cellophane.

Iryne came to see me that morning, two hours before takeoff, to say that in my outer office were a pair of exhausted and slightly bedraggled young women who were members of our embassy staff in Tokyo. They had managed — in spite of General Clark's edict against "unauthorized women in the war zone" — to sneak across for a weekend with friends, who had promised to get them back and then defaulted on that obligation. Learning of the trip of the Constellation, they were begging for a ride back to Japan before they became AWOL from embassy Tokyo. They were, declared Iryne, waving her eyelashes persuasively, really members of Ambassador Murphy's staff; she had checked their identities and credentials. She said they were respectable if slightly irresponsible young women, and — showing that Iryne did her homework — she said there were thirty-three spare seats in the Connie, not counting the quarters in the suite, all empty. Could the wayward maidens occupy two of the spare seats?

Giving the matter no particular thought, I said, "Sure," and went back to the documents on my desk. Iryne, as was proper, informed Flight Control at K-9 that there would be five embassy passengers instead of three.

Twenty minutes later my "red light" phone buzzed, and Iryne popped her head in to say, "General Clark on the line." The "red light" phone was a military scheme devised, as far as I could make out, for the specific purpose of offending our Korean allies. It was a gimmick whereby, whenever General Clark wished to make a call to Korea, all other telephone communication was automatically cut off, without warning or explanation, until the general had finished instructing, admonishing, or upbraiding some subordinate on the peninsula — or merely passing the time of day with him. General Clark had insisted on having the Signal Corps install one of these contraptions in the chancery and another in the residence, but the only time I remember using it was that morning, following General Clark's call.

The Clark conversation was brief, to the point, and unpleasant. In the tone of voice he might have used on an enlisted man who reported for duty with an unbuttoned tunic, the general informed me that he had just been apprised by Flight Control in Pusan that I had added two unauthorized passengers to fly to Tokyo "on my plane." He said he was calling to let me know that their flight was disallowed. He had authorized as passengers myself, my wife, and my secretary. No others. Period.

Keeping my temper, I inquired whether I had been correctly informed that there were accommodations for over thirty persons outside the main suite. The general replied that the capacity of the plane had nothing to do with the case, which involved the unauthorized presence in Korea of two women whose return "on my plane" he would not permit.

"In other words," I said, "the government plane now at K-9 is not at the disposal of the American ambassador, as I had perhaps naively assumed, but is regarded as his personal vehicle by the commanding general, who now proposes to dictate the passsenger list to the American ambassador."

"If you put it that way, that is correct," said General Mark Wayne Clark.

"In that case," I said, "I have two things to remark." I looked at my watch. "The only way I can attend your meeting is to fly to Tokyo as scheduled. I propose to do so. The second is that thereafter I propose to have nothing whatever to do with any airplane under your jurisdiction." And I hung up on General Mark Wayne Clark, which I am told had not happened to him since the Anzio campaign.

Next, I used the same "red light" phone to call Ambassador Murphy, who answered in a matter of seconds. Bob greeted me cheerfully, and said that he and Mildred were expecting Lucy and me to spend the night with them at the residence. He'd see me at the meeting. "And what can I do for you now?"

To my bewildered humiliation, I got nowhere with my colleague in Japan. He was sympathetic and plausible, and he conceded that yes, the two stranded young ladies were in fact members of his embassy staff. But to go to bat for them with the touchy commanding general, whose regulation they had incautiously violated, when there were national issues at stake requiring the closest collaboration between the embassy and headquarters — where was my sense of proportion? Bob said he was sorry, but he was not going to jeopardize his own relations with General Clark, which he reminded me went back a good deal farther than mine did, over a matter that, in the last analysis (meaning "no unauthorized women in Korea") was within the general's jurisdiction. End of that conversation.

Iryne again appeared in the doorway. She said my wife was waiting in the car, and that we had better be starting.

"Not," I said, "until I make another phone call. Get me Lieutenant General Sam Anderson, commanding the Fifth Air Force. He's probably at Kimpo, outside Seoul."

That connection took longer, and I realized I would probably be late for the Tokyo meeting. When I reached General Anderson, he laughed immediately.

"Look," he said, "do you know how many Eighth Army GIs I fly back and forth to Japan each day on R and R? Hundreds and hundreds of them. I don't have the duplicate of Wayne Clark's Constellation — bucket seat transportation for the soldiers. But I get them to Tachikawa in one piece, and get what's left of them back to Korea. Tell your secretary to give my aide the names of the two girls, and have them stand by at K-9; I'll have them in Tokyo for supper. And by the way," Sam concluded, "looks as though the American ambassador to Korea could use some Fifth Air Force transportation pretty soon. I'll send over a plane to bring you back tomorrow."

General Anderson was as good as his word. My wife and Iryne Codon and I flew to Tokyo in the luxurious empty Constellation, but we returned the next day in a veteran bomber, with the bomb bay doors long since sealed, and plenty of comforts for the run between Tokyo and Pusan.

At the meeting General Clark greeted me civilly enough and there was no further utilization of his transportation during the balance of our Far East association. We remained on a first-name basis, supplemented on his departure by a signed photograph with the famous Barrymore profile, but matters discussed between us were thereafter largely confined to official business.

If I have dwelt upon this episode, which I still regard as not creditable to the Tokyo participants, it is not that I considered General Clark a two-bit Douglas MacArthur, even though he did share much of the latter's egotism, vanity, and adoration of adulation. Clark was an able commander. The Far East assignment, with an unwinnable war, was a tough one and, at the moment he took over, the POW issue suddenly flared with the capture, within the prisoners' stockade, of the American brigadier who was responsible for the most hard-bitten captured North Koreans. Clark liquidated that problem with firmness and dispatch.

What stuck in my craw and remained in my memory of the incident, which I was often to recall in my military dealings during the balance of my career, was the power exercised, often arrogantly, by these three- and four-star officers serving a nation half of whose gigantic budget was soon absorbed by the Department of Defense. It was President Eisenhower, at the end of his second term, who warned his fellow citizens against the dangers of the already immense influence of the "military-industrial complex." I had merely stumbled across a minor manifestation of the self-importance bred by power, and I had not liked it. Moreover, on a far more important level, it was that same arrogant self-confidence that, notwithstanding the experiment of Korea, helped our military advisers lead the country into the far worse morass of Vietnam.

While the fighting in Korea continued, I sought to play my embassy role in the minor key suggested before my arrival, and I continued to cultivate President Rhee. This was not difficult, for I admired the old gentleman from the start, as Lucy did his Viennese wife. He encouraged me to commute frequently to Seoul for discussions with him while the work of reconstruction and repair went forward on the old American embassy residence. By then the battle line north of the capital, with the First Marine Division between us and the Communists, had become fairly stable.

One of our earliest and most welcome visitors during this period was Adlai Stevenson, who came at the president's sugggestion in the vain hope of softening up President Rhee on his opposition to an armistice, presumably by representing the United States's attitude as a nonpartisan affair. That, in the light of the campaign speech that had preceded Eisenhower's own Korean visit, seemed somewhat ironic, but Stevenson held patriotism above personal resentment and he came. The governor, whom I had known casually during his State Department service several years before, was our guest in Pusan for several days, and a more delightful companion never crossed our threshold. In early morning walks on the hillside above Pusan, we talked of the affairs of men and the things that affect them. We rarely agreed, partly because of Stevenson's persistent belief in the justice of the "rising tide of expectation," but that did not prevent the development of a friendship that grew with the years. His arguments about the rights (and the presumed virtues) of the underdog reminded me of my heated arguments fifteen years before with Larry Duggan.

Governor Stevenson's popularity with the Koreans everywhere he went touched and astonished him: Don't they know I *lost* the election?" But he got no farther than previous envoys with President Rhee, who told me he had enjoyed talking with "Mister Stevenson" because he was a gentleman, even if he did not agree with him.

In the spring of 1953 President Rhee decided, without consulting the military, that it was time to move his capital back to Seoul, and did so. I insisted on following him, greatly to the irritation of the generals, and as soon as the buildings were made habitable, the embassy moved back.

In Washington, that spring, the Republicans were organizing their administration, and the shadow of Senator Joseph McCarthy fell heavily across the Foreign Service. To their discredit, neither President Eisenhower nor Secretary Dulles intervened to curtail the senator's capacity for evil before he picked up the momentum and the publicity that were to carry him briefly to the heights of influence and the depths of depravity.

Mine was a Democratic recess appointment as ambassador, valid only until the end of the next session of the Senate unless resubmitted for confirmation. Weeks and months were to go by before I received word indicating that favorable action was forthcoming. President Trujillo had once branded me a Communist for harboring Gustavo Durán for a weekend, and Senator McCarthy had demanded that anyone in the Foreign Service with that tag anywhere in his dossier, for whatever reason, should be subject to a searching reinvestigation.

I knew Secretary Dulles fairly well, but his character remains an enigma to me. His early call for "positive loyalty" from senior officers, most of whom had received their first commissions not from Presidents Roosevelt or President Truman but from Republican Presidents Coolidge or Hoover, and who took genuine pride in the nonpolitical aspects of their profession, seemed inexplicable, and his hostility toward John Paton Davies and John Carter Vincent, vindictive. I nevertheless regarded the secretary as a friend, and the record supports that belief: he not only recommended me for three ambassadorships after Korea, but also was instrumental in circulating a gratifying number of copies of my first book, *Shots Heard Round the World,* as he swooped around the world on his indefatigable travels. Seen after the day's work, with a glass of Old Overholt in his hand, he could be a relaxed and delightful companion, and his wife, Janet, was a lady of rare charm and distinction.

Perhaps the most telling criticism of Mr. Dulles's administration is that on his travels he tried to carry the State Department around in his pocket. That cannot be done. If the premises are to function, the secretary himself must put in an appreciable part of his time "tending store" instead of constantly rushing all over the world, an inevitable victim of the effects of changes of time, gastronomy, cultures, and climate.

Finally, Foster Dulles accepted as his assistant secretary for Far Eastern affairs a disciple of yo-yo diplomacy who was to prove the most persistent raspberry seed between my teeth since the Eagle Scout from Pocantico Hills. This official, a Republican banker from Virginia named Walter Robertson, had been junior to me as a wartime "auxiliary officer" on the staff of Pat Hurley in Chungking. Because Walter was in charge of economic work, our official duties rarely overlapped, especially since it was my view that the economic problems of China were mostly insoluble, and in any case could not be tackled effectively until after the war. However, I had thought sufficiently highly of Walter's general competence to recommend him for chargé d'affaires when Pat Hurley abruptly abandoned Chungking, thus assuring him a berth the next year with the Marshall Mission.

Robertson was first and foremost a "professional Southerner," still fighting what he constantly referred to as "the War between the States" (which, to irritate him, in Chungking I used occasionally to call "the War of Northern Aggression"), but what rendered Walter an impossible chief was his habit of misinterpreting any opinion at variance with his own as insubordination, coupled with his propensity for rushing abroad at the dropping of a code group. Upon arrival at a foreign capital, he would try to take the play away from the resident representative, thus often affecting the prestige and future usefulness of the envoy as well as creating more confusion than progress. Since his Far East bailiwick at the time extended from Karachi to Seoul, the area afflicted by his meddling was considerable. I found this somewhat tiresome, although my relations with President Rhee by the time of Walter's first Korean visit were sufficiently firm to remain unaffected. Robertson was also a strong Chiang Kai-shek man, reportedly remaining convinced throughout the Eisenhower administration that someday the G-mo would return in triumph to the mainland.

Assistant Secretary Robertson appeared in Seoul shortly after the Stevenson visit, possibly to verify my reports or to smoke out whether I had neglected to record something of importance. He was accompanied by the assistant secretary of state for public affairs, the genial Carl McCardle, a personal friend of Secretary Dulles. Certainly two more incompatible individuals could not have been fitted into one airplane, and Walter Robertson was scarcely speaking to his traveling companion by the time they reached Seoul, to which Lucy and I had just moved. We were still on a camping-out basis, using GI utensils and plates, kindness of General Maxwell Taylor, who by then had succeeded General Van Fleet. We installed Robertson and McCardle as roommates in the single guest room of the residence. To Walter's relief, Carl shortly went off to inspect the troops.

The elderly president did not take greatly to Robertson, who was guilty of the discourtesy to me of trying to negotiate with Rhee without the American ambassador present. Rhee used to send me word via his foreign minister, Mr. Pyun, concerning what had occurred so that I was able to anticipate the contents of Robertson's first-person telegrams to Secretary Dulles. But Robertson got no further with the old gentleman than previous visitors had, even though he thought he had obtained an assurance that when an armistice was signed, Rhee's ROK troops would not violate it. I doubted whether that was what the president had meant, and was on the receiving end of a rebuke for my obtuseness when a "qualifying statement" by President Rhee reached us. It left matters almost exactly as they had been before the Robertson conversations, although I was privately of the opinion (shared by General Taylor) that bluster though he might, President Rhee had little intention of committing his troops to the suicidal venture of attacking the Communists without American support.

I did, however, derive one substantial dividend from the Robertson/McCardle visit. Carl McCardle expressed astonishment when I told him that unless my appointment was confirmed by the Senate by the end of the session in July — and it was now well into the spring of 1953 — one ambassador to Korea would be out of a job. He volunteered to look into it on his return to Washington. He did not tell me what steps were taken, but a few days before the Korean armistice was finally signed, my nomination was confirmed, along with that of my equally nonpolitical contemporary Fletcher Warren, who had gone to Turkey in circumstances similar to mine.

Before the armistice was agreed upon, however, President Rhee was to create one further crisis that threw Washington into an uproar because it threatened, in Potomac opinion, to terminate the negotiations with the Communists at Panmunjom. Throughout those long, drawn-out talks the Communists had persistently sought to use the POW issue as a bargaining counter, a maneuver with which our military found it difficult to cope because in previous twentieth-century wars POWs were live bodies, captured during the course of hostilities, exchanged sometimes as a matter of mutual convenience while hostilities continued, but more often held until the war ended, when each side delivered its POWs to the other side under a formula designed by the victor.

In Korea there was to be no victor; besides which, a Communist war is an ideological war that goes on and on regardless of what the parchment says. And the Communists had reached the conclusion, which proved erroneous, that from the POW issue they could derive substantial political advantage.

The prisoners themselves were divided into four groups. First, on the Communist side, the Americans, plus a few other UN soldiers, most of whom had been captured by the Communists during the Allies' ignominious retreat from the Yalu River in December 1950. Then, on our side, the captured Chinese "volunteers," who were in stockades on the island of Cheju, fifty miles off the south coast. They gave relatively little trouble, and in the end most of them elected to go to Taiwan rather than to return to the utopia of Mao Tse-tung and his jolly agrarian reformers — clearly a blow to

Communist expectations. Third, the North Korean Communist prisoners, who included the hard-core, Soviet-indoctrinated leaders. They were on a different island, also off the south coast — tough, disciplined Comrades; they were the ones who captured and endeavored to hold as hostage the American brigadier general guarding them.

A final group, about twenty-five thousand strong, was likewise made up of North Koreans, most of whom had not espoused communism. They were the farm boys and industrial workers who had not enjoyed the Russian occupation or the rough Communist dictatorship that followed. They had been thrust into uniform when the North Korean levies were being organized. They were housed on the mainland, and President Rhee's agents had circulated extensively among them, convincing themselves (and the president) that those prisoners ought to be set free. Many in fact had indicated their intention, if freed, of enlisting in the growing ROK forces. This fourth group of POWs was guarded by ROK troops, whereas the Chinese and the pro-Communist North Koreans were in the hands of the Americans. In theory, of course, everyone, including President Rhee's ROK guards, was subject to the United Nations Command now exercised by General Taylor.

One fine spring night, without anyone's authorization but his own, President Rhee ordered his ROK guards to open the stockades in which the twenty-five thousand anticommunist North Koreans were confined. They were invited to come out and disperse. Inasmuch as these men promptly discarded their uniforms and insignia, by daylight they had melted into the general Korean population, impossible for United States or any other non-Korean forces to identify. It was a coup, the success of which, from Rhee's point of view, was total.

With respect to that triumph I was amused. General Taylor — his military command flouted — was annoyed, but Washington (especially Walter Robertson and the Pentagon) became almost hysterical with rage, inflamed on receipt of General Taylor's and my telegrams confirming the impossibility of rounding up those whom Rhee had set free.

General Taylor and I went together to admonish the president, our telegraphic instructions smoking in our pockets, but the only satisfaction we had from the old gentleman, warming his stiffened fingers around his teacup and wearing the unrepentant expression of the cat that had swallowed the canary, was the statement that his action ought to have been taken long ago. Our cabled report to Washington was not soothing to the recipients.

The Communists at the conference table at Panmunjom, except for increasing for several days the decibel level of their vilification, did nothing. In the end, the POW problem was settled by a complicated formula whereby the Communists hoped, if not to reap propaganda, at least to save face. The main point was that each individual POW could elect to remain with his captors or to return to his original side. To accomplish this, some five thousand Indian troops were to be brought to Korea by ship. They were to be assisted by a Neutral Nations Supervisory Commission made up of representatives from Switzerland and Sweden, who were in fact neutral, and Czechoslovakia and Poland, who were not.

The last weeks before the armistice saw the fiercest fighting since the Ridgeway offensive of 1951, inspired this time by the Communists, who were seeking — not without some measure of success — to counter the American claim that "aggression had been repelled; therefore our objective has been achieved. The Korean War was a success." The war in fact ended in a stalemate with the Demilitarized Zone or dividing line between North and South Korea closely approximating the 38th parallel that the Communists first crossed on June 25, 1950. Future historians, surveying the ravages of the so-called credibility gap that became a feature of the Vietnam War in the next decade, may decide that the gap was conceived in the official declarations of the Eisenhower administration following the armistice signed on July 27, 1953.

Generals Clark and Taylor came to luncheon with Lucy and me that day, after the signing ceremony at Panmunjom, and a more dismal pair it would be hard to imagine, even though each officer had probably done all it was possible to do, given the limitations imposed by instructions from Washington.

Secretary Dulles arrived in Seoul a week later, bearing a defense pact highly favorable to South Korea, since it committed the United States to intervene on behalf of the ROK if that country were again attacked and, in the meantime, to continue to maintain United States troops on the soil of the Republic. Its purpose was clear: to warn North Korea against future adventurism and to placate President Rhee.

Even though President Rhee did not carry out his threat to upset the armistice with ROK troops, he did almost everything else to show his contempt for that agreement, including forbidding the transportation across ROK territory to the Demilitarized Zone of the five thousand Indian troops who would handle the exchange of prisoners. As a consequence of this intransigent act, the Indians had to be moved from their ship to a United States aircraft carrier, and thence by American helicopters, the largest troop movement by chopper up to that time. Fortunately for the operation, the Indians were commanded by General Thimaya, a Sandhurst graduate of superior competence.

The Indian presence involved me in one of my fiercest altercations with the State Department. I report it not because of its influence on events (which was nil), but because it so clearly describes how *not* to conduct American diplomacy. While the Indian troops were at sea, approaching Korea, I was startled to read in the press that my colleague from New Delhi proposed to visit Korea. Ambassador George V. Allen made this announcement on the eve of his departure from India by air. I knew Allen well and considered him something of an articulate lightweight except in matters of personal publicity. He was several years my junior in the Foreign Service, but even if that situation had been reversed, elementary politeness coupled with bureaucratic common sense would have indicated advance communication with Seoul to ascertain the views of the incumbent ambassador in Korea. Instead, the visit had been cooked up between Assistant Secretary Robertson and Ambassador Allen without any reference whatever to the views of Seoul.

These views were now made known by cable in prose of unambiguous vigor. I demanded that George be diverted to Tokyo, where I would meet him. I did so on the neutral territory of our embassy (now in charge of Ambassador John Allison, who had succeeded Ambassador Bob Murphy when the latter was assigned to the State Department).

I pointed out that it was my responsibility, and not Allen's, to deal with President Rhee; that the whole situation with respect to the armistice was not yet stabilized and was still in precarious balance; and that no possible profit could be achieved by having the American ambassador to India suddenly barge into the affair, the details of which could not possibly be known to him.

"How would you like it," I concluded, "if I suddenly announced I was flying to New Delhi to help settle the problem of Kashmir?" In George's presence I dictated a telegram to Washington, reiterating my objections to his Korean adventure. Ambassador Allen then dictated one of his own, referring to his previous correspondence with Robertson (which had not been repeated to me) and declaring that it would be "highly embarrassing" if, after the public announcement in New Delhi of his "mission to Korea," he should return to India without having visited the Indian troops and without making a courtesy call to discuss Indian matters with President Rhee.

Washington — that is to say, Walter Robertson — promptly cabled back, supporting Ambassador Allen. Still refusing to have any part of this imbecile charade, I did the opposite of Achilles sulking in his tent: during the two days George Allen spent in Korea, I remained in Tokyo, cheerfully drinking sake and eating Japanese goodies with my close friend Jeff Parsons, number two in Allison's embassy, and his spirited wife, Peggy. In Seoul, Lucy put Ambassador Allen in the embassy guest room. I returned, unappeased, just as he was leaving. As predicted, he accomplished nothing.

The armistice and the defense pact naturally marked important milestones in the relations of the embassy with the ROK government. The Pentagon, after maneuvers to which once again I was not privy, persuaded the State Department that the nonmilitary aid program — a vast and impressive design for the rehabilitation and the industrialization of the Republic of Korea — should be initially under the military, "to be gradually phased into embassy control." Here was a situation with as many built-in booby traps as the Communists were installing on their side of the Demilitarized Zone. In other hands that multibillion dollar aid plan could have left the unhappy American ambassador to Korea in permanently boiling oil.

Better things awaited me. General Clark had retired to The Citadel to teach the Charleston boys to do squads right, and his replacement in the Tokyo High Command was four-star General Ed Hull, a gentleman in the Omar Bradley mold, who was helpful in every aspect of our relationship, which soon became close, cooperative, and friendly. It was, furthermore, my everlasting good fortune that the program itself was placed in the honest and capable hands of C. Tyler Wood, a friend from my last tour of duty in the State Department after World War II. Max Taylor continued in command of the now shrinking Eighth Army on the peninsula.

Ty Wood's, Max Taylor's, and my views did not always coincide, but our recommendations for action — sometimes relayed to Washington for approval — were never reached without open discussion among ourselves, frequently followed by a joint call on President Rhee.

I emphasize "joint," for the old gentleman developed an uncanny ability to identify the point at which divided views might lie. He endeavored to exploit such situations by inviting us in, one or sometimes two at a time, hoping to face the third with a fait accompli. President Rhee never took it amiss, however, when having invited General Taylor to discuss some military matter loaded with economic or political gunpowder, the general would turn up with Briggs and Wood in attendance. "Since it would doubtless save time," General Taylor would say politely, "to have my colleagues learn directly from Your Excellency what are the President's views . . . ."

These matters moving peacefully along, I had hoped for some slackening of business, with a larger proportion of my time spent round the rice paddies flushing Korean pheasants, but again I counted without Washington. Who should appear in the autumn of 1953 but the vice president of the United States and Mrs. Nixon, making an official visit during which they invited President and Mrs. Rhee to go to Washington in mid-1954? A more comfortable guest room had been completed before their arrival at the embassy; however, the best we could offer the Secret Service man was a cot outside their door, while his off-duty mate slept on a mattress down the hall, outside the kitchen.

This was one of the first of the foreign safaris undertaken by those in high Washington position and, like nine-tenths of the ones I participated in, witnessed, or studied, it was largely a waste of time and money. Not much money, to be accurate, for in those days propeller planes were still in use, so over-water hops were long and tedious, with much fatiguing noise and vibration. A decade later, with jets, there were backup planes in case the first one should conk out, and separate planes for armored limousines and for newspaper correspondents, as well as advance parties to scout routes and accommodations, to install special communications equipment, to confer with brother "security personnel," and generally to act like a battery of power drills at a busy intersection, oblivious to the traffic of either the host government or the host public.

That 1953 Nixon visit was muted by comparison, with the vice president not even boasting an accompanying staff, and the pleasant and unobtrusive Mrs. Nixon learning to cope with the trappings of power and acting as her husband's secretary. Vice President Nixon himself, still apparently involved in the aftermath of the Hiss case, spent a good deal of his limited unscheduled time trying unsuccessfully to reach Washington by telephone, for purposes not explained. He was not a person who projected the easy warmth of Adlai Stevenson — but then, few people did.

President Rhee naturally sought to capitalize on the vice presidential presence, and the spontaneous demonstration that he organized between Kimpo Airport and the capital, complete with schoolchildren in colorful Korean costume waving little American flags, might have aroused the envy of the Benefactor of Santo Domingo himself. I do not recall that any official business of great moment was transacted, but the Korean president was flattered by the attention and rank of his guests, as well as by the invitation conveyed on behalf of President Eisenhower to visit Washington the following year. During the Nixon visit Rhee behaved in exemplary fashion, with no threats about tearing up the armistice even though he continued to view that instrument with implacable distaste.

The year 1954 saw a conference at Geneva that mired the United States more deeply in Vietnam but did little for the other half of the agenda, which was converting the Korean armistice into a treaty of peace. That failed largely because the North Koreans balked at UN supervision of elections, aware that in an honest count not one Korean in ten would vote for Communist domination.

The visit of President Rhee to the United States in 1954 was a personal success. He received a prolonged ovation at the joint special session of Congress in his honor. In contrast, little applause followed the "North to the Yalu" declaration in his speech, in which he reiterated the conviction that the only solution that would prevent the Communists from again attempting to dominate his country was to expel them by force. To the extent that he may have become convinced of American apathy toward renewing the Korean War, that trip may have served a useful purpose, as well as constituting a tribute to a brave and patriotic man. Certainly in New York, at the United Nations, as well as in Washington, President Rhee was received with the admiration and respect he deserved.

In Korea itself, his "On to the Yalu" exhortations to his troops had an amusing culmination. It was the president's custom, at fairly frequent intervals, to accompany the commanding general on trips to inspect the troops who remained along the south side of the Demilitarized Zone long after the fighting had stopped. On those occasions he often addressed the soldiers and expressed most graciously in English the gratitude of his country for the timely assistance rendered in 1950, without which the ROK might have been overwhelmed. President Rhee did it well, his command of English being almost perfect, and the picture presented by the indomitable old leader was an appealing one. Having spoken in English, he would turn to General Taylor, and with a most humble and ingratiating smile would ask if he might now say a few words to his troops in their own language, "because not all of them have learned English." He would then make a speech in Korean that invariably evoked loud cheers. President Rhee had been accustomed to follow this sequence since the days of General Ridgway, who preceded Van Fleet, who was followed by Maxwell Taylor.

Taylor was a most unusual soldier by any set of criteria, and one of his talents was languages, which he seemed to pick up with extraordinary speed and facility. As a captain he had been a Japanese language officer in Tokyo in the 1930s. Somewhere along the line — he was a paratrooper with an enviable World War II combat record — Taylor had found time to learn German, French, and Spanish, so that it did not seem unnatural to him, when he was given the Korean command in 1953, to have a crack at that language. For a whole year he spent his lunch hour working at the difficult and complex language of the Land of the Morning Calm. He never claimed great fluency, but soon he could follow a speaker and recognize the general content of his remarks.

President Rhee, unaware of the progress the general was making, used two carefully prepared patriotic speeches when he addressed the troops. The English one, described above, invariably produced genuine applause. The second speech, in Korean, was to the effect that notwithstanding faint-hearted allies, who, although he was grateful to them for their initial support, had declined to back up his demand for victory, his country would know no real peace until the hated Communists were ejected by force and Korea's white flag with the sacred red and blue yin and yang flew over all the territory from Cheju to the Yalu. Prolonged cheers.

After listening to these dual efforts on a number of occasions, General Taylor remarked to the president one day that, being a student of languages, his work had convinced him of a remarkable truth: the extreme difficulty of rendering in one language exactly the thoughts expressed in another language, even though the speaker commanded a high degree of proficiency in each.

The diminutive president did not bat an eye. But thereafter, when General Taylor was present with him on the platform, the Korean speech was a closer approximation of the one just made in English. It was definitely a score for General Taylor.

Thus passed the first year after the fighting stopped. At Panmunjom all sorts of arguments continued to simmer and not infrequently to boil, so that at one time Secretary Dulles sent his senior law partner, Arthur H. Dean, to cross verbal swords with the Communists. On this occasion the latter became so insulting that Dean walked out on them — a favorite tactic the Communists had not expected to be used against themselves. Dean thus earned much stature. Dean's adventures, flowing in part from the fact that Secretary Dulles insisted that the Pentagon accord him the assimilated rank of general, may someday be made of record, preferably by the principal protagonist. He was one of the few "special emissaries with assimilated rank" who, in my experience, accomplished anything worthwhile, if it was only to leave the Communists grinding their teeth over having been beaten at their own game.

It should not be inferred that what little I myself accomplished in Korea was done without a more than adequate supporting staff. My first deputy and close friend, Allan Lightner, was succeeded by Niles Bond, an exceptional drafting officer from New England, who was in turn followed by Carl Strom from Iowa, a serious-minded mathematician who knew about cybernetics as well as diplomacy.[1]

My political officer, Arch Calhoun, was as able as any man in the Foreign Service. So much so, in fact, that much later, when the good Christian Herter succeeded Foster Dulles as secretary on the latter's death in 1959, at which time Arch was completing his term as Herter's special assistant, I connived with the secretary against the Personnel Board to wrest Calhoun from the European Bureau to serve with me in Athens.

It is a matter of continuing pride to me that no fewer than five of my colleagues in embassy Seoul were to become chiefs of mission, each in due course in charge of an embassy of his own.

My economists, the mysteries of whose craft often escaped me, worked well with their military opposite numbers and later with Tyler Wood's assistants, thus relieving me of many chores and burdens. Iryne, mowed down by ambition-plus-romance, soon satisfied both undertakings: she went home to law school, became a practicing lawyer, and married a lawyer in California. Her successor, Moselle Kimbler, abandoned diplomacy for a responsible position in one of the great foundations, thus paving the way for Emma Drake, who had been Jim Penfield's secretary in Prague in 1949. On her transfer from Prague, Emma had been incautious enough to volunteer that if I ever needed a secretary, she would like to be considered. She served with rare devotion and efficiency, first in the final months of my Korean assignment and then at the three ambassadorial posts that followed.

1. Bond, who came to us from Tokyo, fared badly in Korea, in that Syngman Rhee, who could be as unreasonable at times as he was benevolent at others, reached the unjust conclusion that because of his Japanese service, Bond was pro-Japanese. Nothing could have been further from the truth. Furthermore, it was Niles Bond who wrote the first draft of perhaps the most reckless telegram I ever signed: one denouncing the program, instituted because of fear of Senator McCarthy, to fumigate United States Information Service libraries abroad of "ideologically objectionable books." My protest against that pusillanimous folly, dispatched to the State Department while I was still a recess appointee and before President Eisenhower's book-burning twitter at Dartmouth, was leaked by someone to Joe Alsop, who gave it such wide and favorable publicity that, as I look back on it, I am surprised that the unclean demagogue from Wisconsin did not declare a personal vendetta against me.

My Korean experience is as rich in memories as those provided by any of my sixteen posts, too many to recount all. There is the story of Chung Kook Sung, the embassy chauffeur, who, when waiting at Kimpo with a dozen American military drivers who wanted to know "How many stars does your boss rate?" pointed to the Blue Jack on my fender, that then being the ambassadorial emblem, and shattered his colleagues, whose sedans carried two, three, or at the most four stars, by replying: "Forty-eight stars."[2]

There was the work that my wife did in helping organize Korean war widows into a guild whose handicrafts Lucy arranged to have sold at the army and air force stores, to the delight of many a veteran's household in the United States today; and my daughter's extracurricular labors on behalf of a children's hospital; and the orphanage sponsored by a company of tough American MPs who became so interested in the success of the venture that when the company was moved to the front, a member would return to Seoul by motorcycle once a week and report to his friends on how things were going with the youngsters.

There were the many hunts that I had, and the spirited Korean friends that we made, and the delights of the changing seasons, and the charm of our ex-imperial garden with an immense azalea so brilliant in color it seemed impossible that heat as well as brilliance did not emanate from its heart. There was the persimmon tree behind our house, its leaves gone by November but the fruit still ripening — bright orange against the pale blue sky.

The other day I reread my Korean chapter in *Farewell to Foggy Bottom*, published ten years before this is written. With most of my conclusions I would still agree, except that I now doubt whether the push to the north, toward the narrow waist of the peninsula (which, if achieved, would have given a basis for the "We have repelled aggression" thesis), would really have been, militarily and politically speaking, a feasible proposition. However, the 1953 stalemate probably did encourage the Chinese and perhaps embolden the North Vietnamese, but beyond that lay the deep frustration of the American military, who wanted a chance in Vietnam to prove that, given the resources, the defeat of a distant Asian enemy could be assured. That frustration derived from Korea, and with the propellant accorded the military by the 1947 legislation that created the National Security Council (according it

2. Chung's daughter received her medical degree from the University of Pennsylvania; one son graduated from Dartmouth and Yale; and three other sons — one of whom was valedictorian of his high school class — graduated from Harvard.

and the CIA preponderance over the State Department in advising the president), led us into the tragic mess in Southeast Asia.

By the end of 1954 rumors began circulating that I was up for transfer, and at a chiefs of mission meeting in Manila early the following year, Secretary Dulles asked me if I would accept Peru — a polite way of imparting the news that I would soon return to the post where I began my service as vice consul in 1926.

Although sorry to leave our Korean friends, we were pleased at the prospect of Lima, and a few weeks later we paid a farewell call on President and Mrs. Rhee at their island retreat at Chinhae. It was a fine spring day and the president, having caught a mess of little fish that morning, was in a benevolent and reflective mood. Lucy wore her best Korean dress, with the white silk bow at the shoulder, below which the president pinned a decoration, reading for her in English the citation that acknowledged her friendship and her work with the Korean women whose husbands had been killed in the war.

To me, remarking that he was aware of the regulation of my government forbidding the acceptance of decorations, he gave a lacquered cane with a dedication in Hangul, done in inlaid mother-of-pearl. The cane is too fragile for use in New England, but it makes a talking point with snowbound visitors.

As we ate his little fish, of which he was mightily proud, I thought of the simplicity of this elderly gentleman, twenty years beyond the age at which most men retire (I remember a speech he made once on his birthday: "Now that I am seventy-eight — or eighty-seven . . . ."), who almost single-handedly guided the fortunes of a nation of more than twenty million people, a nation for whose independence and welfare he had struggled since he was a teenager in the nineteenth century. But instead of reminiscing about his achievements, he asked questions about Peru, and seemed genuinely interested in the answers. Then he made a prophetic observation:

You have often been instructed to reproach me for my declaration of the "Rhee Line," sixty miles offshore, within which Korea does not permit the Japanese to fish. I know your government is angry with me for using patrol boats given by the United States to form a Korean Navy to enforce that declaration. Perhaps sometimes my judges have been harsh with the Japanese fishermen apprehended within my line, even though perhaps those judges cannot forget the forty years when not a single Korean fisherman was permitted to fish anywhere off our own coastline. Now the situation has changed and we think that Korea, a poor country, has a right to the resources off our shores, which resources the Japanese have been destroying faster than they can be renewed. We are putting a stop to that and it is the right thing to do.

Now I don't know Peru, but I read the weekly magazines from the United States, and I see that Peru now believes as Korea does, except that the Peruvian government goes three times farther than we do. Peru has declared a *two hundred-mile* limit and I expect your government is three times as angry as it is with me.

President and Mrs. Rhee accompanied us to the wharf when we prepared to return to the mainland for our last night in Seoul. We were sad, for in the probability of things, it was doubtful whether we should see that strong old gentleman again.

"One final thing," President Rhee told me as we shook hands on the jetty, beside which was tied his diminutive fishing boat. "Tomorrow morning, when you fly from Kimpo Airport, do not be surprised not to see American soldiers. I have arranged for an honor guard of Korean troops. Korean troops only. They will salute you in my name as good friends of Korea." He and Mrs. Rhee stood waving on the pier as our launch surged away from them.

Two days later, having fought off the Bureau of Inter-American Affairs, which wanted me to reach Lima day before yesterday, we sailed from Osaka for San Francisco on the SS *President Wilson,* our ambition to make a Pacific crossing by ship at last on the way to fulfillment.

After Thirty Years

Peru

The State Department to which I returned in 1955 was a different place from the one I had left in the closing days of the Truman administration. It was much worse. Compared with its condition today, it was possibly an ideal establishment — taut, tidy, and sophisticated (instead of sprawling, uncoordinated, and full of "grievants") — but in the three years I had been in Korea, the entire top echelon had been replaced, the department was suffering from absentee management, and a blight known as "Wristonization" (after Henry Wriston, the former president of Brown University, who had chaired the committee that bore his name) had defoliated the permanent staff, hordes of whom had been forced into the Foreign Service. The State Department was to spend the next several years "dedesignating" — as the quaint bureaucratic word had it — several hundred of those home office slots, and many of the former occupants returned to Foggy Bottom.[1]

I bade an untearful farewell to the Far Eastern Bureau and reported for duty to Henry Holland, assistant secretary for inter-American affairs. Henry was a sharp Texas lawyer, bilingual in Texican Spanish, with whom I had a slight acquaintance dating back to his work as an auxiliary officer during the war. He was a staunch private enterprise man, and we got on well during his Washington exposure.

The first thing I found out, as I sat in Henry's office admiring the photographs of his predecessors, was that President Rhee had been right, as usual. The reason for Potomac grumbling over my having returned from Korea by ship, instead of flying back, was that the State Department was running a fever over the pretensions of Peru (abetted by Chile and Ecuador) not only in claiming a two-hundred-mile limit for fishing rights, but also in enforcing that claim by seizing a foreign fishing vessel on the high seas. An extortion-

---

1. Those interested in this undertaking are referred to *Anatomy of Diplomacy*.

ate fine (the equivalent of several million dollars) had been levied against a whaling ship recently intercepted 180 miles off the Peruvian coast.

A stop had to be put to that sort of nonsense, declared Henry, and he had Secretary Dulles's endorsement of a plan to send me immediately to Lima to tell President Odría where to head. That accomplished, Henry assured me, I would be instructed to return to Washington "for consultation," after which I could take my overdue leave. And how soon could I depart for Lima?

That sort of hazard often catches up with officers when they switch from one jurisdiction to another. The accompanying cliché is invariably "That is one of the exigencies of the service." So I told Henry Holland, yes, I could take off practically at once, and that an early autumn vacation would be eminently satisfactory. But I said I wanted one thing understood in advance: I thought the chances of persuading the Peruvian government to abandon its stand on fishing rights were not good. In fact, they might be microscopic.

"What makes you say that?" demanded my new assistant secretary, not without irritation. "In international law Peru hasn't a leg to stand on."

"In international law, maybe so, maybe not," I answered. "I'm not a lawyer. But, just the same, General Odría may think he's riding a wave of the future. Furthermore, he may believe justice is on his side." I pointed out that Peru is a relatively poor country, and its west coast all the way from Tumbes to Tacna is desert, except for the little rivers, often hardly more than trickles, where the irrigation system of the pre-Incans hasn't been much improved. Subtract sugar and cotton in those valleys and the petroleum wells around Talara, and the "riches of Peru" were mostly stolen by the Spaniards during the first century after the conquest, or else they lie locked in the Andres, or on the Atlantic side of the cordillera. For another example, history's accumulation of guano was mined out in a single generation but the birds are still there, attracted by millions of little fish, anchovetas, which also represent the principal food of the big tunas and marlins. Peru has no continental shelf. The ocean is thousands of feet deep within sight of land.

"Besides," I said, "we taught the Peruvians to fish. Back in the late thirties, when it looked as if the European war might spread and the United States might be asked to feed some of the Latinos in exchange for wartime cooperation, we sent to Peru a special mission organized by the Bureau of Fisheries. We — the United States — got the Peruvian fish-meal industry started. Now it's one of their most important assets.

"Or take the tuna fishing," I went on. "That needs capital, which Peru lacks, and expensive ships designed since the war, with all sorts of gadgets, some of them developed by the Japanese. How would we like it if we were the Peruvians and a fleet of those big California tuna operators, using vessels and equipment we couldn't afford, started taking fish right in our own front yard, and even coming into our ports to buy the bait used to deplete one of our few natural resources?"

I laid it on fairly thick. Because of my hassle with the president of Korea over his "Rhee Line" and the seizure of Japanese vessels, I had done my share of homework on the so-called Law of the Sea. I found it to be complicated, and the more I studied it, the more it appeared to include a lot of tarnished legends, to which the United States itself had contributed during the "noble experiment" of American Prohibition (1919–1933).

Being immersed in Asian affairs, I had not paid much attention to Peru and its claim to a two-hundred-mile limit, but following President Rhee's tip, I had visited our consulate in Osaka, where I accumulated a pile of documents on fishing problems worldwide. These I had not only studied aboard ship but discussed with Admiral Raymond Spruance, a fellow passenger, who had added to a brilliant naval career a stint as ambassador in Manila. For twelve days the Spruances and the Briggses shared a table on the *President Wilson,* to our pleasure as well as my profit, for as head of the Naval War College after World War II, the admiral was abundantly familiar with maritime limits and jurisdictions.

So in a sense I was laying for Henry Holland, and while I did not object to deferring my leave or taking on the president of Peru, I did not want the State Department to experience any false euphoria about the chances of success. I also had a premonition that Peru might be right, not on the two-hundred-mile limit (that seemed excessive to me) but on the general proposition that a coastal country should enjoy a preferred position with respect to the fishery resources off its own shores, and for a great deal farther out than the three-mile limit or the twelve-mile limit.

At 7 A.M. three mornings later, in the chill mist of the early Peruvian winter, I reached Limatambo Airport, after an all-night flight from Miami. The first to greet me was my old friend from Prague, now the Brazilian ambassador to Peru, Edgar Fraga de Castro, proclaiming loudly, first in English and then in Spanish, for the benefit of adjacent listeners, that the airline ought to be fined for scheduling an arrival at so horrible and indecent an hour. After that blast, Fraga presented to me a nervous Peruvian protocol official, who made the proper little official speech, concluding with the welcome information that the foreign minister would receive me with the office copy of my letter of credence on the afternoon of the following day.

Around us, as the mist lifted, were the gray-brown hills I remembered, and the unforgettable smell of the dust of centuries on the parched land, mingling with the scent of things growing under irrigation from the Rimac River. So much of the river's flow is skimmed off, above the capital, that only a fraction passes beneath the bridge beyond Desamparados Station, on the far side of the City of Kings.

It is a gamble to return to an environment once cherished. Places change with the years, as do individuals. What may have charmed a vice consul in his twenties is not necessarily the favorite fare of an aging ambassador. Yet in our service one retains a special attachment for a first post — be it Haiti or Finland or Thailand — and after a few sniffs of that Peruvian winter air, I felt at home again. It was a satisfaction, too, six years and two posts removed from our hemisphere, to be able once again to understand the language of the country. To me, Peru is still the most varied and interesting place in South America, and I planned to visit dozens of corners of it, exploration of which as a junior official had been beyond me. I was happy to be back.

In 1955, in keeping with Lima's imperial colonial past, when it was the most important city in the Western Hemisphere, the presentation of credentials was still a colorful event, featuring the gorgeous old viceregal coach, a horse-drawn museum piece done in satin and gold, which after independence in 1824 was refurbished and sent to fetch each arriving envoy from his residence to the Plaza de Armas and the Presidential Palace. For escort we had a company of mounted dragoons, in plumed and polished helmets, in uniforms handed down from the victories of General Sucre and the obeisances of Simón Bolívar.[2]

In my vice consular days nine-tenths of the political and commercial life of the capital was concentrated in that small area between the Plaza San Martín and the Plaza de Armas, the center of which was the old Hotel Maury with its high ceilings and immense gilt-framed mirrors that in the nineteenth century reflected the elite of Lima. The city houses of the aristocracy, some containing more than half a dozen patios one behind the other, surrounded the inner city. The most ornate of these, and one of the most

---

2. In 1969 a revolutionary government, made up largely of left-wing military crackpots, abandoned the viceregal coach as being undemocratic. Since then the arriving ambassador, encouraged to wear a business suit, has been taken to the Presidential Palace by automobile.

beautiful of all Spanish colonial buildings, is the Torre Tagle Palace, three blocks off Girón Unión, which now houses the Peruvian Foreign Ministry.

The meeting with President Odría, a diminutive general who received me in uniform, his sash of office conspicuously present, went as I had anticipated. That is, insofar as the two-hundred-mile limit was concerned, the president was as prepared for me and my representations as I had been for Henry Holland. Better, for whereas Henry had casually mentioned that the British were "equally interested," my deputy, Clare (Tim) Timberlake[3] had told me, and the president now confirmed, that the interest of the United States had initially been inspired by London, following Peruvian action against a Greek-owned whaling ship. The American tuna ships, the president reminded me, were already taking out Peruvian fishing licenses when they called at Peruvian ports for bait. That also was true, but they were doing so under mounting protest and beginning to wail loudly to their congressmen about it.

The story of the whaling vessel, owned by Aristotle Onassis, was that this far from unsophisticated owner, hearing of Peru's two-hundred-mile limit, had included in the coverage of his vessel by Lloyd's of London protection against the vicissitudes of that limit, which few then took seriously. Months later his ship was overtaken by a Peruvian warship and escorted to Callao, the port of Lima, where a nationalistic judge assessed a maximum penalty — payable by Lloyd's.

The anguish of the underwriters having been conveyed through the Board of Trade to the British Foreign Office, and thence through simultaneous representations to the American ambassador in Great Britain and by the British ambassador in Washington to the State Department, the bureaucrats of the Potomac awoke to the seriousness of this new hazard on the west coast.

---

3. Clare Timberlake, an honest and courageous official, was the victim of a bad roll of the dice. He left Peru with my recommendation that he was chief of mission material. Appointed by the Eisenhower administration as our first ambassador to the Congo, he quickly (and accurately) decided that Patrice Lumumba and his merry men, to whom the Belgians were turning over the reins of power, were not capable of their sensible use. Saying so to the incoming Kennedy administration, represented on African matters by the ineffable G. Mennen "Soapy" Williams, whose idea of diplomacy was to don native costume and make like a paramount chief, got Timberlake fired from Kinshasa (ex-Leopoldville). He retired without receiving a further appointment — a waste of superior material.

President Odría, from Tarma, high in the Andes behind Lima, was a tough little soldier-turned-politician. We sat on an uncomfortable and ornate viceregal sofa following the presentation of my credentials, which he quickly handed, unopened, to the chief of protocol. In a statement more eloquent than mine to Henry Holland, the president made a plea for sympathetic understanding of the *necesidades,* as he termed them, leading Peru to take a step without which her fishery resources, the extent of which had been recognized internationally only since the war, could be irremediably damaged by foreign vessels traveling from thousands of miles away. Floating factories, he called them, fishing on what they claimed were the high seas but actually often within sight and hailing distance of the Peruvian shoreline. The two-hundred-mile limit, he declared, was irrevocable. He hoped that I, whose reputation as a friend of Peru had preceded me, would make Washington understand that there was no anti-American sentiment behind his government's decision, only the imperatives of self-preservation.

"I understand that you," he told me, "come from the northeast part of your country called New England, where fishing is also important. Your country recognizes sometimes three miles and sometimes twelve miles. But what would you *norteamericanos* say if Russian ships started taking your lobsters and your codfish just outside Boston?"

We parted amicably in a flurry of *Vuestra Excelencia* and *Señor Embajador,* and I promised to convey to Washington the views he had expressed, at the same time voicing the hope that until some sort of amicable accommodation could be devised, his government would recognize the difficult problem that Peru was creating for the United States. I had been with the president so long that the press pounced upon me when I emerged. They were not altogether satisfied when I told them that since I had been an official of my country in Lima a quarter-century before, there had been many things of mutual interest to discuss.

I returned to the embassy in a thoughtful mood, wondering about the extent to which my own plea for forbearance had been accepted by President Odría and mentally beginning to draft a telegram that I foresaw might give Henry Holland and the sea lawyers of the State Department little comfort.

While awaiting an answer to my report, I started my official calls and embarked on a number of diplomatic chores that would save time on my return. The Timberlakes were well informed. Between them, Tim and Judy commanded six or seven languages, including fluent Spanish, and Tim was an energetic, self-confident officer who had long since learned his way around. He said that administrative problems at the embassy were especially irritating. Too many people. The State Department seemed to have no spine in dealing with other Washington agencies sponsoring cockeyed projects, each resulting in more drones in the hive. I said that was an old story, going back to the days of Nelson Rockefeller; I agreed that no tick clings with greater tenacity than the superfluous bureaucrat. I urged him to do his best, and I would back him up. As to the chancery being too cramped — I'd prod the buildings people in Washington; I understood they had plans for a new chancery closer to the residence.

Our head economic man, Tim went on, was a serious, hardworking officer with a thorough knowledge of his job, but he was a "Wristonee," worthless as economic counselor because he could not speak Spanish. I said to encourage him to take as many hours of Spanish lessons a day as he spent at his desk.

One of the attachés had a drinking problem. In his cups he had been heard loudly denouncing "the natives" in public places where many understood English. Suppressing the impulse to say "Fire the bastard," I suggested that Tim warn the offender that the new ambassador was a so-and-so "who ate attachés before breakfast." If that didn't straighten him out, we would take steps on my return.

And what to do about fine old Dr. Giesecke, who knew more about Peru and its archaeology than most Peruvian professors? Since passing the mandatory retirement age, Don Alberto had been employed on a year-to-year basis, renewable every twelve months by the ambassador personally. I said to rehire him, in my name. That was a good decision. When Arnold Toynbee, the great British philosopher-historian, came to Peru, he insisted on spending so much time with the American cultural attaché that the British ambassador, a stuffed shirt, was vastly annoyed.

In other words, we had the usual run of matters that afflict any Foreign Service undertaking. The midcentury difficulties were exacerbated by the crusading spirit that was shortly to produce the ultimate imbecility, the Peace Corps.

I dined *en famille* with the Fragas, catching up with the gossip about all our Prague friends, including the report that Ben Rogers, our former colleague in Prague, was coming to Lima as Canadian ambassador. How Fraga knew that before the Peruvian government, I don't know, but the Brazilian diplomatic service, from the nineteenth century well into the twentieth, was by far the best in Latin America and one of the best in the world. Its officers were highly trained professionals who, although sometimes giving the appearance of dilettantism, kept themselves remarkably well informed on the countries they served in. Fraga, still cursing Panagra for the seven o'clock arrival of its planes from Miami, was a case in point: his family owned large, profitable chunks of the state of Pará at the mouth of the Amazon, an area he rarely visited. He was educated in Europe. His French, English, and Spanish, fluent and frequently profane, were nearly perfect. His enchanting wife, Celina, spoke German. If there was anything about Peru that escaped them, probably President Odría had not yet thought of it.

A colleague of that caliber can be of much help to a newcomer. Fraga was gracious enough to congratulate me on my handling of the two-hundred-mile business, adding that he had already recommended to Itamaraty, the Brazilian foreign ministry, that Brazil consider some similar step, which he predicted would be generally adopted within a decade. (He missed it by ten years: the United States in 1974 tardily joined the procession.)

I spent an afternoon with Timberlake's predecessor, John Paton Davies, whose eviction from the Foreign Service I regarded as a blot on the Dulles administration. John declined to discuss his dismissal with his Peruvian friends, who were uniformly sympathetic. Remaining in the country, he was starting a furniture factory, a wildly improbably venture that nevertheless prospered. Six years later, when I was briefly in Lima accompanying Adlai Stevenson, I failed in my effort to convince John that with the advent of the new management, he ought to apply for reinstatement. I was saddened by his decision not to do so.

I called on Slim Faucett, finding only the debilitated shell of the cheerful American mechanic who came to Peru in the early 1920s and was the first man to fly an airplane over the cordillera from the Pacific to Iquitos, Peru's Amazonian port six hundred miles east and twenty-five hundred miles from the Atlantic. That feat earned Slim almost as much local prestige as Lindbergh was to achieve, internationally, by his New-York-to-Paris flight in 1927. On the strength of increasing confidence in airplanes, Slim Faucett then organized, and for thirty years headed, the Peruvian airline that still bears his name, as good an example of American drive and ingenuity coupled with local confidence as one could find in Latin America. Now Slim looked old and was gravely infirm, but he seemed glad to see me. We had often upended a pisco sour together in the days when he was outlining his plans and raising money for his first single-engine plane, at about the time Harold Harris, with Grace and Company and Pan American Airways backing, was founding the international carrier that became known as Panagra.

At Slim's suggestion I was to spend ten days on the eastern fringe of the cordillera, flying to Pucallpa in one of his excellently maintained DC-3s, unpressurized but with oxygen brought to each passenger through a tube connected with a central tank. This began on signal from the pilot when he reached ten thousand feet, still far below the jutting peaks of the Andes. At the same altitude the captain and crew donned portable oxygen masks for the crossing.

The eastern foothills of the Andes, nearly three thousand miles from the Atlantic, are as lovely as any land that I know, rich and fertile valleys and uplands, where a farmer can grow anything agriculture can name and live in a climate at once stimulating and benign. Only one problem: the market lies on the other side of the mountains and few of the producers of the Peruvian *montaña* could pay even the reduced rates that Faucett Airlines quoted.

It took me two hours to fly to Pucallpa on the Yurimaguas River, an Amazon tributary, altitude six hundred feet above the level of the distant Atlantic. It took me six days to return by jeep and automobile via Cerro de Pasco, with its copper mines, and the Central Railroad of Peru, which at Ticlio nearly touches sixteen thousand feet, from which the descent to Lima is precipitous and spectacular.

Messages from Washington, churlish in tone, awaited me. My failure to persuade President Odría was a disappointment to the maritime stalwarts in the State Department. They were still being chivied by our British friends, bruised by having to pay Aristotle Onassis the amount of the fine levied against his whaling ship, and by the increasingly vocal representatives of the big California tuna clippers who had to choose between possible confiscation and the stiff Peruvian license fees.

This dilemma was repeated to me, fortissimo, when I paused in Washington at the beginning of my overdue vacation. We had a splendid leave, interrupted only by a pleasant ceremony in Groton, Connecticut, where Lucy was invited to lay the keel of a brand new Peruvian submarine.

As we prepared to return to Lima, it was suggested that we pause for two or three days in the Canal Zone for discussions with the commanding general, Caribbean Command, who was responsible for the operation of our military missions in South America. That I was happy to do, because Quarters One at Quarry Heights was occupied by Lieutenant General Harrison, the lay preacher who had outlasted the Communists at Panmunjom, and had received the Panama command as a well-merited reward. It was valuable to receive an overall picture of the Pentagon program, with which I did not entirely agree. Harrison, however, was the sort of officer who encouraged frank discussion. He was well aware that military missions, a decade after World War II, did not always attract the best officers, many of whom preferred to be nearer the center of things, meaning the United States or Europe. He said that if I found anyone within my jurisdiction who did not measure up to my requirements, a personal note would effect a change without the delay and red tape involved in going through official channels. That was a generous concession that I told him I would use sparingly; I remain grateful to a fine officer and a good friend.

In addition to wiping the eye of the General Accounting Office by using four airplane berths for two people, Miami to Panama and Panama to Lima, thus paying them back for swindling my bride out of a steamship ticket twenty-seven years before, I was able to be of some unexpected use to General Harrison during our visit. Juan Domingo Perón, dictator of Argentina and destroyer of its economy, had finally been overthrown. He fled, first to Paraguay and then to Nicaragua; he was en route to the latter haven when we reached Quarry Heights. Perón's plane had radioed for permission to land at Allbrook Field in the Canal Zone, and he was getting closer at the rate of five miles every minute.

General Harrison was disturbed, and nothing I volunteered about Perón reassured him. He was reluctant to pass the buck to Washington. I could imagine the tizzy in my old bailiwick in the State Department if they suddenly received a call from the Pentagon: Should we let Perón land in the Canal Zone, or should we not? The ex-dictator was still a ticking bomb with an explosive following in many countries, and it did not seem that involving the Canal Zone in possible demonstrations for or against the discredited leader of the *descamisados* was likely to advance the interests of the United States. My host agreed, but time was pressing.

"Why not close Allbrook Field," I suggested, "and let him land in the Republic of Panana? You can explain that Allbrook is now entirely military and that the facilities on the Panamanian side are adequate. In fact, to hear the Panamanians tell it, their commercial field is the best in the Caribbean. If they want to give Perón an honor guard or if they decide to throw him in the clink, we couldn't care less, and our government would not be involved."

So Juan Domingo Perón did not light down beside the Panama Canal. In the Republic of Panama he embarked a female passenger, and they became the uninvited guests of the Somozas in Nicaragua, who soon encouraged them to leave for Madrid — which is a separate story. Telling Perón "no" on landing at Allbrook Field got the general off the hook, and he was grateful to me for the suggestion.

When I first saw Lima, it was a city approaching a quarter of a million people and there were only two paved roads outside the city, one connecting

Callao with Lima (a toll road built by an American company for the centenary of independence), and Avenida Leguía (now Arequipa), originally named in honor of then president, from Lima to the southern suburb of Miraflores. A paved road to Chosica, a resort village up the Rimac Valley at above two thousand feet, was completed in 1928, the year Lucy and I reached Lima as bride and groom. The hitherto sleepy Chosica, geared for half a century to the comings and goings of trains, had the most elegant houses near the tracks so families and friends could exchange greetings from verandas and from the car windows of the Ferrocarril Central del Perú. The place had long since burst at the seams, encouraging the growth of a sort of suburbia all the way down the widening valley. Lima itself, with over four times the inhabitants of the 1920s, was now ringed by the slum huts of Indians lured off their native altiplano by tales — largely false — of easier living near the capital.

Now, in 1955, the Pan American Highway was paved for its entire coastal length, Ecuador to Chile, and lateral roads were being pushed into the interior, including one paralleling the railroad, already ruining the passenger business of the railroad company.

But the overriding problem of Peru, just as it had been when Ambassador Poindexter outlined it to me a generation earlier, was still the Andean Indian: often sullen when faced with a culture not his own, frequently exploited (although never so cruelly as under the Spaniards), repeatedly a prey to demagogues of the left, continuing to multiply faster than the halting economy could advance, and thus condemning a growing proportion of the Andean inhabitants to a miserable, marginal existence. The deteriorating efforts of successive administrations to mesh democratic self-government with the machinery created by geography, Spanish colonization, and the indigenous population were responsible for the political tensions, of which I was to experience merely preliminaries: the twenty-first century inexorably intruding itself into the twentieth.

The embassy residence, on land acquired before 1930, when Ambassador Moore had tried, without success, to persuade the State Department to buy an adjoining cotton field in order to give the diplomatic premises breathing space, was already as close to "downtown" as the rented Barreda mansion had been in the 1920s, when downtown had been the Plaza San Martín, two hundred yards away. Nevertheless, we moved into our new home with satisfaction, with a covey of servants inherited from my predecessor, the good Harold Tittman, whose fortune it had been to serve as ambassador to Peru during the previous seven years. I doubted if we would stay that long. It seemed to be my lot to be forced to play musical chairs, but that did not obscure the pleasure of our return to the City of Kings, in September 1955, early spring.

We found ourselves sliding smoothly into a life we enjoyed, in a profession that had now claimed exactly thirty years, more than half my life. Many old friends were still in the Rimac Valley. The young mayor of Lima, who genially officiated at the marriage of numerous American couples heading for the Andean mines, which ceremonies I witnessed and then certified in my official consular capacity, was now a senior senator, and still genial. Maggie Conroy, as Peruvian as Bernardo O'Higgins was Chilean, who thirty years before had taught Sam Reber, Jack Cabot, and me Spanish for an hour each day, was still driving golf balls, but at a new course miles from the Lima Country Club, which had become the center of a residential district. Bob Koenig, who as a junior mining engineer with the Cerro de Pasco Copper Company had been fired by the manager, had returend as president of the company.

The Timberlakes were presently transferred to Buenos Aires, a promotion for Tim, and they went with our blessing. Assistant Secretary Holland was good enough to let me choose as Timberlake's successor Henry Dearborn, of proven worth and diligence; we had known him and his wife, María Rosa, in Washington. The noxious attaché was removed, kindness of General Harrison, and his replacement fitted well into our official family. The economic counselor, the "Wristonee" who came knowing no Spanish, was at last becoming intelligible to the people with whom he was working.

The forces slowly fermenting within the Republic were responsible for most of the problems that faced me. They turned out to be three in number. The fishing problem I was lucky to keep from boiling over, but it remained unsolved and capable of erupting, lava-hot, at any moment. Here, relations with the Peruvian Navy, which for over thirty years had been assisted by one of our earliest naval missions, proved a valuable factor. Both the prime minister and the foreign minister during my incumbency had been Peruvian admirals who knew and had confidence in the United States. They were as uneager as I was to see our two countries come to blows over the maritime issue.

The protection of the rights of American capital abroad next claimed my attention. That did not arise in the acute form of expropriation during my Lima service, but I was nevertheless aware of it after the first ride we took in the automobile we had acquired on our way from San Francisco to Washington, after our recent Pacific crossing. The car ran splendidly in the United

States, and at the end of our leave we shipped it to Peru, but the first time we tried to take it uphill to Chosica, the sound from under the hood was that of empty bottles being shaken together.

Peruvian gasoline, I discovered, was 70 octane. Our automobile had the usual American high-compression engine, demanding an octane rating many points higher. I had ordered the car while we were still in Korea but I had neglected to say where it was to be used. Dismayed by its performance, I invited in the Lima manager of the International Petroleum Company, a Canadian subsidiary of Standard of New Jersey.

I told the manager that I had first been to Talara in northwest Peru in 1926, then the first Peruvian port of call. I had gone ashore to visit the desolate company area, part of which I found deserted because the foreign personnel had swarmed aboard the *Santa Luisa* to enjoy such amenities as the vessel provided during its call at that barren port. Various petroleum installations were then abuilding, along with houses for the staff, on the headland a mile from the town. Talara evidently had not changed since the colonial era: an impoverished fishing village, huge on the edge of the continent near where the Humboldt Current meets the warm flow called El Niño, spinning out of the Gulf of Guayaquil. Behind Talara, on the Sechura Desert, were the oil wells.

"And what," I asked, "is all this about 70 octane gasoline?"

My guest could not have responded more positively had I been a dentist poking an exposed nerve. "Of course we could make high octane gas," he told me. "And we do, for export. But because the Peruvian government is afraid to buck the Union of Chauffeurs, the local price has been frozen. The highest octane we can make at that price, and break even, is what you buy at the pumps. About 70 octane. I know, with your high-compression engine, that when you put a strain on the motor — going uphill, for example — it sounds like you have a case of Coke bottles instead of your horsepower.

"But," he continued, "you are one of the lucky ones, Mr. Ambassador. Most people who are stuck with high-compression engines have to take the motor down and put in new gaskets. Reduces the efficiency of the engine and is not always successful. But you have an air attaché with an airplane. Borrow a few gallons of this 100 octane avgas and mix it in a proportion of three gallons of ours and one of his. You'll be amazed at the difference."

I accepted his recipe, and my car perked up. Thereafter I investigated his story. It was as he had said: the Union of Chauffeurs was a Communist-dominated organization with enough trained characters shouting for nationalization to make the government cautious. There had already been one destructive strike with rioting and burned cars and threats of violence at the refinery. It was a part of the familiar anti-capitalist conspiracy; in the demagogic appeals to nationalism, facts were distorted, the truth was ignored, and the real interests of Peru were betrayed.

I found the record of the company singularly good. Before investing, more than thirty years earlier, it had carefully investigated title to the producing area, even to the point of submitting the antecedents to the Peruvian Supreme Court, which endorsed the enterprise. The amount of money needed was considerable, and since Peru did not possess that kind of capital, it came from North America and was entitled to a fair return. The policy of the company in its relations with Peruvians had been sensible and enlightened. At the beginning, the ratio of foreigners was comparatively high, local technicians being unavailable. But as the project developed, the company actively encouraged Peruvians to participate. By midcentury the percentage of non-Peruvian personnel was minimal. Even as early as 1930 the Lima manager was not from North America; he was a Colombian engineer whom I remembered with respect.

In the IPC compound outside Talara, what house an employee occupied depended on his rank in the company, not on his nationality. Membership in the club facilities was not restricted. By now practically the entire payroll was Peruvian. And the benefits to the little fishing village of Talara, which I had found so squalid in 1926, were extended in all directions as roads multiplied and gas stations sprang up, and the Republic of Peru became motorized and motor-conscious. Peru owed a debt to the International Petroleum Company, not the other way around. And now the company was being prevented by self-styled patriots from making a product commensurate with the engineering advances that had occurred during its lifetime.

I was reminded of President Leguía's troubles at Callao when he tried to build modern port facilities to replace the antiquated discharge into lighters, half or three-quarters of a mile offshore. The ships were served by launches whose owners were members of a fiercely radical union that fought so viciously against the port improvement project that the government finally bought them off with lifetime pensions. The inflation following the Depression wiped out most of the value of the pensions, so the *fleteros* did not win much, except that they had established a dangerous precedent of being paid for doing nothing.

This background is included because in 1967 an anti-American, left-leaning Peruvian government did expropriate the International Petroleum

Company, its action accompanied by the customary barrage of false charges and unproved allegations with the stamp of Moscow upon them. Secretary of State Dean Rusk, inert about almost anything that did not have to do with Vietnam, should automatically have applied to Peru the provisions of the so-called Hickenlooper Amendment and let the hemisphere chips fall where they might. Rusk did nothing. His successor in the Nixon administration, even more inert than Rusk, accorded more importance to "hemisphere relations" than to American rights.

My high-compression automobile fared as badly as the company, and much sooner. The embassy chauffeur, with little understanding of the workings of an internal combustion engine, decided by himself that if a mixture of one-quarter avgas and three-quarters local gasoline was good, reversing the proportions would be four times as good. Thus his stature would be enhanced and he would be honored for his independence and ingenuity. The result was burned-out valves, and my chariot was disabled for an extended period.

Meanwhile, I was seeing little of the president of Peru, who was busy scheming to defeat the constitution and get himself an additional term of office, but not receiving much support from the military, which suspected him of seeking to establish a dictatorship. General Odría was sufficiently cordial when I met him at official functions, but the mutual rapport that existed between me and the chiefs of state in Uruguay and in Korea (and was conspicuously absent in Czechoslovakia) was lacking. Nor was the handling of my next problem calculated greatly to soothe the official to whom I was accredited.

In the middle of the Peruvian summer of 1956 — early that calendar year — my wife and I were on the point of departing on a trip to Cuzco when President Odría announced he had uncovered a plot against his government. He accused one Pedro Beltrán of heading the conspiracy. Without trial Beltrán was imprisoned on the desolate, guano-covered island of San Lorenzo, south of Callao harbor.

Pedro Beltrán was an Oxford-educated Peruvian citizen who had served with distinction as ambassador in Washington shortly before becoming prime minister in the immediately preceding government. He owned Montalvan, the great cotton hacienda in the Cañete Valley, one hundred miles south of Lima, where Harold Harris in 1927 had conducted the first spraying of cotton by airplane in South America. More important, Beltrán was the owner-publisher of La Prensa; it and El Comercio were Peru's two leading newspapers. Finally, Pedro and his American wife were our intimate friends.

For an American ambassador to make representations because of the treatment by the Peruvian government of a citizen of Peru was to court the kind of rebuff no sensible ambassador wants to experience. Busybody diplomacy, which has since been adopted by Washington as if it were a prime asset in the conduct of foreign affairs, was still looked upon with some suspicion. Yet decency, justice, and friendship all clamored to be heard.

The only peg on which I could possibly hang an official interest, albeit one that might readily be misinterpreted as interference in Peru's internal affairs, was that Beltrán, in addition to publishing *La Prensa,* published on the same presses the Latin American edition of the *New York Times* — a venture later killed by international postal bureaucracy, but at that time in full swing. The Inter-American Press Association and the *Times* were already demanding that Pedro Beltrán be freed.

And so, first warning the State Department of my intention (in one of those "in the absence of instructions to the contrary, I propose" telegrams, the purpose of which was to permit Washington to head me off if it wanted to), I went to see not the foreign minister but the prime minister, Admiral Saldías, who had been a lieutenant commander when I was in Peru with Ambassador Moore. I did not go to the prime minister's office, where my presence might have caused speculation on the part of the local press, but to his home. And I told the admiral that I came not as "el embajador norteamericano" but in my private capacity. That was clearly eyewash, because in the country of his accreditation an envoy has no "private capacity," but Saldías took it in stride. I went on to point out the potentially destructive effect on the relations between our two countries caused by the incarceration of his own predecessor in office, a man only slightly less known and respected in the United States than he was in Peru itself.

Saldías was a civilized human being. He must have known the fanciful nature of the charges brought by President Odría against Beltrán, and have suspected the impact of that vindictive action not only in the United States but also in other countries of the hemisphere. I do not think he was enthusiastic about my intrusion, but he heard me out politely, merely commenting that the problem was much on his mind.

The extent to which my expression of interest facilitated Beltrán's release, after several weeks of imprisonment among an unlaundered aggregation of common criminals, can only be surmised. I hope it helped. Miriam Beltrán was kind enough to say she thought it did. In token thereof I have long been the possessor of a signed photograph that I immediately tagged the "Hemingway Beltrán" — it was taken when the ex-prisoner was still wearing the luxuriant whiskers that sprouted during his incarceration on that rainless, treeless island, with no ration of water for washing, much less for shaving.

In the wake of these events, we were still settling in and enjoying the Peruvian summer — a delight of brilliant sunshine by day and clear, cool nights beside the chill Humboldt Current. Our Canadian friends, the Rogerses, arrived, and Ben in his turn rode in the viceregal carriage on his way to present his credentials. With the Fragas we promptly established a club for the revival of our shared Prague memories, much to the amusement of our respective staffs. It was in those contented circumstances that I unexpectedly received a special emissary from the secretary of state.

He informed me that I was slated to go to Brazil as soon as James Dunn, the incumbent, should choose to retire. That would probably occur soon, because legislation had been enacted creating the grade of career ambassador, a new title to represent the topmost run of the diplomatic ladder. Just as career minister outranked Class One and the rest of the professional hierarchy, so career ambassador was to be reserved for a very few officers.

Jefferson Caffery and Norman Armour, whose names would have lent added distinction to any first list, had already retired, but Secretary Dulles insisted that Jimmy Dunn, whose service included ambassador to Italy, France, and Spain before Brazil, and who had entered the Foreign Service at the end of World War I, be one of four officers to be raised to the new rank before his retirement. (The others chosen were Loy Henderson, Bob Murphy, and Doc Matthews, each of whom deserved the honor.)

So scarcely eight months after I first returned to Lima, we were about to be moved across the continent to Portuguese-speaking Brazil, our fifteenth transfer. We had hoped for at least three or four years in Peru, but Brazil was Brazil, more than half South America and larger than the United States before the statehood of Hawaii and Alaska. A professional did not turn down that kind of assignment.

The emissary was Cecil Lyon, himself soon to be appointed ambassador to Chile, where we had served together on the eve of World War II. I told Cecil that it would be a privilege to accept the embassy in Rio de Janeiro whenever the Dunns decided to leave and the president decided to make the appointment. Cecil emphasized that in the meantime mum was the word, for there were the mechanics to be followed, and premature publicity was not one of them.

Those proceedings took several months, with additional days to wind up my Peruvian affairs, making it fifty-three weeks from the presentation of my credentials to the time of our departure. Fraga did not learn of Foggy Bottom's intention until the request for my *agrément* was made by Washington to his government in Rio, shortly before the nomination was made public. To say that he soundly berated me for not telling him sooner would be tautology, inasmuch as anything Fraga did was accompanied by sound effects. In fact, he denounced me in Spanish, English, and Portuguese, which last he declared I was not smart enough to dominate — an accurate prediction. He nevertheless must have given me a clean bill of health to his government, because Brazil granted the *agrément* with gratifying promptness. Fraga likewise informed me, in confidence he said was undeserved, that he was shortly to be transferred as ambassador to Sweden.

As things worked out, by departing almost simultaneously, Fraga and I were to save the Lima diplomatic corps the cost of two farewell banquets. Being senior to me on the Lima diplomatic list, Fraga produced a remarkable speech. His oratory was built around the premise that I had deliberately remained in Peru long enough — exactly one year plus one week — to be eligible to receive from the corps one of those big, handsome plates of softly shining Peruvian silver. They were costly objects, having the coat of arms of Peru on one side and the facsimile signatures of all the other chiefs of mission on the other. With rising prices, the "quota" payable every time an ambassador departed became so onerous that a one-year rule was established, the purpose of which, declared Fraga, was to keep out the short-term pikers.

"But *colega* Briggs," Fraga shouted, "has beaten the game. He has stayed in Peru one extra week when he could, I am sure, have left Lima a fortnight ago and saved you all that money."

At the time my nomination to be ambassador to Brazil finally became public, Lucy and I were in the midst of entertaining, in the embassy residence, an improbable assortment of guests. We had simultaneously under our roof, which fortunately was capacious, the American vice admiral who commanded the National War College (his two dozen wards on their annual outing, colonels and navy captains and a few civilians, were distributed around the town); Marian Anderson, whose voice and whose human warmth we had so greatly admired in Korea, who was touring South America under cultural auspices; and Mary Hemingway, whose husband was at Cabo Blanco, the famous fishing club beyond Talara, hoping to catch a marlin. Marian Anderson's accompanist took his meals with us but lodged in a hotel.

We gave a reception for the admiral and his colleagues, inviting the Peruvians we thought they should meet, with Marian Anderson and Mary Hemingway as added attractions. We gave a dinner party for Marian and

Mary, with the vice admiral and his aide as added attractions. And, those agreeable chores accomplished, I fled for a weekend at Cabo Blanco, for I had not seen Ernest (considerably knocked about by two airplane accidents, three days apart) since a party on Gardiner's Island when Winston Guest rented it, back in 1947. Ernest's current project was to hook one of those giant black marlin of the Pacific, and to provide footage of the struggling fish jumping for a film of his epic *The Old Man and the Sea,* being done by Warner Brothers. That would then be spliced into shots of Spencer Tracy and his little boat off Cojimar, near the north coast of Cuba. Ernest was assisted in this enterprise by the old Cuban fisherman from his boat, the *Pilar.* His *viejo* was the prototype of the Old Man of the story.

I leave for another occasion an account of those sunbaked days, eight or nine hours a day, in the long Pacific swell half a degree south of the equator and five miles off the Rainless Coast, and of the four marlin caught during Ernest's stay of a month, two of which were gaffed during my visit, including a monster that weighed 1,075 pounds. That was not a record — someday someone hopes to boat a one-ton fish — but it was still a giant thing of iridescent beauty, fabulous to see. But not one of the four jumped out of the water, and since Ernest was not to be in the picture, the only return on the Cabo Blanco investment was the big fish itself, which was stored in the freezer in the nearby town of Paita until the shark season started. When the sharks began running, the marlin was carefully thawed and roped to a craft identical to the Cuban fishing boat of the Old Man. The theatergoers who thrilled at the picture were watching Spencer Tracy, plus Ernest's biggest fish being torn to shreds by sharks, not in the Gulf Steam but on the edge of the Humboldt Current, three thousand miles from Cuba.

And so, although we saw no American tuna clipper, nor any whaling vessel, and no Peruvian patrol craft, my departure from Peru, like my coming the year before, had to do with the high seas and high adventure.

"It is always a good idea," said Ernest, "to quit while you are ahead."

World Power or Fumbling Giant?

The hardest weeks I can remember, since studying for the Foreign Service examinations with Angus Crawford in 1925, were those I spent trying to absorb Portuguese for seven hours a day in the State Department language school.

Portuguese is a beautiful Latin language, with a great richness of conjunctives and conditionals, but if you approach the tongue as I did, with thirty years of intermittent Spanish behind me, almost every word is offbeat. The best I was able to do — even by following my State Department immersion with a daily 8 A.M. session after I reached Rio de Janeiro, was to memorize a five-minute extemporaneous speech to be used again and again with a few nouns and verbs changed, depending on whether I was dedicating an atomic reactor, replying to a toast pledging inter-American solidarity, or accepting a gift of Bahia *charutos*.

I felt better about it when I discovered that my Spanish-speaking colleagues in Rio, with the exception of the Uruguayan who lived next door to Rio Grande do Sul, made no effort whatever to learn Portuguese. To my Peruvian and Venezuelan and Mexican colleagues, Portuguese was nothing more than *español mal hablado* — Spanish badly spoken. On the other hand, I have yet to meet the Brazilian diplomat in a Spanish-speaking land who did not speak excellent Spanish.

Of my briefing in Washington not much stuck, probably because of my language preoccupation. Henry Holland was on the point of bowing out as assistant secretary for Latin America, and no successor of comparable talent was in sight. The premises were left for months in the hands of his deputy, the inexperienced and well-intentioned Dick Rubottom, who the following year was selected for the appointment. He tried diligently to be of assistance to me in Brazil, and in fact he often was.

My most vivid Washington recollection is of a luncheon given for me by Eugene Black, the formidable head of the World Bank. The purpose was to warn me against the debt-incurring propensities of Brazil. According to my host, Brazil was in hock up to its ears but already clamoring for more credits, which, he said, no sensible private banker would grant in such circumstances. That was possibly true, but Brazil, a nation of sixty-five million people in 1956 (which was to pass one hundred million less than twenty years later), was hardly a private customer. Brazil was a country that was clearly going places, even if a sympathetic foreigner did occasionally wonder whether the Brazilians themselves knew in which direction.

Brazil turned out to be — for all its improbable and sometimes incredible achievements in architecture, in music, in road-building, in urban and rural development, and, perhaps most significantly of all, in multiracial living — the Land of Original Snafu, including chaos cheerfully multiplied by confusion.

Consider some unrelated samples that occurred during my own experience: one had to do with my reception as ambassador and another with international finance.

On my arrival in Rio I was not received by President Juscelino Kubitschek because he was in Panama attending a convocation of presidents, an affair promoted by President Eisenhower for no useful or intelligible purpose. In the absence of the Brazilian chief of state, I presented my credentials to the vice (and acting) president, João "Jango" Goulart, a left-wing *político* one of whose few redeeming features was that, coming from the southeast corner of the country close to the Argentine and Uruguayan borders, he could be conversed with in Spanish instead of my still inadequate Portuguese. That ceremony completed, I was ushered into the president's private elevator, which would take me to the street level and the saluting troops. But the nervous operator pushed the UP button by mistake. Two floors above the Catete Palace state reception room I had just quitted, the elevator door automatically opened upon the president's private dressing room, revealing a startled acting president standing on one foot, pulling off his striped trousers and displaying cerise silk shorts. An unnerving experience but a fitting introduction to the rest of the script: later that day at the international airport, on the arrival of President Kubitschek from the presidential conclave in Panama, Vice President Goulart would duly present me to the president of Brazil, thus completing the protocolary requirements for official recognition.

The reason for this complicated scenario was that thereafter everyone would attend a reception in honor of the visiting president of Argentina, General Aramburu, in the embassy of Argentina. It seemed a somewhat roundabout way for the president of Brazil and me to meet, but as a newcomer I was prepared to do as I was told.

So, divested of my credentials-presenting regalia, I, in due course, hied myself to the international airport at Galeão, then a forty-minute drive from downtown Rio, only to find a amiable, unruly mob of several thousand of President Kubitschek's political adherents waiting to greet the returning chief of state. No one met me, and once incautiously out of my official automobile, I was swallowed up by churning humanity and unable to penetrate to within one hundred feet of the disembarking president, who shortly drove away behind a motorcycle escort of special police with red caps secured under the chin and huge crimson balloon tops that quickly filled with air as their speed increased.

Later that day I did meet my new chief of state at the Argentine embassy. The Argentine ambassador presented the American ambassador to the president of Brazil in a room where the two presidents and their host, plus an occasional favored visitor, had repaired for refreshments. While sharing a *copo de champanha* we were joined by José Macedo Soares, the dignified and experienced Brazilian foreign minister, who was horrified to learn of my airport "ordeal," as he termed it. He considered the whole Goulart idea of an airport greeting as the height of undignified folly that he would have blocked had he known of it in time. The foreign minister was a gentleman of the old school of Brazilian diplomacy that produced the Baron de Rio Branco and a long line of illustrious successors who added to the stature of the Republic. Macedo Soares did not believe in airplane travel, mingling with crowds, summit meetings, or the invasion of professional diplomacy by amateurs. We got on very well together. Only in Brazil could the formal reception of a foreign envoy depart so far from the norms of official behavior, with everyone involved blithely unaware that there was anything unusual about it, or that all might not come out happily in the end — though in this case it did.

The scene now shifts to the American embassy residence, on a Friday evening of Brazilian midsummer, eighteen months later. It was the weekend immediately preceding the famous Rio de Janeiro Carnaval. Much has been written about that gaudy three-day *festa* that ends on Ash Wednesday, when Lent shuts down upon the havoc of seventy-two hours of fun and games, with many of the participants not having been to bed (except for purposes other than sleep) since the preceding Saturday. Most of what is written about Carnaval in English emanates from advertising firms along Madison Avenue on behalf of cruise tours, omitting reference to the suffocating heat of Rio in midsummer, the incessant noise, the aroma of hot bodies, and the interminable processions of costumed samba dancers.

The gentry of the capital flee the surroundings of Guanabara Bay well before the celebrations begin, taking refuge at Petrópolis and Teresópolis, resorts inland from Rio de Janeiro where at two to five thousand feet above sea level the air is soft and stimulating, instead of torrid and soggy.

My wife and I had planned a Carnaval away from Rio, only to be deflected by a telegram from Washington reminding me that the *Caronia*, queen of the round-the-world cruise ships of the 1950s, was spending those three days in Rio harbor, with certain citizens aboard who had claims upon the hospitality of the United States representative to Brazil. My grumbling about the *Caronia* turned out to be superfluous, because who should wish to visit me that Friday night after dinner but his excellency the finance minister of Brazil, José Maria Alkmin, a politician from the president's home state of Minas Gerais, who understood less about finance — domestic or international — than any fiscal official with whom I had dealt during the past thirty years.

I avoided Alkmin whenever I could, sending my treasury attaché to the Finance Ministry, but that attaché had left Rio for the holidays, so I received the finance minister in my paneled private study in the embassy residence at 10:30 that night.

I could guess what the minister wanted, but not the amount. The Brazilian government desired the loan of $30 million, to be available Wednesday— Ash Wednesday — morning. And would I kindly telegraph a message to Washington to his friend Robert Anderson, secretary of the treasury, requesting that the corresponding arrangements be made? And could he use my phone a minute?

When I indicated the instrument on my desk and made as if to leave the room, the finance minister waved me back.

"Friends do not have secrets," he said.

The minister then proceeded to ask for the international operator, and placed a call to the Brazilian ambassador in Washington, Senhor Amaral Peixoto. The call came through so fast I suspected a setup; they talked for forty minutes, in a Cariocan jargon that left me not much wiser than before except that Peixoto was "vigorously to supplement the friendly efforts of Senhor Briggs, *o embaixador americano* — from whose home, the minister repeated several times, he was calling.

It was after midnight when I saw my guest to his waiting automobile. And where, I asked, could I reach the minister when I had a reply from Washington?

"Oh, at the ministry. Just call my office," was the airy reply, as though a substantial installment of the thirty million was already in Alkmin's pocket.

I routed out the duty officer and, while that sleepy colleague was en route to my house, I composed the promised telegram, trying to keep my communication as deadpan and factual as possible. It was after two o'clock when I got to bed, thankful for the air conditioning.

On Monday night my wife dragged me to a samba parade followed by the dreadful Municipal Ball, featuring fantastic feathered costumes under burning lights and TV cameras. The reply to my telegram, filed that afternoon in Washington, came as I was wearily getting into bed.

The reply was, as I had anticipated, a turndown but a politely sympathetic one, tactfully suggesting that if the crisis were as serious as represented, why not pledge some of the Brazilian government's gold that, Secretary Anderson understood, was on deposit in a New York bank in an amount in excess of the $30 million allegedly required. (I deleted "allegedly" in the translation I made for Alkmin.)

I then spent all day Tuesday — the final frantic day of Carnaval — in futile efforts to find his excellency the minister of finance. Tuesday night I had a Portuguese-speaking member of my staff telephone the residence of the president of the Republic, with the result that I found myself invited to appear at Larangeiras Palace, the presidential residence in Rio, at nine the following — Ash Wednesday — morning.

Next day, as the embassy automobile stopped at the presidential doorway, out popped not a uniformed flunky but José Maria Alkmin, who led me immediately to the long *sala* where President Kubitschek was already waiting. I handed the Portuguese translation of the Anderson telegram to the president.

The two Brazilians read the message with gloomy faces. They had possibly been warned of the contents by the Brazilian ambassador in Washington. Then the president got to his feet and began pacing up and down the *sala*. Without reference to our turndown, the president embarked upon a speech about the economy of the country. He dwelt specifically on the need to retrench, to eliminate unnecessary budget items, to come to grips with inflation, and to scrape unavoidable expenses to the bone.

The president would tolerate no more sloppy accounting. The word would go forth today, the very beginning of the holy period of Lent — here Kubitschek paused to cross himself — to all the ministries and agencies of his government. Everyone, even the private citizens, would have to take heed and to be governed accordingly.

That was the general purport of a performance lasting for six or seven uninterrupted minutes, accompanied by wide forensic gestures. I watched goggle-eyed, for President Kubitschek might have been addressing a packed auditorium instead of one foreign ambassador, plus his own minister of finance, who kept nodding his head and repeating, "Sim, Senhor Presidente" with the monotonous regularity of a metronome.

Finally, the president paused in front of us. In his pacing about, he had unbuttoned his double-breasted jacket. "There comes a time," he declared in a resonant electioneering tone of voice, "when every citizen of this Republic must be called upon to tighten his belt. Everyone must share in the sacrifice. . . . Belt-tightening it must be!" The president illustrated by opening his jacket and moving his right hand to his left hip, as if to demonstrate the belt-tightening technique about to be adopted by each and every compatriot. Solemnly he looked from his American guest to his guardian of the finances of the Republic, and finally to the top of his trousers.

"Good God," President Kubitschek exclaimed. "How can I tighten my belt when I'm wearing suspenders?" Whereupon the president of the Republic and his minister of finance dissolved in a gale of laughter, the idea of belt-tightening when there was no belt on the president's trousers being too much for either of them to contemplate seriously.

And that was the end of the $30 million loan project.

It would be easy, but an oversimplification, to infer from the foregoing that the largest country in South America is simultaneously the world's largest lunatic asylum, except that the inmates, instead of being under restraint, not infrequently occupy official position. I found myself fighting the temptation to think so myself several times. When I made my official call upon the governor of São Paulo, Brazil's richest and most industrialized state, I was received by Jânio Quadros, who before calling in a television crew to capture the visit for posterity, rummaged in his desk, retrieved a glass object, and proceeded to sprinkle white table salt over his shoulders and coat collar. He was simulating dandruff, he explained, to demonstrate to his constituents that he was a man of the people, without false pretensions of elegance. (In 1961, Quadros was to follow Kubitschek as president of the Republic.)

Notwithstanding these occupational vicissitudes, I found that operating a large embassy in a big country did not differ very greatly from what I had been doing for the past dozen years in places that loomed smaller on the map. Remembering George Messersmith in Havana, I was at pains to delegate my authority. That was accomplished during a 10:30 meeting every morning, attended by half a dozen senior officers, including my minister counselor for economic affairs, who simultaneously wore the hat of aid mission chief; Howard Cottam was a Ph.D. in economics as well as a Foreign Service officer. He did everything that was needful, includig efforts to shrink instead of expand our overblown aid program, which I applauded.[1]

At that 10:30 meeting, at which discursiveness was not encouraged, reports were rendered and tasks apportioned. By that time I would have survived my eight o'clock Portuguese lesson, skimmed the Rio press plus *O Estado de São Paulo,* and read the telegrams to and from Washington. My colleagues were expected to have done likewise. That session was followed by one I did not attend, chaired by the senior political officer. It involved the so-called intelligence community: the attachés, my principal spook (a knowledgeable and sophisticated officer), and the representatives of my grossly overstaffed military establishment, Brazil having a large equivalent of a military assistance advisory group.

My principal problem was putting a senior staff together. My able predecessor, Jimmy Dunn, pleading for retirement, had been persuaded to remain long enough to collect his deserved career ambassadorship. His, and now my, deputy departed two weeks after my arrival to become deputy in Bonn. His successor, a month after arrival, suffered so serious a breakdown that it took a year at home for him to mend. My stalwart consul general, Donald Edgar, the same officer who as vice consul in Havana many years before had registered our son as the offspring of American citizens, suffered a heart attack that soon invalided him from the service.

These unhappy rolls of the individual dice meant that for seven months I was my own number two. It meant also that I familiarized myself with a number of operations I might otherwise have left largely to others. I became more convinced than ever — to the subsequent annoyance of the Department of State, which I was to oppose and combat almost every time a Potomac bureaucrat dreamed up some new scheme involving additional personnel — that diplomacy, professional experienced diplomacy, could be conducted twice as efficiently with less than half the people.

Embassy Rio was grossly and disgracefully overstaffed. Although my efforts to prune the diplomatic list were largely futile in the 1950s, I like to

---

1. Howard Cottam, on one occasion, for the impending arrival of Crawford H. Greenwalt, chairman of the DuPont Company, organized at least three separate task forces of embassy economists, only to discover that the sole magnet drawing Mr. Greenwalt to Brazil was not petrochemicals but hummingbirds, on which he proved to be a world authority. This did not prevent Howard Cottam from later becoming ambassador to Kuwait.

think that my campaign may have been of assistance to a successor, Jack Tuthill, whose achievements in that direction in the next decade were considerable.

As to a deputy, I was finally able to snatch Woodruff Wallner from the jaws of a NATO assignment. He and his wife, Monica, were bilingual in French and inclined to regard service outside metropolitan France as slumming. Nevertheless, they fit into the Cariocan scene, and although Woody deliberately shunned regular Portuguese lessons, he learned more of the language in a few weeks by some arcane method of his own than I had with months of painful travail. Woody was high-strung, intolerant, and brilliant — assets that commended him both to the Brazilian Foreign Office and to me. Not universally popular with subordinates — he did not suffer oafs with patience — he soon became a most valuable assistant and colleague, thus freeing me to pursue my ambition to learn something about Brazil.[2] To me this meant traveling in the vast country and poking into places as out of the way as Porto Velho on the Madeira River, as spectacular as Iguaçu Falls, or as historic as Ouro Prêto — meaning "black gold" — the colonial capital of Minas Gerais, now deliberately abandoned to the historians and the tourists by a government sufficiently imaginative to recognize the worth of that lovely old city to the archaeologists and anthropologists of the future.

There were then twenty-two states in Brazil plus two immense and trackless territories in the Amazon basin. Now that the chancery was in good hands, I saw no reason why I should not visit them in succession, an ambition quickly endorsed by President Kubitschek because it tied in with his plans for Brazil's *desenvolvimento* (development). He may have reasoned that if he could get the American ambassador hooked, for example, on the power potential of the Paraná River, he would have an ally for its development later on.

As far as I know, that sort of forest-hopping had not been indulged in by any previous American ambassador. Nothing I could have done could have produced comparable rewards in satisfaction and experience. Most of the state governors (who were elected officials enjoyed more autonomy than the majority of their opposite numbers in Spanish America) insisted on putting up my wife and me, or in organizing either a banquet or a reception, fre-

2. To my disappointment, Woodruff Wallner never received an ambassadorial appointment although his talent was unquestionably greater than many of those rewarded with missions of their own. He retired as deputy chief of mission in Paris, a position of considerably more importance than ambassador to many countries.

quently with local theatrical talent. These affairs had the advantage of leaving me indebted to each successive host, and in a position to pay back his hospitality when next he appeared in Rio de Janeiro, so that before long I had a large assortment of far-flung gubernatorial friends whom it would have been impossible to reach on a personal basis in any other way. I recall being flattered when the papal nuncio, a cosmopolitan gentleman who had a superlative Venetian chef, accused me of invading more dioceses in the Republic than he had.

In addition to my wife and me and the four-man crew of the plane, my secretary, Emma Drake, usually accompanied us, and one junior officer, a different one each time in order to spread the experience, which was exacting. The junior, under Emma's demanding eye, was responsible for such arrangements as hotel reservations, paying bills and distributing tips, luggage, and arranging local transportation, which last invariably included a lecture upon the theme of *devagar* — an essential word meaning "slow down" in Portuguese.

It required two years to visit all twenty-two states and the two territories of Brazil, but by the time I had done so, I felt I had a fair working knowledge of the country. A good many of the seeming aberrations of the government, I decided, resulted from the intense preoccupation with quickening physical development at the same time that Brazil, far more than any other Latin American country, kept a weather eye on the world beyond its borders. Thus Kubitschek experienced a kind of exhilaration that — along with the wonderful capacity of Brazilians to laugh at themselves — accounted for his inability to take seriously the tightening of his nonexistent belt.

Of all the achievements of the Kubitschek administration (1955–1961), the one of which the president was the most proud was Brasília, the new capital of his country. It was a project in enthusiasm for which I ran him a close second, inasmuch as the notion of moving from sizzling, favela-ridden, congested, and unhygienic Rio de Janeiro — for all its natural beauty when seen from afar — appealed almost as much to my imagination as it did to that of the chief of state. Brasília, inland some six hundred miles northwest of Rio, would occupy a plateau nearly four thousand feet above sea level.

Moving the capital inland (on the sound premise that it would stimulate development of the trackless hinterland) had been in the constitution establishing the Republic in 1889. Three factors, plus inertia, combined to delay the project. First, the bureaucrats of Rio de Janeiro dearly loved their Atlantic beaches (polluted though most of them had become by the 1950s). Second, the red soil of the *planalto* was so unproductive that nothing but brush and bushes grew upon it, and when the new capital finally became a fact, tons of dark imported soil were spread over the initial coating. Last, there was the expense of building a huge city where until 1955 there had been nothing but a long, dry depression that was scheduled to become a lake, twenty-five miles long, fronting the metropolis.

As for money, the president declared that a great and growing country like Brazil could borrow it. Look at São Paulo, a tea plantation at the turn of the century; look at Belo Horizonte, open fields in 1900. Poof! The president snapped his fingers. (He did not, I noticed, follow that with a gesture of tightening his belt.) I arranged, after some argument with Sam Waugh, president of the Export-Import Bank, for the first Brasília credit: a modest $5 million for structural steel.

I visited Brasília often, and on the first occasion we landed on a grass strip beside shanties housing the first few hundred workers. I was able to shoot *codornas,* the little quail-like birds I had hunted in Uruguay, within a mile of the site of the capitol. Later, when the president built a guest house, I slept in it before he did — enjoying the large double blanket with the monogram J.K. upon it. By then there were at least ten thousand men at work, and I had to travel miles before I could unlimber my shotgun.

Today the Palace of Dawn, the president's house, looks out on its artificial lake, with broad green lawns sweeping toward the impounded water. There are trees and shrubbery and a stout iron fence not unlike the one enclosing the estate at 1600 Pennsylvania Avenue.

Brasília, the president was convinced, would be his monument. Once he completed his new capital, he could begin the far greater task of opening up the interior. That plan included a highway to connect the new capital with the mouth of the Amazon at Belem, one thousand miles north, and another highway, at right angles, running west to the border of Peru, cutting across the valleys of a dozen north-flowing Amazon tributaries, several of which carry a flow of water almost equal to the Mississippi.

Whether Kubitschek was a seer, a statesman, or merley spooked, the future will decide. Nor will it be a distant future, because at the present birthrate, the Brazilians will either have to find productive use for the great empty Amazon basin or spread over all the rest of the continent, across borders that Brazil already has with every country of South American except Ecuador and Chile.

It took approximately 120 years from independence to the closing of the American frontier in the 1890s. But whereas the United States uprooted its soil and "subdued the land" with picks and shovels and hand labor, along with teams of horses and oxen, Brazil is accomplishing that devastation with huge machines that are to the primitive implements of our North American forefathers what the chain saw and bulldozer are to the hoe and spade; uprooters of trees, earthmovers, giant scrapers and skidders, all feverishly at work tearing the surface of Brazil to pieces.

Politically, the country has been almost equally sacrified. It has gone from a Portuguese colony to a kingdom, to an empire (a leisurely process that absorbed nearly four centuries), to a republic, a dictatorship, a representative democracy (more or less the Kubitschek administration from 1955 to 1961), and in 1964 a military dictatorship. The twentieth-century role of democracy in Brazil has not been heartening, with the demagoguery of the civilian leaders equaled only by the indiscipline of the electorate.[3]

To get back to my own responsibilities in the late 1950s — of which the most important was the maintenance of our relations on the even keel that had long characterized the affairs of Brazil and the United States — my most trying problem was of such small intrinsic importance that the only reason it reaches this chronicle is that once again it illustrates the unwisdom of permitting the American military — as they are empowered, if not encouraged, by the National Security Act of 1947 to do — to usurp the functions of diplomacy.

After the first orbital flight of the Russian sputnik, temperatures in the Pentagon shot up and the entire Potomac community was in a dither. A part of the spin-off was the atomic scientist program sponsored by the White House, whereby embassies already top-heavy with amateur whatnots were to be saddled with atomic attachés with unspecified responsibilities. It was in connection with this program that, hardily protesting that embassy Rio needed an atomic attaché "like a cigar store Indian needs a brassiere," I found myself deeply in the White House dog house, since I had not been aware of President Eisenhower's personal interest, nor of the fact that all embassy replies to the circular telegram in question were automatically routed to the Executive Office.[4]

---

3. Since its return to civilian, democratic government in the early 1990s, Brazil has joined a regionwide trend — marred only by the continued military dictatorship of Cuba's tyrant, Fidel Castro.

4. Further details concerning this small contribution to diplomacy are included in *Farewell to Foggy Bottom*.

I was somewhat chastened when I received peremptory instructions from Washington to obtain from Brazil the right, on behalf of the air force, to install on the remote island of Fernando da Noronha, what the message called a "guided-missile tracking station" — whatever that might be. What was required, my directive continued, was a certain amount of acreage on which would be installed various classified electronic gadgets, to be transported to Fernando da Noronha by ship, and thereafter in charge of air force personnel who would not be subject to Brazilian jurisdiction.

Fernando da Noronha is a rocky and precipitous escarpment, some two hundred miles off the bulge of Brazil in the direction of Dakar. It is more than one thousand miles from Rio de Janeiro. Used as a penal colony in the nineteenth century, the island had a brief period of importance when the French started a seaplane service in the 1930s, crossing from Africa to Natal, with Fernando da Noronha as an emergency fueling stop. But since we flew land planes from Natal to Africa all through World War II, with seaplanes shortly thereafter abandoned, Fernando da Noronha quietly slid back to its placid colonial days with the handful of inhabitants living a lush life from the abundant fishery resources, plus their small garden plots on the very limited arable land.

Brazil had no objection to a guided-missile tracking station, whatever they thought I meant, and they suggested what I considered to be a minimum of conditions: the Brazilian flag should fly beside the American emblem on the acreage selected; there would be a Brazilian liaison officer of rank equal to his American opposite number in order to iron out local problems; and should Brazil so request, the United States would undertake to train a handful of Brazilian technicians in the nonclassified aspects of what was going on. Brazil suggested a five-year executive agreement (i.e., one not requiring senatorial confirmation), renewable unless denounced by either party. All of this seemed reasonable to me. A page and a half of typescript should cover it, and the navy could start unloading boxes and bundles day after tomorrow. I was grateful to the Brazilian Foreign Office and not unpleased with my own sagacity.

Not so the air force. Their ideas covered pages of telegraphese, which meant that in some Pentagon cubbyhole lieutenant colonels were indulging in contingency planning. What had started out as a simple and straightforward exercise in bilateral diplomacy within a fortnight produced a file of documents as thick as a suburban telephone directory and twice as complicated. Every time I thought I had some foolish loose end finally tied down, the script would be changed, the justification being that the development of telemetry was now proceeding so fast that the gospel of last Monday was the heresy of the following Friday.

Even so I persevered, being greatly aided by my friend Dirceu Moura, now secretary-general in the Foreign Office, whose command of English was of incalculable assistance. Moreover, the project had President Kubitschek's blessing. Dirceu and I soon had a text we thought was watertight, and I informed Washington we proposed to sign the agreement the following day.

It was 2 A.M. when Assistant Secretary Richard Roy Rubottom reached me on the telephone to report that "on further consideration," Cape Canaveral had decided that a Fernando da Noronha landing strip suitable for cargo planes would be preferable to depending upon the United States Navy. The pending text should accordingly be redrafted. Sleepy as I was, I knew the answer to that one. Suspecting some such gambit among the armed services, which often acted as though they thought they were sovereign states suspicious of one another, I had already visited the island. I had taken along the agricultural attaché, a knowledgeable young man with a Ph.D. of his own, albeit not in missiles or rocketry. The agricultural attaché quickly confirmed that to enlarge the thin strip on which we had landed into a field capable of handling cargo planes would leave the inhabitants of Fernando da Noronha with no gardens whatever. We had also taken the trouble to examine the docking facilities left by the French when they forsook their seaplanes. These appeared entirely adequate. Cape Canaveral, in short, could go climb a tree, preferably an Arizona cactus, and Assistant Secretary Rubottom was encouraged to quote me to that effect.

That brought matters to a boil. The next Washington message informed me that the lieutenant general, USAF, commanding at Cape Canaveral — that is, the ranking officer concerned with the missile program — was en route to Rio de Janeiro. He would overfly Fernando da Noronha to examine it from the air, but would not attempt a landing. Suppressing the temptation to suggest a parachute drop, together with a month's supply of K-rations, I warned Dirceu Moura of what was up and sent my air attaché to Galeão Airport to greet Lieutenant General Donald Yates in my name.

As now and then happens when bureaucrats stop dictating messages to one another and start using their heads instead of their typewriters, the general and I turned out not to be the malevolent ogres each had pictured the other. Don Yates was from Bangor, Maine, ninety miles from my then legal residence; he was a West Pointer who graduated while airplanes still bore army insignia. His row of ribbons from aviation to rocketry had included meteorology and hurricane surveillance with more than a dash of cybernetics. He and Dirceu Moura and I found no difficulty in agreeing, first, that a vodka gibson outranks a vodka martini for the reason that a pearl onion displaces less alcohol than an olive; and second, that it would cost a fortune to carve out a cargo landing field on an island that from a distance looked not unlike the entrance to Rio harbor — to say nothing of depriving the inhabitants of Fernando da Noronha of their pitiful farmland. The agreement, as drafted, was dandy. It was duly signed, and the next day a satisfied Lieutenant General Yates flew back to Florida with a certified copy in his pocket.[5]

On the broader stage of inter-American relations things were not proceeding smoothly. A majority of our ambassadors, if properly queried, could have come up with the answers, but the fretful Good Neighbors, who had come through the war not only unscathed but relatively prosperous, were now carping about being taken for granted. President Eisenhower — who had no real understanding of the problems of the hemisphere — preferred to send his brother Milton (who spoke no Spanish and knew even less about Latin America than the president) on a fact-finding mission, with my friend Jack Cabot holding his hand. Then came the 1956 meeting of presidents in Panama, during which Eisenhower spent as much time riding his electric golf cart on the Quarry Heights golf links as he did pondering the problems of the hemisphere. In 1958, it was the turn of Vice President Nixon to take a poke at the problems.

The Nixons did not come to Brazil. The vice president excused himself with the legitimate observation that he had been in the country to attend the Kubitschek inauguration in 1955, on behalf of President Eisenhower. But he went almost everywhere else in South America, the announced purpose being to ascertain the facts — as if those had been carefully withheld from those in authority.

The Nixon trip was a disaster. It was a futile and cockeyed conception to start with, but it became a disaster because instead of playing the expedition in the low key it deserved and confining his interviews to responsible government officials plus those recommended by our respective diplomatic missions, the vice president did exactly the opposite: he stopped his cavalcade to harangue crowds, he engaged in public debate with stevedores, and he argued on street corners with students, for all the world like an American candidate touring the boondocks. When he wound up the target of brick-

5. A sequel to my pleasant acquaintance with General Yates occurred the following year, when we each received an honorary degree from Bowdoin College.

bats and bottles in Caracas, the American people, confused and badly informed by Washington, leaped to the idiotic conclusion that somehow it was all the fault of Uncle Sam.

The first Latino president who was smart enough to recognize that there might be gold in the hills of American self-accusation was President Kubitschek, who scooped up the guilt complex like a loose football on the inter-American gridiron. Quickly Kubitschek advanced the proposition that the reason for Vice President Nixon's troubles was that the United States did not understand the natural right of the have-not nations (now called the "underdeveloped nations") to be developed at the expense of the already developed nations. He named this doctrine Operação Pan América, the new revelation that would henceforth illuminate relations among members of the hemisphere family.

That, of course, was a distant chant from what I had been promoting on behalf of John Foster Dulles, whose view of Brazil was that such slogans as Work Hard, Cultivate Thrift, and Do Not Borrow More Than You Can Afford to Pay Back were more valid than invitations to slip a hand into Uncle Sam's pocket. It was also the view of Mr. Dulles (and of a great many sensible people before and after) that the treatment a country extends to existing investments from abroad has an inevitable bearing upon the willingness of foreign citizens (and their governments) to make further capital available.

All this was now to be superseded by Operação Pan América, on behalf of which Kubitschek proceeded to launch a formidable campaign with a surprising number of adherents in the United States. The Eisenhower administration was still squirming about what role to play in this Lusitanian sport when President Kennedy was elected, and he in turn stole the pigskin from Brazil, renaming it Alliance for Progress, with a charter contained in a special address to the Latin American diplomats assembled in the White House on March 17, 1961.

That speech, which in effect tried to commit the United States to extending the welfare state from Alaska to the Beagle Channel, is undoubtedly one of the silliest ever delivered by a chief of state to the representatives of the hemisphere gathered together. Fortunately for my own peace of mind, I had by that time exchanged the problems of the New World for those of Greece.

My eviction from Brazil was possibly an embarrassment for John Foster Dulles, who had assured me in 1958 that "there would be no change in Rio representation during the balance of the Eisenhower administration," which still had over two years to run. That may be why he sent an emissary with a letter in February 1959 to inform me that Clare Boothe Luce, the consort of the *Time/Life* empire, wanted my job, and would I accept an appointment as special assistant to the secretary of state to counsel him on Latin American matters? By that time Foster was a very ill man (he died that May), and I do not know whether he even read my reply, which was to the effect that I believed I could be more useful to our government serving in a post abroad than in a departmental capacity.

Greece followed.

In the meantime, however, there had been some spectacular publicity, first over Mrs. Luce's confirmation by the Senate (she was endorsed by a comfortable majority); then by her aiming a verbal horseshoe at Senator Wayne Morse, then chairman of the Latin American subcommittee of the Foreign Relations Committee; and finally by the publication of a letter to the candidate from her publisher husband warning her of pitfalls ahead. Mrs. Luce, who needed only to take the oath of office in order to become ambassador to Brazil, resigned instead. My curiosity has continued to simmer as to why, in those circumstances (which for weeks paralyzed the transaction of substantive business between the United States and Brazil), Mrs. Luce, a highly gifted as well as articulate lady, desired the Rio job in the first place.

Foster Dulles, who knew more about it than anyone else in the department, was seeing only members of his family by the time I reached Washington a few weeks before his death. President Eisenhower, whom I questioned on the occasion of my call before going to Greece, implied that he thought it an odd appointment, "but it was all Foster's idea." Henry Luce, with whom I held brief conversation, confined his remarks to an acknowledgment of the assistance rendered by Lucy to his wife in regard to household and related matters in Rio de Janeiro. But none of that clarified the underlying question.

I hoped that Mrs. Luce, who was capable of prose that was both eloquent and memorable, would see fit someday to enlighten the record.[6]

On July 15, 1959, on the island of Corfu, I presented my credentials to King George of Greece.

6. She did not do so before her death in 1987.

And Last a Monarchy

Greece

Serving as American ambassador to Greece in the early 1960s ought to have been 80 percent picnic and 20 percent work. Instead, Greece turned out to be one of the most arduous assignments I had. This was due essentially to two circumstances: the Greek character and the hordes of supernumerary official American personnel, in and out of uniform, many of whom hoped to prolong indefinitely their stay in a country with over three hundred days of sunshine a year and $2.75 liquor at the PX. Dealing with the Americans proved the more time-consuming.

A Greek is a mixture of Hellene, Macedonian, Phoenician, Egyptian, Arab, Saracen, Roman, Turk, Visigoth, and Crusader, to whom a ribald Creator added a dash of Tabasco sauce and Lord Byron, plus the stinging honey bees of Mount Hymettus. The result is a creature in almost constant political agitation. The Greeks are so lively, intelligent, sophisticated, cynical, quarrelsome, and intolerant of each other that no matter how serene the horizon may look, some sort of political tempest is perpetually brewing on the far side of Parnassus, ready to blow up in your face like a trick cigar in a vaudeville act. Whenever someone remarks that "Democracy was born in Greece" (which happens at least once at every academic gathering), the standard retort should be "and so was Chaos."

To imagine a permanently tranquil Greece would be as naive as to argue that Euclid or no Euclid, a straight line is the shortest distance between two points. To a Greek negotiator nothing could be sillier. Nevertheless, I was fortunate to be there during a period between political convulsions. The Caramanlis government was probably the best administration the country had enjoyed since independence from Turkey in 1830, if not since Pericles. Greece was greatly beholden to the United States and, at the time of my service, a staunch NATO ally.

In addition to a competent Greek government, resting at that time upon a solid base of public support, I enjoyed other valuable assets. To follow an accomplished predecessor is a boon of great value, for it meant that I inherited tidy premises and a smoothly operating embassy machine, notwithstanding the fact that it was vastly inflated in size. My predecessor, Jimmy Riddleberger, was a friend of thirty years. He had been in Athens only a few months when he was dragooned into putting a finger in a Washington political dike — the ever-leaking, ever-septic aid program. Jim left me his deputy, Samuel D. Berger, one of the ablest officers in our service, already known and respected by Greeks and Americans alike.

The view of Greece from the Potomac was less cheering, for the country, having been rescued from the Communists in 1949, again loomed small among the Washington agencies wielding power. Since the effectiveness of an envoy in an era of practically instantaneous communication depends on local recognition that he has the backing of his government, the declining power of the State Department eroded the effectiveness of more than one representative of that period.

A graph of this waning prestige of the State Department, beginning with the inauguration of Franklin Roosevelt, should someday occupy the talents of a respectable historian. The line, unlike Euclid's, would be far from straight. In the prewar days of Secretary Hull and Undersecretary Welles it rose, notwithstanding the acrobatics of Adolf Berle, Nelson Rockefeller, Henry Morgenthau, and Mrs. FDR, but the line of State Department influence practically disappeared during the war and it experienced its sharpest decline with the National Security Act of 1947, which in effect transferred diplomacy to the military and created the Central Intelligence Agency as a sharp-toothed duplicate State Department with an added skulduggery department. The graph showed a brief upward trend under Dean Acheson (following Marshall, who had tried to run the State Department like a graft on the tree of the General Staff) and Dulles, who with the backing of Eisenhower ran his own show from 1953 to his death in 1959. Under Kennedy, abetted by a cabal of presumptuous professors lodged in the White House cellar, the State Department was to take further punishment, including the ineptitude of two succeeding secretaries of state, neither of whom appeared to know the difference between Cleopatra's Needle and the Washington Monument. Professional diplomacy inevitably not only suffered in the measure of the decline of the prestige of the State Department, it practically went into eclipse.

My Potomac briefing was therefore not an outstanding success, although I prowled dutifully around the corridors of the State Department, trying to make like an Aegean sponge while dodging former cronies who wanted to gossip about Brasília. One of my troubles was that Mr. Greece, the young man on the Greek desk in the Near Eastern Bureau, was an Iranian expert, with no Acropolis experience at all. He was diligent, but he lacked competence in his subject, a great limitation on his usefulness.

The assistant secretary of state for our area had just been named ambassador to Pakistan. He was more interested in the building of Rawalpindi than he was in the chores facing embassy Athens. His successor, a man of sincerity and goodwill, who had served in Greece, lacked the bureaucratic backing that might have helped him spar successfully with those mobilized against him (or me) by other Potomac agencies.

I knew Secretary Herter well and I respected him for his experience, his ability as a statesman, and his personal charm. But the president was not exactly a tower of strength on behalf of Foster Dulles's successor. Furthermore, no secretary of state was able to spend much time discussing the affairs of only one of the hundred countries composing the burgeoning United Nations.

I survived my protocolary visit in New York to the Orthodox archbishop of North and South America, impressively whiskered, who offered me hard candy and coffee on top of Metaxas brandy. Back in Washington the next day I became a cropper on no less a playground than the White House itself, where I went for my farewell call on President Eisenhower. The president had already entered a phase of mounting inertia induced partly by declining health and partly by the loss of Sherman Adams, who in his abrupt, acerbic way had known how to keep the bureaucratic machinery functioning. During that period — the last years of the Eisenhower administration — the president enjoyed being head of state but often failed to function effectively as chief executive.

However, the president remembered enough of his NATO days to come fully alert when I observed that certain military gadgets installed in Greece, pointing to the north, could hardly be soothing to Moscow, even though the detonating button remained firmly in the presidential pants pocket. I said I had the impression that the gadgets were already becoming obsolete, and that a new set — placed, for example, in Ethiopia — would be just as effective as "deterrents," without the provocation of their presence in Greece.

The president asked some sharp questions and scribbled notes on a pad: he would raise the matter with the joint chiefs. In the meantime, I'd better be on my way, and he wished me luck. It ought, the president said genially, to be a more pleasant assignment than Korea.

An hour later, my final Washington luncheon was abrasively interrupted by an angry Bob Murphy, who was acting secretary of state. He accused me of rocking the boat and even of wetting some of the carefully ballasted State/Pentagon cargo, of which I gathered the gadgets in Greece were a part. Not altogether penitent, I inquired why I had not been warned what corner of the White House rug I was not supposed to walk on. I resisted Bob's suggestion that I postpone my departure for Greece "until the matter is cleared up," and Bob finally agreed, grumpily, that my scheduled NATO briefing with General Lauris Norstad in Paris should include some schooling in the proper point of view.

NATO headquarters in those happier days were still just outside Paris. Lucy and I denned up at the Crillon, across the alley from the chancery, where we had many friends, and I received a prompt appointment with the four-star head of our NATO establishment, whom I had known and respected since his fewer-star days in the Pentagon. Notwithstanding Murphy's jitters, I found Larry Norstad relaxed about his gadgets in Greece, which he agreed had become obsolete. He said he was prepared to remove them anytime the Greeks suggested it. The difficulty was, he conceded, that once you got something installed — whether it was in Norway or in Portugal — interest soon built up around that installation, causing the bureaucrats to dig in.

General Norstad promised to keep the matter in mind, along with intelligence about duck shooting on the marshes on the Greek side of the Maritsa River. This was not the last of my brushes with NATO, some of whose moguls regarded Greece as a part of *their* bailiwick, with the American ambassador largely a figure of protocol, trained to jump through the military hoop on command.

Historians may recall that one of Khrushchev's excuses for provoking the Cuban missile crisis two years later was the presence of these gadgets in northern Greece. I should have had the foresight in 1959 to insist to General Norstad that they be removed.

Following this pleasant French interlude, we moved to Stuttgart to pick up a car, since we planned to enter Greece from the north, across Yugoslavia, simultaneously seeing what we could of the Balkans, where I had not set foot since 1922, before I entered the Foreign Service. That expedition was uneventful. We stopped overnight at Salzburg, which is exactly five hundred kilometers from Stuttgart, so that the first maintenance check on our car could be made.

We had a gay dinner with Rebecca Wellington, our consul general in Salzburg, and at 1:30 the next afternoon the car was delivered by the manager himself, who impressed on us that a Mercedes was not a car but a "purr-cision instrument," adding several admonitory paragraphs. We were to recognize as we bounced across Serbia in the ruts of Albanian oxcarts, inhaling Balkan dust by the lungful, that our "purr-cision instrument" lived up to the Salzburg panegyrics. Few things looked better to us than the first frontier post of Greece, with the blue and white flag waving, a modern gas station just beyond, and a long ribbon of smooth macadam highway stretching south, with Athens only a day and a half away. We had seen nothing like that since leaving Austria.

The preceding twenty years had been rough times for the Greek people, but their revival with the assistance of American aid had been phenomenal. Soon after World War II began, Benito Mussolini, jealous of the ease with which Hitler overran Poland, thought he saw a chance for some easy loot nearer home. Great Britain, for over a century the protector of the Hellenes, was otherwise engaged. Mussolini first seized Corfu, the island where the Greek royal family had their summer residence. He then moved against the mainland, intending to conquer Epirus before marching triumphantly south.

The expression "rose as one man" accurately describes the Greek people facing the overconfident Italian invasion and the Italian demand for surrender. The *Oxi* of the Greek general is still celebrated as Oxi Day, the anniversary of his resounding "No!" So savagely did the Greeks defend their homeland that soon Mussolini was appealing to Hitler for aid. That was in the spring of 1941, the year Hitler decided to attack Russia. Oxi Day accounts for the Greek boast that Greece won the war, a modest assertion based on the fact that Hitler, instead of leaving Mussolini to stew in his own minestrone, sent German divisions that had been scheduled for an invasion of Russia to overrun Yugoslavia and Greece. Those combat troops were replaced by occupation troops (and later by the hated Bulgarians), but the weeks it took the Nazi regiments to reach Athens were those of the scheduled 1941 advance into the heart of Russia.

Many Greeks escaped to fight against the Nazis elsewhere. Others went underground to join bloodily competing, often Communist, guerrilla movements that fought one another until 1949.

When the Greeks referred to "the war," they were rarely talking about the period before 1944, most of which they regarded as the era of the repulsed Italian invasion and the ensuing German occupation. "The war" to the Greek people dates from the Nazi withdrawal until the final defeat of the Communists by Greek troops under General Van Fleet (later of Korea) at Mount Grammos, near the Serbian-Albanian frontier.

This is a period abundantly covered by historians, from the Christmas visit of Churchill and Eden in 1944, when half of Athens was in the hands of the Communist guerrillas, to Churchill's disposal of Prime Minister Papandreou, whose antics twenty years later were to lead to the coup d'état of the colonels.

The British soon admitted to Washington that their country, bled white by the war, could no longer carry the burden of Greece. It is to President Truman's credit that he picked up that burden, and American assistance led to the victory of 1949. When we reached Greece a decade later, the difference between a new building and an older one in Athens was not the cleanliness of the former but the scars left by machine gun bullets on the walls and around the window frames of pre-1944 construction. Nearly every town and village in Greece thus testified to the bitterness of the fratricidal strife.

The royal family had gotten out one jump ahead of the panzers. King George died, to be succeeded by Paul and Princess Frederika, a most personable pair with two children, soon joined by a third born in South Africa, with Field Marshal Smuts as her godfather. They later went to England, where their London refuge had its unfortunate aspects because among the welter of "governments in exile" being supported by the British government were these five royal Greeks — connected by family ties with the British royal family — unaccustomed to penury. It became Queen Frederika's conviction, or perhaps hallucination, that Winston Churchill deliberately kept them on short rations. From that time forward Queen Frederika had nothing good to say of the man who, more than any single individual except perhaps President Truman, was to save Greece from communism.

The United States then undertook to help the Greeks rebuild their shattered country, and in fact to usher Greece into the twentieth century. Over $2 billion were funneled into Greece in the 1950s. For several years the Communists perched inside the Yugoslav and Bulgarian borders, with hundreds of kidnapped Greek children as hostages, hoping that the American miracle was a mirage. It was not a mirage. Although the dollars came from overseas, the men who mixed the mortar and the hands that squared the bricks were Greek, and the planning of the highways and roads was a joint Greco-American venture. Like the Marshall Plan next door, the rehabilitation of Greece resulted from the fusion of strong and determined human raw material, Greek as well as American.

The program of rehabilitation was for practical purposes finished by the end of the 1950s, but the aid program remained in being and hundreds of American bureaucrats stayed on. A part of my task, to the extent that anyone spelled it out to me in Washington, was to liquidate the aid operation and at the same time see to it that the volatile Greeks, who were then passionately "on our side" (and had in fact joined NATO, as well as sending a contingent to Korea while their own capital was still smoldering), remained dedicated to the Free World. Granted the friendly and cooperative attitude of Greek officials, the latter objective presented no problem, provided I could rid the premises of the superfluous Potomac crusaders before they soured the pudding. Irritants — such as running a bus line from downtown Athens to the suburb of Kifissia, where an American school had been established, with "no indigenous personnel" printed conspicuously over the door of the bus; a post exchange almost as large as Macy's; and an air force freight-forwarding enterprise with five thousand United States personnel — had been tolerated in the busy days of reconstruction but were causing mounting criticism by the time of our arrival.

The foreign minister, Evanghelos Averoff, was the most pleasant and stimulating official I could remember, although he confessed to me one day that it was sometimes more exciting to deal with my Russian colleague even though the latter was admittedly a bastard. When he dealt with the American ambassador or with deputy Sam Berger, he said, it was all straightforward talking. What we said, he could count on. We might not give him the whole story, but what we did say was factual and true, and he would act on it. Not so our Russian colleague. You could listen to him for half an hour (in fact the foreign minister had just done so) and spend the rest of the day trying to figure out what his real objective was, and what was supposed to be derived from the content of his remarks. "Levantine backgammon," Averoff called it. "It is like playing chess blindfolded." The minister spoke five languages as well as I spoke English, and he could be highly articulate in all of them.

Prime Minister Constantine Caramanlis was something else again. To the press he was "the Macedonian Anthony Eden," and he wore the title with distinction. Possibly tougher than his foreign minister, he was a yes-or-no man on whose word you could count, who demanded action from his subordinates and followed through on things he said he would do.

We had been in Greece for only a few weeks when Lucy and I were invited to dine with the prime minister and his radiant wife, Amalia, at their home — "a family meal, dress informal." I had a long session with Sam Berger, going over items of business pending between our two governments and trying to think what subjects the prime minister might choose to bring up. We were the only guests, and not one word of business was spoken by our host. The minister's English was rudimentary but his French was fluent. Amalia Caramanlis, a woman some years younger than her husband, spoke excellent English. It was one of the most relaxed and relaxing introductions to official business that I ever experienced, with one memorable observation by our hostess as we were admiring the gallery of signed photographs of notables cramming the formal reception room of their apartment. The picture of President Eisenhower, in a silver frame with the seal of the United States at top, had a place of honor on the grand piano. It was suitably inscribed and signed, and it was dedicated in the president's handwriting "to my friend, Konstantine Caramanlis" — instead of with two Cs or two Ks. "It seems that your president," said Amalia Caramanlis, "has trouble making up his mind."

A week later I had a business session with Caramanlis in his office that was tough, straightforward, and pulled no punches — the sort of session Sam and I had envisaged before the supper invitation. The prime minister's secretary phoned Emma Drake: Would it be convenient for the ambassador to stop by at three o'clock on Wednesday? No subject was mentioned. Emma assured the secretary that I would be there.

Mr. Caramanlis had things on his mind — some not of overwhelming importance, but protracted by our mixed French/English discussion. Several times his secretary, looking scared, popped in with bits of paper; the prime minister, concentrating on our Greek/American business, swept them off his desk unread. It was 4:40 when our discussion ended, and the prime minister courteously accompanied me into his outer office, whence an aide would conduct me to the elevator.

Sitting in a corner, looking like a football coach whose team trails 30 to 10 in the fourth quarter, sat Aristotle Onassis, whom I had not met, obviously kept waiting for his appointment.

Onassis was greeted by the prime minister, who then switched to French: "Allow me to present to you, Ari, our new friend, the American ambassador."

The only accurate description of the sound made by the caller, accustomed to have people, from maître d'hôtel to bankers, literally fall on their stomachs as they approached him, and who had been waiting for three-quarters of an hour for his appointment, was a noise laden with venom.

Onassis's opposite number in the one-upmanship of who amassed a billion dollars first was his ex-brother-in-law, Stavros Niarchos, who did become a friend. Niarchos owned an island sixty miles south of Piraeus (soon Onassis bought an island off the west coast), and stocked it annually with twelve thousand Mediterranean redleg partridge and three thousand pheasants, with professional gamekeepers and all the fixings for the kind of gracious shooting that had ended in most of Europe in 1914. Niarchos built a comfortable, unornate house and a guest house nearby, but while this construction went forward, guests remained aboard his yacht, the *Creole*, two hundred feet long, with masts and sails that worked, along with auxiliary power for windless days. Although Niarchos maintained offices in various capitals, much of his business was conducted from the *Creole*, which had communications equipment as elaborate and extensive as the *Queen Elizabeth*.

The *Creole* was black, sleek, and beautiful, with a crew of thirty, including a British skipper. The ship flew the Bermudian flag; I never asked why.

Niarchos called on me not long after we reached Athens: a meeting that lasted five minutes, with little time wasted on amenities. Niarchos said he had heard I liked bird shooting. So did he. Would my wife and I like to join them for a weekend, two weeks hence? We would leave on the *Creole* Friday afternoon, returning by noon Monday. He assumed I had my own guns; he had plenty of ammunition — 12 and 20 gauge. Almost as an afterthought, he remarked that the royal family would probably join us on Saturday and Sunday.

The Greek royal family were a cheerful, extroverted group, whose language when they were at home together was English (although the king and queen, when alone, often spoke German), and whose informality we viewed with some caution, never before having served in a monarchy. Queen Frederika was busily engaged in trying to find suitable mates for their now-teenage children, and their private palace at Tatoi, twenty miles north of Athens, was forever buzzing with titled visitors, not all of them solvent, whom they housed and fed with generous hospitality.

Thus began an association that was as pleasant as any that Lucy and I remember. The king and queen traveled on a Greek destroyer, and they slept aboard not half so comfortably, one of the princesses confessed to me, as guests on the *Creole*. But the king had spent much of his preaccession days in the Danish Navy, and besides, he remarked, "it looked better" for them to be on a Greek ship. They took their meals and spent their days on Niarchos's island, Spetsipoula, sometimes shooting, otherwise bathing or sailing. Prince Constantine proved to be a crack sailor. The next year he won the first and only Olympic Games gold medal achieved by Greece since the games were reestablished in 1896. This was probably the high point of the popularity of the royal family between World War II and the coup d'état that lost Constantine his throne in 1967, not long after the death of his father.

{ *And Last a Monarchy* }

Initially I was somewhat puzzled by Niarchos's invitation, and the many that succeeded it. I eventually concluded that we were invited because he admired the way I could shoot, which aroused his highly competitive spirit, and because his wife, Eugenie, and Lucy became friends. But with a bow to our wives, it was the shooting that probably turned the trick. Stavros had taken to raising birds not long before I was appointed to Greece. Someone told him that I was a good wing shot. When he found out I could knock down more birds than he could, his sense of rivalry became so acute that he practiced constantly and kept inviting me in the hope that someday he could outshoot his ambassadorial guest. These invitations were, incidentally, made known to the Department of State, which was aware of Niarchos's altercation with the Justice Department over the use of certain World War II vessels he had purchased. State did not object. Throughout our association I cannot recall a single instance when business matters were discussed, much less did Stavros ever ask a favor of the embassy.

The reason for my prowess with a shotgun was the speed with which I could get off a shot, and that in turn was the result of twenty Octobers in the alder thickets of eastern Maine, chasing woodcock, a bird no one in his right mind would pursue, but to the fanatic the finest game on the continent. The woodcock, a target scarcely larger than a robin, sits well for a dog, but in flight it is the zaniest thing that moves: erratic, unpredictable, irrational, and usually out of sight — especially in early season with the leaves still on — before the hunter can get the shotgun to his shoulder.

At the age of fifteen I lost the sight of my right eye, and rather than give up shooting, I determined to shoot off my left shoulder, using my one good eye. That is not an easy thing for a right-handed person to learn, and I found that the only way I could be sure of getting the gun to my left shoulder was to carry it with my right hand around the forearm, and my left behind the trigger guard. This was awkward in thick cover, but it eventually beat the right-shoulder reflex. In the process of carrying the gun almost in position to fire, I became a fast shot.

The redleg Mediterranean partridge is a fine game bird and no tied balloon for a target, but it is twice the size of the American woodcock, and when flushed, it indulges in few acrobatics: it merely seeks, in fast, direct flight, to get out of the proximity of the hunter. The island of Spetsipoula, seven miles long and forested to a degree unusual among the Greek islands, was covered with heavy, low brush, out of which the partridge were flushed by beaters augmented by some members of the crew of the *Creole*. By the time I had run off a string of a dozen redlegs, most of them crumpling in flight before Stavros could fire his shot, my reputation was made, and no matter how many misses I had thereafter, my host was sure he had something to show his friends. These included the duke of Marlborough (one of the finest wing shots I ever met) and King Paul, who, like me, suffered from a bad right eye but used a specially made shotgun, with the stock set over so far that with the butt against his right shoulder, the left eye could be used.

This is not to imply that I became a regular Spetsipoula weekender, although we did enjoy the Niarchoses' hospitality on many occasions during our years in Athens. I recall one occasion of considerable frivolity just after the engagement had been announced of Princess Sophie, the oldest of the three children, to Juan Carlos, the prince of the Asturias, whom Franco had reportedly picked as his successor. Queen Frederika regarded this as a notable achievement, and I suppose it was, taking into account the dwindling ranks of reigning royalty. Being outside of the second or third martini, I asked the queen why she didn't find some attractive young Greek for their second daughter, Irene, who was my special favorite.

This was an impertinent question that might remind her highness of how shallow the roots of the family were in Greek soil. The queen's prompt rapping-my-knuckles reply was, however, revealing. "That," said the queen sharply, "would be the most unpopular thing we could do. One Greek family would be delighted, and all the rejected suitors would try to foment a revolution."

All these activities were diverting and diplomatically useful. We met a great many Greeks both on those visits and on the independent trips we soon started taking to explore the country. Greece may look small on the map, but the land is so mountainous and hides so many folds and valleys that if it could be spread flat, it would cover half of Europe. Nor did lack of a knowledge of Greek prove the handicap I had apprehended: three minutes after our arrival in any village, there would appear the inevitable Greek returned from America, who had owned a restaurant in Fall River, or shined shoes in Cleveland, or worked in a flower ship on Madison Avenue. Lucy said her most useful Greek phrase was "Have you any relatives in the United States?" The largest American Legion post outside the United States was in Athens. Ten thousand Veterans Bureau and Social Security checks a *month* were distributed through the embassy to beneficiaries scattered all over the mainland and among the islands of the Aegean. Thus we found no lack of volunteer interpreters.

Our amicable relations with the Greeks were not matched with our fellow Americans, my project being to render them less numerous, and therefore less conspicuous. Within a few weeks they considered me the most unpopular representative since before the war because I thought the post exchange a good place to start reducing numbers. As not many private citizens know, the PX system is the largest retail business in the U.S. The original PX idea was a good one, closely tied to military morale: namely, to furnish our fighting forces as many as possible of the comforts of home at taxfree prices. Cigarettes, cola, beer, toothpaste, razor blades, chewing gum, salted peanuts, soap, paper handkerchiefs — a modest list, but it burgeoned with incredible speed, and it soon became a behemoth.

After the war Europe was prostrate, and in many places starvation loomed. The PX, raided by generous GIs on behalf of the vanquished (including the female vanquished), was the corner drugstore, the local dry goods emporium, and the town liquor store, all rolled into one conveniently located establishment. The argument for its remaining, years after the economy of Europe had revived, was that the occupation troops were entitled to enjoy a small slice of the American way of life, at cut-rate prices.

By the time we reached Greece, the small slice had grown into a monumental helping, with a correspondingly punishing effect on private retail trade within the country. The PX on the Piraeus Highway was selling not only taxfree American products of every description, but Italian and Spanish leather goods, Portuguese laces, French perfumes and wines, British woolens, Norwegian sardines, and even Belgian shotguns at lower prices than in the United States.

I complained to Washington against the whole proposition (and got nowhere); I summoned the local air force colonel (who was cooperative, albeit bewildered), and had him take down the huge sign and move the main entrance to the PX to the rear of the building, thus removing the glut of parked American automobiles often threatening to choke the highway. I called in all outstanding PX cards against a new issue that tightened eligibility regulations. It was this last move that produced the most howls, for upward of one hundred freeloaders who no longer had any connection with the American government lost their PX privileges, to their extreme and vocal annoyance. Restrictions on wholesale purchases by individuals were also introduced, in the hopes of reducing the black market. As far as I could ascertain, they had little effect; the GIs and their Greek clients developed a special talent for cutting corners.

I reaped a fine crop of friendly editorials in the local press, which had been complaining on behalf of Greek merchants, although the bloom on this minor triumph was soon carelessly erased by the royal palace itself. One day a few weeks before our first Greek Christmas, Emma reported that the grand mistress of the court, Mary Carolou, was on the phone. Mary was born an American citizen, heiress to one of the Greek-American tobacco fortunes that flourished until overshadowed by the shipping magnates. She did countless helpful things in the relations between the palace and the embassy. In the absence of a court in the British sense of the term (with titles galore and *Burkes Peerage* for the newcomer to study), the Greek counterpart was a modest affair, with only a handful of relatives with titles and little "court life" as such. Hence Mary Carolou's importance to us and my eagerness to be of such help as I could to her.

The grand mistress of the court proceeded to drop a chunk of Pendelikon marble on the gouty ambassadorial foot. The queen, explained Mary, accompanied by the two princesses, desired to do some Christmas shopping at the American PX, preferably at a time when the emporium would not be too crowded.

That request set me back on my heels; in fact, it practically had me floored. I had a horrible mental picture of the teeming post exchange, full of aggressive American wives, likewise engaged in Christmas shopping, where within thirty seconds some bright-eyed customer would recognize the royal family, and within thirty more, pandemonium would ensue.

The embassy wiggled out of that one by persuading Mary Carolou that it would be ever so much easier for the queen and her daughters to come in on a Sunday afternoon (when the PX was normally closed); and I persuaded the air force colonel to have a bevy of Greek salesgirls, who were suitably impressed, rack up some overtime. But the story leaked, and a rich crop of ambassadorial kidding ensued. There were also venomous letters to congressmen from some of those recently dispossessed of their PX cards.

That experience, however, was nothing compared to the far more fundamental battle over "how many official Americans there were in Greece," and the termination of the aid program. My attempt to get rid of two officers and a handful of enlisted men of the Coast Guard, whose excuse for a presence in Athens was "there might be an accident in the Aegean Sea involving an American merchant ship," required considerable time and investigation, but my case was airtight. There was no more excuse for a Coast Guard contingent in the Athens embassy than there was for the taxpayers to underwrite a saxophone quartet on the island of Papua. But the State Department, instead of endorsing my complaint and joining me in demanding the withdrawal of the Coast Guard unit, merely forwarded my document to the admiral commanding, who went off like firecrackers, telling the chastened

State Department to mind its own business, while he minded his. In a private communication, I was advised to pipe down.

In addition to my unsuccessful hassle over the Coast Guard, my relations with the American military soon became strained. I doubted whether my army attaché needed seventy-seven officers and men — the largest attaché office, the colonel told me proudly, in the world. My eviction of the two-star general who headed the military assistance advisory group from an embassy house was followed by an altercation over the desire of the Pentagon (which I was able to block) to increase still further this 250-man Pentagon appanage, theoretically dedicated to teaching Greeks to use American NATO armament. The embassy maintained the full-time services of a government lawyer whose sole function was the handling of claims arising from the extracurricular activities of our uniformed personnel, mostly automobile cases. These were complicated by our "status of forces" agreement, which gave immunity to our men in uniform while they were performing their duty, but not when they were off duty. Thus a corporal transporting an official pouch from Ellinikon Airport to the chancery was immune until he delivered the bag. If he stopped for a beer on his way home and then ran into a baby carriage, the simplest solution was to pay a claim and get the GI out of Greece on the first westbound plane. (It was sometimes alleged that one of the most profitable activities in Greece was pushing baby carriages in front of GI jalopies.)

My war with the navy was on a different level. I resented the making of political speeches involving Greece by Sixth Fleet admirals, without previously clearing those passages with the embassy. The admirals, whose top luminary wore four stars and operated out of Naples with approximately the pomp of a viceroy of India in the days of Queen Victoria, were constantly sounding off, often in a clearly belligerent fashion. Their invariable retort, when I complained, was that they were speaking in their NATO rather than in their national capacity, and what they said was therefore none of my business. On that one, I got no more help from General Norstad than I had from Bob Murphy over General Clark's airplane. Larry Norstad said, with considerable frankness, that he was too busy trying to maintain order and morale among sixteen sovereign allies to get himself involved in what was essentially an American family problem. I had his "moral support," but he was not going to tangle with the titans of the Sixth Fleet.

My other gripe was over the frequency of naval visits to Greek ports, especially Piraeus, the port of Athens, by these same admirals, who rarely had the courtesy to consult the embassy about timing. They would barge in with a flattop and escorting destroyers (with upward of five thousand bluejackets).

While the Greeks showed remarkable forbearance and courtesy, each such visitation produced turmoil, causing the Greek naval officials to spend money (probably borrowed from the United States) on repetitive receptions and dinners and other maritime ceremonies.

Getting nowhere with hints and later with more overt representations, I took to staging trips out of Athens when what I regarded as a superfluous naval visitation loomed, thus leaving my deputy, plus my naval attaché, a mere four-striper, to handle the Sixth Fleet brass. The brass responded with complaints about "ambassadorial indifference." Once again I got nowhere, partly because my campaign received little State Department support and partly because King Paul was a sailor at heart, his torso covered with Danish tattoos acquired during his youth.

The episode of the nuclear submarine illustrates the point. On that occasion, navy headquarters in Naples did inquire whether there was any objection to a nonadvertised call of a nuclear submarine on the Attic Peninsula, for purposes not disclosed. I objected, not to the visit but to its proximity to Athens, and the likelihood of publicity with spectacular or slanted stories. The Communist party had been officially barred and had gone underground, but there were still many Communists in Greece; their intelligence service was excellent. I had a mental picture of the scare stories they would invent involving the alleged peril to Athens of contamination due to the presence of the vessel. The Greek press did start screaming, but not at me.

Through Greek NATO sources King Paul learned of the visit. He became all sailor, sending word through his naval aide to the American naval attaché that the royal family would be happy to be invited to inspect the atomic vessel. What was more, the king asked if they could return the next day and go for a short cruise and a dive in the vessel, a wildly hazardous proposal inasmuch as that type of warship was not far beyond the experimental stage. If anything had short-circuited, the entire dynasty might have been wiped out.

Another source of mounting tribulation was the invasion of Greece by traveling Americans who wanted to call on the queen. Nine-tenths of those visitors had no business to transact but wanted to brag that they had shaken the hand of royalty. It was futile to explain to most of these good people that with the situation reversed — Greek visitors desiring to invade the White House — not one in one hundred thousand would have penetrated the gates at 1600 Pennsylvania Avenue.

With Mary Carolou, the grand mistress of the court, the embassy cooked up a system that might have worked better had we been able to depend fully on Queen Frederika. Instead, she proved an unpredictable ally. With Mary's collaboration we drafted three separate form letters, third-person notes from the ambassador to the grand mistress (or, if the king was involved, to the chamberlain). All three letters were equally polite and protocolaire, in fancy stuffed-shirt English, so that a copy could be furnished to the disappointed petitioner (or his congressman or senator) as evidence that the embassy had done its best. The undisclosed purport of these letters varied, however, to a formidable degree. Type A letter was sent on behalf of someone whose importance, in the embassy view, merited an audience. Type B, equally eloquent and impressive, meant (to the palace) that it was a matter of indifference to the embassy whether Oscar Coonskin, president of the Coonskin Nuts and Bolts Company, was or was not received. Type C, which matched the other two in persuasiveness of tone, meant that if their majesties wasted time on that one, they needed to have their heads examined.

These arrangements were only moderately successful. The fault lay in the unpredictable nature of her majesty, who was genuinely friendly to the United States but who did not like to be told what to do. Thus she received a delegation of wives of mayors of a dozen small towns in Texas (clearly Type C material), who marched in waving Lone Star flags while singing "Deep in the Heart of Texas."

About that same time an important, if obnoxious, congressman (Type A letter, plus a phone call) cooled his increasingly sensitive heels for several days before giving up and going home, convinced that the embassy had shortchanged him and that the State Department appropriations ought to be pared still further.

The case of Chester Bowles illustrates another aspect of the problem. Chester, half of the famous advertising team of Benton and Bowles, had been ambassador to India in the Truman administration. He was currently congressman from Connecticut and a member of the Foreign Affairs Committee. Later, under President Kennedy, he was to be undersecretary of state, and after that ambassador to India again. Obviously he was Type A material, and an audience with the king was quickly arranged, although the royal family was at its country palace in Tatoi, in the Attic hills north of the capital. I was told to appear, with Chester, at 6 P.M. for "an informal audience."

Bowles and I set out in the embassy limousine. The driver, from Kifissia on, was fighting a midwinter snowstorm that made our progress slow and hazardous. It soon became clear that Chester had given the interview much thought. For most of the ride he outlined his views on the Balkans, inquiring whether there was anything in his proposed presentation that might be embarrassing to the embassy. I assured him to the contrary, warning him, however, that the subject was exceptionally complex.

Mr. Bowles was returning his notes to his pocket when his majesty himself greeted us in the hall, remarking that it was a foul night but that he had a fire going in the living room. There he proceeded to build us three monumental highballs in glasses almost as challenging as kegs: there must have been a half-quart of scotch in each glass, plus a squirt of soda. The ex-sailor attacked his with gusto, while Chester sipped, and I wondered whether my gold inlays would survive. Just as Chester was about to launch his first question, there was a stir behind us, and who should appear but Queen Frederika. Ordering tea, she plunked herself down in an armchair and started to talk. Forty minutes later, her tea consumed, her majesty was still talking and Mr. Bowles — an articulate character in his own right — had not, as the saying goes, been able to get a word in edgewise.

Suddenly the queen looked at her wristwatch and got to her feet. She addressed her husband exactly as wives do in the suburbs.

"Dear," she said, "if we aren't going to be frightfully late, we must go dress. Such a pleasure to meet you, Mr. Bowles, and to get, firsthand, your views on foreign affairs."

Another episode was the opening of the film *Never on Sunday,* starring the Greek actress Melina Mercouri. The idea of the producing company for what the producers called the "woil primeer" was to hire the biggest theater in Athens and have the royal box occupied by the royal family plus the American ambassador and his wife, plus the actress herself, on all of whom the spotlight would play during the intermission. The champagne would be on Hollywood.

The first I knew of this bomb ticking under my table was a phone call from the grand mistress of the court to say that a very fancy invitation had arrived, outlining the project and emphasizing that the leading artist was the daughter of a former mayor of Piraeus. *Viva Greece!* would be the theme of the evening. The royal family was tempted, but Mary, being a sagacious grand mistress, had prevailed on them to check with the embassy, which shortly received a comparable invitation on stiff paper almost an eighth of an inch thick. I told Mary Carolou I would call her back, and asked Emma please to summon Monty Stearns, a talented junior officer married to the beautiful and knowledgeable daughter of my predecessor, Ambassador Riddleberger. I figured that this attractive couple, whose Greek was fluent and who mingled vigorously in Greek society, would have movie news at their fingertips. I also consulted my chief spook.

In short order I was able to inform Mary that the theme of *Never on Sunday* was the harlot-with-a-heart-of-gold, and that the role was extremely well played and very funny. But was it, Mary interrupted, the kind of picture suitable for the queen and two teenager daughters? I told her that was for her majesty to decide. And, I added (a piece of paper just having been pushed under my nose by Emma), the director of the picture, reported to have more than a casual relationship with the star, had recently been accused in the United States of Communist sympathies and affiliations.

The upshot was that there were only three people occupying the royal box on the night of the "woil primeer" (which turned out to be Hollywood hokum, because the picture had already been released, amid hearty applause, in the United States). They were Crown Prince Constantine (representing the royal family), myself (without Lucy, who reportedly had a bad cold), and the star of the performance, who was as angry as a young lady could be, even when the crowd cheered her to the rafters, which it soon did. While our hostess glowered, Prince Constantine and I discussed, across the spacious decolletage of the lady, last weekend's hunting at Spetsipoula.

The Eisenhower administration fumbled its way into its last year, culminating in a visit to Greece by the president himself; but of much more significance to me was a spring visit by Secretary and Mrs. Herter, which bore on much broader international relations. A NATO ministerial meeting was scheduled to be held in Istanbul. Those intermittent affairs were attended by ministers for foreign affairs and the secretary of state. They invariably concluded with a communiqué emphasizing solidarity, following long harangues by European members demanding more aid, and arguments by the United States declaring that the allies ought to do more for their own protection. I suggested to the secretary that at the end of this meeting a short vacation in Athens might recharge his batteries and would give Lucy and me the pleasure of hosting him and his wife. I guaranteed that there would be no official banquets, although their majesties might propose a family meal. There would be a minimum of protocol.

Chris Herter arrived exhausted. For years he had suffered much arthritic pain, and travel was not easy for him. It was almost the end of the era of propeller planes, and although special aircraft for high officials (civilian Washington belatedly copying the Pentagon) had comfortable executive quarters, these long trips were tedious affairs at just half the speed that was about to be provided by jets. The secretary's assistants were bedded down in Athens hotels, the aircraft crew were told they could have forty-eight hours off duty, and the secretary and his wife were the first occupants of a new guest wing constructed at the embassy residence. Our only other guests the evening of their arrival were Sam and Margie Berger. It was a relaxed meal, and the participants retired early, but not before I had a private conversation with my chief. The secretary accepted a snifter of brandy and a pillow under his long, arthritic legs. "I have," he said, "some news for you — good news and bad. First, the good. You are one of six senior officers who are about to be promoted to career ambassador, and I want you to know how pleased I am. Greece is, I think, your seventh post as ambassador, already a record."[1]

As one of the original cast of career ministers, a rank established in 1946, in which I had vegetated for nearly a decade and a half, I was much gratified as well as amused by Chris's account of the confusion created by the White House because the president had refused for four years to appoint *any* career ambassadors after the initial group of four. The career ambassador legislation dated from 1955, and the only men thus far promoted to it were those original four (Loy Henderson, Bob Murphy, Jimmy Dunn — my predecessor in Rio — and Doc Matthews, as mentioned in the preceding chapter).

The president had agreed to the original list with reluctance, said the secretary, because it omitted the name of Livingston Merchant, then serving as ambassador to Canada. It was patiently explained, on several futile occasions, that although Merchant was clearly a superior candidate, he had joined the Foreign Service relatively late as a lateral entrant, and he did not have sufficient time to render him eligible under the conditions laid down by Congress for this "five-star diplomatic rank." It was not until 1960 that Livy Merchant became eligible, and during the four intervening years Eisenhower had stubbornly refused to approve any other candidates.[2]

1. A friendly exaggeration: Norman Armour was also chief of mission in seven countries, and in addition saw much distinguished service as assistant secretary of state. And of course no one could approach the record of Jefferson Caffery (1886–1974), whose career concluded with twenty-eight consecutive years as chief of mission. Unfortunately, both outstanding officers had retired before career ambassadorships were established.

2. The secretary then told me in confidence that in addition to Livingston Merchant and me, the following four officers were on the new list: Russian experts Chip Bohlen and Tommy Thompson; George Allen, whose attempts to kibitz my Korean adventures have been mentioned, and who later was ambassador to Greece; and Jimmy Riddleberger, my immediate predecessor in Athens. (Foreign Minister Averoff was to remark cheerfully to me a few days later, after the White House sent in the nominations, "I see Greece got three of you.")

"End good news," said my guest genially. "Now for the bad. You are probably in the dog house with more agencies in Washington than anyone in the entire Foreign Service. In general, I heartily approve your objectives, which, if I understand them, include terminating the aid programs and getting rid of what you regard as superfluous personnel, especially among the military. Correct?"

"That's right," I said, "thus incidentally reestablishing the prestige of the ambassadorial office. As to the aid programs, Jimmy Riddleberger agrees: our government has invested more than $2 billion in Greece since the end of the Communist fighting eleven years ago, but if the Washington bureaucracy has its way, their programs will go on forever.

"They have a special vocabulary," I went on. "They will agree, for example, that such-and-such a project might be 'wound down,' meaning that as soon as your back is turned, it will be business as usual. The next steps, if pressed, include arguing for 'just six months more' on a given project, or else all the progress thus far made will be jeopardized. When you slap that one down, such a project can be 'phased down' as an initial move toward 'phasing out.' I demanded a specific personnel roster for a 'phased out' program, and so help me, it called for almost exactly as many people as there were before, 'in order to tie up loose ends.' Did you know, Chris, that for the last five years there has been on the aid payroll a so-called expert on international banking? On international banking, mind you, for a country that practically invented banking. All Greece needed was some money to put in the kitty, not some American bureaucrat (who had possibly failed in banking at home) to explain the law of supply and demand."

We were still at it, half an hour later, when Mrs. Herter, in dressing gown, stuck her head in and said time was up. I had just admitted to the secretary that a message I had recently sent to Washington, to the effect that "every pipsqueak vice admiral in the Mediterranean thinks he can pipe himself up the Acropolis with the embassy gathering pebbles so he can make like Demosthenes," was provocative, even if labeled "Eyes Only," which (the secretary had said) practically assured that a copy would turn up in the Pentagon.

I asked for the only official favor I ever requested of a secretary of state. Could I have John A. Calhoun, the head of the secretary's secretariat, for Athens when he finished his current stint in the State Department?

"Not our Arch," protested Mrs. Herter. "Chris couldn't do without him."

The secretary uncurled his long frame, wincing as an arthritic twinge caught him. He explained to his wife that a Foreign Service officer was precluded by law from indefinite departmental duty, and Arch's tour would soon be up. He understood the personnel people wanted to send him to Berlin, but he would ask Arch where he wanted to go.

The next day was one that ended in calamity, but this we did not know until it was almost over. The only item on the Herter agenda was "a family luncheon" at Tatoi, at which the only guests were the Herters, Lucy, and I, an event as cordial and friendly as one could wish. Furthermore, it became apparent that Queen Frederika, who, it may already have been inferred, possessed a whim of steel, was determined to have several hours alone with the American secretary of state, and as she was determined, so she arranged it.

Having ascertained by a series of questions that the Herter program for the afternoon was a floating affair, she promptly tied the royal barge to it; that is to say, she proposed that she herself drive the secretary back to Athens in a palace car, via Sunion, at the tip of the Attic Peninsula, where we would all be her guests for tea. The rest of the family would follow in another of the palace automobiles, which the crown prince promptly offered to drive. Only the king was able to squirm out of that one, alleging monarchial desk duties. His majesty saw us off at the door, poor Chris Herter wedged into the crown prince's Italian roadster with the queen, looking both gay and lovely, behind the wheel.

The rest of us, including the princesses Sophie and Irene, distributed ourselves in a Rolls Royce, the crown prince driving, with the empty embassy limousine tagging along in third place. The queen, often gesticulating, drove at a leisurely pace, which bored Prince Constantine to the extent that he took to holding back and then catching up with such bursts of reckless speed that his sisters finally protested they would rather walk. Thereupon the crown prince subsided to a sulky sixty kilometers an hour. We had a pleasant tea at Sunion.

On our return, following a pause at the Athens palace, farewells were said and the Herters and Briggses changed into the embassy automobile for the short ride back to the embassy residence. We arrived there to find the secretary's senior staff waiting in a state of unzipped morale verging upon consternation. They were standing just inside the doorway with the news that a U-2 plane was missing, presumably shot down over Russia.

I can still recapture the shock and alarm this intelligence produced among my colleagues. The U-2 flights had been kept so highly classified that this was the first I had heard of that secret project. It was also the first that the State Department had heard of the incredible folly of arranging a flight so close to the impending summit meeting of President Eisenhower with Chairman Khrushchev in Paris.

It was known through our Washington intelligence sources that the Kremlin was aware, from its monitoring devices, of the U-2 flights, even though they might not have known of the incredible accuracy of the special photographic equipment that from sixty or seventy thousand feet could pick out an old man on a park bench reading *Pravda,* and then read the fine print on the page. Thus far the speed and altitude of the plane had been so great that although the Russians were surely working at it, previous flights — from Southeast Asia to a distant safe haven, clear across the breadth of the Soviet Union, with special attention to critical areas and installations — had not been intercepted.

Half a dozen of us moved into my office in the residence, a retreat just examined by one of my spook technicians, who had declared it free of listening devices, and I sent Yannis the houseboy for ice and the makings. The secretary was exhausted and in considerable pain, but he accepted a scotch and soda, while Ted Achilles of the Herter staff outlined what little information we had thus far received.[3]

Two telegrams had arrived. One reported that the plane, hours overdue at its destination, was presumably missing; the second was that in response to a question which later turned out to have been inspired by TASS, a brief statement had been given out in Washington that a weather plane, on a routine flight from Pakistan, might perhaps have strayed off course, possibly crashing in the mountains. Achilles drafted an urgent telegram to the president, which the secretary promptly signed, expressing concern over the potential for trouble in the situation and suggesting that there be an absolute minimum of official comment or attempted explanations until the matter could be discussed "at the highest level," which was secretarial politeness for imploring the president to keep his trap shut and to give orders that everyone else follow suit. The secretary added in his message that he would depart for Washington "soonest."

"Soonest" unfortunately turned out to be not until the following morning, because the crew of the secretary's plane, told they could have forty-eight hours of leisure, could not instantaneously be rounded up. Further-

---

3. Theodore Achilles, as a vice consul in Havana in 1930, imported the Model-A Ford I bought in 1934, from a successor vice consul, for $65. After a long stand as number two in Paris, Ted followed me as ambassador to Peru, where in 1956 he gave the sound but unheeded advice to Vice President Nixon that he had better stay away from San Marcos University. Ted became counselor of the department following Lima, and was now one of the secretary's principal assistants.

more, a short stop at Madrid had already been promised, during which renewal of certain important (to our military) base facility agreements would be discussed. Hence, Washington arrival was at least twenty-four hours away.

"Check me on my recollection," said the secretary wearily. "Aren't those U-2s equipped with destruction devices that the pilot is supposed to use if there is any chance whatever of the plane's falling into Soviet hands? He can bail out, but not until after he pushes the 'destruct button.'" His staff assured him that was the case, and on that less than optimistic note the meeting adjourned.

The Herters got away from Athens about 8 A.M., and after a grueling trip with the touchdown at Madrid and a pause to refuel at Goose Bay, arrived in Washington about 6 P.M., which was midnight, Athens time. In the meantime, in spite of the secretary's warning telegram, several official and conflicting versions of the disappearance of the plane had been issued in Washington. The Communists, after waiting until the administration had lodged itself on a conspicuously fragile limb, suddenly sawed it off by producing pictures of plane and pilot, both intact, downed and captured in the heart of Russia. Chairman Khrushchev then waited until the Paris summit meeting to administer the most painful personal humiliation that any president of the United States has suffered at Communist hands, breaking off the summit negotiations after figuratively spitting in the Eisenhower eye.

It remains my conviction that if Secretary Herter had not paused for that well-earned rest in Athens — had he, in short, been in Washington at the time when the U-2 disappeared — he could and would have prevented that barrage of conflicting statements which were to make publicly ridiculous the United States and personally to shame an American chief executive.

Today the incident still makes interesting speculation. In Christian Herter the president had a sagacious, competent, patriotic, and experienced secretary of state, but as Dean Acheson was cogently to point out in reference to his own career, no secretary can be more effective than the president who appoints him, and who is ultimately responsible for the conduct of foreign affairs. By allowing the Pentagon and the Central Intelligence Agency to call the turns in foreign affairs and to mount such a dangerous project on the eve of such an important international meeting — without even notifying the secretary of state, much less seeking his authorization — President Eisenhower was to prove once again that he was hardly the greatest statesman since Benjamin Franklin.

Although the Eisenhower administration still had some six months before Kennedy nosed out Nixon the following November, nothing of great moment occurred during that time in Athens. The Eisenhower visit to Greece accomplished nothing, although it used up a tidy sum in transportation, equipment, and mobilization of personnel and security, including some tearing up of the royal palace in order to render more safe and cozy the bedroom and bathroom occupied for one night by the president of the United States.

A pox on international diplomacy by chiefs of state — the most hazardous way of conducting foreign relations!

In November 1960, when Kennedy followed Eisenhower, all the chiefs of mission dutifully wrote: "Dear Mr. President-elect: Together with congratulations upon your victory at the polls, I have the honor to submit herewith my resignation as Ambassador to . . . ." These messages were sent to the State Department, which sat on them until the new secretary of state carried them to the White House, along with his proposed revised ambassadorial roster. This game of musical chairs might begin from one to six weeks after the inauguration of the new chief executive. Most of the politicos, interpreting the omens, promptly departed, but it was a trying period for professional diplomats, who under our Constitution are just as vulnerable as the politicians to being remanded to the ashcan.

I was therefore favorably impressed by the briskness of young President Kennedy, who let scarcely a week go by before sending personal telegrams to each chief of mission. Unfortunately for my neighbors in Southeast Europe, the president made a clean sweep of almost everyone in the vicinity except Doc Matthews in Vienna and me in Athens. Furthermore, the retained ambassadors soon received personally inscribed presidential letters, improving (so I naively hoped) the chances of an ambassador's being in fact boss of his own ship, to the detriment of military hangers-on, superfluous dispensers of aid for the backward, the spook fraternity, the propagandists, and other accretions, most of them accumulated since Franklin Delano Roosevelt's time.

On the whole, the forced resignation system had worked fairly well, with certain exceptions exemplified by the State Department's servitude imposed on behalf of that pious old gossip Bernard Baruch. By way of reward, for sixteen long years Barney had first one, and then a second, incompetent relative serving as ambassador abroad.

The new president soon created another favorable impression by acting upon a long-standing Athens recommendation that the prime minister of Greece be invited to be the guest of the United States on an official visit including Washington and New York. This was a trip originally urged by my predecessor, and we were pleased at the prompt action by the new president. April was the date fixed, and since it was the first such visit since the inauguration of President Kennedy, the Greeks regarded it as a fine feather in the national cap to have Prime Minister Caramanlis the primary recipient of such an honor.

I was to discover that progress had been made in the mechanics of these official enterprises since that initial one in which I had participated in the 1930s, in honor of Tacho Somoza of Nicaragua. The Greek prime minister's program called for a formal welcome by the secretary of state, flanked by the Greek ambassador and his staff, plus ranking State Department officials, including the American ambassador to Greece, summoned to Washington a day or two in advance. The foreign guests stayed at Blair House, across the street from the White House, and attended a white tie dinner there that night. The next night the secretary of state was host at a slightly less formal affair, and the third night the guest of honor was host to President and Mrs. Kennedy at a dinner and reception at the Greek embassy.

Three days in New York followed. The prime minister was housed in one of the tower suites at the Waldorf, a motorcycle escort waiting on 50th Street below and plainclothes types scrutinizing all those entering or leaving by the side door. The first night in New York, the State Department, represented by the chief of protocol, was host at a theater party for the prime minister, followed by an informal nightclub supper. The next night there was a huge banquet attended by several thousand in a hotel ballroom, the mayor of New York as host.

That banquet was the climax of the New York stay, and after that, for a week or ten days, the prime minister toured the country, visiting Greeks, seeing the sights, and, presumably, catching his breath.

Such official business as was transacted on official visits usually took place the first afternoon at the White House, with subsequent discussions at the State Department. Since the end of the war a certain sordidness had crept into those proceedings, because the question almost inevitably arose as to the amount of the credits to be extended to the visitor's government in order to have the visit regarded, back home, as a success. Most statemen, it may be remarked, returned with promises of subsidy — tons of wheat for India, a steel mill for Zamboanga, or a tunnel under the Andes to bring moisture to lands arid since Inca times.

Washington was a heady place that spring of 1961, during the annual miracle of the cherry blossoms. There was an electricity in the air, a feeling of self-confidence in youthful leadership that had been lacking in the 1950s, and of a country on the move, preparing to tackle great issues. The inspiring words of the inaugural address still echoed. America was strong and vigorous. It was the high tide not only of the new administration but of the optimism and self-confidence of the country.

Initially, I was much attracted to the young president. Prime Minister Caramanlis was due to arrive on a Monday morning, and the previous Saturday morning Lewis Jones, the outgoing assistant secretary of state for Near Eastern affairs, and I had been summoned to the White House to tell the president what Caramanlis was likely to have on his mind. I was told to prepare a two-page memorandum; Lewis Jones, to my horror, brought a "briefing book" almost as heavy as a metropolitan telephone directory, bristling with statistical tables and tabs — several hundred pages that led me to suspect that the only thing omitted might be the Spartan boy with the fox in his shirt — and I wasn't sure I couldn't find him if I looked in the appendix.

Outside on the lawn the blades of a helicopter turned lazily, awaiting the impending presidential takeoff for a spring weekend at Glen Ora. Kennedy winced slightly when handed the briefing book, which an aide promptly stuffed into a briefcase. The president said he would dig into it over the weekend, and would we please return at nine Monday morning (three hours before the prime minister was due at National Airport in Washington), prepared to answer questions. After dealing with President Kennedy's predecessor, who possibly read his last briefing book on the eve of D-Day, this was an encouraging sign. Kennedy — evidently a lightning reader — was as good as his word, with pointed questions for us to answer on Monday morning.

Two incidents punctuated the New York visit. The first was produced by Aristotle Onassis, who crashed the after-theater supper party. A more serious crisis faced me the following morning when I turned up for duty at the prime minister's suite in the Waldorf Towers, from which loud sounds were audible. These seemed to be the prelude to, or perhaps the accompaniment of, a game involving the prime minister, the foreign minister, the Greek UN representative, and the archbishop of North and South America — complete with whiskers, robes, incense, and upside-down black bonnet. Everyone was shouting at once. The general drift appeared to be that Prime Minister Caramanlis had declared he was damned if he would go, while the other three pleaded with him not to run out at the last minute on the huge New York banquet in his honor scheduled for that evening. It turned out, the foreign minister interpreting, that the prime minister had that morning been informed that among those at the head table would be the defeated presidential candidate, Richard M. Nixon. Furthermore, Nixon was scheduled to speak.

It was the thesis of the Greek prime minister that for him to attend a banquet in those circumstances would be an unforgivable insult to President Kennedy that would destroy any vestige of goodwill thus far created by his visit to the United States. He had maintained this position for some time before my arrival, with several broken coffee cups testifying to the strength of his convictions.

This was one of those unrehearsed occasions when you have to act fast. Disregarding my position outside the hierarchy of visitors, I plunged into the game like a substitute quarterback in a borrowed helmet, throwing passes in all directions. I said this was New York and not Thessaloniki, and that I knew more about American political customs than he did. What was more, far from resenting the presence of his erstwhile opponent, President Kenendy would be flattered as well as gratified at this demonstration of the bipartisan nature of Greek-American friendship — as witness the fact that another occupant of the head table would be Adlai Stevenson, the presidential candidate of almost a decade ago who had been defeated by Eisenhower.

Caramanlis was an admirer of Governor Stevenson; that, and the eloquent interpreter services by his colleagues of my remarks finally won the ball game, with the somewhat sulky assurance of Prime Minister Caramanlis that his proposed attack of influenza would accordingly be deferred. It also earned me, on the way down in the elevator, the hirsute and Orthodox equivalent of a Latin American *abrazo,* since his eminence was scheduled to preside that night along with the mayor of New York and to perform various chores designed to promote celestial approval of an event that featured three thousand guests.

And there, as far as I was concerned, my United States visit as ambassador to Greece should have ended and I ought to have returned to my normal diplomatic duties. I should have flown back as scheduled to my post in Athens. Instead, by the sheer chance of being seated only a few places away from Governor Stevenson at the banquet, I was shortly backed into a corner, and it would be several weeks before I was again to admire the Parthenon.

By coincidence, the Greek official visit had begun on the day of the landing of the Cuban boys at the Bay of Pigs. I had marveled at the concentration of the president on our Attic affairs, as well as at his composure, as more and more bad news from Cuba was handed him by Secretary of State Dean Rusk, who kept excusing himself to take phone calls the tenor of which became increasingly tragic.

Having breakfasted that previous Monday morning with Allen Dulles, I was privy to these Cuban events and only less disturbed by them than the head of CIA. I reminded Allen of my seven years in Cuba and asked if I could be of any service. I was told that matters were being handled directly by the president and his brother. That reckless offer on my part may, however, have trickled back to Stevenson and encouraged the following project.

Governor Stevenson, a patriot as well as a gentleman, and the chief American delegate to the UN, was the angry man. A lesser man than Stevenson might have resigned or thrown rocks through White House windows for placing him in an impossible position facing the invectives of the Castro delegate to the UN. Notwithstanding which, President Kennedy (now all public penitence and "I will take the blame") had asked Stevenson to make on Kennedy's personal behalf a tour of Latin America to canvass the post–Bay of Pigs state of feeling within the hemisphere. The governor phoned me, shortly after the Greek banquet in New York, asking me to join him on the tour.

By that time I had read the president's March 17, 1961, speech whereby (a few days before the Bay of Pigs enterprise) Kennedy sought to launch Alianza para el Progreso, an idea stolen from the Republicans, who had stolen it from President Kubitschek of Brazil. It was by all odds the worst speech delivered by a chief executive on the subject of Pan-Americanism in years, and it had been made at the White House before the assembled Latino diplomats at a white tie reception. The abolition of poverty was to be the responsibility of the United States, from Point Barrow to Cape Horn. "Viva Alianza para el Progreso," chirped the guests until they started reading some of the fine print thereafter emanating from the White House cellar, the effect of which admonitions, if taken literally, would have been to promote a revolution in practically every country from El Salvador to Chile.

At that point, I repeat, I should have held Governor Stevenson off — if necessary, with a boat hook. I should have returned to the Acropolis and gone about my Greek business. Common sense and the voice of experience should have served me better. Against that, however, were my high regard for Adlai and recognition that, within my over three decades in professional diplomacy, seventeen years had been spent either in Latin America or working in Washington on problems involving the hemisphere. Stevenson knew nothing of the Good Neighborhood, except for a private trip with Bill Benton the year before, during which one of them was to coin the unfortunate phrase "the revolution of rising expectations," which was to be hitched to Alianza like bubblegum to a school desk. What else Stevenson learned about the continent you could hide under an acorn.

Maybe, I thought, I could do something useful, something that might make the inter-American system more practical or less like a Macy's Thanksgiving Parade balloon. That was my mistake, which I recognized too late when I attended the single "briefing session" for Stevenson in the State Department. Attending was a professor from Harvard — an economist, I shortly discovered, who was to succeed Jack Cabot as ambassador in Rio — with whom I quarreled incessantly on the tour over his efforts (to which Adlai finally put a stop) to monkey with my draft reporting telegrams.

The Stevenson expedition was not a success. Not only is it impossible to visit seventeen capitals in eleven days without experiencing such numbing exhaustion that soon you cannot remember where you slept night before last, but there is no opportunity between stops to recoup your energies — as there used to be between ports aboard ship. Roused at 7 A.M. after three or four hours of sleep, with no opportunity to inscribe, much less edit, your notes on the two hours with the chief of state you saw the day before, you were projected from the farewell ceremonies in the country last visited directly into the speech of greeting to be made an hour later in Asunción or Santiago or La Paz.

Stevenson was wonderful in the impromptu charm of his arrival statements and in his durability, but his ideas soon convinced me that had he become president, I should have climbed the nearest ceiba tree. His conviction that "the underdog is always right" was the thesis I had argued two decades before with Larry Duggan, to as little avail.

We had survived a long day in Chile, where Bob and Ginny Woodward had just become our representatives, to the satisfaction of the Chileans. By the special presidential plane at Adlai's disposal it was a short flight to La Paz, at over 12,500 feet above sea level. We went from the world's highest landing strip to the house of the Bolivian president, which was heated by a fireplace that burned eucalyptus, giving off a pleasant smell but exhausting the small amount of oxygen still existing at that altitude. To make matters worse, our incompetent La Paz embassy had paid no attention to my telegram demanding flasks of oxygen in the hotel rooms of the visitors.

I folded — that is, I passed out. It was *soroche,* the affliction that often attacks those who move too quickly from sea level to the altiplano, probably aggravated in my case by fatigue and the frayed nerves of one whose advice had been repeatedly rejected. We still had three capitals ahead of us, and although I recovered sufficiently to warn Governor Stevenson that the president of Ecuador was crazy (one of the few bits of intelligence with which Adlai readily agreed), I continued to feel like an undried dishcloth all the way back to the Potomac.

As far as I am aware, no written summary of the Stevenson trip was undertaken. We did, however, report to President Kennedy, who received us in his second floor bedroom, where he was recovering from a back wrenched, so the press reported, playing touch football at Glen Ora. Stevenson, whose private view of the chief executive I knew to have been affected by White House handling of the Bay of Pigs mortification, appeared to be as buoyant self, although he dwelt largely and disproportionately on the plight of the disadvantaged, meaning Andean Indians, dwellers in the Brazilian favelas, and the masses generally. He contrasted this with the position of the surviving old families, who in a number of countries continued to govern as heirs of the Spanish conquerors whom they had evicted in the first quarter of the nineteenth century.

As a small footnote to history I recall that the president detained me for a few moments at the end of the session to thank me for making the South American trip, and to remark that according to the letters from his wife, ostensibly enjoying a private spring visit to Greece, she was enjoying an exceptionally enjoyable vacation. Mrs. Kennedy was residing in the embassy residence in Athens under the chaperonage of my deputy, Tap Bennett, and his wife, Margaret, who, as the daughter and granddaughter of eminent American ambassadors, knew how to cope with exalted visitors. President Kennedy authorized me to convey the observation to the Greek ambassador: "My wife is having the time of her life. She says Greek hospitality is tops."

Later that day I concluded my Stevenson episode by presiding over a State Department session. On presenting Governor Stevenson, I confided my admiration for the survival potential of my recent traveling companion. Stevenson, looking as fresh as a June strawberry, replied that having engaged in two presidential campaigns, and having lost both of them, there was no form of human exhaustion he had not learned to defy.

Whereupon Stevenson proceeded to advocate a policy toward our southern neighbors that was the negation of practically every recommendation I had made, although he had the honesty to pause from time to time and with a friendly smile in my direction observe, "The contrary views of Ambassador Briggs are worthy of study."

And so we returned to Greece, but not in the leisurely fashion anticipated. One of the few stipulations I had been able to inject into the

South American scenario was that we would return to Europe by ship, but a strike by one of the prehensile maritime unions canceled steamship sailings. After a one-night sleepless airplane flight we found ourselves facing protocol at Frankfurt, plus the sad news in a *Stars and Stripes* someone handed me of the suicide the day before of Ernest Hemingway in faraway Idaho. I had received a cheerful letter from him shortly before leaving Washington.

Dodging immense German trucks down the Autobahn on our way back to Greece did little to revive me, although a short pause in Belgrade with George Kennan, who had recently taken over the post as a Kennedy ambassador, undoubtedly did. However, there I had a wire from Tap Bennett in Athens, urging hasty return, for reasons continued in a long State Department telegram he was repeating to our consul general in Thessaloniki, to await my arrival there.

That telegram proved a further demonstration of how a basically good idea (in this case, a meeting of chiefs of mission) can be converted by bureaucrats into something dreamed up by a patient in an asylum. Chester Bowles — he of the Balkan discussion with Queen Frederika — abetted by Soapy Williams, the crazy former governor of Michigan who had been appointed assistant secretary for African affairs, wanted to stage in Athens some four weeks hence (at the height of the Greek summer tourist season, with every hotel room within miles of Constitution Square in Athens already reserved and often already paid for) a super chiefs of mission meeting. This would include all the Near East embassies and most of those on the east and Mediterranean coasts of Africa, plus a delegation from Washington. Ambassadorial wives were to be included, along with "certain senior administrative officers" — the latter a camel's-nose-under-the-tent proposition that I had been fighting against for a decade, inasmuch as administrative personnel, while essential to the operation of an establishment, have nothing legitimate to do with policy or with the diplomacy that implements policy.

My telegram to Washington from Thessaloniki (if it survives somewhere in the archives, it is possibly kept in an asbestos folder) was only partially successful. It saved Athens from the invasion, but instead of postponing the affair until, say, October, a pleasant and relatively tourist-free time of year in Greece, Chester Bowles and Soapy Williams moved the location to Cyprus. A worse spot could not have been chosen.

Cyprus, independent scarcely a year, was already seething with Greco-Turkish animosities. Any other island would have been better, and most of them except Spetsipoula and Skorpios, which were owned respectively by Niarchos and Onassis, were available.

It proved to be a circus, with clowns but with little laughter. I remember a pompous American political appointee from a Muslim post who dwelt laboriously on "empathy," which he illustrated by telling how he banished from the main reception room at his embassy residence the galaxy of signed photographs of Washington and foreign notables, substituting for the lot of them a single object, a copy of the Koran, open no doubt to an appropriate passage, resting upon a tiny prayer rug on the large expanse of the top of the grand piano. There was also an aging ingenue from Washington who harangued the ambassadorial wives about not referring to the inhabitants of the host country as "the natives," or mentioning classified subjects during conversations at mealtimes, "because so many of the servants understand English."

The only persons I can remember who made any sense were Julius Holmes, our ambassador to Iran (who had joined the Foreign Service in 1925); our wretched and beaten-down host, a junior officer just appointed to Nicosia; my ex-chief spook from Macedonia (who had been filched from my staff and sent to try to bring some order into the competing CIA and Defense Department hordes); and Ed Murrow of World War II broadcasting fame, who had just been appointed by President Kennedy to head the propaganda apparatus officially known as the United States Information Agency. Ed chain-smoked cigarettes and coughed, but what he said between coughs was worth listening to.

One of the worst moments of my career occurred when the fatuous and futile proceedings, after three gruesome days, were grinding to a halt via a final harangue by Undersecretary of State Chester Bowles. It was produced by Ambassador Holmes, who reminded me, in a whispered aside, that as senior Foreign Service officer present, it would be my duty to address the Washington delegation on behalf of all those who had attended, expressing, as Julius gleefully put it, "suitable appreciation."

Enveloping myself in a cloud of cigar smoke, I remember declaiming that I was sure that for each one of us it had been an unforgettable experience, and that each of us would return to his post filled with memories. It was a feeble effort. A few weeks later I found myself in an oxygen tent at the tiny but excellent air force hospital that occupied a corner of Ellinikon Airport, victim of a coronary attack that had been building up ever since I was felled by *soroche* and frustration in the capital of Bolivia.

For the next six weeks Tap Bennett ran the Athens embassy efficiently while I wrestled with an ulcer (the occupational disease of many professional diplomats) and an attack of gout. The latter, acquired two decades before, is bad enough when the victim is otherwise intact. In an oxygen tent the phenomenon was sufficient to mobilize an air force medical colonel from Wiesbaden, whose prescription — originated by the ancient Greeks over two millennia before — was identical with that being administered by the air force captain in charge of my case.

My hospitalization was notable for a visit of sympathy from Larry Norstad, whose four stars and gaggle of accompanying NATO brass threw the local GIs into such astonished excitement that the orderlies, on entering and departing my ward, thereafter saluted so often that I was tempted to put up a sign: "Don't salute the ambassador; he can't salute back."

After six weeks I was discharged, and crept about our garden on shrunken shanks, spending the next month with my staff coming to the residence for official business. Since I was deprived of cigars, my ensuing ill temper was hard on Lucy and my colleagues. After Fidel Castro, I had been unashamedly obtaining my cherished *tabacos* from England.

Nevertheless, I was gradually building back my depleted forces and contentedly settling back into the crystal gazing and fire fighting that constituted much of ambassadorial diplomacy in Greece. I had a new military attaché who spoke Greek and did not incessantly feud with my highly experienced chief spook, and a new naval attaché with an amphibious plane and a matching penchant for bird shooting. Although I missed the closeness of my association with Sam Berger and Arch Calhoun, both now ambassadors (the one in Korea and the other wasted on Chad), Sam's replacement, Tap Bennett, likewise came out of the top drawer of the Foreign Service. And I was making slow but steady progress in reducing the spectacular conspicuousness of the American official presence in Greece.

At which point, just as 1962 began, I received a telegram from Dean Rusk (who must have taken time out from Vietnam to sign it) informing me that the president had decided to transfer me to Madrid, with instructions — as soon as possible after my nomination had been submitted to the Senate — to pause in Spain en route home long enough to case the joint and prepare some recommendations. (The bureaucratic telegraphese probably read "to assess the situation with a view to participation in the formulation of future policy.") I was reminded that Franco was seventy-two years old and said to be failing, and that our military and naval base arrangements (which were huge and expanding) were shortly due for renegotiation.

Spain would have been my eighth post as ambassador, and as a career ambassador in grade, retirement — normally three years in the future — could be deferred at the discretion of the president. Moreover, the pleasant relations we had with the Greek royal family had been expanded to include Prince Juan Carlos, whose engagement to Princess Sophie had been announced along with tidings from Madrid that, upon Franco's retirement, the monarchy would be restored with Juan Carlos on the throne. By leaving Greece when we did, we missed the royal wedding, an ecumenical affair involving both the Orthodox and the Catholic churches. (The French ambassador, dean of the diplomatic corps, browbeat the Greek palace into inviting the diplomatic corps to attend both religious ceremonies, to the boundless rage of the majority of his colleagues.)

Our own departure from Athens was muted by the sadness of leaving friends, but enormously facilitated by my still being on the recuperation list, which provided an excuse to eliminate the major part of the interminable official dinners, banquets, and other forms of farewell tortures to which a departing envoy is exposed. We had a final weekend at Spetsipoula, the air force kindly assigning the same young captain who had inflated my oxygen tent to accompany me. The luncheon with the royal family at Tatoi had as other guests only the foreign minister and his wife, for whom we had much affection. In his remarks preceding the toast, King Paul referred to the impending transfer to Madrid of his elder daughter, who would be able to report, he hoped, upon the continued well-being of the Briggs family. He also informed me privately, over a brandy in his study, that he was disappointed that the regulations of my government (since changed) precluded his awarding the customary Grand Cross of the Order of Phoenix, which would have considerably brightened the austere pinafore in which I was expected to present credentials in Madrid.

Our first and only relationship with royalty thus ended on notes of sympathy and friendship. King Paul died two years later, and the monarchy ended in 1967 when his son attempted to defy the usurping colonels.

En route to Washington we did, as scheduled, spend ten busy days in Spain, and sailed from Algeciras for a week aboard the *Independence*, which went some way toward compensating us for the failure of our plans for an Atlantic crossing on the *America* seven months before. I did not see Franco, both for reasons of protocol (I had not yet been confirmed by the Senate and was technically in Spain incognito) and because he was temporarily incapacitated by the loss of a finger when one barrel of his shotgun exploded, inflicting a not dangerous but exceedingly painful wound. The bird shooting in Spain was fantastically good for those few fortunate enough to enjoy it, and I hoped soon to be among them.

Instead, the State Department medical fraternity, which in view of my recent coronary record in Greece examined me with what seemed at the time to be extravagant thoroughness, did not approve of what they thought they saw, including a growing listlessness. Resisting the demand that I go to Bethesda for observation, I was able to persuade the State Department medical director to approve of Johns Hopkins, one of whose leading physicians had looked after the Briggs family for years. Thus I found myself on a train to Baltimore on the day I should otherwise have been appearing before the Foreign Relations Committee for the customary scrutiny by Senator William Fulbright and his colleagues.

Weeks later I was still at Johns Hopkins, having barely squeaked by after a debilitating bout with infectious hepatitis. It might be a long time, said the medicos, before I could again undertake ambassadorial duties. In fact, recommended our medical director — who had generously visited me several times in Baltimore — I should accept medical retirement as provided for in Foreign Service legislation, and turn in my uniform.

Meanwhile, not unreasonably, my nomination as ambassador to Spain had been withdrawn by President Kennedy, my replacement being my old and devoted friend Bob Woodward, who the year before had entertained Adlai Stevenson and me in Santiago de Chile.

On June 30, 1962, after thirty-seven years, the last half of them spent in embassies on three continents, I sadly relinquished my frayed ambassadorial toga.

Pride Dwelt Upon — A Time for Reflection

The human liver is an arrogant, eccentric, and unpredictable piece of machinery that, when incited by hepatitis, can give the owner a protracted period of incarceration, accompanied by much wringing of hands on the part of the medical profession. The three months I was hospitalized became a period of meditation upon the career I had followed and the life I had led, and the changing status of the United States in world affairs during the period when I had been a participant.

These speculations have continued during the years since my retirement, sometimes with anguish, sometimes with anger and contempt, but rarely without the optimistic hope that the United States, having at long last purged itself, still possesses the stamina to forge ahead.

Mine had been a congested career. Seventeen transfers in thirty-seven years and eight ambassadorial appointments in the last two decades of my service did not impress me then, or since, as the most efficient utilization of manpower. The 750 individuals comprising the State Department of Charles Evans Hughes and President Coolidge (who signed my first commission) had grown to 1,900 by September 1939, when World War II erupted. With the coming of the Cold War, diplomacy was plundered by the Pentagon, but this did not prevent thousands of additional bureaucrats from climbing aboard the top-heavy and at times rudderless ship of state.

The multiplicity of our transfers, and all those successive staffs my wife and I had at so many different posts, provided us with an inexhaustible warehouse of memories, only a fraction of which could adorn the book I hoped someday to write. What, I wondered, had become of those thirteen brides, on whose absent parents' behalf and at their request, I had given in marriage: thirteen daughters in seven countries, beginning in the ancient cathedral of Santo Domingo, with Columbus's bones almost within the shadow of the altar, and ending in Athens with Toni Riddleberger and Monty Stearns, preceding by only a few months the wedding of my temporary secretary — the girl who had written, in place of "Man does not live by bread alone" (which I had rather pompously dictated), "Man does not love in bed alone" in an official document dispatched to Washington before her improvement of the text had been discovered. That same maiden, as she took my arm in the aisle of the Athens church, muttered in her ambassador's ear, "The countdown has begun."

Then there had been a sumptuous wedding in Rio in our beautiful embassy residence, with the president of Brazil as best man, and a visiting United States senator, who was a shutterbug festooned with cameras, happily snapping picture after picture. He was a dreary and unpleasant little man who had probably cadged more free lodgings and free meals from the Foreign Service than any other member of the Congress, but he had such a lovely time watching President Kubitschek participate in the nuptials of my wife's lush Brazilian secretary to her American groom that the senator's account of the virtues of the American ambassador to Brazil left the corresponding desk in the State Department in an almost comatose condition. (When the senator departed, we tipped the residence servants on his behalf, giving them the impression that our dismal guest had left us the money.)

And there was the wedding of Gloria, of our Korean embassy staff, to a marine captain, in a chapel on the edge of what a few days before had been the front line. It was so soon after the armistice signing that the marines were still in battle dress. A marine, when he is not fighting, is likely to be among the most sentimental of creatures; in Seoul we enlisted the sympathetic interest of the major general commanding. He not only attended the wedding, but he supplied a helicopter to transport the bride, himself, and Lucy and me to the chopper pad beside the chapel, only a few hundred yards from the edge of the truce zone. Giving the matter further attention, the general likewise loaned his own cook, a mess sergeant, who produced a wedding cake of noble dimensions to grace the table at the Officers' Club after the chaplain had completed his business.

The sergeant, with the hash marks of many enlistments on his sleeves, was no novice at helicopter-riding. In icing his cake he was mindful of the vibrations to which it would be subjected on the half-hour flight to the front.

Gloria was a very pretty girl, with Spanish brown eyes and a figure that would have attracted attention in whatever environment. The ceremony in the chapel was both dignified and martial, with all the groom's fellow officers converging thereafter on their club, and the enlisted men, many of whom had not seen an American girl in months, lining the road and cheering with spontaneous if envious goodwill.

Presently it was time to cut the cake — the bridal couple were catching a late plane for honeymoon leave in Tokyo — and, since this was a frontline enterprise, there were no dress uniforms and there was no ceremonial sword. The cake was cut with a marine bayonet, a powerful and wicked-looking instrument that was handed to Gloria by the mess sergeant himself. What the sergeant had added to the icing so the helicopter ride would not shake his cake apart remains his culinary secret. If there is any form of edible cement, he used it. Tapping this formidable carapace with the tip of the bayonet produced a sound not unlike striking a hubcap with a tire iron, nor did pressure exerted thereafter produce even a dent in the shining surface. The bride, with all admiring eyes upon her, appealed to her husband to guide and strengthen her hand. At that moment the sergeant, placing his own interpretation upon the bride's hesitation, declared in the tone of voice a sergeant of marines acquires over the years, "That's all right, lady. That's a bran'-new bay'nit; it ain't been used."

I wondered, in my isolation ward at Johns Hopkins with the vigilant eye of my night nurse upon me, what had become of those thirteen couples, and whether I would ever see them again. For several Christmases after each wedding we received cards, and not infrequently little oblongs of stiff paper with either a blue or a pink ribbon attached. But with so many moves to so many countries, we gradually lost touch with most of them, although at least one of the grooms since became an ambassador.

Thinking of Korea, I also remembered the ordeals of Arthur Dean, Foster Dulles's senior law partner in Sullivan and Cromwell, who was dispatched to my bailiwick soon after Gloria's wedding to perform some unperformable magic at Panmunjom, where the interminable military negotiations leading to the armistice had been held, and which was again the scene of acrimonious debate over certain of its terms. I was delighted to welcome Arthur, who, unlike nine-tenths of the "special emissaries with the personal rank of ambassador" to whom I had been exposed, was sagacious, cooperative, and a wonderful companion. He used to emerge at least once a week from his Quonset hut and fly back to Seoul, where he would accompany me to call on President Rhee, recounting the results of his activities.

Secretary Dulles, having informed the Pentagon that Arthur Dean was to have the equivalent of three-star rank and the Far East Command having been instructed accordingly, Mr. Dean was not only accorded singular deference by the military but his presence occasioned comment on the part of the GIs, whose compound adjoined the restricted area set aside for the colonels and generals. On his first visit to Seoul, Dean recounted having overheard the following conversation:

First GI: "Who's this civilian bird wandering around the VIP area?"
Second GI: "That's the American ambassador."
First GI: "Maybe so. But I thought we had an American ambassador.
    He was around here last month with General Taylor."
Second GI: "Yeah, that's right. But that ambassador is too smart to hang
    around this dump, so they had to find them a special one."

That story delighted Ambassador Dean, who retold it with relish.

Dean's negotiations were predictably unproductive, but instead of sitting around indefinitely, listening to reiterated Communist invective and abuse, Dean suddenly broke off the session, after making observations to his opposite numbers that must have made Uncle Joe Stalin, recently deceased, squirm upon his bed of embers. Ambassador Dean paid a farewell call on President Rhee (who was delighted that nothing had been completed) and was homeward bound by airplane before Foster Dulles's irritated comments caught up with him.

Not all of my memories were as cheerfully sustaining as these incidents culled from my cornucopia of treasures, although it remains my conviction that the Diplomatic Service can, and does, produce the largest quota of improbable and diverting experiences that any profession could provide. It was a wise senior officer who told me early in my career, "Always take your job seriously, but never yourself." It was sound advice, and my good memories helped to smooth over some of those days in Baltimore when anxious faces peered through my doorway. I remembered an observation made to me in Prague by Sir Pierson Dixon, one of England's most gifted diplomats of the century. Bob Dixon and I became close friends, and I asked him one day if he were disappointed that local official duties had prevented his attendance at the recent coronation of Queen Elizabeth II. "Yes," said Bob. "I hated to miss all those perfectly dreadful things that always happen."

But not all my memories were happy. The death of my friend Larry Duggan came floating out of the dark caves of memory to plague me. I found myself heavy with doubts over that still unexplained event in 1948. Duggan, my immediate chief in the late 1930s, after fifteen years in the State Department jumped, fell, or was pushed to his death from his office window in New York. Larry was a human being of great personal charm for whose patriotism and integrity during the three years when I served as assistant chief of the Latin American Division I would unhesitatingly have vouched, even though our views about humanity in general and international affairs in particular remained separated by an unbridgeable gap. Larry worried constantly about the downtrodden masses, and I doubt whether he ever got over the suspicion that American companies abroad were the exploiters of the people. My own experience in foreign lands (whereof Larry had none except as a traveler or attendee of international conferences) convinced me that nine out of ten American enterprises were conducted with a greater degree of social conscience and a keener awareness of the importance of the welfare of the workers than many corresponding firms operated by nationals of the countries concerned.

Larry was, and we used to argue the point repeatedly, a sucker for the underdog, whereas my thesis was that the underdog got under, along with his mange and his fleas, just as often through indolence, incompetence, or failure to grasp his opportunities as he did through oppression or exploitation. Larry and Adlai Stevenson would have seen eye to eye on many a social issue. Moreover, his behavior toward Ambassador Spruille Braden in Cuba, over the latter's torpedoing of a pet project of Harry Dexter White of the Treasury Department, had always seemed to me strange and not in character with the man I remembered with affection. Larry's liberal views were bound to have attracted the attention not only of New Dealers, as the leftists of the 1930s were called, but also of professional Communists. Larry and Noel Field (who undoubtedly became a Party member shortly after abandoning the State Department for the League of Nations in the early 1930s) were intimate friends. For several years their apartments were side by side on Judiciary Square. Larry and Alger Hiss also were friends. Communist recruiters, whose freedom of action was increased by the Soviet-American alliance following Pearl Harbor, must inevitably have eyed Larry Duggan as promising, if not uniquely valuable, material. That was so partly because his honesty and his unquestioned patriotism, along with his liberal attitude toward society, must have rendered him susceptible to their publicly proclaimed objectives while at the same time perhaps dulling his perception of the actual status of "the masses" in countries already under Communist domination.

There are three possible explanations of Larry's death: first, that foreign agents, apprehending dangerous disclosures by an awakened Duggan, gained access to his office (which would not have been difficult for trained operators) and hurled him to his death. No evidence to substantiate this conjecture has, to my knowledge, been uncovered. Or it may have been a case of suicide triggered by depression induced by tardy recognition of the real character and objectives of some of his friends and associates: a sudden impulse in response to some overwhelming inner compulsion. Again, there is no evidence to support that conclusion. Those who were with Larry on the last day of his life (December 20, 1948) reported him as cheerfully preparing for Christmas with his wife and children, and that his plans included a brief trip to Washington in connection with international students. He was at the time director of the Carnegie Endowment for International Education, an agency with which I had tangled — although not with Larry — over the nomination for study in the United States the year before of two Communist Uruguayan youths, on the theory, according to my birdbrained attaché, that exposure to the United States would soon cure their malady. The suicide theory rests solely upon supposition, for which, as far as I know, no tangible evidence has been produced.

Last, there is the theory, apparently accepted by his wife and parents, that his fall was an accident. Larry was not in robust health, it was 7 P.M., and his office was deserted at the end of a long and tiring winter day. He had one overshoe on, and the other rested beside his hat and coat. According to this explanation, Larry, feeling faint, had gone to the low open window for fresh air and, leaning too far forward, had somehow managed to fall out. The street was sixteen floors below the window.

The case was immediately seized upon and cruelly exploited by two members of the House Un-American Activities Committee (Karl Mundt and Richard M. Nixon) who a few hours later released an out-of-context segment of testimony, given a few days before in executive session, that purported to link Duggan's name with the Communist apparatus. This produced such morning headlines as "Fall Kills Duggan, Named with Hiss in Spy Ring Inquiry." The Mundt-Nixon press release, on examination, proved nothing whatever discreditable to the man who could no longer answer in his own defense, although it did succeed in making much publicity, and hence perhaps some political capital for Messrs. Mundt and Nixon, the latter in 1948 a fledgling congressman.

Fourteen years later I found the case occupying my feverish if debilitated attention in my hospital room in Baltimore. Insofar as I am aware, the circumstances of Larry's fall were, and still are, uncertain. The case was to figure in the campaign launched a few years later by Senator McCarthy.

Larry himself — whether he was pushed, fell, or jumped — symbolized the conflict between liberalism and conservatism — a conflict where partisans of the former have succeeded in weakening the United States and in reducing its stature as a world power. I know of no clearer definition of "liberal" and "conservative" than that attributed to Professor Jeffrey Hart of Dartmouth College: Whereas liberals tend to judge a society according to its solicitude for real or imagined victims, conservatives tend to judge a society on how it rewards effort and merit.

Oversimplified as that definition may seem to some, there is much in it to ponder as we expend our resources on the underdeveloped, the underprivileged, and the underpar segments of societies differing fundamentally from our own.

My father, who was born on a Wisconsin farm in 1865, did not go to college, but by the age of thirty-five (one year after I was born) he was a successful businessman in the East. Father would probably have dated the decline of our country from the two amendments to the Constitution in 1913 (the Sixteenth and Seventeenth), which provided, respectively, for the income tax and for the direct election of senators. Especially the income tax. On my own calendar, as I tried in 1962 to formulate it with an uneasy mind, the date could have been 1933, when President Franklin Delano Roosevelt violated the pledged word of the United States in the unilateral devaluation of gold. Visit a numismatic museum today and read with shame the unqualified promise of the United States government to redeem the gold certificates (which Roosevelt promptly confiscated) in gold of a certain weight and fineness.[1]

Second, Roosevelt so stacked the domestic cards in favor of labor that the latter grew and grew in power at the expense of capital, until the cost of production in the United States became so high that, had the value of the dollar not still further declined because of profligate and spendthrift fiscal policies, little of United States production could have been sold abroad. Soon no American vessel could sail the seas except supported by a subsidy — coming, of course, from the taxes levied on the American people.

---

1. One of the few legitimate complaints Panama ever had against the United States was when Franklin Roosevelt tried to pay the annual rental in his debased dollars. Panama rejected the payment and in effect threatened to sue, citing the text of the treaty. Rather than let the matter get to the Supreme Court, which might have overturned the devaluation, Roosevelt directed the State Department to draft a new treaty in which the rental would be raised from the original $250,000 in gold per annum to $430,000 per annum in Roosevelt dollars, that being the precise equivalent, at that time, of the amount stipulated in the treaty. The new arrangement was ratified in 1936.

Franklin Roosevelt prepared the citizens of our country for war; he is entitled to credit for that. But in international affairs he was an almost unmitigated blight. He pictured himself as the Great Statesman ("I can do business with Uncle Joe"), but Roosevelt was in fact outmaneuvered throughout his relations with Soviet Russia, which violated practically every pledge it made, beginning with the undertakings resulting in recognition in 1934 and ending with the Yalta meeting in 1945, the results of which Roosevelt did not live to see. Subsequent research indicates the president was losing his grip, sinking physically if not almost moribund, in that winter of 1945. He died the following April.

From the pinnacle of military victory in 1945 (with the notable exception of the success of the Marshall Plan in Europe, the Truman Plan in Greece and Turkey, and NATO), the decline of United States prestige proceeded steadily, and 1962 found me the somber spectator of an almost uninterrupted slide, with the Southeast Asia disaster still ahead of us. Although not always at the center of great events, I had nevertheless been close enough to the machinery of political power and American diplomacy to observe with dismay developments that appeared to me (and to many of my fellow professionals) to point toward trouble.

President Truman was the most competent chief executive since Theodore Roosevelt, but he made two egregious mistakes. The uniquely enchanting "oral biography" by Merle Miller was still more than a decade away from my hospital bed, but in that account Miller was to quote the former president as considering a certain political appointment as "the worst mistake" of his administration. I wish I could agree, but the facts simply cannot be molded to fit that conclusion.

The worst mistakes President Truman made, both in the term of office he inherited from Roosevelt, were the National Security Act of 1947 and the creation of Israel in 1948. Each criticism deserves some amplification.

The National Security Act (although its unification of the armed services was overdue) created the National Security Council and the Central Intelligence Agency, which between them transferred diplomacy from the State Department to the White House and the Pentagon, with consequences wholly unpropitious.

The United States unquestionably needs an intelligence agency, which should, however, have been placed under the policy direction of the secretary of state, with its activities defined and strictly limited, and with its operations abroad under the jurisdiction of the American ambassador in the country concerned. Furthermore, its functions should have concentrated on *covert* activities abroad, inasmuch as the gathering and interpretation of overt foreign intelligence has since the dawn of the Republic been a primary responsibility of the State Department.

The National Security Council began cautiously, under two strong secretaries of state, Acheson and Dulles, each of whom possessed the confidence of his president and maintained the authority inherent in his own office. Not so Dean Rusk under Kennedy and Johnson, nor Rogers under Nixon. By the end of the Kennedy administration (1963), the national security adviser was calling more shots than the secretary of state. His assistants, separated from and not accountable to the State Department, were infinitely more influential because of their proximity to the decision-making center of power. Under Kissinger, the NSC secretariat figure rose to nearly 150 persons, and almost no substantive foreign affairs business was conducted in Foggy Bottom.

During its first fifteen years my own relations with the Central Intelligence Agency were good.[2] The original upper echelon were recruited mostly from the Office of Strategic Services (OSS); many of them were personal friends. I took the position that the closest coordination should be maintained with respect to intelligence reporting, and that no assessments, as they were then called by the bureaucrats, should be cabled to Washington that were at variance with embassy political reporting. The CIA and the service attachés had their own communication systems, separate from that of the Department of State, which in itself is an invitation to freewheeling. On covert projects it was understood that the ambassador was boss, not in the sense that he was entitled to become privy to the details of a given operation but, as the president's representative in the country concerned, he was entitled to know what the objective of the operation was and to decide whether that objective, if gained, was worth the risk in terms of general relations if the operation blew up in our face. Had such a regulation been in effect in 1960, no U-2 flight on the eve of a summit meeting would have been permitted.

By no means have all chiefs of mission shared my interpretation of ambassadorial responsibility. Some have refused to become involved with the CIA at all, on the theory that they can then dodge a Foreign Office complaint by declaring they have no information on the subject. Others, seeing themselves as amateur James Bonds, have wanted to kibitz. At every post except Korea (where the CIA operated as a supposedly invisible tentacle of the military), I was served by sophisticated and cooperative station chiefs, my prime objection to their activities being that each had staffs several times

2. As detailed in *Anatomy of Diplomacy*, chapter 6.

larger than needed. There are few things worse than idle hands in an embassy, especially if they are patriotic hands full of unvouchered funds.

Genuine covert intelligence operations (not the monkey business promoted by the Nixon administration at Watergate nor some of the childish goings-on of the Defense Intelligence Agency) are as old as the Trojan Horse, and precisely as important today in terms of our national security.

But I can find little to show that the dangers inherent in the National Security Act were recognized by either the chief executive, or General Marshall or Secretary Acheson, who were Truman's two principal advisers. On the contrary, Truman wrote in his official memoirs that the passage of the National Security Act and its strengthening amendments represented one of the outstanding achievements of his administration.

The most charitable conclusion I can reach is that the president was thinking primarily of the unification-of-the-armed-forces aspects of the legislation rather than of its diplomatic implications.

Much of the blame for the follies of the 1960s in Southeast Asia must, and should, be laid at the feet of our military, who, in addition to their diplomatic inexperience, apparently learned so little from the Korean War that they could hardly wait to try once again on terrain even more difficult and distant than before, and on behalf of a population who lacked one-tenth of the toughness of spirit of old President Rhee and the people of Korea. True, the ultimate responsibility rested upon successive chief executives, especially Eisenhower, Kennedy, and Johnson, but the dominant counsel came from the Pentagon. It was as bad counsel as the advice given by the military to President Roosevelt at Yalta, whereby, at the instance of uniformed advisers, Stalin was bribed to enter the war against Japan at a time when recognition of the impending and inevitable defeat of Japan merited, if anything, a bribe to Stalin to stay out of the conflict.

Support for the establishment of Israel was a different matter altogether. Although the problem is too complex for consideration here, the effects of that support have proven as deleterious as any step taken by the United States in foreign relations. The creation of Israel has hung around the neck of the American government, a millstone loaded with explosives that have been detonating intermittently ever since, with no end in sight.[3] It is conceivable that some interim accommodation between Israel and the Arabs

---

3. In the original text the author noted the exploitation of this situation by the Soviet Union. He did not foresee the development of Islamic extremism that helped focus anti-American sentiment throughout the Arab world.

may be devised, and that accommodation, should it last long enough, might lead to stability. But it is hard to be optimistic given the apparent intractability of the issues in dispute between Israel and the Palestinians.

Turning to the Eisenhower administration, the greatest mistake in foreign affairs was not Secretary Dulles's acquiescence in the virtual destruction of the morale of the professional Foreign Service, nor his lack of interest in the multiplication of bureaucratic drones, nor the expenditure of millions of dollars in aid programs, nor the growing indifference of our government to the deliberately bad behavior of "developing" nations, but the failure of the American government to help prevent the seizure of the Suez Canal by Egypt in 1956.

It will be remembered that 1956 was the year of the brave but pitiful attempt by the Hungarians to regain their freedom. The American people were outraged by the brutality of the Soviet suppression of the Hungarian effort to escape from bondage, and the air was still reverberating with American denunciations of Communist behavior when Nasser of Egypt made his decision to tear up the Suez Canal treaty and to operate the waterway himself, without reference to his country's pledged obligations. The Israelis, whose ships were prevented by Nasser from transiting the canal, allied themselves with the French and British. They organized a joint military operation that was spectacularly successful. It would probably have ended with the occupation of Cairo and Alexandria, and the elimination of Nasser altogether, had the United States not intervened. That is to say, the United States, in precisely the tone of voice just used in denouncing the Soviet conduct in Hungary, barged into the Near East conflict, foot in mouth and Sixth Fleet rattling. It was John Foster Dulles at his holier-than-thou worst. At the ensuing conference the role played by the United States was sanctimonious and unedifying. More, it was diplomatic idiocy. The upshot was that Nasser succeeded in holding the Suez Canal.

In the Near East the situation created by Egyptian control was to lead directly to the 1967 war, and then to the throbbing dilemmas of the present era.

Another foreign affairs error dating from the 1950s was United States tolerance of "bad behavior as an instrument of national policy," indulged in with increasing impunity as the European colonial period drew to a close and the previous wards of the no longer Great Powers began flexing their muscles in emulation of Tarzan. Along with this indigenous swinging from branch to branch of the tallest forest trees came conduct nourished by stimulants supplied by the Communists, both Russian and Chinese. Not long thereafter came the problem of "urban guerrillas" and the failure of successive governments to give protection to diplomats — a situation that today renders the conduct of international relations infinitely more difficult if not, in some areas, impossible.

Since retiring from the Foreign Service, I have watched with dismay the defeats we have suffered since World War II. Leaving aside for the moment the sinister contributions of the Communist world in creating many of the perils facing the U.S., it is evident that a large segment of the human race is incapable of handling the tools of representative democracy, the bright visions of the nineteenth century having dissolved in the abrasive realities of experience. Not only are many peoples not able to master those tools, but they show little eagerness to make the effort to do so.

Turning to the United States itself, I am by no means unaware of the pessimistic prediction of a British historian, in the 1820s, when a still young United States had just celebrated its golden anniversary of independence. That historian doubted the existence of democracy as a *permanent* form of government, declaring that "It can only exist until the voters discover that they can vote themselves largesse from the public treasury. From that moment on, the majority always votes for the candidates promising the most from the public treasury, with the result that a democracy collapses over loose fiscal policies, always followed by a dictatorship."

Cognizant of that hazard, the Founding Fathers instituted a system of checks and balances whereby, inter alia, it was sought by the framers of our original Constitution to protect the nation from the discovery by the majority that they could elect candidates promising the largest handouts. The twentieth century has witnessed a progressive whittling down of those safeguards, to the point where an astronomical deficit is now taken for granted by a dangerously large proportion of the American people.

Unless, therefore, the United States can tidy up its own premises, protecting the elements who produce from the raids of the representatives of those who produce not but hope to continue being paid for idleness, our vaunted democracy may become a bankrupt machine, grinding to that halt predicted many decades ago, when ours was a nation of untapped resources with a population of scarcely twenty-five million.

Assuming that we possess the intelligence and the hardihood to put our nation in order, the following observations seem pertinent to the conduct of foreign relations, bearing in mind that in the shrunken world in which we exist, the United States cannot function alone.

First, systems of government-by-oppression are incompatible with individual freedom, and that is what will eventually destroy communism. The overthrow of Allende in Chile, the first piece of real estate to gain its freedom once the Communist claw had closed upon it — may be regarded by future historians as a watershed, as well as a demonstration of the house-of-cards nature of the Moscow Communist empire.

Second, our relations with Latin America (a prime concern of the author for approximately half his career) have often been marked by considerable disorder. There is undoubtedly blame on both sides. During the 1960s successive administrations were so bogged down in Southeast Asia that the New World received only peripheral attention, often from the wrong sorts of officials. Neighbors have had valid things to say about the raw materials on which they live or go hungry, and about their inability to control, or even in some cases largely to influence, the price of copper, sugar, cotton, corn, bananas, cacao, coffee, or meat: items literally vital to millions of Latin American producers. On the other hand, their record of the treatment of American firms (and the American government's record of indifference to that treatment) has often been execrable.

Then, too, the Good Neighbors have been incredibly slow to recognize the dangers inherent in their galloping birthrates and their impact on the environment (behind every felled tree is a machete-wielding man) that present today's world with a menace equaled only by the proliferation of atomic capabilities.

"Hemispheric solidarity" is an outworn objective, no longer relevant to present conditions. It may have been a useful formula for obtaining collaboration during World War II (although its ornamental facade never included Argentina), but it has little meaning at present, and that should cease to worry the American people. The first thing to remember is that Latin America is merely a convenient label for a group of nations as highly diverse as the imagination can conceive. Moreover, they are nations that the United States should treat individually on their merits or demerits.

Castro's Cuba illustrates the point. Castro remains primarily a Cuban problem, which I am confident the Cuban people will someday solve. In the meantime, despite persistent liberal establishment efforts to rewrite Cuban history — an effort that has already succeeded in luring dozens of simple-minded Americans (legislators, journalists, and academics, mostly) into enjoying the privilege of having a bearded tyrant blow cigar smoke in their faces — let us not forget the citizens whom he murdered, nor the thousands whom he jailed, nor the millions of dollars of American property that he stole, nor the endless sewer of vilification and falsehood concerning the United States in which he continues to wallow.

Third, few would take issue with a statement of former Secretary of State Henry Kissinger, echoing the words of many predecessors, when he declared that the purpose of the State Department "is to preserve the peace, the security, the well-being of the United States, and — since America cannot live in isolation — to contribute to just international agreements for all mankind." An eloquent generality, but an ounce of specifics is often more effective than a ton of self-righteous prose.

The United States needs to pay more attention to its own interests, and less to remodeling the rest of the world. It cannot be proclaimed too often that a crusading spirit is not a foreign policy, no matter how well intentioned that spirit may be. Never in recorded history has a nation acted with greater generosity or with greater regard for its fellow man than has the United States in the post–World War II period. Never has a nation been more generous with a former adversary than the United States has been with Japan and Germany.

It is in the matter of assistance to primitive or undeveloped lands that the United States has fallen upon its face, not once but again and again; it will continue to fall on its face until Congress dismantles the AID bureaucracy, which has had its snout in the public trough ever since the Marshall and Truman plans ended. There is little to show for their efforts in backward lands but rusted and broken pieces of machinery, abandoned warehouses and silos and sheds, wells with the pumps long since disabled, cooperative schemes that lasted only so long as loans continued to be forthcoming.

In the matter of aid to certain marginal segments of the international body politic, let us likewise consider "doing as we are done by," assisting with compassion in the case of natural disasters but declining to assist those countries that steal American property or habitually vilify the United States. And when we do extend aid, let it be done prudently, a careful step at a time, with no more shoving whole programs down the throat of a bewildered foreign government merely because Congress appropriated the money — and if those dollars are not spent, the appropriation may lapse.

There is nothing in the record to demonstrate that internationally administered programs are superior to bilateral ones. On the contrary, the international bureaucrat seems less likely to be amenable to reason and experience than the national representative upon whose activities there is always the possibility that at long last a chill congressional eye may be cast. In addition, the American portion of the aid (which is usually the major component of whatever international program you may choose) is either diluted or lost sight of altogether when it is merged in what is often grandiloquently termed an international program.

Fourth, perhaps the greatest folly of the last generation has been the penchant of presidents for so-called summit meetings, in which the chief executive personally engages in negotiations. That is the most dangerous thing a president can do, since it forces him either to accomplish something (when the raw materials of accomplishment are often lacking) or to attempt to create the illusion of accomplishment — as Chamberlain did in 1938 after Munich. In a constitutional monarchy the danger is somewhat less, for a ruler can make ceremonial visits and, if he or she is sufficiently astute, achieve something on the side. A visit to Paris by Edward VII paved the way for the Entente Cordiale. But in the United States the president is simultaneously chief of state and head of government; as such his foreign excursions — notwithstanding the temptations inherent in the luxury of Air Force One and the speed with which it can whisk him from here to there — should be limited to those rare occasions when a truly important agreement, already negotiated and complete in every detail, can have its importance emphasized by the presence of the chief executive. Such occasions occur infrequently. Even though he may spend a substantial part of his Washington time wrestling with the complexities of foreign affairs, a president should stay at home and leave the conduct of diplomacy to those best qualified to deal with the intricacies of foreign affairs — the diplomats

Fifth, secretaries of state have greater latitude, but they also have succumbed to the purr of the ubiquitous jet. One inescapable effect of simultaneously negotiating abroad and trying to operate a government bureaucracy in Washington is that the bureaucracy wilts and, abroad, the American ambassador is so miniaturized that frequently he becomes almost invisible. That is a bad thing, for the ambassador is the personal representative of the president, and if he is ignored or treated like a shoeshine boy by the secretary of state or other high-level Washington visitors, the ambassador's prestige is destroyed and his future usefulness is compromised.

Sixth, another reduction in the effectiveness of ambassadors has resulted from the multiplication of their numbers, beginning over fifty years ago, first by abolishing the title of minister (for generations the top representative of the United States in most countries), and then by giving every accredited representative, whether he serves in Moscow or Barbados or Rwanda, ambassadorial rank and title. My conclusion is that there should be a new title, such as emissary, given to our chiefs of mission in the dozen or so countries genuinely important to us.

Seventh, I leave to others, with my blessing, such projects as can be devised for fumigating Foggy Bottom and reducing its personnel to manageable proportions, say to half the present population, as an initial step. I turn instead to the activities of an ambassador, as separate from the question of his prestige, or his rank in the hierarchy. Here I speak from experience at twelve posts, in seven of which I served as chief of mission.

If a diplomatic mission is to function efficiently, the ambassador must have unquestioned authority over *all* segments of his establishment: the various attachés, CIA, the military missions, the Information Service, and, most important, in certain underdeveloped countries afflicted with AID and Peace Corps operators, over their projects also. In theory and on paper, such authority exists, but it is impossible to exercise so long as the representatives of the nonstate agencies have separate budgets and separate communications facilities, often utilizing the later at cross purposes to the reports of the chief of mission, and so long as the State Department will not assert itself at home.

Finally, since the days of Franklin Roosevelt, the Foreign Service has been subjected to too many blows, too much harassment, and too little attention from secretaries of state. It has been unappreciated or disparaged by the political leadership and the citizenry at large. For the good of our country, the integrity of the officer corps of the Foreign Service must be restored so that its members can continue to function as "proud servants of the great house" of the United States.

It was my privilege to do so, for almost four decades.

Index

155–56, 158–59, 161, 171–72; and Perón, 266–67; in Peru, 15–45, 332–48; retirement of, 399; and Rhee, 307, 315, 322, 328–29; on Rockefeller's projects, 132–33, 198; on Roosevelt administration, 106–7, 133, 172, 406–7; in Senate confirmation struggle, 270–72; steamship travels of, 14, 29–30, 74, 78, 154, 272, 273, 329; and Stevenson, 315, 392–96; and Trujillo, 188–91, 316; on Truman administration, 407–10; in Uruguay, 256–68; and Welles, 118. *See also* American Republic Affairs Division; Western European Division

Briggs, Lucita, in Korea, 304–5

Briggs, Lucy, 50, 114; in Cuba, 86, 91n, 105, 161; in Czechoslovakia, 285, 295; in Dominican Republic, 188; in Greece, 371, 374, 375; in Korea, 305, 306, 307, 314, 315, 320, 322, 327, 328; in Peru, 29, 33, 40, 45; in Uruguay, 261

Britain: and Greece, 370; and Mexican oil-field expropriation, 138; rubber monopoly of, 49, 65, 66; and State Department, 47

Brooks, Clarence, 152

Brown, Bim and Caroline, 259

Bruce, David, 267, 302, 303

Bruce, James, 267

Bullitt, William, 107–8, 109

Business interests: expropriation from, 137–43, 343–44; in Latin America, 126–27, 137–43, 264–65, 341–43, 412; in Liberia, 63–68; New Dealers' view of, 124, 126–27; in Spain, 58–59. *See also* Trade

Butt, Archie, 72

Butterworth, Walton, 2n

Byrnes, James F., 224, 230, 238, 241, 247, 248, 252

Cabot, Elizabeth, 161

Cabot, Jack, 161, 191n, 196, 236–37, 362

Caffery, Jefferson, 85, 86, 91, 98, 99, 383n; achievements of, 103–4; in Brazil, 104–

5, 124; and Gómez impeachment, 102, 103; inarticulateness of, 82; marriage of, 105; meeting with Hull, 90; relations with Cubans, 87–88; staff selection of, 81–82; working style of, 88

Calhoun, John A. "Arch," 326, 384–85, 397

Callao (Peru), 12, 15, 17–21, 30

Caramanlis, Amalia, 371, 372

Caramanlis, Constantine: and Briggs, 371–72; official visit to U.S., 389–92

Caraway seed import case, 52–53

Carnegie Endowment for International Education, 405

Carol, King of Romania, 163–66

Carolou, Mary, 377, 380, 381, 382

Carter, John, 55

Carton de Wiart, Adrian, 225, 281

Carton de Wiart, Hubert, 281–82

Carton de Wiart, Noelle, 283

Casablanca Conference, 111–12

Castle, Bill, 47

Castro, Fidel, 94, 140, 412

Caterpillar Club, 23

Cecil, Viscount, 73–74, 76, 79

Central Intelligence Agency (CIA), 181–82, 249, 366, 387; and ambassadorial responsibility, 408–9; in Korea, 302–3

Céspedes, Carlos Manuel de, 84

Chaco War of 1932–36, 44n, 116–17, 231

Chapin, Selden, 249, 250, 252n

Chapultepec Conference, 201n, 236

Chennault, Claire, 218

Chiang Kai-shek, 203, 205, 212, 218, 222, 227, 317

Chiang Kai-shek, Mme., 208, 222

Chile, 132, 134, 393, 412; Antarctica claim of, 151–52; Bowers' ambassadorship in, 145–49; Cardinal Daugherty in, 149, 150; embassy reorganization in, 153–55; embassy staff in, 152–53; expropriation of American property, 141; German presence in, 144, 147–48, 151; Rockefeller emissaries in, 150–51; in Tacna-Arica dispute, 28–29, 36–45

China: Chungking chancery, 207–25; Chungking-Yenan relations, 223; embassy residence in, 215; and Far Eastern Division, 205–6, 219; foreign correspondents in, 218–19; intelligence operations in, 219–21; in Korean War, 300; Lend-Lease in, 216–17, 221–22; "loss" of, 227; Marshall Mission to, 226, 317; Operation Coronado in, 220n; policy change demands of "old China hands", 215–16, 219, 228; postwar objectives in, 224; Roosevelt memorial service in, 210–12; Wallace Mission to, 207n

Chou En-lai, 23

Christy, Cuthbert, 69n

Christy Report, 69, 70

Chung Kook Sung, 327

Churchill, Winston, 65, 106, 112, 265, 370

Clark, Mark Wayne, 280, 305, 307, 309–13, 320, 322

Clarkson, Anne, 120

Class One posts, 251–52

Cochran, Merle, 291, 292

Codon, Iryne, 311–12, 313, 314, 326

Colombia, 131, 231

Colonos Association, 96

Congo, 334n

Connally, Tom, 271

Conroy, Maggie, 341

Conservative, definition of, 406

Constantine of Greece, 373, 382, 385

Consular work, 7, 12–13, 17–19, 34

Coolidge, Calvin, 9, 10, 34, 400

Coordinator of inter-American affairs, 132–36, 150–51, 200

Co-Prosperity Sphere, 8

Cottam, Howard, 355

Crawford, Angus Macdonald, 1–6, 10, 36

Crook Factory, 173–74

Cuba, 81, 121, 133, 134, 208–9; airport construction in, 179; Auténticos in, 85, 91, 96; Bay of Pigs invasion, 391–92; Braden ambassadorship in, 172–83, 231; Caffery ambassadorship in, 86–105;

Carol of Romania in, 163–66; under Castro, 412; consul general embassy merger, 158, 159–60; corruption and graft in, 176, 177; Crook Factory in, 173–74, 181; and depression of 1930s, 82–83; diplomats of, in U.S., 118–19; divorce law in, 98; electoral law in, 98–99; embassy chancery in, 86, 162–63; embassy relations, 87–88, 96–97, 173; expropriation of American property, 140; Gómez regime in, 99–103; Guantánamo Bay base in, 92, 168–70; Havana Conference in, 113–16; intelligence operations in, 173–74, 181–82; Japanese internees in, 180–81; Laredo Bru regime in, 103–4; Machado's ouster in, 84, 91; Mendieta regime in, 89, 90–93, 98–99; Messersmith ambassadorship in, 155–72; and Platt Amendment, 83–84, 91; political repression in, 83; political unrest in, 84–85; Presidential Palace in, 89–90; refugees in, 159, 164; school-building program in, 100–101; sugar agreement with, 176–78, 235; sugar production in, 90, 93–94; sugar regulation in, 95–96; trade agreement with U.S., 92–93; treaty with U.S., 91–92; war effort of, 168, 175–76, 183; wartime communications in, 172–73

Cuban American Sugar Company, 90

Cuban Sugar Stabilization Institute, 96

Culbertson, Paul, 39, 42, 43, 48, 49, 271

Cultural attachés, 130

Cumming, Hugh, 196

Czechoslovakia: arrest of embassy staffer, 273, 275, 276; arrest of foreign correspondent, 292–94; under Benes, 269–70; Briggs appointment to, 268, 269, 270–72; consulates in U.S., closing of, 279; diplomatic community in, 281–84, 295–96; diplomatic passports in, 288–90; embassy personnel in, 273–74, 276–278, 280–81; expulsion of embassy staffers, 278–80; frontier crossing, 274, 292; and Gottwald,

274–76; military attachés in, 278, 280; Petschek Palace chancery in, 284–88, 295

Grow, Jasper, 22, 41, 42
Guantánamo Bay base, 92, 168–70
Guerra, Ramiro, 96n
Guest, Winston, 210, 211, 217, 221, 348
Guggenheim, Harry S., 86
Guiteras, Antonio, 91

Hacdendados Association, 96
Haiti, 8, 121, 135, 201
Hajdu, 279–80
Halla, Blanche, 253
Hamilton, Maxwell, 219
Handbook of South American Indians
　(Smithsonian Institution), 128
Harris, Harold, 22–23, 24–25, 337, 344
Harrison, General, 338–39, 341
Hart, Jeffrey, 406
Havana Conference, 113–16, 121
Hemingway, Ernest, 159, 191, 268, 395;
　Crook Factory of, 173–74, 181; marlin
　fishing of, 348
Hemingway, Mary, 347–48
Henderson, Loy, 250, 346, 383
Herter, Christian, 326, 367, 382–87
Hevia, Carlos, 82, 89, 90, 176
Hibbard, Freddy, 46, 47, 48
Hickenlooper Amendment, 344
Hickerson, Jack, 250
Hiss, Algerand Duggan, 404; Panama
　Canal Zone document of, 243–45, 247
Hitler, Adolf, 369
Holland. *See* Netherlands
Holland, Henry, 330–31, 341, 349
Holmes, Julius, 396
Hoover, Herbert, 9, 45, 48–49, 57, 165; in
　Peru, 40; and Platt Amendment, 83–84;
　and rubber market, 49; speech writing
　for, 53, 55
Hoover, J. Edgar, 164n, 181–82
Hopkins, Harry, 197, 201
Horak, Mary, 289, 290, 293
Hornbeck, Stanley, 205
Hosmer, Charles, 128–29
House Un-American Activities Commit-
　tee, 405

Howell, Williamson, 254
Hughes, Charles Evans, 10, 13, 28, 114–15,
　272, 400
Hull, Cordell, 104, 127, 178, 235, 253; back-
　ground of, 117–18; and Cuba, 85, 90, 101;
　Declaration of Havana, 116, 131; on
　expropriation without compensation,
　137–38, 143, 231; at Havana Conference,
　113–16; and Latin American policy, 116,
　121–22; and Liberia, 79; at Montevideo
　Conference, 115; and Paraguay, 116–17;
　resignation of, 196–97; and Rockefeller
　appointment, 133; and Roosevelt, 113;
　and trade policy, 92; and Welles, 87, 236
Hull, Ed, 308, 322
Hurley, Patrick: achievements of, 227; and
　Briggs, 204–5, 225; and Chiang
　Kai-shek, 222; and Chungking-Yenan
　parley, 223; diplomatic style of, 226–27;
　Foreign Service relations with, 203–4,
　215–16, 227–29; and Lend-Lease, 216–17,
　221–22; in New Mexico, 229; objectives
　in China, 205; physical appearance of,
　204; press relations with, 218–19; resig-
　nation of, 225–26; staff of, 213–15, 217

India, 303, 320–21
Indonesia, 54; aid program in, 290–91;
　Cochran ambassadorship in, 291, 292
Integralista revolution, 123–25, 172
Intelligence operations: in China, 219–21;
　in Cuba, 173–74, 181–82; in Czechoslo-
　vakia, 277; limitations of, 284; policy
　direction and function of, 407–8; State
　Department unit, 248–49. *See also* Cen-
　tral Intelligence Agency (CIA)
Inter-American Defense Board, 240
Interior Department, and musk oxen
　case, 50–51
International Cooperation
　Administration (ICA), 290
International Petroleum Company, 342–
　44
Irene, Princess of Greece, 375
Isolationism, 8

343–44; fishing rights in, 329, 330–32, 335, 338; geography of, 16; Hoover's visit to, 40; Indian problem in, 16–17, 340; match monopoly in, 31–33; Moore ambassadorship in, 23–25, 27–45; Poindexter ambassadorship in, 15–17, 26–27; ship voyage to, 29–31; in Tacna-Arica dispute, 28–29, 36–45; transportation in, 338, 340

Petschek Palace, 284–88, 295

Phillips, Billy, 72

Pierrepont Moffat, Jay, 61, 72, 81

Platt Amendment, 83–84, 91

Plaza, Galo, 242

Poindexter, Miles, 15–16, 17, 27

Potocki, Count, 210

Present at the Creation (Acheson), 139, 239n, 246n, 249, 253

Prisoners of war (POWs), in Korea, 318–20

Program of Cooperation with American Republics, 127–30

Prohibition, 11

PX system, in Greece, 376–77

Quadros, Jânio, 354

Reber, Sam, 64, 70, 72

Reed, Harry and Germana, 193

Resolution 14, 116

Reynolds, Lacey, 217

Rhee, Mrs., 305, 307, 308, 315

Rhee, Syngman: and armistice, 320, 403; and Briggs, 307, 315, 322, 328–29; and CIA, 302–3; and High Command, 310–11; and Nixon visit, 323; objectives of, 307; POW release by, 319; and Robertson, 317–18; speech to troops, 324–25; in U.S., 324

Riddleberger, James, 383, 366, 384

Ridgway, Matthew B., 301

Rivero, Pepín, 92

Rivière, Jean, 281

Robert College, 2

Robertson, Walter S., 225, 316–18, 321

Rockefeller, Nelson, 191, 236, 316; as assistant secretary of state, 201–2, 224; as coordinator of inter-American affairs, 132–36, 151; in Dominican Republic, xiii, 197–201; in Haiti, 201

Rogers, Ben, 282, 336, 346

Rogers, Frances, 282

Rogers Act of 1924, xi, 2, 7

Romeyn, Nina, 122–23, 124

Roosevelt, Franklin D., 90, 101, 104, 116, 126, 127, 145, 164, 197; Chinese memorial service for, 210–12; critique of administration, 106–7, 406–7; and Cuba treaty, 91; diplomatic adventurism of, 107, 133, 172; emissaries of, 112; and Foreign Service, 106–12, 250–51; Good Neighbor Policy of, 84, 85, 121, 138; and Hull, 113; and inter-American cooperation program, 129–30; and Liberia, 71–72; and Welles, 118, 122; at Yalta Conference, 222

Roosevelt, Quentin, 221

Rowberg, Brynhild, 289, 290

Rubber-gathering program, 135

Rubber plantations: in Brazil, 49; in Liberia, 49, 63–64, 65–68

Rubottom, Richard Roy, 349, 361

Rusk, Dean, 344, 391–92, 408

Russ, Mr., 12, 13

Russell, Lillian, 28

Saladrigas, Carlos, 168, 177

Saldías, Admiral, 345

Salomoni, Dr., 117

Sandino, Augusto, 8

San Francisco Conference, 224, 243

Savoy, Eddie, 10, 12, 13

Schoen, Baron von, 144, 148

Seaman, consular work with, 18–19

Searles, Fred, 241–42

Senate, Briggs confirmation struggle in, 270–72

Sevareid, Eric, 218

Sevilla Sacasa, Guillermo, 233

Seymour, Horace, 210

Shipley, Ruth, 288, 289, 290

{ *Index* }

PROUD SERVANT:
was designed by Rich Hendel;
composed in 10½ /14 Minion with Castellar display
by Focus Graphics;
printed by sheet-fed offset lithography
on Turin Book 50-pound natural vellum stock
(an acid-free, totally chlorine-free paper),
Smyth sewn and bound over binder's
boards in Roxite A cloth,
and wrapped with dust jackets printed
in three colors on 100-pound enamel stock
finished with polypropylene matte film lamination
by Thomson-Shore, Inc.;
and published by
THE KENT STATE UNIVERSITY PRESS
Kent, Ohio 44242